GOOD
BOTTLED
BEER
GUIDE

Jeff Evans

BOOKS

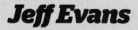

Published by the Campaign for Real Ale Ltd
230 Hatfield Road
St Albans
Hertfordshire AL1 4LW
www.camra.org.uk/books

© Campaign for Real Ale 2009

First published 1998
Second edition 1999
Third edition 2001
Fourth edition 2003
Fifth edition 2004
Sixth edition 2006
Seventh edition 2009

ISBN 978 1 85249 262 5

A CIP catalogue record for this book is
available from the British Library

Printed and bound in Singapore by KHL
Printing Co. Pte Ltd

Managing Editor: Simon Hall
Project Editor: Katie Hunt
Editorial Assistance: Emma Haines
Design/Typography: Linda Storey
(Top Floor Design Ltd)
Cover Design: Dale Tomlinson
Marketing Manager: Kim Carvey

Picture Credits
The publisher would like to thank the
contributors and breweries who have kindly
given permission for their photography to
be published in this publication.
Front cover: Top: CAMRA archive; Bottom:
Matthew Wright; page 3: Katherine Longly;
page 13: CAMRA archive

Acknowledgements

Jeff Evans would like to thank all the brewers who kindly provided
information about their beers for the compilation of this book, and
particularly brewers who took the time to forward samples for tasting.
Brewers who would like to make sure their beers are considered for the
next edition are invited to contact Jeff via CAMRA at: 230 Hatfield Road,
St Albans, Hertfordshire AL1 4LW. Alternatively, they can e-mail Jeff via
camra@camra.org.uk.

Thanks are also offered to CAMRA's many brewery liaison officers
and branch members for their comments, tips and advice.

Contents

Introduction

Britain's brewers have gone bottling crazy. The Local Brewing Industry Report 2009, compiled by the Society of Independent Brewers from a survey of its members, reveals that the volume of bottled beers produced in 2008 increased by more than 50 per cent on the year before. In short, there are more bottled beers than ever now on sale and bottle-conditioned beer – or real ale in a bottle as CAMRA has styled it – is playing a major role in this expansion.

It's not a scenario I could have envisaged when I put together the first edition of the *Good Bottled Beer Guide* back in 1998. At the time, I wasn't exactly scraping around to find beers to include in the book, but at the same time the bottle-conditioned beers that were out there took some time to track down. In the end, I came up with around 180 and the *Good Bottled Beer Guide* was born. Sitting down to plan this seventh edition, I quickly realized that we were now in a completely new ball game. Not only has the number of brewers in the UK increased dramatically, but the number of bottling brewers, and the variety of bottled beers they produce, has also rocketed.

More than 1,300 beers are listed in this book. All are bottle conditioned, which means that they contain yeast and enjoy a secondary fermentation in the bottle, just like real ale on sale in the pub, which tastes fresh and complex because of the life-giving yeast in the cask. This was how all beers were once bottled, until the industrial revolution brought us filtration and pasteurization, both useful devices in their own way, but used for so many years to ensure convenience and stability, at the expense of true character and flavour. When CAMRA was founded in 1971, there were only five bottle-conditioned beers in regular production. It was, by any measure, a niche product. With so many examples on sale today, real ale in a bottle has left the niche behind and is now commonplace, more than justifying a book all to itself.

Developments in the bottled beer sector have largely come from the smaller breweries, a sector that has grown and flourished since the then Chancellor Gordon Brown introduced Progressive Beer Duty back in 2002. This tax break for the smallest producers has allowed companies to invest in their business, reward themselves and their staff appropriately and, in some cases, put money into bottling beer. They've seen bottling as a valuable add-on to their cask beer business at a time when the pub market has become ever tighter. With dozens of pubs now closing every month, the market for draught beer is under threat. Bottling, therefore, has provided a convenient solution to the problem of spare brewing capacity and lost trade.

However, increased bottling is not just a response to difficulties in the pub market. It has been fuelled also by new infrastructure for selling the product. Farmers' markets are a relatively recent development, and brewers now take stalls alongside cheese makers, organic vegetable growers and local butchers to present a fresh, hand-crafted product that stands in sharp contrast to the heavily-advertised, international brands that dominate the world of brewing. It's the same story at farm shops and garden centres, as these retail outlets have begun to diversify from their traditional wares. Increasingly, too, the small grocer/off-licence has realized the value of stocking something local and interesting. It draws in customers, who will then stock up on other commodities while there, and offers an opportunity for them to compete in beer sales, as they stand no chance of matching the supermarkets on the price of canned lagers. Some shops have become Aladdin's caves for the bottled beer enthusiast, often stocking several hundred beers from the UK and overseas. Then there is the phenomenon of the internet, with its proliferation of mail order websites that provide yet another route to market for bottled beers.

All of the above have combined to generate a new interest in beer among the general public. More and more people now understand that beer is not just something to be swilled down by the pint, but that it can be easily as complex and as fascinating as wine. They are becoming more discerning and are keen to discover new and unusual brews. They are beginning to talk about malts, hops and beer styles, and to look for interesting beer and food matches. This, in itself, is a positive influence on the market, encouraging brewers to keep on turning out interesting bottled beers.

The mood has even extended to some of our major breweries. Well-established regional breweries now recognize the importance of having at least one bottle-conditioned beer in their portfolio. The brewers love creating these: it often gives them a chance to develop something remarkable, over and above the bread-and-butter beers (however fine) they turn out on a daily basis. Fuller's, Wells & Young's, Greene King, Harveys, St Austell and Shepherd Neame have been doing this for some time, and they've now been joined by the likes of Hook Norton, Samuel Smith, Sharps and Thwaites.

This edition of the *Good Bottled Beer Guide* divides its coverage of beers into two parts. At the back of the book is a listing of all UK breweries producing bottle-conditioned beers and details of the beers they offer. The main section of the book, however, is devoted to the highlights, several hundred beers that have been taste-tested and are recommended here by beer style. This, hopefully, makes it easy for readers to select a mild, a

wheat beer or a barley wine, for instance. A full index of beers is then provided at the end of the book for easy reference.

The pursuit of excellence in bottle-conditioned beers continues with the stars and rosettes system that was introduced in the last edition of the book. A star placed in front of a beer name in the main section of the book highlights a beer of outstanding quality, a great example of a real ale in a bottle. A rosette displayed alongside a brewery name in the reference section at the back of the book indicates that we consider the brewery produces a consistently high standard of bottle-conditioned beer. These accolades are not awarded lightly. The benchmarks have been set high, to encourage all brewers to strive for these standards. They will be under continuous review. More stars and rosettes may be awarded in future, but some may also be taken away.

CAMRA sees bottled beers as supplementary to cask-conditioned beers, beers to enjoy when you are not able to visit the pub and drink the best draught ales. They allow experimentation, offer great dining options and are perfect for social gatherings where cask beer is not an option. There's a beer for every occasion in this book, so it's time to be adventurous and join the bottled beer party. We are, after all, spoiled for choice these days.

Jeff Evans

Brewing for the Bottle

The journey from fields of golden barley to the glorious beer in your glass is long and complicated, but at the same time a wonderful illustration of how man can take the bounties of nature and turn them into something even more special. Although the largest breweries with their giant factories do their best to suggest otherwise, beer is not an industrial product. It's an agricultural one, with most beers laboured over by farmers, maltsters and brewers with years of experience and a deep understanding of the ingredients and how to get the best from them. To simply describe the brewing process in a matter-of-fact, step-by-step fashion does nothing to recognize the science and artistry that goes into making a great beer, but we'll do so here anyway, to at least offer a basic explanation of how the colours, aromas and flavours we enjoy so much find their way into your glass.

Malt, Hops and Yeast

The process of brewing begins with malt. Malt is barley grain that has been partially germinated to help release starches and enzymes needed for the brewing process and then kilned to prevent further germination. The degree of kilning also dictates the character of the malt; the more 'baked' the malt, the darker the colour and the more roasted the taste. Some malts are toasted dark for bitter, chocolate- and coffee-like flavours; others are just lightly crisped for a sweeter, nuttier taste. At the brewery, the malt is crushed and then combined in a vessel called a mash tun with hot water (known as 'liquor' in the trade), which has usually been treated to adjust its chemical balance.

After an hour or so's mashing and stirring, a thick, sweet liquid called wort is formed. This is run off from the mash tun, leaving behind the spent grains, and diverted into a boiler known as a copper. Here the wort is boiled up with hops, which add bitterness and sometimes herbal, spicy, citrus or floral characters. Like malts, hops come in many varieties. Some are very bitter; others milder. Some make themselves known in the aroma; others express themselves in the taste. Hops also act as a preservative. They can be added as whole hop flowers or as compressed pellets. Some brewers use hop oils (concentrated extract), but these can be astringent. The hops are added at various stages of the boil and sometimes 'adjuncts' are introduced in the copper, or earlier in the mash tun, too. These include sugars, which add to the fermentability of the wort, and maize, which helps produce a good head on the beer. Sometimes fruits and spices are added at this stage, too, but these can also be introduced later in the brewing process.

After an hour or two in the copper, the hops are strained out and the wort is run off and cooled, before being pumped into a fermenting vessel, where yeast is added ('pitched'). Yeast is a single-celled fungus that turns the sugars in the wort into alcohol and carbon dioxide (the gas that gives beer its natural effervescence). Each yeast, however, also has its own character which is harnessed and preserved by brewery chemists. Many breweries use the same yeast for decades and it plays a large part in developing the 'house flavour' of their beers.

During the first few days of fermentation, the yeast works furiously with the wort, growing quickly and covering the top with a thick, bubbly layer of foam. Most is skimmed off, but some sinks into the brew and continues to work, eating up the sugars and generating more carbon dioxide and alcohol. Lager beers are known as 'bottom fermenting', because the yeast they use sinks to the bottom of the wort, rather than lying on the top. A few days later, this 'primary fermentation' is deemed over and bottle-conditioned beers and processed bottled beers go their separate ways.

Bottling Options

Processed, or 'bright', beers are chilled, filtered and pasteurised, killing off and removing any yeast still in the brew. They are then put into bottles and carbonated. Some of these beers are given time at the brewery beforehand to mature. Other breweries follow a halfway-house system whereby the beer is sterile filtered to remove the yeast, but is not

pasteurised. Such beers, strictly speaking, do not condition in the bottle and have a fairly short shelf-life, but they do have a fresher taste than heavily pasteurised beers.

For bottle-conditioned beers, however, the next stage varies from brewery to brewery. Some adopt the simplest form of bottle conditioning, running the beer from a cask or tank into the bottle, yeast and all. This can be a rather hit-and-miss affair, as not enough yeast may get into the bottle to ensure a good secondary fermentation and the beer may be rather flat when opened. Other breweries take greater pains to ensure their beers have the right level of fizz. They fine or filter out the tired old yeast and replace it with fresh yeast, which may be a special strain that works well in bottles. In both procedures, the technically precise check the yeast and fermentable sugar levels to guarantee that the right amounts are present.

9

Some brewers 'kräusen' the beer ready for bottling. This involves adding some partially fermented wort to the beer to introduce some fresh yeast but also to give the existing yeast new sugars to feed on. Others prime the beer, using sugar solutions for the same purpose. Once capped and labelled, bottles are often warm-conditioned at the brewery for a few weeks, to ensure that the secondary fermentation gets off to a good start and are then released for sale.

Getting the Best out of Your Bottled Beer

Bottle-conditioned beer is a living product, so it just needs a little care and attention to be enjoyed in perfect condition. There's nothing too complicated involved, just a few simple ground rules that will enable you to get the best out of your bottled beer.

1 Make sure you buy fresh stock. Check the best before dates and choose bottles that still offer a long shelf life. While some bottle-conditioned beers can mature wonderfully over time, most are designed to be drunk young and fresh, particularly the weaker ones.

2 Store your bottles in a cool, dark place. Temperature and light can play havoc with bottled beer and low temperatures and a dark environment will help your beer stay fresher longer. In particular, avoid direct sunlight, especially if the beer is sold in a clear- or green-glass bottle. Light causes a chemical reaction to take place among the hops to create 'skunky', unpleasant aromas, and heat will rapidly change the character of the beer.

3 Keep bottles upright. There is a natural sediment in bottle-conditioned beer which may stay in suspension if the beer is shaken up or laid down, making the beer cloudy and chewy (although it is otherwise harmless). If you do lay a beer on its side, make sure you stand it upright well before you plan to open it. Some beers include a sticky yeast that won't cause much of a problem if the bottle is laid down but in others the yeast is much looser and it may take a few days for the sediment to settle again. As a rough rule, the only bottles that you should consider laying down are those with cork stoppers, which may dry out and shrink if kept upright, allowing air in to spoil the contents.

How Real Ale in a Bottle is Brewed

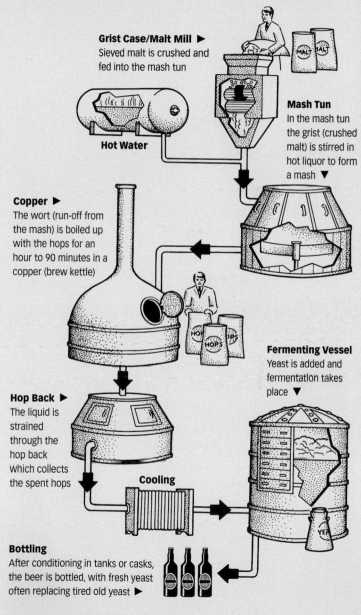

Grist Case/Malt Mill ▶
Sieved malt is crushed and fed into the mash tun

Hot Water

Mash Tun
In the mash tun the grist (crushed malt) is stirred in hot liquor to form a mash ▼

Copper ▶
The wort (run-off from the mash) is boiled up with the hops for an hour to 90 minutes in a copper (brew kettle)

Fermenting Vessel
Yeast is added and fermentation takes place ▼

Hop Back ▶
The liquid is strained through the hop back which collects the spent hops

Cooling

Bottling
After conditioning in tanks or casks, the beer is bottled, with fresh yeast often replacing tired old yeast ▶

11

The Champions

Below is a list of the most recent winners of CAMRA's Champion Bottle-conditioned Beer of Britain contest. Judging takes place during the Great British Beer Festival, held in London in August each year.

1996
1 Marston's Oyster Stout
2 Bass Worthington's White Shield
3 Courage Imperial Russian Stout

1997
1 Hop Back Summer Lightning
2 King & Barnes Festive
3 Fuller's 1845

1998
1 Fuller's 1845
2 Burton Bridge Empire Pale Ale
3 Hampshire Pride of Romsey

1999
1 Young's Special London Ale
2 Salopian Entire Butt
3 Hampshire Pride of Romsey

2000
1 King & Barnes Worthington's White Shield
2 Hampshire Pride of Romsey
3 King & Barnes Festive

2001
1 RCH Ale Mary
2 Hop Back Summer Lightning
3 Fuller's 1845

2002
1 Fuller's 1845
2 Brakspear Live Organic
3 Hop Back Summer Lightning

2003
1 O'Hanlon's Original Port Stout
2 Fuller's 1845
3 RCH Old Slug Porter

2004
1 Titanic Stout
2 Young's Special London Ale
3 Yates' YSD

2005
1 Durham Evensong
2 Young's Special London Ale
3 Titanic Stout

2006
1 Coors Worthington's White Shield
2 Greene King Hen's Tooth
3 Titanic Stout

2007
1 O'Hanlon's Original Port Stout
2 Titanic Stout and Wye Valley Dorothy Goodbody's Wholesome Stout (joint)
3 Wapping Baltic Gold

2008
1 Wye Valley Dorothy Goodbody's Wholesome Stout
2 Fuller's 1845
3 Wells & Young's Special London Ale

Message on a Bottle

The labelling of bottled beer continues to improve. In fact, Britain is very much leading the way in providing information on bottles about ingredients, brewing processes, strengths, beer styles and even food matches. Compare the labels of German or American beers and the difference will be obvious.

It hasn't always been this way, however. Words to inform, educate and inspire drinkers were few and far between on beer labels not so long ago, and one area in which UK beers particularly fell down was in identifying which ones were bottle conditioned. Even where this is declared today, there is often no supportive information to explain exactly what that means and what it entails for the drinker.

That is why in 2004 CAMRA launched the Real Ale in a Bottle accreditation scheme, a simple system through which breweries can acquire special logos to display on their bottle-conditioned beers. These advise customers that the beer is a living product that contains a yeast sediment and needs a little care to enjoy at its best. So far, more than 150 breweries have signed up. When seen on bottle labels, the 'CAMRA says this is real ale' logo reveals that the method of production has been recognized by CAMRA and that the beer is a bottle-conditioned product. The logo is therefore a technical endorsement and should not be seen as an award that reflects on the taste, style, ingredients or any other aspect of the beer. Consult this book, or the results of CAMRA's Champion Bottle-conditioned Beer contest for that.

A second logo available to accredited breweries provides some succinct advice on handling real ale in a bottle. It reads: 'Yeast is the hallmark of a natural beer and produces a sparkle and sediment characteristic of all living beers. Store upright, serve lightly chilled and pour with care to leave the natural sediment in the bottle.'

CAMRA is also working to raise awareness among retailers about bottle-conditioned beer, with display packs available to help promote the product. Part of this initiative is the Real Ale in a Bottle Retailer Awards, first presented in 2008 and scheduled to run every two years. Entrants are judged on their range of products, their sales methods, the value for money for the consumer, and the attitude of staff in promoting bottle-conditioned beer.

Three categories were recognized in the inaugural awards. The prize for Large Retailer went to Booths, a supermarket chain of 26 stores in the North of England. It was described by the judging committee as a perfect example of what a multi-site retailer should be doing to promote real ale, with a good range even in the smaller outlets. The Small Retailer award went to The Offie in Leicester, which was singled out for its unparalleled commitment to stocking rare brews and its welcoming staff who are keen to offer advice and discuss bottled real ale. The third award, for Mail Order/Online Retailer, was given to The Real Ale Shop in Wrentham, Suffolk, for having an excellent website that gets straight to the beer and for promoting localism through its selection of bottled real ales from East Anglia.

With brewers and retailers now working together to promote bottle-conditioned beer, the future for real ale in a bottle looks ever more promising.

When looking to identify beers from other countries that are bottle conditioned, there are a few phrases that will help. These generally translate as 'with yeast' or 'bottle-fermented'. Bear in mind, however, that – particularly for some big brand German, Belgian and Dutch wheat beers – the beer may still be pasteurised even if it contains yeast, meaning that the yeast is not living and the beer has not conditioned in the bottle. 'Bottle-fermented' is therefore a more reliable guide.

	With Yeast	Bottle-fermented
German	mit hefe/ naturtrüb	flaschengärung
Flemish/Dutch	op gist/met gist	hergist in de fles/ nagisting in de fles
French	sur levure/sur lie	refermentée en bouteille/fermentation en bouteille

Growing Old Gracefully

It is often thought that all bottle-conditioned beers mature well in the bottle. The truth is that only certain types of beers can be relied upon to develop in this way. For the majority of real ales in the bottle, the advice is always to drink the beer fresh and young, when their advantage over tired, pasteurised beers is greatest.

Weaker beers are unlikely to mature well. They become dry, thin and gassy as the yeast eats its way through the fermentable sugars and creates more carbon dioxide. They may also be prone to off-flavours as the yeast dies and other chemical and biological changes take their toll. However, strong beers can prove to be a revelation over time and there are plenty of beers with which it is fun to experiment.

The wine industry calls this maturation process 'laying down', but it's a rather inappropriate term for bottle-conditioned beers as these are generally better stored upright, so that the yeast sediment stays tight to the bottom. But the principle is the same. The liquid is kept somewhere cool and dark and, over a lengthy period of months or years, it develops interesting characteristics not found in the beer while it is still young.

Apocryphal stories about bottles of Worthington's White Shield, Thomas Hardy's Ale and Gale's Prize Old Ale have floated around the bottled beer world for decades, relating

15

how, if tucked away for a decade or two, these already wonderful beers suddenly emerge from a long slumber more stunning than ever. As beer ages, it certainly undergoes a steady, gradual change in flavour, but such changes are not always for the better. If you experiment, expect some disappointments as well as some delights.

It was, however, delight all the way at a structured tasting of Fuller's Vintage Ales held at the Chiswick Brewery in 2006. All of the first ten 'vintages' were available for sampling, with not a 'bad' beer among them, despite their age. More importantly, there were some truly sublime discoveries in the selection. Even the original, 1997 Vintage Ale was in fine form.

With Vintage Ale, Fuller's has followed the lead of Belgian Trappist breweries in creating a beer specifically designed to lay down. It's a beer that has had to be devized and brewed with care. The chemistry and biology of the ageing process are complicated, with both positive and negative changes there to be managed during a beer's long life.

Bottle conditioning is the starting point for long-life bottled beer, according to Fuller's head brewer, John Keeling. Pasteurization, the process that was brought in to kill bugs and wild yeast and to give a stable product, can be responsible for negative flavours, he explains. It speeds up staling and oxidation. In time, oxidation can develop interesting flavours like Madeira, but in the short term the impact is less welcome, giving rise to unpleasant papery notes. Live yeast eats up stray oxygen and brings out the best in his beers and Fuller's yeast can live for up to three years in the bottle.

Sometimes off flavours develop because of yeast breakdown in the beer – 'autolysis', in technical terms. But, explains John, the amount of yeast involved controls this. 'A lot of people put too much yeast in,' he says. 'You do get some autolysis but, if you don't put too much in, it doesn't really come out as a negative flavour.'

With the yeast live and active, flavour fluctuations occur in the beer, with peaks and troughs of quality developing. 'It's like a sine wave going up and coming down,' John reveals. 'Each peak, for a while, is better than the peak prior. You can get a bottle of Vintage Ale at the bottom of its sine wave. It's not as good as it was five months ago. Then you'll taste the same beer five months later and you'll find it's even better than the beer you had ten months ago. Then it will start to fall slowly off that peak again. It's all about biochemical cycles.' This would explain why seasoned White Shield drinkers reckoned that the beer had a 'sickness period' several months into its shelf life, but then bounced back to taste better than ever.

Strength Matters

Hygiene at the brewery is also absolutely crucial when it comes to how a beer develops in the bottle. 'Any infection is going to vastly change the flavour of the beer, and the infection will be inconsistent, so your beer will be inconsistent,' Keeling explains. 'That can range from over-conditioning the beer so it just pops out of the bottle and it's too fizzy, or it can make a beer that shouldn't be acidic go acidic. That's why weak beers don't mature very well. They're meant to be drunk fresh and they are very, very susceptible to any small infections, because you've got no alcohol to fight against them.'

Generally speaking, beers mature better the stronger they are, because there's more flavour to undergo biochemical changes in the maturing process. 'You have a reaction called the Maillard reaction, which is found in food and beer, between reducing sugars and amino acids,' John adds. 'When you cook something, or in the case of brewing, boil it, you greatly speed up this reaction, so you get different flavours and colours coming through. At the end of the boil your wort is darker than at the beginning of the boil. That's due to these Maillard reactions. These reactions don't stop: they continue, but very slowly. So over a period of years in the bottle, the beer will get naturally darker. It also changes the flavour.'

Biology, chemistry and the wonders of brewing science aside, for the drinker the first thing to notice as a strong beer grows older is that the hop character starts to disappear. Next, gradually, the malt character gets thinner as the yeast works its way through the fermentable sugars, turning a once full-bodied beer into something slighter and drier. With oxidation perhaps kicking in to add some fortified wine notes, and those Maillard reactions causing other flavour changes, it's easy to see how beers bearing the same label, but a number of years in age apart, can taste rather different. And – if you select the right beers – rather wonderful, too.

How the Guide is Organized

As ever, the *Good Bottled Beer Guide* contains details of all known bottle-conditioned beers in production in the UK. However, the ever-expanding number of real ales in a bottle has led to changes in the way the *Good Bottled Beer Guide* is organized for this edition.

Coverage of the beers is now arranged in two sections. At the back of the book is a full reference listing of all breweries producing bottle-conditioned beers and the names of the relevant beers, along with an indication of strength and beer style. Before this, in the main part of the book, you will find an extensive selection of highlights – in the view of author Jeff Evans the best bottle-conditioned beers currently in production. These are arranged by beer style. For the first time, therefore, the finest real milds in a bottle, real stouts in a bottle, real barley wines in a bottle and so on are collected together. Outstanding individual examples of real ale in a bottle – beers that are consistently good and full of character – are marked out by a star ✳ in front of the beer name.

At the start of each section, some historical detail is given about the style of beer, together with notes on ingredients, some food matching suggestions and recommended serving temperatures. Within each section, the history and description of each beer is presented, along with information such as strength and bottle size, plus tasting notes, compiled by Jeff. But, because bottle-conditioned beers are living, maturing products and are likely to change character during their shelf life, these notes are offered only as a basic guide to what you might expect in the bottle.

If a beer has a listing with a major retailer (supermarket or off-licence chain), this is indicated in this section, but beers featured in the book are mostly sold locally, through farmers' markets, small grocers, craft shops and delicatessens. Some breweries also sell directly to the public, but this may be by the case only. Some also offer a mail order service, which, if relevant, is mentioned in the full, reference listing of breweries at the back of the book. Otherwise, beers can be obtained through specialist off-licences or mail order companies (see Beer Shops).

Also in the reference listing of breweries, look out for the coveted rosette symbol 🍺, which highlights breweries that in Jeff's opinion – based on years of tasting real ales in a bottle – produce consistently good bottle-conditioned beers. This, of course, does not mean that all other breweries are bad, just that breweries awarded rosettes set a very high standard. Hopefully, we can award even more rosettes in future editions.

Milds & Brown Ales

Mild: the style of beer that dare not speak its name. A few years ago a Midlands brewer reported that he had produced a new dark mild and put it on sale at a local pub. Customers came and went. They perused the pump clip and decided on something else. What was it that was disturbing the wary public? The word 'mild' it seemed.

Not to be outdone, the resourceful publican reached for his toolkit and drew out a reel of masking tape. Slicing off a little rectangle, he carefully positioned it over the offending word on the pump clip, leaving just the headline name of the beer – Black Bulldog, Ruby Goat or whatever it happened to be – to catch the drinker's eye. This sleight of hand worked a treat. Within a couple of hours, the cask was empty.

There is clearly something about mild – or, more precisely, the image of mild – that leads customers to shy away from it – until they try it and discover it's one of the most tasty, refreshing drinks a pub can stock. Mild was once the most popular beer style in Britain, right up to the 1950s in fact. It was a drink closely associated with heavy industries, the beer that miners, steelworkers, foundry men and farmers reached for in search of both refreshment and nourishment at the end of a sweaty day's toil. The decline in such industries has been mirrored in the decline of mild. Being 'mild' in alcohol, it offered tired workers the welcome opportunity of sinking a few pints without feeling too much the worse for wear, although this is not where the name comes from. Neither does it come from the fact that the beer is traditionally not as highly hopped as other beers, so it is milder in bitterness, although both these attributes do sum up what mild is about. Historically, mild was a beer that was fresh, as opposed to one that had been allowed to age and therefore had a more demanding, sour flavour. This, of course, doesn't explain how the beer is made today, or the ingredients that shape its character.

Mild's complexion is based on a generous use of malt – both pale malt to provide most of the brewing sugars and darker malt to add roasted grain character and colour. Hops provide a gentle balance of bitterness rather than taking over. But these are not rules, just generalities. Some milds are, perversely, fairly bitter, and some milds are not even dark. There's a type of ale, with the traditional amber hue of a bitter, but with only gentle hopping, that falls into the category known as 'light mild', and then there are also milds that are not so easy on the alcohol. Historically, milds would have been much stronger than most are today, heading up towards 6% and more. Quite a few of this ilk have been revived in recent times and are featured in this section, along with other variations of a beer style whose name should be shouted from the rooftops rather than whispered guiltily whenever we seek out a pint.

Brown ales share mild's malty character, but generally without such a deep roasted grain influence. Some of these can be fairly bitter, but on the whole are mellow on the palate, or indeed are rather sweet. Look more deeply and you'll discern a distinct North-South divide in brown ale styles, in that the southern-brewed version tends to be rather sweet and low in strength, while the northern (perhaps more precisely north-eastern) is stronger, hoppier and more robust.

Most bottle-conditioned milds should be drunk young, as alcohol and hops – which are both known for their preservative qualities in beer – are in short supply. Stronger milds and brown ales may mature well in the bottle for several months and the very strongest are even worth trying after a year or two, to see how the flavours have changed.

At a Glance

Strength: ABV 3–3.5% for standard milds and southern brown ales, but higher for strong milds and northern brown ales

Character: Dark milds have a red-brown colour and a malty, often roasted flavour. Bitterness is generally subdued. Lighter milds have an amber colour and may be a little more hoppy. Brown ales are red-brown in colour, with modest bitterness and a good malt profile that brings toffee and nut to the taste. Some may be rather sweet.

Serving temperature: Cool (12° C)

Food matches: Lamb, pâtés, barbecues, mushrooms, pizzas, chocolate puddings

Butts ▪ Golden Brown

ABV 5% 500 ml Ingredients not declared

Berkshire brewer Chris Butt confesses to being a Stranglers fan, hence the use of one of the band's song titles for this beer's name. In the lyrics there is reference to 'tied to a mast', which explains the illustration of a girl tied to a mast of a ship on the label. Chris always declines the invitation to reveal more about his beers, but he does say that this amber-brown ale contains three different malts and just one hop strain.

A malty, nutty, lightly fruity aroma is followed by a smooth, nutty, malt taste with a touch of caramel and a hint of citrus fruit. Nut and caramel feature in the dry, malty finish that becomes increasingly bitter and hoppy.

Cannon Royall ▪ Fruiterers Mild

ABV 3.7% 500 ml Cocktail pale malt, chocolate malt, wheat malt, Challenger, Golding, Fuggle and Northdown hops

West Midlands Mild of the Year for 2007. This quaffable, chestnut-coloured beer is named after The Fruiterers Arms pub, behind which Cannon Royall Brewery can be found. It was first brewed back in 1997.

Soft chocolate leads in the aroma, soon joined by blackcurrant and other berry fruits. Fruity overtones continue in the taste, which is otherwise softly malty and nutty with light chocolate and a gentle bitterness. Fruit also lingers for a while in the drying, nut-and-chocolate finish.

Conwy ▪ Mulberry Dark

ABV 3.8% 500 ml Pale malt, Munich malt, crystal malt, chocolate malt, roasted barley, torrefied wheat, Pioneer and Cascade hops

This red-coloured, easy-drinking, nutty mild takes you back to the year 1944, when prototypes of the Mulberry temporary harbours, later used in the D-Day landings, were tested at Conwy, North Wales. Drink with sausages and casseroles, suggests the brewery.

A welcoming aroma of nutty, toasted malt and faint caramel leads on to similar flavours in the sweetish taste, with a freshening fruity acidity. The finish is dry, nutty and gently bitter. A light-bodied mild.
Major stockists **Local Co-op and Thresher**

Corvedale ■ Katie's Pride

ABV 4.3% 500 ml Maris Otter pale malt, crystal malt, chocolate malt, wheat malt, Golding hops

In its cask-conditioned form, this mild from a brew pub in Shropshire has won a host of medals in SIBA (Society of Independent Brewers) regional and national beer competitions. It was named after landlord/ brewer Norman Pearce's daughter, who helps run the pub and is now pictured on the label. When first brewed, the beer incorporated a new, trial hop strain called Jenny, but this is no longer available and has been replaced with Goldings.

An amber-red beer with an aroma of chocolate and nut. Nut again leads in the taste, which is also slightly floral and sweetish, with just a hint of tartness from fruity hops. Dry, nutty, pleasantly bitter finish.

Cropton ■ Balmy Mild

ABV 4.4% 500 ml Pale malt, crystal malt, chocolate malt, Fuggle hops

Described by this North Yorkshire brewery as 'a refreshing new take on the most traditional of Northern beer styles,' Balmy Mild was added to the Cropton range in 2001 and is also available in cask form.

An orange-red beer with biscuity grain in the aroma. Nutty, crispbread maltiness follows in the bittersweet taste, along with a touch of chocolate and a gentle, citrus acidity. Dry, malty, bitter finish.

Elmtree ▪ Nightlight Mild

ABV 5.7%   500 ml   Pale malt, roasted malts, First Gold hops

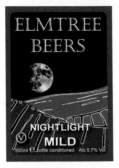

Beers from this Norfolk microbrewery are produced, like numerous other beers in the region, using barley grown at Branthill Farm near Wells-next-the-Sea. Nightlight is the latest addition to the range. It's acceptable to both vegetarians and vegans.

A dark brown mild with an inviting, biscuity, chocolate and caramel aroma. The taste is bittersweet, chocolaty and fudgy, but perhaps a little thin for the strength, rounding off bitter and dry, with coffee and dark chocolate notes.

Hoggleys ✳ Mill Lane Mild

ABV 4%   500 ml   Pale malt, mild malt, crystal malt, black malt, torrefied wheat, Golding and Challenger hops

This very drinkable and satisfying dark mild takes its name from the road on which Hoggleys brewery was originally situated. It is now brewed twice a month for bottling and is acceptable to both vegetarians and vegans.

A ruby mild with plenty of body. Biscuity, dark chocolate and a touch of caramel feature in the aroma, while the taste contrasts sweet malt with smoky, bitter, roasted malt flavours, including coffee and nut. The gently bitter finish is dry and nutty, with more roasted malt.

Kingstone ✳ 1503

ABV 4.8%   500 ml   Pale malt, brown malt, chocolate malt, smoked malt, wheat malt, oat malt, Fuggle hops

'Is this the taste of Tudor England?', asks the label. It might be. The label goes on to reveal that, in the year 1503 – hence the name – one Richard

Arnold chronicled this recipe, which offers one of the earliest recorded examples of the use of hops in British brewing. Kingstone has followed the recipe as closely as possible and come up with a satisfying beer that, brewer Edward Biggs says, makes a good partner to a chocolate dessert.

A chestnut-coloured ale with nutty, chocolaty, toasted malt in the aroma. The taste is sweet, malty and nutty with suggestions of coffee-cream chocolates. There's a slowly increasing bitterness in the dry finish, where more malt, nut and coffee can be found.

Oakleaf ▪ Maypole Mild

ABV 3.8% 500 ml Pale malt, crystal malt, chocolate malt, roasted barley, Golding hops

The cask version of this traditional dark mild from Gosport picked up a gold medal at the SIBA (Society of Independent Brewers) national championship in 2004.

A deep ruby beer with a biscuity, lightly smoky aroma of plain chocolate and gentle liquorice. The taste is a nice balance of smoky malt, chocolaty sweetness and the bitterness of roasted grain, with a hint of caramel in the background. Roasted grain builds pleasantly in the dry, moderately bitter finish, where dark chocolate lingers.
Major stockist **Local Thresher**

Old Chimneys ▪ Meadow Brown

ABV 3.4% 500 ml Pale malt, crystal malt, wheat malt, roasted barley, Fuggle and Challenger hops

Meadow Brown takes its name from a rare butterfly but is in fact a bottled version of Old Chimneys' cask Military Mild. The beer is usually parti-gyled (brewed as part of the same batch) with Black Rat Stout.

A ruby-coloured beer with biscuity, chocolaty malt in the aroma. The taste is thin but pleasant and sweet, with clean chocolate and nut flavours, before a dry, bittersweet, nutty finish.

Pitfield ■ 1824 Mild Ale

ABV 6.5% 500 ml Maris Otter pale malt, black malt, wheat malt, Golding hops

This particular beer serves as a reminder that, in days gone by, mild was not only Britain's most popular brew but a rather potent drink, too. It's part of a range of beers from Pitfield that illustrates historic beer styles.

Ruby, with light fruit in the creamy, malty nose. Smooth malt leads in the mouth, with hints of darker malt and some fruit. Dry, bitter, roasted malt finish.

Spire ✳ Dark Side of the Moon

ABV 4.3% 500 ml Pale malt, dark crystal malt, roasted barley, Fuggle and Golding hops

Many of this Chesterfield brewery's beer names are musically themed and the inspiration this time is Pink Floyd's enormously successful 1973 album that contained tracks such as 'Money' and 'The Great Gig in the Sky'. The beer is also available in cask-conditioned form.

A red/dark amber mild with an aroma of toffee and butterscotch. The smooth taste also features toffee-like malt but it's not sweet, thanks to a bitter backnote from the hops. There's a moreish malt character to the dry finish, which is bitter for a mild, with chocolate and roasted grain notes building.

Teignworthy ■ Edwin Tucker's Choice
Old Walnut Brown Ale

ABV 6% 500 ml Maris Otter pale malt, brown malt, amber malt, chocolate malt, wheat malt, Fuggle and Golding hops

Teignworthy Brewery is housed in part of the historic Tucker's Maltings in Newton Abbot, Devon. The Maltings is also home to an excellent bottled beer shop, and the management has commissioned Teignworthy to produce a number of re-creations of historic beer styles for the shelves. This dark ale was added to the range in 2004, echoing a style of beer in circulation during the 19th century.

The big malty aroma of this claret-coloured ale has lots of nut, chocolate and coffee. The bittersweet taste is also malty, with earthy, nutty and alcoholic notes. Nutty malt lingers in the coffee-like finish.

Teignworthy ▪ Martha's Mild

ABV 5.3%   500 ml   Pale malt, crystal malt, amber malt, chocolate malt, wheat malt, Fuggle and Golding hops

Martha's Mild is one of a small range of beers that Teignworthy Brewery has created to celebrate the birth of the four children of brewer John Lawton and his wife, Rachel. This one is for Martha, born on 27 March 2002.

A strong red-brown mild with coffee, chocolate and nut in the rich, inviting aroma. The taste falls on the sweet side, with coffee, liquorice, hazelnuts and a touch of fruity hop all in the mix, before a dry, bitter, coffee and nut finish rounds off.

Thwaites ▪ Very Nutty Black

ABV 3.9%   500 ml   Pearl pale malt, crystal malt, sugar, caramel, Golding, Fuggle, Whitbread Golding Variety and Challenger hops

Thwaites Dark Mild has a chequered history. The cask version was judged Champion Beer of Britain by CAMRA in 1978 (joint) and 1980, but gradually sales dripped away as mild fell out of favour. In 2008, the name was changed to Nutty Black in a bid to save the beer. It worked: sales soared. Then, in 2009, along came this stronger, bottle-conditioned version, brewed to mark CAMRA's Mild Month (May). Whether it continues in future years remains to be seen, but it's a very welcome addition to the real ale in a bottle scene, from a brewery that has bottled a number of fine bottle-conditioned beers for other breweries.

A dark ruby beer with a biscuity, surprisingly fruity aroma of blackcurrants with a pinch of liquorice. Blackcurrants and smooth, dark malts fill the bittersweet taste, which again has a hint of liquorice. The finish is dry and fruity, with some roasted grain bitterness pushing through.

Major stockists **Booths, Morrisons**

Tipple's ■ The Hanged Monk

ABV 3.8% 500 ml Pale malt, crystal malt, chocolate malt, Golding and Bramling Cross hops

The Hanged Monk is the first of three 'ghost beers' brewer Jason Tipple has devised (the others are called Lady Evelyn and Jack's Revenge). Each is based on a spooky tale from Norfolk, and this beer relates to St Benet's Abbey, that was built near Ludham in AD 816. The prosperous settlement was much envied by William the Conqueror, who enlisted the help of an inmate to help him take it. The resident offered to let the Normans into the abbey if they promoted him to abbot in return. His side of the bargain fulfilled, the treacherous monk was pleased to see the Normans being true to their word. But, no sooner had they elevated the monk to abbot status, they promptly elevated him in a different sense, hanging him for being a traitor. It is said that, on 25 May each year, his ghost can be seen writhing in agony from a beam above the now-ruined abbey arch.

A deep garnet-coloured beer with a welcoming aroma of chocolate and nut with a touch of both coffee and toffee. Nutty, coffee-like dark malt flavours feature in the mouth, along with bitterness that stems from both the roasted grain and the hops. Roasted grain comes to the fore in the dry, moderately bitter finish. Drinks like a light porter.

Tryst ▪ Brockville Dark

ABV 3.8%   500 ml   Optic pale malt, crystal malt, amber malt, chocolate malt, roasted barley, Challenger and Golding hops

This ruby-coloured mild was introduced in 2003 and, like this Scottish brewery's other bottled beers, is also sold in cask form. The name is taken from Falkirk's old football stadium. CAMRA's Champion Bottle-conditioned Beer of Scotland in 2006.

Rich chocolate leads in the aroma, with orange-citrus notes emerging, along with biscuity malt. The taste is bittersweet, with chocolaty malt flavours, an orange-hop bitterness and some peppery spice. The finish is dry and bitter with chocolate lingering and hops slowly building.

Vale ▪ Black Swan

ABV 3.9%   500 ml   Maris Otter pale malt, crystal malt, chocolate malt, Perle and Fuggle hops

The name and the label of this mild play on Vale Brewery's logo (actually based on the Buckinghamshire county emblem) of a swan, but making it black to match the darkness of the beer.

A ruby-brown mild, with chocolate and nut, plus a whiff of coffee, in the malty aroma, which also features a hint of pear. Drying, dark malt flavours feature in the bittersweet taste, along with a touch of chocolate and a sharp, fruity, almost pear-like acidity. Chocolaty roasted grains linger in the dry, bitter finish.

Woodforde's ▪ Norfolk Nog

ABV 4.6%   500 ml   Maris Otter pale malt, crystal malt, chocolate malt, Golding and Styrian Golding hops

Pre-dating the same success of Woodforde's popular Wherry bitter by four years, Norfolk Nog was CAMRA's Champion Beer of Britain in 1992. To earn

Milds & Brown Ales

29

the supreme CAMRA accolade with two different ales is a remarkable achievement, especially for a small brewery. (For the record, only one other brewery, Fuller's, has claimed the top prize with more than one beer.) The only caveat when citing this achievement is that drinkers should be gently reminded that cask beer and bottled beer are not quite the same thing. The level of carbonation can make a difference to the nature of the beer, as can the maturing process in the bottle. A nog is thought to have been an East Anglian type of stock ale, stored for enjoyment many months after brewing.

A ruby-coloured beer with an aroma of a chocolaty, treacly malt and light, sharp citrus fruit. The taste is bittersweet, with chocolate and treacle at first, then hints of orange. Chocolate and nut feature in the dry, bitter finish.

Bitters

Bitters

An American colleague once summed up in one word why he loves coming to Britain. 'Bitter,' he said. He then went on to remark how the drinkers of this country just don't realize when they're on to a good thing.

Visit other countries and the emphasis, you'll find, is usually on much stronger ales or lagers, but in the UK we have this wonderful style of beer called bitter that is both packed with flavour and not too alcoholic, a drink that oils the wheels of conversation without leaving the drinker reeling.

Bitter arrived in the UK in the 19th century, as brewers looked for an alternative to well matured beer, which demanded time and space at the brewery, both of which were in short supply. With improvements in yeast handling, it had, by now, become possible to produce weaker beers that didn't go sour quickly, so bitter was born as part of a breed of so-called 'running beers', designed for a fast turnover. Reflecting the beer's clear complexion, gained through improvements in malt production, the brewers called it pale ale, but drinkers, recognising its difference to the prevalent heavy porters and sweet milds, called it bitter.

Today's typical bitter falls into the 3–4.1% ABV bracket. It is brewed with a high proportion of pale malt and often a good dose of crystal malt. This slightly darker, stewed malt brings a biscuity character to the beer, sometimes along with nut and toffee notes, as well as turning the beer that welcoming shade of light brown that characterizes this type of brew. Hops are gainfully employed, and generously added, contributing the flavour from which this style of beer takes its name.

Bottle-conditioning bitter (as for weak milds) is a little more tricky than bottle-conditioning stronger beers. There is less alcohol, obviously, which means the beer is less able to fight off any flavour-marring infections that might grow over time in the bottle, but this shouldn't be a problem in a brewery where hygiene and careful yeast management are second nature. The action of the yeast inside the bottle is also more marked than in most other beer styles, in the way it eats up the sugars in the beer, turning them into a little more alcohol and carbon dioxide. In stronger beers with fuller bodies, sugar loss is not so significant, but bitters can become dry and markedly less sweet after only a few months in a bottle, with carbonation also rising. The best advice with bottle-conditioned bitters is to drink them as young as possible. While some beers benefit from ageing in the bottle, bitters need to be consumed fresh, when their considerable advantage over pasteurised beers is most obvious.

At a Glance

Strength: ABV 3–4.1%

Character: Crisp, light-to-medium bodied, hoppy and bitter, but with some sweetness and other flavours from the malt, perhaps biscuit, nut and toffee. Hops may also bring fruit, herbal or floral notes. Colours may vary from pale amber to dark brown (see also Golden Ales).

Serving temperature: Cool (12° C)

Food matches: Battered fish, cold meats, sausages, pies, cheeses

Concrete Cow ▪ Cock n Bull Story

ABV 4.1%   500 ml   **Pale malt, crystal malt, amber malt, Challenger and Fuggle hops**

Milton Keynes, home of the Concrete Cow brewery, is a new metropolis built around a number of much older towns and villages. One of these is Stony Stratford, home to coaching inns named The Cock and The Bull. It is said that coach travellers taking lodging at these pubs in centuries past would exchange fanciful tales from across the country, so giving rise to the original 'cock and bull story', and the name of this amber-coloured beer.

Nutty, toasted malt with a touch of caramel and a sharp hop note feature in the aroma, with more nutty, caramel flavour found in the bittersweet taste. The finish is nutty, drying and bitter.

Concrete Cow ▪ Fenny Popper

ABV 4%   500 ml   **Pale malt, crystal malt, Cascade hops**

The strange name of this light amber ale relates to six, small ceremonial cannons that have been fired each St Martin's Day (11 November) at Fenny Stratford, Milton Keynes, since 1770.

Zesty grapefruit from the Cascade hops dominates the aroma, also taking charge of the sharp, drying, mildly bitter taste. The dry, hoppy, bitter finish lingers well. Overall, a fresh, clean-tasting bitter.

Cropton ✳ Two Pints Bitter

ABV 4%   500 ml   **Pale malt, crystal malt, Challenger and Golding hops**

A pint of Two Pints was first served at the New Inn, home of Cropton Brewery, in 1984, the brewery's first year, but the beer did not find its way

into a bottle until 1996. It's now this Yorkshire brewery's biggest selling beer, taking its name from the idea that one pint of Two Pints 'is worth two of any other'.

A dark golden-amber beer with light caramel-like malt in the aroma, along with hints of orange marmalade from the hops. The crisp, bittersweet taste features oranges and creamy caramel, before a moreish finish that is dry and malty but increasingly bitter and hoppy.

Fox ▪ Branthill Best

ABV 3.8%   500 ml   Maris Otter pale malt, amber malt, chocolate malt, torrefied wheat, Phoenix, Cascade and First Gold hops

A beer using Maris Otter barley from Branthill Farm at Wells-next-the-Sea, Norfolk. A back label on the bottle explains how the farm's location close to the sea and its geology – sandy loam over chalk soil – provides an ideal environment for quality barley production. The label even quotes a map grid reference for the field in which the barley used in the beer is grown.

An amber ale, with an aroma of lightly chocolaty, nutty malt and a floral note from the hops. The taste is malty, nutty and mostly bitter, with a light fruity acidity, before a dry, nutty, bitter finish.

Hoggleys ▪ Kislingbury Bitter

ABV 4%   500 ml   Pale malt, chocolate malt, torrefied wheat, Fuggle, Challenger and Golding hops

Named after the brewery's original home village in Northamptonshire, this was the second ever brew, and is described by brewer Roy Crutchley as a 'traditional English pint'.

A bright amber-coloured beer with orange marmalade and a little chocolate as well as nut in the aroma. The taste is bittersweet and lightly orangey, with a good mix of hops and faintly nutty malt. The drying finish features nutty malt and bitter hops.

Humpty Dumpty ▪ Humpty Dumpty Ale

ABV 4.1% 500 ml   Maris Otter pale malt, crystal malt, caramalt, wheat malt, Challenger and Fuggle hops

Several of Humpty Dumpty's beers are named after the golden age of steam railways and the name Humpty Dumpty itself also has locomotive connections, being a class of steam engine that once plied routes in East Anglia. Humpty Dumpty Ale is the brewery's flagship bitter.

An orange-gold beer with orange and floral notes, plus hop resins, in the nose. The fruity, floral taste is rather sweet but with hop resins in the background, while the finish is bittersweet, but increasingly hoppy and dry, with lingering fruit and floral notes.

Itchen Valley ▪ Fagins

ABV 4.1% 500 ml   Maris Otter pale malt, crystal malt, wheat malt, Whitbread Golding Variety, Golding and Fuggle hops

Depicting the Dickensian villain on the label (trading on Dickens's connections with Hampshire, where Itchen Valley is based), Fagins is one of the company's earliest beers.

A dark golden ale with a creamy, orange marmalade-like aroma with hints of grapefruit. There's more faint grapefruit in the taste, which is otherwise crisp, hoppy and gently bitter. Bitter hops feature in the dry, but not deep, finish.

King ▪ Horsham Best Bitter

ABV 5% 500 ml   Maris Otter pale malt, crystal malt, chocolate malt, enzymic malt, Golding, Whitbread Golding Variety and Challenger hops

The King family has a long association with brewing in the Sussex town of Horsham, with Bill King, founder of this brewery, formerly managing

director of King & Barnes, the regional brewer that was sold to Hall & Woodhouse and closed in 2000. This session ale, named after the town, is a solid, traditional British bitter.

Amber, with a malty aroma that has hints of chocolate, plus a light hoppy sharpness. The taste features both malty sweetness and good bitterness, and is slightly nutty, with some gently floral hops. The finish is dry, hoppy and creamy-malty.

Kingstone ▪ Tewdric's Tipple

ABV 3.8% 500 ml Pale malt, crystal malt, Fuggle and Northern Brewer hops

Kingstone's popular session ale is named in honour of a 6th-century King of Gwent, who abdicated his throne to become a hermit. He was then forced to leave his life of solitude in the hills above Tintern to lead the Welsh to triumph over the Saxons at the battle of Pont y Saeson. He didn't survive the conflict. Fatal injuries saw him die – legend has it – at the spring now known as St Tewdrig's Well in Mathern, where the Rivers Wye and Severn meet (today beneath the first Severn Bridge). Tewdric is also known as St Theodoric in Catholic circles.

An orange-golden beer with a light orange and pear fruitiness to the soft, malty aroma. The taste is drying and bittersweet, but with a good, tart, hoppy bite. Orange-citrus notes are again present. The dry, firmly bitter and hoppy finish lingers well. Robust for a beer of this strength.

McGivern ▪ Amber Ale

ABV 4% 500 ml Pale malt, crystal malt, Bobek and Pilot hops

McGivern Ales is a very small business, operating out of a garden shed in North Wales, so you can be sure this is genuinely a hand-crafted beer! The strength of Amber Ale, and other beers from the brewery, may vary.

Bitters

A light amber-coloured bitter with mellow malt and an orange fruitiness in the aroma. Juicy oranges feature in the bittersweet taste, while the finish is slow to build but winds up dry and nicely hoppy-bitter.

Old Chimneys ▪ Great Raft Bitter

ABV 4.1%   500 ml   Pale malt, crystal malt, caramalt, Challenger and Target hops

One of the brewery's three original draught beers, Great Raft has been available in bottled form since 2002. The beer takes its name from Britain's rarest and largest spider, which inhabits a local fen. Also sold as Brockford Bitter at the Mid-Suffolk Light Railway, Wetheringsett.

A dark golden-hued ale with a spicy, toffee-like aroma, with faint orange and peach notes. The dry, rather understated taste is also spicy and toffee-like with a gentle citrus accent. Malty, toffee flavours feature in the dry finish that becomes gradually more bitter.

Pen-lon ▪ Lambs Gold

ABV 3.2%   500 ml   Maris Otter pale malt, light crystal malt, Target, Tettnanger and Willamette hops

This light bitter from West Wales was a gold award-winner in the Wales True Taste competition for 2005–6. At 3.2%, it's one of the weakest bottle-conditioned beers in production.

A dark golden-coloured beer with a clean, malty and floral aroma tinged with apricot-like fruit. The taste is light in body but on the sweet side, with hints of orange and a mild, hoppy bitterness. The finish is slow to develop but is eventually dry, gently hoppy and bitter.

Pen-lon ▪ Tipsy Tup

ABV 3.8% 500 ml Maris Otter pale malt, light crystal malt, Target, Tettnanger and Willamette hops

Tipsy Tup continues the sheep theme of beers from this farmhouse brewery in West Wales.

An amber-golden ale with tart citrus fruit and gentle malt in the aroma. The taste is rather sweet, but with tart, orange-like fruit and light malt, while the finish is dry, bitter and hoppy.

Pitfield ▪ Bitter

ABV 3.7% 500 ml Pale malt, crystal malt, wheat malt, Fuggle, Challenger and Golding hops

Pitfield's popular session bitter – now organic, like all Pitfield's beers – was one of its first ever brews and has survived the brewery's various changes of address in recent years.

An amber/dark golden-coloured beer with an aroma that is malty at first, with clean hop resins then taking over. There's a good, slightly nutty, malt foundation to the taste, with plenty of sharp hop resins on top. The finish is dry, bitter and firmly hoppy.

RCH ▪ PG Steam

ABV 4% 500 ml Optic pale malt, crystal malt, Fuggle and Progress hops

This version of RCH's draught bitter was launched as part of a pack of beers for sale in British Home Stores in 1998. It was labelled then On the Tiles. PG Steam is named after brewers Paul Davey and Graham Dunbaven and the fact that this was the first beer they brewed on steam-heated equipment.

Bitters

A golden-amber bitter with tart citrus and berry notes in the spicy, hoppy aroma. Tart oranges join bitter hops and sweet malt in the mouth, rounded off by a dry, hoppy, bitter finish.

Red Squirrel ▪ Conservation Bitter

ABV 4.1%   500 ml   Pale malt, dark crystal malt, chocolate malt, Challenger hops

This interesting and successful beer lends its weight to the fight for red squirrel conservation, with a penny a pint donated to the cause, which is important to Hertford brewer Gary Hayward.

A chestnut-coloured ale with a soft, malty, nutty aroma. Squirrels would love the nutty, creamy, smooth and bittersweet taste, which also has traces of chocolate and a citrus and berry fruitiness. Dry, nutty, bitter finish.

Ridgeway ▪ Bitter

ABV 4%   500 ml   Maris Otter pale malt, Challenger and Boadicea hops

This bitter features the new Boadicea strain of aphid-resistant hops. The label pictures the Ridgeway long-distance footpath from which the business derives its name.

An amber beer with bitter orange marmalade in the aroma. The taste is floral and bitter-sweet, with light orange-citrus notes. Dry, floral, hoppy finish.

Sambrook's ▪ Wandle

ABV 4%   500 ml   Maris Otter pale malt, crystal malt, Boadicea, Fuggle and Golding hops

The first bottled beer from a brewery founded at the end of 2008. It takes its name from the river that flows through the part of South London where Sambrook's is based and is a slightly stronger version of a regular cask beer of the same name.

A dark golden bitter with fruity hops, caramel and toffee in the aroma. The taste is sweet, with a slightly sour caramel-like note from the malt and a good, tangy, peppery hop balance. The finish is dry, nutty-malty and firmly bitter.

Stonehouse ▪ Station Bitter

ABV 3.8%   500 ml   Pale malt, crystal malt, chocolate malt, Styrian Golding hops

Based near Oswestry In Shropshire, Stonehouse's brewery stands next to the Cambrian railway line, so all the beer names have a railway theme. Station Bitter is the only bottle-conditioned beer in the selection, brewed by Stonehouse but bottled by Oxfordshire Ales.

A bright amber bitter with a juicy aroma of bitter oranges and grapefruit, along with lightly toffee-like malt. The bittersweet taste is big and fresh, blending juicy grapefruit and orange with floral notes, while the finish rounds off dry, hoppy and a little bit chewy, but with more citrus fruit. Lots of flavour for the strength.

Suthwyk ▪ Bloomfields

ABV 3.8%   500 ml   Optic pale malt, crystal malt, Challenger, Fuggle and Golding hops

Sidney Bloomfield was the man who tended the Hampshire land now farmed by Suthwyk's Martin Bazeley back in the 1920s. He died at the tender age of 40 in 1926 – a sad consequence perhaps of the fact that, in those pre-tractor days, the 700 acres in his care were farmed only with horsepower. One field on the estate still bears his name and it is here that the barley turned into crystal malt used in this session ale is grown.

An amber-golden beer, with spicy hops, malt, melon and citrus fruit in the nose. The taste is clean, crisp and spicy, with malt sweetness and a light melon and peach fruitiness. The dry, bitter and fruity finish gradually turns more hoppy.

Teignworthy ▪ Reel Ale/Edwin Tucker's Devonshire Prize Ale

ABV 4%   500 ml   Maris Otter pale malt, crystal malt, Fuggle, Golding, Bramling Cross and Challenger hops

Reel Ale is Teignworthy's standard cask bitter. When bottle conditioned, it is sold under the same name and also as Edwin Tucker's Devonshire Prize Ale in the Tucker's Maltings bottled beer shop, adjacent to the brewery, largely as an attempt to catch the eye of the Devon holidaymakers the Maltings attracts.

Amber-coloured, with a malty aroma that has hints of nut, chocolate and orange. The taste is a bittersweet mix of malt and hops, with a touch of toffee, a light, citrus sharpness, a hint of pear and a drying backnote. The finish is dry, hoppy and firmly bitter.

Teme Valley ▪ That

ABV 4.1%   500 ml   Maris Otter pale malt, crystal malt, wheat malt, roasted barley, Challenger and Fuggle hops

You can see the logic behind some of the simple beer names from this Worcestershire microbrewery, based next to The Talbot pub in Knightwick. You just have to enter the bar and say 'I'll have a pint of That'. That is a perfect match for stews or game dishes, according to The Talbot's beer menu, the hop bitterness lightening rich sauces and gravies.

An amber-coloured bitter, with a malty aroma that has a touch of toffee. There's a malty moreishness to the bittersweet taste, along with a light, hoppy sharpness and hint of burnt grain. Burnt grain continues into the dry, bitter, malty aftertaste.

Tryst ▪ Antonine Amber

ABV 3.9%   500 ml   Pale malt, crystal malt, caramalt, oats, Challenger and First Gold hops

As the name reveals, an amber ale first bottled by this award-winning Scottish brewery in 2008. It's based on an old recipe.

Appley fruit, hop resins and malt figure in the aroma. The taste is mostly bitter (but not lacking sweetness) and malty, with some faint orange fruit. Dry, malty, bitter and hoppy finish.

Vale ▪ Wychert

ABV 3.9%   500 ml   Maris Otter pale malt, crystal malt, chocolate malt, Fuggle and Perle hops

'Wychert', meaning 'white earth', is the substance from which the walls of many of the oldest buildings in the lovely village of Haddenham (this Buckinghamshire brewery's first home) were constructed. You see them all around the village green – and on the bottle label.

An amber-orange ale (the label says 'auburn'), with an appealing, slightly chocolaty, aroma of toasted malt and light hop resins. A little toffee and nut from the toasted malt feature in the crisp, bittersweet taste, with a sharp, fruity acidity and light hop notes. Dry, hoppy and gently bitter finish.

White ▪ 1066 Country Bitter

ABV 4%   500 ml   Maris Otter pale malt, crystal malt, chocolate malt, Munich malt, wheat malt, Golding hops

A beer inspired by White Brewery's proximity to Hastings, 1066 and all that. It is now brewed weekly.

A dark golden bitter with light chocolate and nut in the malty aroma. The taste is crisp, bitter and orchard-fruity, with nutty malt behind. Dryness and a firm bitterness figure in the finish.

Bitters

Wickwar ▪ BOB (Brand Oak Bitter)/ Dog's Hair

ABV 4%   500 ml   Maris Otter pale malt, crystal malt, black malt, torrefied wheat, Fuggle and Challenger hops

BOB, one of Wickwar's most popular beers, took its name from Brand Oak Cottage, where one of the founders was living at the time the beer was created. This brew – which is sometimes packaged under the name of Dog's Hair – has also been sold in a filtered version called BOB Sparkling.

An orange-amber ale with toasted malt and gentle, floral hops in the aroma. The taste is malty and fairly sweet but with a bitter hop edge. Light toffee, pear drop and apple notes also feature. The drying finish is bitter and hoppy, but still malty.
Major stockist **Local Thresher**

Woodforde's ▪ Wherry

ABV 3.8%   500 ml   Maris Otter pale malt, crystal malt, Golding and Styrian Golding hops

This is a bottled version of CAMRA's Champion Beer of Britain of 1996, and very well does it reflect the success of its cask-conditioned equivalent. A wherry – as depicted on the label – is a type of shallow-draught sailing boat once commonly seen crossing the Norfolk Broads, close to Woodforde's home. After brewing, this beer is now taken to Hepworth's in Sussex for bottling, where it is filtered and then re-seeded with fresh yeast.

An orange-amber beer with a fresh and fruity aroma of oranges, mangos and a touch of elderflower. Bitter oranges and other citrus fruits lead the way in the crisp, clean taste, balanced by a light sweetness, before a dry, bitter, hoppy finish.

Best Bitters

The story of best bitter is the story of bitter, recounted in the previous chapter. The origins of the beer are the same, but the difference lies in the strength and body. Until the late 1970s (even later for some), most brewers only produced a handful of beer styles. There would be a mild, a bitter and then a best bitter. Where the divide actually falls between the last two is not possible to say with any accuracy. Some brewers declare beers of around 4.5% to be a bitter, rather than a best bitter, but for the purposes of this book, the line has been drawn at 4.1% for bitter, with stronger examples of the same, broad beer style featured
in this section for best bitters. Some beers here are described by brewers as pale ales, and others are labelled 'premium ales'. Also included in this section are more malty beers, such as red ales and Scottish-style 80/- beers, that fall into the same strength bracket.

At a Glance

Strength: ABV 4.2–5%

Character: Medium-to-full bodied, hoppy and bitter, but with some sweetness and other flavours from the malt, perhaps biscuit, nut and toffee. Hops may also bring fruit, herbal or floral notes. Colours are generally amber to brown (see also Golden Ales).

Serving temperature: Cool (12º C)

Food matches: Battered fish, roasted meats, sausages, pies, casseroles, barbecues, cheeses

Adur ▪ Velocity

ABV 4.4%   500 ml   Maris Otter pale malt, crystal malt, black malt, Perle and Hallertauer hops

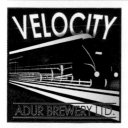

The label of this Sussex beer features the ultra-streamlined shape of the historic steam locomotive Mallard, which set the world-record steam engine speed of 126 mph in 1938, a record that still stands.

An orange-amber ale with a slightly appley aroma of soft toffee-malt. Toffee-like malt continues in the bittersweet taste, with a hoppy backnote, floral tones and more hints of apple. The finish is dry, malty and increasingly bitter.

Atlantic ▪ Red

ABV 5%   330/500 ml   Pale malt, crystal malt, wheat malt, Fuggle and First Gold hops

Fully known as Red Organic Premium Ale, this was Atlantic's first ever beer, introduced in January 2005. The inspiration, according to brewer Stuart Thomson, were the 'the malty red beers of Scotland and Ireland' and their copycats in New Zealand, Canada and Australia.

An orange-amber beer, with oranges featuring in the slightly tart, creamy aroma. The taste is bittersweet and filled with juicy blood orange character, with malt support and a drying hoppy note. The finish is also dry, hoppy and bitter, with more orange.
Major stockist **Local Asda**

Beachy Head ▪ Legless Rambler

ABV 5%   500 ml   Cocktail pale malt, crystal malt, Challenger and Bramling Cross hops

Beachy Head brewery is based in an old farm building among Sussex's South Downs – wonderful rambling territory, hence this beer's name. Like

Best Bitters

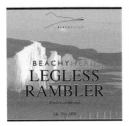

other ales, the recipe was created as a home brew, before brewer Roger Green turned professional, and has been fine-tuned since Beachy Head opened in November 2006.

An orange-amber ale with a zesty aroma of bitter orange peel and light background malt. Bitter orange contrasts with sweet malt in the satisfying taste, with hints of caramel, plus floral notes from the hops, adding to the mix. Citrus and floral elements feature alongside malt and hops in the dry finish.

Major stockist **Local Waitrose**

Beachy Head ▪ Original Ale

ABV 4.5% 500 ml **Cocktail pale malt, crystal malt, Perle and Challenger hops**

The first ever beer produced by Beachy Head when it opened on the East Sussex coast in 2006, this deep amber best bitter began life during brewer Roger Green's successful home-brewing days. It's also available in cask-conditioned form.

A complicated aroma of orchard and light citrus fruit with smooth, gently toasted malt leads to nutty malt, red apple and floral notes in the taste, along with a citrus sharpness, piney hops and a hint of bubblegum. The finish is nutty, malty and drying, becoming more hoppy and bitter.

Major stockist **Local Waitrose**

Blythe ▪ Chase Bitter

ABV 4.4% 500 ml **Pale malt, crystal malt, Challenger and Golding hops**

This amber-coloured ale is named after Cannock Chase, Staffordshire's famous area of forest and heathland, not far from Blythe Brewery's home on a farm at the edge of the quiet village of Hamstall Ridware.

A light floral, citrus aroma of faintly caramel-like malt leads to caramel malt notes in the bittersweet, slightly perfumed taste, along with sharp, citrus hops. Malt also lingers in the dry, bitter, hoppy finish.

Blythe ▪ Old Horny

ABV 4.6% 500 ml Pale malt, crystal malt, black malt, torrefied wheat, Challenger, Golding and Styrian Golding hops

Blythe's strongest bottled beer celebrates the Horn Dance, a morris dancing-type ritual that dates back to medieval times and is performed every autumn in and around the Staffordshire village of Abbots Bromley. The beer is also only an autumn performer, but bottles may be available a little longer.

An amber-coloured ale with light malt and citrus featuring in the aroma. The taste is fairly crisp and bitter, supported by sweetish malt, and hops soon take over in the dry, malty, rather bitter afterpalate.

Blythe ▪ Palmer's Poison

ABV 4.5% 500 ml Pale malt, crystal malt, black malt, flaked malze, Challenger and Golding hops

This dark best bitter has a dark connection with Staffordshire's history: it recalls in its name Dr William Palmer, a notorious serial killer from Rugeley who was hanged for his crimes in Stafford in 1856. He features, top-hatted, on the bottle label.

A copper-coloured ale with caramel-like toasted malt, earthy hops and and traces of orchard fruit apparent in the aroma. The mostly bitter, drying taste is earthy-hoppy and caramel-malty with just a hint of almond. The finish is both bitter and very dry, but with malt character still in evidence to the end.

Breconshire ▪ Red Dragon

ABV 4.7% 500 ml Pale malt, crystal malt, dark crystal malt, wheat
malt, Pioneer, Golding and First Gold hops

'Blending the red ale traditions of the North East
and Ireland with a hint of Welsh flair', declares
the label of Red Dragon. When first produced, the
beer included the trial hop known as 93/50, or
Susan, but this is no longer grown, so the recipe
has been modified to focus on three hop strains.
First bottled in winter 2004.

Soft, zesty oranges join slightly savoury malt in the aroma. The biscuity
taste features savoury malt up front, with sweet oranges and grapefruit
behind, along with a touch of chocolate. A big hop presence lingers in
the dry, malty, bitter finish, with more chocolate.

Buffy's ▪ Norwegian Blue

ABV 4.9% 500 ml Maris Otter pale malt, Fuggle, Golding and
Mount Hood hops

There's a gentle parrot theme running through Buffy's beer range. This
Norfolk brewery produces an ale called Polly's Folly and then there's
this Norwegian Blue, named after a species of colourful bird that Monty
Python once made the star of a memorable sketch. Being fresh and bottle
conditioned, this is no dead parrot, however. It was first brewed back in
1996 and is also sold in cask form. A favourite among the Buffy brewers.

Golden-amber with a melon and peach aroma, with a hint of chocolate.
The bittersweet taste has a caramel-like malt note, a light citrus
sparkle and fresh hop resins. Dry, bitter, hoppy and nutty-malty finish.

Butts ✳ Barbus Barbus

ABV 4.6% 500 ml Ingredients not declared

Barbus Barbus is the Latin name for the barbel fish and this beer
celebrates the sport of coarse fishing, the chief pastime of Berkshire

brewer Chris Butt. In cask form, it has quickly become the brewery's most popular ale. Three hop strains contribute to the flavour, but no further information about the make up of the beer is available, except that all ingredients are organic.

A dark golden beer with peppery grapefruit, orange and tropical fruit notes from the hops in the aroma. The taste is crisp, bittersweet and hoppy, laced with more orange and grapefruit, while the finish is dry and bitter, with citrus notes again from the plentiful hops.
Major stockist **Local Waitrose**

Cannon Royall ▪ Muzzle Loader

ABV 4.2%   500 ml   Cocktail pale malt, crystal malt, wheat malt, Challenger, Golding, Fuggle, Northdown and Willamette hops

The military weapon theme adopted for its beers by Worcestershire brew pub Cannon Royall continues with Muzzle Loader, an ale first brewed in 2000. It's also available in cask-conditioned form and features a blend of no fewer than five hops.

A deep golden beer with sharp, piney hops in the aroma, plus a light orange-like backdrop. The taste is earthy and bittersweet, with more orange zest and piney hops. Fruit lingers in the slowly drying, increasingly bitter and hoppy finish.

Cheddar ▪ Gorge Best

ABV 4.2%   500 ml   Maris Otter pale malt, crystal malt, chocolate malt, roasted barley, wheat malt, Challenger and Golding hops

What used to be Cheddar Best Bitter gained a packaging make over (like all Cheddar's beers) in 2008 and adopted the new name of Gorge Best (cheesy pun intended). It was one of the first beers Cheddar ever brewed and, says brewer Jem Ham, appropriately makes a good companion for mature cheeses.

51

An amber ale with tangy, sappy hop resins well to the fore in the aroma with soft malt behind. The taste is also hoppy and resin-like but not too aggressively so, with a hint of toffee coming from the light malt and a slightly briney character emerging. The finish is dry and malty at first, but hops soon build to leave a tangy, bitter finish.

Concrete Cow ■ Old Bloomer

ABV 4.7%   500 ml   Pale malt, crystal malt, amber malt, chocolate malt, Northdown and Fuggle hops

Wolverton, today a suburb of Milton Keynes, home of the Concrete Cow brewery, is a railway town. It was once home to a class of locomotive known familiarly as the Bloomer, allegedly because its lower parts were exposed in the style of ladies' fashion at the time. This fine best bitter recalls the Bloomer's heyday.

An amber beer (the label says ruby) with amber malt supplying nutty, toffee and milk chocolate notes to the aroma. Toffee-like malt runs on into the taste, which is smooth and bittersweet but with a hoppy sharpness, floral notes and a pruney dried fruit character in the background. Malt lingers in the dry, bitter, hoppy finish.

Coniston ✳ Bluebird Bitter

ABV 4.2%   500 ml   Maris Otter pale malt, crystal malt, Challenger hops

Bluebird is the beer upon which the fortunes of the Coniston microbrewery in Cumbria have been built. The cask version (3.6%) was judged Champion Beer of Britain in 1998, just three years after the brewery was set up, and this stronger, bottled version began to win accolades of its own soon after, with gold medals at London's International Food Exhibition and the Beauty of Hops competition. In 2001, the beer picked up yet another Beauty of Hops gold, this time judged by a panel of female experts as The Ultimate Fem'ale in a Bottle, and in 2003 it earned a silver in the International Beer

Competition. Bluebird – which brewer Ian Bradley sees as an ideal partner for fish and curry dishes, because of the spicy hop character – takes its name from the famous land and water speed machines used by Donald Campbell, who was tragically killed on Coniston Water in 1967.

A copper beer with a fruity hop nose. Pepper, spice and the zest of citrus feature in the clean, crisp taste and the dry, bitter, hoppy finish.
Major stockists **Asda, Booths, Tesco, Thresher**

Coniston ✳ Bluebird XB

ABV 4.4% 500 ml Maris Otter pale malt, crystal malt, torrefied wheat Challenger and Mount Hood hops

This version of Coniston's Bluebird has a pronounced American accent. Pitched just a touch stronger than the original bottled Bluebird (see above), this beer also includes Mount Hood hops from the USA in a coals-to-Newcastle bid to capture a slice of the American beer business. Now it's also on sale in the UK and was runner-up in the northern section of the Tesco Drinks Awards for 2009.

Copper-coloured, with piney hops at first in the nose, then a lime and grapefruit accent. The taste is nicely balanced with gentle, toffeeish malt in the background and a prevailing citrus sharpness. Dry, bitter citrus fruit leads the way in the aftertaste.

Coniston ▪ Old Man Ale

ABV 4.8% 500 ml Maris Otter pale malt, crystal malt, roasted barley, Challenger hops

Named after the mountain overlooking Coniston, Old Man – described as 'an old style bitter' – was first produced in cask in 1995, although at a lower ABV than this bottled version. The inclusion of roasted barley helps the beer to nicely complement beef and venison dishes, as well as black pudding, reckons brewer Ian Bradley.

53

A copper-coloured ale with juicy oranges and hop resins in the lightly malty aroma. Sharp, juicy orange notes from the hops lead over soft, nutty, treacly malt in the taste, before a dry, bitter, hoppy finish that has a gently-roasted, nutty malt character.

Conwy ■ Cwrw Gwledd/Celebration Ale

ABV 4.2%   500 ml   Maris Otter pale malt, crystal malt, chocolate malt, torrefied wheat, Cascade, Golding and Styrian Golding hops

Featuring Conwy Castle on the label, this was the first beer off the brewery's production line. The distinctive hoppy aroma comes from American Cascades which are allowed to stand in the copper after the boil has finished to impart their citrus qualities. The English name is not a literal translation of the Welsh. Cwrw Gwledd actually means 'feast ale'.

A dark golden beer with sharp grapefruit in the aroma, backed by gentle malt. In the crisp taste, a smooth, honeyed malt base is topped by zesty grapefruit from the hops. The finish is dry, increasingly hoppy and bitter, with more grapefruit notes. Well balanced, with the hops not overbearing.

Major stockists **Local Co-op and Thresher**

Corvedale ■ Farmer Rays Ale

ABV 4.5%   500 ml   Maris Otter pale malt, crystal malt, wheat malt, Fuggle hops

Farmer Ray is Ray Morris, the only hop farmer in Shropshire, who produces the hops that Corvedale uses in this amber-coloured best bitter. The beer is based on an earlier Corvedale beer known as Secret Hop. The hop at the time was Susan, a trial hop that is now no longer available.

There's a savoury malt note to the aroma, with light tropical fruit as a contrast. The same savoury character continues in the sweet taste, along with big flowery and tropical-fruity flavours. The finish is dry and a little chewy, but with more malt and floral notes.

Corvedale ▪ Norman's Pride

ABV 4.3%   500 ml   Maris Otter pale malt, crystal malt, wheat malt, Northdown hops

Norman Pearce is the landlord/brewer at The Sun Inn in Corfton, Shropshire. His family has been running the establishment since 1984 and this was his first commercial brew, introduced in 1999, when the tiny brewhouse behind the pub was commissioned.

A dark golden/amber ale with soft fruit – hints of apricot, pear and orange – in the aroma. There's a crisp bitterness to the taste, but also a floral, fruity (apricot) sweetness and some light background malt. The finish is floral at first, becomingly increasingly bitter and drying, with malt still evident.

Cropton ▪ Yorkshire Warrior

ABV 4.4%   500 ml   Pale malt, crystal malt, Fuggle hops

A dark golden-amber beer brewed to commemorate, and draw attention to, the achievements and sacrifices of the Yorkshire Regiment, with donations from sales going to support the unit's benevolent fund.

Toasted malt features in the aroma, followed by a bittersweet taste of malt and tart citrus fruit. Hops come through pleasantly in the dry, bitter finish, with more toasted malt. There may be a strong sulphurous presence in younger samples.

Dow Bridge ▪ Fosse

ABV 5%   500 ml   Maris Otter pale malt, crystal malt, chocolate malt, Challenger, First Gold, Northdown, Fuggle and Golding hops

An amber-coloured ale named after the famous Fosse Way, the Roman road that ran from Exeter to Leicester. Like Dow Bridge's other bottled beers, this strong bitter is also sold in cask-conditioned form. It was first brewed in 2003 and then first put into bottle two years later.

Best Bitters

Treacly malt and raisin notes feature in the spicy aroma. Sweet, treacly malt leads in the full-bodied, slightly creamy taste, but with hop bitterness and a gentle fruity sharpness coming through for balance. The finish is dry, bitter, malty and nutty.

Farmer's ▪ Captain Ann

ABV 4.5%   500 ml   Maris Otter pale malt, crystal malt, chocolate malt, Fuggle and Golding hops

 Local history is the inspiration for this ruby-coloured ale from Maldon, Essex. The Captain Ann in question is Ann Carter, who led two grain riots in the town in 1629, following a bad harvest. Grain was still being exported and Carter urged hungry townsfolk to raid a Flemish ship waiting to take the goods away. Ann was arrested, tried and hanged for her crime, which – as the bottle label suggests – was not so much her act of sedition as daring to call herself 'Captain'.

Toffee notes from the malt feature in the aroma and the taste, which is full-bodied and mostly bitter. Toffee and malt then linger along with some roasted grain in the dry, bitter finish.

Grainstore ▪ Ten Fifty

ABV 5%   500 ml   Maris Otter and Pearl pale malt, Fuggle, Northdown and Bramling Cross hops

The second ever draught beer from this Rutland brewery, first brewed in 1994 and taking its name from its original gravity (1050). A SIBA (Society of Independent Brewers) award winner in its cask form (among numerous awards).

A pale amber-coloured best bitter with a lightly hoppy aroma. The taste has a musty, appley, sweetish character, with a liquorice-like bitterness and also just a suggestion of almond. Malt flavours then linger in the dry, hoppy and bitter finish.

Hobsons ▪ Manor Ale

ABV 4.2%   500 ml   Maris Otter pale malt, amber malt, wheat malt, Cascade and Challenger hops

Originally brewed and bottled on behalf of the Severn Valley Railway, Manor Ale is also sold in cask-conditioned form under the name of Steam No.9. In the same fashion as other bottle-conditioned beers from this award-winning Shropshire brewery, it is presented in a smart package complete with a neck sleeve as found on wine bottles.

An unusual, golden-amber-coloured beer, surprisingly malty, almost chocolaty, in the aroma with tart orange-citrus notes then emerging. A nutty, malty flavour comes to the fore in the bittersweet, crisp taste, backed by a light citrus sharpness that is derived from the hops. The dry, bitter, hoppy finish features some faint, lingering, lemony sweetness.

Major stockist **Local Co-op**

Hoggleys ▪ Pump Fiction

ABV 4.5%   500 ml   Pale malt, crystal malt, roasted barley, torrefied wheat, Golding, Target, Chinook, Challenger and First Gold hops

One of two beers from this Northamptonshire brewery that share a humorous Quentin Tarantino movie theme. Pump Fiction features no fewer than five hops in the copper but also has plenty of crystal malt character. Like Reservoir Hogs (overleaf), it is now produced a couple of times every month.

A bright amber-coloured beer with some barley sugars and zesty oranges in the otherwise floral aroma. The taste is gently bitter, clean and fairly crisp, with nutty, toasted malt flavours overlaid with spicy hops. Hops then bring more bitterness to the dry, malty aftertaste.

Best Bitters

Hoggleys ▪ Reservoir Hogs

ABV 4.3%   500 ml   Pale malt, crystal malt, Golding and Target hops

This 'Quentin Tarantino' beer, like Pump Fiction (overleaf) was developed initially as a cask-conditioned ale for a beer wholesaler.

A bittersweet, copper-coloured beer with an aroma of peach, lemon and melon. The taste also majors on fruity hop flavours – peach, lemon and lime jelly – with good malt support and a dry backnote. The burnt malt in the bitter, dry finish is a bit of a surprise.

Hogs Back ▪ BSA (Burma Star Ale)

ABV 4.5%   500 ml   Maris Otter pale malt, crystal malt, chocolate malt, Fuggle and Golding hops

Introduced in 1995 for the 50th anniversary of VJ Day, and as a tribute to members of the Burma Star Association and prisoners of war in the Far East, BSA was re-labelled to mark the 50th anniversary of the founding of the Association in 1951. The label depicts servicemen of the day (actually the brewery partners' parents – one of whom served in the Burma Star movement) and recalls the famous and poignant quotation: *'When you go home tell them of us and say – For your tomorrow we gave our today'.*
The Imperial War Museum has taken stocks for its visitors and, for every bottle sold, Hogs Back pledges a donation to the BSA's welfare fund.

A robust amber ale with a sweet, spicy, earthy-malty aroma that has hints of orange and sultana. The taste is bittersweet and moreishly malty, with tangy hops and little bursts of citrus fruit. Some roasted grain and a hint of liquorice pop up in the dry, bitter, malty finish.
Major stockists **Budgens, Harrods, Londis, local Sainsbury's, Tesco, Waitrose**

Hogs Back ▪ TEA (Traditional English Ale)/Gardeners Tipple

ABV 4.2% 500 ml Maris Otter pale malt, crystal malt, chocolate malt, Fuggle hops

TEA – or Traditional English Ale, to give it its full name – is one of Hogs Back's longest established brews and was launched in bottle in 1997. It is now brewed weekly. The cask-conditioned version claimed the Best Bitter title at the 2000 Champion Beer of Britain contest. The beer has also been sold under the name of Gardeners Tipple at the Royal Horticultural Society in Wisley, Surrey, and various farm shops, and is also a big export to Russia.

An amber-coloured best bitter with malt supported by smoky orange notes in the nose. Lightly nutty malt and smoky, fruity hops feature in the well-balanced, bittersweet taste. Bittersweet, drying finish of malt and hops.
Major stockists **Budgens, Harrods, Londis, Sainsbury's, Tesco, Waitrose**

Hopdaemon ✳ Skrimshander IPA

ABV 4.5% 500 ml Pale malt, crystal malt, caramalt, Golding and Challenger hops

Inspired by Herman Melville's classic novel, *Moby Dick*, and its references to skrimshander (the craft of carving whale ivory), this beer, like this Kent microbrewery's other bottled beers, is also sold in cask form.

There are hints of chocolate in the malt in the aroma of this amber-golden-coloured beer, along with floral hops that continue into the mostly bitter taste. Other flavours include suggestions of milk chocolate and some grapefruit notes from the hops. Malt then lingers in the otherwise hoppy, bitter aftertaste.
Major stockists **Local Sainsbury's, Tesco and Thresher**

Best Bitters

59

Islay ▪ Angus Og Ale

ABV 4.5%   500 ml   Pale malt, crystal malt, Golding, Mount Hood and Styrian Golding hops

Angus Og was Lord of the Isles in the 14th century and resided on the Isle of Islay. He was an ally of Robert the Bruce. This beer is broadly based on Islay's session beer, Finlaggan Ale, and was first brewed in 2004.

An amber beer with oranges and floral notes, plus a touch of toffee from the malt, in the aroma. The taste is gently bitter, with citrus fruit and both hops and malt in evidence. Drying, bitter, hoppy finish.

Itchen Valley ▪ Hampshire Rose

ABV 4.2%   500 ml   Maris Otter pale malt, roasted barley, Target, Millennium, Galena and Pilgrim hops

Drawing on associations with the rose emblem of the county of Hampshire, where the brewery is based, Hampshire Rose was added to the Itchen Valley range in 2000 and is now one of the brewery's five core beers.

A dark golden ale with tinned pears and hints of orange in the aroma, along with light hop resins and subtle malt. The drying taste is firmly bitter and hoppy from the start, with traces of pear in the sharp fruit and a smooth malt backdrop. The finish is bitter, hoppy and dry.

Itchen Valley ▪ Wat Tyler

ABV 5%   500 ml   Maris Otter pale malt, crystal malt, Golding and Progress hops

Recalling, in its name, the famous leader of the Peasants' Revolt of 1381, Wat Tyler is described on the dark red label as 'a rebel of a beer'. A seasonal beer in its cask-conditioned form.

This red-brown ale has a fruity, malty nose, a bitter but balanced taste of smooth malt and hops, and a dry, bitter, hoppy finish.

Itchen Valley ▪ Wykehams Glory

ABV 4.3%   500 ml   Maris Otter pale malt, crystal malt, wheat malt, Whitbread Golding Variety, Golding and Fuggle hops

Wykehams Glory is named after William of Wykeham, who founded Winchester College (not far from the brewery) in the 14th century.

An amber ale with marmalade, malt and a hint of tropical fruit in the aroma. Gentle pear drops and sharp citrus/marmalade notes feature in the taste, along with a light hop bite. Dry, hoppy and bitter finish.
Major stockist **Local Waitrose**

Keystone ▪ Large One

ABV 4.2%   500 ml   Maris Otter pale malt, crystal malt, amber malt, wheat malt, Golding, Pilgrim and Pioneer hops

Alasdair Large is the name of the founder/brewer at Keystone Brewery, based near Salisbury, Wiltshire. That explains why this well-balanced, light-amber-coloured best bitter – Alasdair's first commercial brew – is called Large One.

There's a good malt presence in the aroma, with hints of chocolate and toffee, as well as orange-citrus notes from the hops. The taste is a good mix of nutty malt and tangy hops, with a slightly orangey note and plenty of body. The drying, hoppy finish is also moreishly malty.

King ▪ Five Generations

ABV 4.4%   500 ml   Maris Otter pale malt, crystal malt, chocolate malt, wheat malt, Golding and Cascade hops

A beer brewed to celebrate five generations of King brewing in Horsham, Sussex. The label depicts brewer James King (1808–79), who founded the family beer business back in 1850.

An amber beer with tart oranges and malt in the aroma. Roasted grain features in the bittersweet taste, along with tart orange-like fruit, and continues into the dry, fruity, bitter and hoppy finish.

Best Bitters

61

King ▪ Red River Ale

ABV 5%   500 ml   Maris Otter pale malt, crystal malt, chocolate malt, enzymic malt, Golding, Whitbread Golding Variety and Challenger hops

This strong beer takes its name from a tributary that runs from a mill pond in Horsham and is one of a few such 'red rivers' coloured by rust from the region's old iron workings.

An amber ale with hints of red that has a touch of chocolate in the roasted, malty aroma, along with hop resins. The taste is bittersweet and nutty-malty, with more roasted grain and modestly citrus hops. Roasted grain continues in the dry, bitter, hoppy finish.

Kingstone ▪ Classic Bitter

ABV 4.5%   500 ml   Maris Otter pale malt, crystal malt, Northern Brewer, Cascade, Willamette and Bramling Cross hops

'A classic farmhouse brew', was how original brewer Brian Austwick described this beer, hence the name. This was Kingstone's first ever beer, introduced in October 2005. The brewery has since changed hands and moved location, but Classic remains a core member of the ever-expanding range of cask- and bottle-conditioned beers.

An amber ale with juicy oranges and smooth, toasted malt in the aroma. More juicy oranges from the hops lead in the taste, which is pleasantly bitter with smooth malt behind. Oranges also linger in the hoppy, bitter, drying finish.

Little Valley ▪ Cragg Vale Bitter

ABV 4.2%   500 ml   Pale malt, crystal malt, wheat malt, sugar, Challenger, Golding and Pacific Gem hops

Cragg Vale is the peaceful corner of the Pennines that Little Valley calls home. Back in the 18th century, it was famous for its band of coin

counterfeiters, who sneakily chipped bits of gold off legal coins for use in making forgeries. Today, Cragg Vale Hill is a magnet for cyclists, who are drawn to the longest continuous gradient in England, climbing nearly 1,000 feet over five and a half miles. As with all Little Valley beers, Cragg Vale is organic and vegetarian friendly.

An amber beer with lightly toasted malt and mildly citrus hops in the aroma, which is also resin-like and nutty. The taste is grassy and dry at first, with a sugary toasted malt character behind and a refreshing grapefruit sharpness. Toasted malt continues into the dry, bitter finish in which hops linger.
Major stockist **Booths**

Lizard ▪ Bitter

ABV 4.2%   500 ml   Maris Otter pale malt, crystal malt, Fuggle hops

Bottled beers from this Cornish brewery are very attractively packaged, with the black and white flag of Cornwall's patron saint, St Piran, well in evidence. Lizard Bitter has been available in bottle since 2005.

Orange-amber, with pear and orange fruit in the aroma and light, smooth malt behind. The slightly savoury, bittersweet taste is also pear-fruity, with good body and malt support. The finish dries straight from the swallow, leaving a malty, bitter flavour.
Major stockist **Local Asda**

Meantime ▪ London Pale Ale

ABV 4.3%   500 ml   Pale malt, crystal malt, Munich malt, Golding, Cascade and Cluster hops

An award-winning creation, broadly based on a beer this Greenwich company used to offer called simply Pale Ale, but with a revised recipe and strength. It is matured at the brewery prior to bottling.

Best Bitters

An amber-golden beer with orange zest and tangy, earthy hop resins in the aroma. Earthy, sappy hops dominate the taste, overshadowing zesty citrus notes and malty sweetness, and continue into the dry, hoppy, tangy finish.

Major stockist **Tesco**

Nethergate ■ Augustinian

ABV 4.5%   500 ml   Maris Otter pale malt, crystal malt, torrefied wheat, Challenger and Styrian Golding hops

This golden-amber beer was originally brewed in 1998, to celebrate the 750th anniversary of the founding of Clare Priory, the mother house of the Augustinian friars in the English-speaking world, which was close to Nethergate's first home in Suffolk. It is now Nethergate's main bottle-conditioned beer, although small runs of the brewery's other cask beers are also produced on a monthly basis. To confuse matters, Nethergate used to produce two beers called Augustinian: one bottle-conditioned at 5.2% that included coriander, and was mostly sold to the USA, and this present beer, for the UK, which was only sold in cask form. This new bottled Augustinian still has a good US market, and is imported by Artisanal Imports of Austin, Texas.

Oranges and peaches feature in the aroma, followed by the same fruitiness, plus a touch of pear, in the bittersweet taste. The finish is dry, hoppy and bitter, with more pear.

O'Hanlon's ■ Royal Oak

ABV 5%   500 ml   Optic pale malt, crystal malt, torrefied wheat, Challenger, Northdown and Golding hops

Like Thomas Hardy's Ale (see Barley Wines), Royal Oak – first brewed in 1896 – was a great beer that Eldridge Pope, the Dorchester brewer, threw away when it left brewing in favour of pub retailing. O'Hanlon's has revived the brew and made it bottle conditioned for the first time. The label recommends it with grilled meats or a cheeseboard.

An amber beer with malt and floral notes on the nose. The taste is
bittersweet and malty, with apricot/orange notes. Dry, bitter finish.
Major stockists **Booths, local Asda, Majestic, Morrisons and Sainsbury's**

Oakleaf ✳ Heart of Oak

**ABV 4.5%   500 ml   Optic pale malt, crystal malt, chocolate malt,
Styrian Golding, Brewer's Gold and Golding hops**

Brewed initially to mark the 200th
anniversary of the Battle of Trafalgar, Heart
of Oak is named after the Royal Navy's
famous marching theme, composed by
Dr William Boyce in the 19th century, with
words added later by actor David Garrick.
Oakleaf Brewing sits on the edge of Gosport
harbour, just across the water from Portsmouth's active naval base.

An amber ale with nutty, toasted malt and fruity hops in the aroma.
Rich, toasted malt in the bittersweet taste is overlaid with juicy
grapefruit and tropical fruits. Tangy hops last longest in the dry, malty,
bitter finish.
Major stockist **Local Thresher**

Oakleaf ▪ Pompey Royal

**ABV 4.5%   500 ml   Pale malt, crystal malt, Golding and Styrian
Golding hops**

Brewed to celebrate Portsmouth's win in the 2008 FA Cup Final, Pompey
Royal is also an interesting re-creation of a lost beer. The original Pompey
Royal was a beer that emanated from Brickwoods brewery in Portsmouth,
which was closed by Whitbread in 1983. The beer lingered a while longer,
brewed elsewhere in the Whitbread empire, but was finally phased out.

An orange-amber ale with hints of banana and orange in the fruity,
malty aroma. The taste is full bodied and mostly bitter, but with some
malty sweetness, a hoppy edge and more banana, before a dry, malty,
hoppy and firmly bitter finish.
Major stockists **Local Asda and Thresher**

Best Bitters

Old Luxters ▪ Dark Roast

ABV 5% 500 ml   Maris Otter pale malt, crystal malt, chocolate malt, Fuggle and Golding hops

This cask and bottled ale was added to the range of beers produced by this Buckinghamshire vineyard-cum-brewery back in 1997. The name's a little deceptive: the beer is not as strong in roast flavour as it implies.

A dark chestnut beer with a malty aroma tinged with cocoa and citrus hops. The crisp, malty and gently roasted taste is well balanced and has orange-citrus notes. Dry, bittersweet finish, with roasted grain.

Outstanding ▪ OSB

ABV 4.4% 500 ml   Pale malt, crystal malt, roasted barley, Pacific Gem and Bramling Cross hops

First brewed in summer 2008, this amber ale, like other Outstanding bottled beers, is also available in a cask-conditioned version.

A chocolate orange aroma, followed by juicy, bitter oranges in the taste, over smooth malt that has hints of chocolate. Tea-like hop notes provide contrast. Good, dry, bitter and hoppy finish.

Pen-lon ▪ Twin Ram

ABV 4.8% 500 ml   Maris Otter pale malt, light crystal malt, Target, Tettnanger and Willamette hops

This is the beer the brewer drinks, which is as good a recommendation as any. Twin Ram from West Wales is Stefan Samociuk's favourite evening tipple and marries perfectly with thick-cut ham, granary bread and mustard, he reckons. This strong ale earned a commendation at the Wales True Taste awards for 2005–6.

An amber-coloured strong ale with a good mix of malt and orange/peach fruit in the aroma. Oranges and spicy hops

join light malt that has a hint of toffee in the bittersweet taste, while the drying finish is malty and bittersweet, turning more bitter, with an almost liquorice note from the hops.

Pitfield ■ Red Ale

ABV 4.8%   500 ml   Pale malt, crystal malt, chocolate malt, caramalt, Challenger and First Gold hops

A recent addition to Pitfield's selection, this red ale is, like all the brewery's range, produced from organic ingredients. Challenger hops are used for bitterness, with the popular dwarf hop First Gold added later and at the end of the copper boil for aroma.

Amber-red in colour, with a lightly nutty and toffee-like aroma, with hints of red apples and hop resins emerging. Lightly nutty malt features in the bittersweet taste, too, with an apple-like fruitiness on top, before a dry, bitter, nutty finish.

St Austell ✷ Admiral's Ale

ABV 5%   500 ml   Cornish Gold malt, Styrian Golding and Cascade hops

First brewed for the Celtic Beer Festival in 2004, this innovative dark ale was then bottled for the first time at Easter 2005, ready for the 200th anniversary commemorations of the Battle of Trafalgar. The innovation lies in the malt, which has been specially created from Cornish barley for St Austell by Tucker's Maltings in Newton Abbot. The barley is kilned at a high temperature to achieve a dark colour and nutty flavour but with humidity retained so that the sugars in the malt do not crystallize and become useless for brewing. As a result, St Austell doesn't need to include pale malt in the recipe. The same malt is also used in St Austell's main guest cask-conditioned beer, Tribute. Admiral's Ale was judged Supreme Champion in the International Beer Challenge 2008, organized by trade newspaper Off Licence News. The beer has been sold also as Smuggler's Ale in Asda stores.

Best Bitters

A copper ale with zesty oranges in the otherwise malty, nutty aroma. The taste nicely balances sweet, lightly nutty malt with a zesty, citrus hop crispness. Dry, nutty, bitter finish with lingering fruit and hops.

Sharp's ■ Single Brew Reserve

ABV 4.5% 500 ml Cocktail pale malt, crystal malt, roasted barley, Northdown, Hallertauer, Brewer's Gold and Bobek hops

Brewed once a year from new season barley and hops, this is the Sharp's harvest ale, if you like. The beer is matured at the brewery for two months and is then shipped from Cornwall to Hepworth in Sussex for bottling.

2008 version An amber ale with an aroma of caramel-like malt and tangerine citrus. The taste is bittersweet, with more juicy tangerines, light tangy hops and smooth, unobtrusive malt. The hoppy, bitter finish is slow to develop but has a faint caramel flavour and some lingering citrus fruit.

Sharp's ✳ Special

ABV 5% 500 ml Cocktail pale malt, crystal malt, roasted barley, Northdown, Brewer's Gold and Northern Brewer hops

Brewed at Sharp's in Cornwall and bottled at Hepworth in Sussex, this bottle-conditioned version of the brewery's slightly stronger (5.2%) cask ale of the same name was launched in 2009. The beer is matured for two months before bottling and then warm- and cold-conditioned in bottle for another two months before release.

An amber beer with orange marmalade and biscuity malt in the aroma and generally bitter taste, with hints of caramel and a good hoppy backbone. The finish is dry and bitter with a prolonged, leafy hop character. Clean and satisfying.

Spinning Dog ■ Mutley's Revenge

ABV 4.8% 500 ml Pale malt, crystal malt, Target and Fuggle hops

Mutley's Revenge carries on the dog theme established at this Hereford pub-brewery. It all began when ex-paratrooper Jim Kenyon named his business after his pet dog, Cassie, and started labelling cask beers with names like Chase Your Tail and Top Dog.

An amber ale with an aroma of chocolaty malt and floral orchard fruits. The taste is nutty, malty and fairly sweet but with a good bitter balance. The dry, nutty, malty finish has a good smack of hops.

Spire ■ 80 Shilling Ale

ABV 4.3%   500 ml   Pale malt, crystal malt, caramalt, roasted barley, Fuggle and Golding hops

First brewed for St Andrew's Day in 2007, to a traditional Scottish recipe, this beer from Chesterfield is one of the few 80 Shilling-style beers still in production, even in Scotland. The peculiar name is related to a Victorian method of taxing beer, with barrels being landed with 60, 70 or 80 shillings' worth of duty, depending on their strength. Brewery founder David McLaren is a former Scots Guardsman, which adds to this beer's credibility.

An orange-red beer with a deeply malty nose, rich in toffee. The taste is smooth and malty, with smoky toffee notes and a subdued, lightly fruity hop balance. After a velvety swallow, the finish is dry and bitter, but still malty and toffee-like. Not too heavy for a malty beer.

Spire ✳ Chesterfield Best Bitter

ABV 4.5%   500 ml   Maris Otter pale malt, Vienna malt, caramalt, wheat malt, Northdown, Progress and Hallertauer Mittelfrüh hops

While some of the ingredients of this orange-amber-coloured, Derbyshire beer may seem exotic – including continental malts and hops – the end result is, as Spire brewer David McLaren declares, a 'traditional, old-fashioned best bitter'.

The intriguing aroma of fruit cocktail and smooth malt features also a not unpleasant pinch of celery. In the mouth, there's a lively start from the resin-like hops, which are then balanced out by plenty of soft, background maltiness. The finish is dry, malty and hoppy, with hops soon running out the winners, leaving a bitter, leafy flavour.

Teignworthy ▪ Harvey's Special Brew

ABV 4.6%   500 ml   Pale malt, crystal malt, wheat malt, Golding and Fuggle hops

First brewed to celebrate the birth of brewery founders John and Rachel Lawton's son, Harvey, on 8 April 2000, Harvey's Special Brew is one of a small series of beers dedicated to the brewers' children (see also Pippa's Pint, below).

An amber-coloured beer with a malty aroma featuring hop resins and orange marmalade notes. The taste is sweet, earthy and malty with more marmalade character, some floral notes and a suggestion of liquorice. Tangy hops take the lead in the immediately bitter, dry, earthy finish.

Teignworthy ▪ Maltster's Ale

ABV 5%   500 ml   Maris Otter pale malt, crystal malt, Fuggle, Golding, Bramling Cross and Challenger hops

This was a innovative brew when first prepared in 1996, as it used the new barley strain Regina, but Teignworthy brewer John Lawton has now switched to the more familiar Maris Otter. The beer is sold on draught in winter and is bottled twice a year.

An amber beer that lives up to its name with a slightly earthy, malty nose. The taste is malty, earthy and bittersweet with a hint of liquorice, while the finish is dry, malty and increasingly bitter.

Teignworthy ▪ Pippa's Pint

ABV 4.7% 500 ml Pale malt, crystal malt, wheat malt, flaked maize, Fuggle, Golding, Bramling Cross and Challenger hops

As mentioned in the entry for Harvey's Special Brew (above), Teignworthy Brewery has developed a range of beers named after the children of brewer John Lawton and his wife, Rachel. Pippa's Pint was added to this range in October 2007, although fourth-child Pippa was actually born two years earlier.

A bright amber ale with an earthy aroma of malt, grassy hop resins and a hint of liquorice. There's more of the same in the unusual, but pleasant, taste, against a sweet backdrop. Hops and liquorice emerge again in the dry, hoppy finish.

Teignworthy ▪ Spring Tide

ABV 4.3% 500 ml Maris Otter pale malt, crystal malt, Fuggle, Golding, Bramling Cross and Challenger hops

Named after the high tides that wash up the Teign estuary close to Teignworthy's brewery in Newton Abbot, Devon, this orange-golden best bitter is brewed every four months or so.

The welcoming, nutty, chocolaty malt aroma also has a light orange fruitiness. Nutty malt and complex fruit (hints of pear and citrus) feature in the pleasantly bitter, slightly warming taste, along with herbal hops. The finish is dry, bitter and malty, with traces of orange.

Teme Valley ▪ Wotever Next?

ABV 5% 500 ml Maris Otter pale malt, crystal malt, chocolate malt, wheat malt, Northdown and Fuggle hops

This beer has found its niche. Initially also available in cask-conditioned form, it always sold better in bottle, so the draught version has now been discontinued. It's a good balance to sweet, sticky puddings, says Teme Valley brewer Chris Gooch.

An amber ale with malt and fruit in the nose (bitter oranges and orchard fruits). The taste is dry and malty, with an earthy bitterness and some light, zesty orange notes pushing through. There's some roasted grain in the dry, bitter, hoppy finish.

Vale ▪ Grumpling

ABV 4.6%   500 ml   Maris Otter pale malt, chocolate malt, Perle and Golding hops

Grumpling stones are the large, foundation stones upon which wychert walls (a mix of mud, straw and stone) are constructed. These walls are striking features of buildings in the picturesque Buckinghamshire village of Haddenham (seen in many a TV series, including *Midsomer Murders*), where Vale Brewery's first home could be found. The beer was first brewed in 1996.

A copper ale with an aroma of creamy, slightly nutty, toasted malt. Creamy, nutty malt also features in the full-bodied taste, but this is not sweet, as floral hops ensure good bitterness. Bitter, floral notes and creamy nut linger in the dry, substantial finish.

Vale ▪ Marks & Spencer Buckinghamshire Ale

ABV 4.6%   500 ml   Maris Otter pale malt, chocolate malt, Challenger and Golding hops

When Marks & Spencer came knocking on Vale Brewery's door in search of a Buckinghamshire Ale to include in its new range of bottle-conditioned beers, the buyers took a shine to Vale's Grumpling, and this, therefore, was given a new label for sale in the high-street stores.

A subsequent shortage of Challenger hops, however, placed Vale in a dilemma. There wasn't enough to sustain the quantity of Buckinghamshire/Grumpling that was demanded. The answer lay in substituting another hop, Perle, and this is what is used in beer branded Grumpling today. So, if you're looking for the original Grumpling, featuring Challenger hops, it's now called Buckinghamshire Ale.

A copper beer with big, flowery hops over smooth malt (hint of toffee) in the aroma, plus just a hint of pear drop. Floral hops lead the way in the bitter taste, but there's a moreish quality to the background malt and plenty of body. The finish is malty, drying and floral.
Major stockist **Marks & Spencer**

Wells & Young's ▪ Young's Bitter

ABV 4.5%   500 ml   **Maris Otter pale malt, crystal malt, Fuggle and Golding hops**

'A pint of Ordinary' is a familiar request in a Young's pub. It's a rather unflattering term afforded to Young's Bitter, the highly quaffable, 3.7% cask ale that has long been a favourite of Londoners. Sadly, in London it is no longer brewed, since Young's closed its Wandsworth brewery in 2006. The beer is now produced at what used to be Charles Wells (now Wells & Young's) in Bedford, where this somewhat stronger, bottle-conditioned version first saw the light of day in 2008.

A clean and fresh-tasting, dry, crisp bitter with gentle orange and soft malt in the aroma, followed by smoky orange notes and a refreshing, spritzy hop character in the taste. The finish is notably dry, hoppy and bitter.
Major stockists **Budgens, Majestic, Sainsbury's, Tesco, Waitrose**

Westerham ▪ British Bulldog

ABV 4.3%   500 ml   **Maris Otter pale malt, crystal malt, Northdown and Whitbread Golding Variety hops**

A blast from the past. Westerham Brewery is housed in a barn only a mile or so from Chartwell, the country residence of Sir Winston Churchill.

The Churchill connections show through in the name of this bottle-conditioned best bitter and in the 1940s styling of the colourful label. The beer is also traditionally English in style, employing plenty of locally-grown Kent hops in the copper boil for a fruity, leafy bitterness.

Dark golden-coloured, with smoky, orange-marmalade hop notes in the aroma, along with smooth, supportive malt and a hint of toffee. The taste is bittersweet, with hops and malt in balance, and more marmalade notes, plus a squeeze of sharp grapefruit. The finish is dry, leafy-hoppy and decidedly bitter.

Major stockists **Local Thresher and Waitrose**

Westerham ▪ William Wilberforce Freedom Ale

ABV 4.8% 500 ml Maris Otter pale malt, crystal malt, Fairtrade demerera sugar, Northdown and Golding hops

William Wilberforce was the passionate anti-slavery Member of Parliament whose great work led, eventually, to the abolition of this iniquitous practice in the year 1807. To commemorate the 200th anniversary of the banning of slavery, Westerham introduced this chunky best bitter, but with a warning. Brewer Robert Wicks was keen to point out that slavery, in the form of people trafficking, still exists, and he ensures that a financial contribution from each pint sold of this beer goes to the multinational charity Stop the Traffik, to aid its efforts in stamping out this inhuman activity. The beer's credentials are sound in another way, too, with Fairtrade demerera sugar from a smallholding in Malawi used as part of the recipe. A cask-conditioned version is also brewed, but at the slightly lower strength of 4.3%.

A dark golden-coloured beer with smooth, biscuity malt in the aroma, laced with floral notes and hints of orange and pineapple. The taste is bittersweet, featuring estery floral notes, some tropical and citrus fruit, a suggestion of almonds and, not least, tart, bitter hops. The finish is dry, bitter, solidly hoppy and tangy.

White ▪ Bottle of Hastings

ABV 4.5% 500 ml Pale malt, chocolate malt, Munich malt, wheat malt, Pioneer and Progress hops

Local history provides the play on words for the name of this best bitter, as it does for a number of this Sussex brewery's beers.

An amber ale with sticky, nutty, caramel-like malt in the aroma. The taste is bittersweet and medium bodied, a balanced mix of malt and hops, giving nutty and floral notes. Very dry, firmly hoppy, bitter finish.

White ▪ Maiden Bexhill Ale

ABV 4.5% 500 ml Pale malt, crystal malt, chocolate malt, wheat malt, Pioneer and Boadicea hops

Brewed to provide a beer souvenir for visitors to Bexhill-on-Sea, the home of White Brewing, this amber ale was also entered into a local best business award competition, in which White finished runner-up.

Nutty malt features in the aroma and taste of this bittersweet beer that has a crispbread-like character and a light floral sweetness. The finish Is dry, nutty, hoppy and bitter.

Major stockist **Local Thresher**

Why Not ▪ Cavalier Red

ABV 4.7% 500 ml Maris Otter pale malt, crystal malt, chocolate malt, Golding and Fuggle hops

A strong bitter with Civil War connections. It has been brewed since the start of the brewery's operations in 2005.

A mostly malty, amber-red-coloured beer with creamy malt and light orange and orchard fruits in the nose. The taste is bittersweet, with gentle caramel from the malt, a pinch of liquorice and some floral, fruity notes that linger for a while in the dry, malty, bitter finish.

Best Bitters

Wickwar ▪ Old Arnold

ABV 4.8%   500 ml   Maris Otter pale malt, Fuggle and Challenger hops

This Gloucestershire beer was named after the Mr Arnold who founded a brewery in Wickwar in 1800 and who merged his business with that of Mr Perrett, his near neighbour, in 1826. Their tower brewhouse was used for cider making from the 1920s and eventually closed in 1969. Brewing resumed at the site when Wickwar was set up in the old cooperage in 1990, and later moved into the old brewery itself. The recipe for this brew is based on Mr Arnold's 'Strong Old Beer'.

Amber-red with toffee notes from the malt in the aroma, and strawberry-like fruit emerging later. The mostly bitter taste is full of smooth, creamy malt with more traces of toffee. Berry fruits, pear drops and tangy hops also feature. Dry, malty, hoppy and bitter finish.

Woodforde's ▪ Admiral's Reserve

ABV 5%   500 ml   Maris Otter pale malt, crystal malt, rye crystal malt, Golding hops

First brewed in April 2002 to commemorate Woodforde's 21st anniversary, Admiral's Reserve is now a permanent member of the bottled range and is also available in cask-conditioned form.

An orange-amber ale with malt, light orange and gentle floral notes in the aroma. The taste is sweetish with smooth malt, floral notes and tart citrus fruit, before a dry, bitter, hoppy finish.

Woodforde's ▪ Marks & Spencer Norfolk Bitter

ABV 4.5%   500 ml   Maris Otter pale malt, crystal malt, caramalt, chocolate malt, Golding, Sovereign, Celeia and Styrian Golding hops

When Woodforde's first produced this beer in 2007 exclusively for Marks & Spencer stores, there was some speculation that it was the brewery's Nelson's Revenge under a different label. A quick comparison of the ingredients proves that it is not.

An amber ale with barley malt sweetness and mild sappy hops in the aroma, along with gentle orange notes. Earthy malt leads in the bittersweet taste, topped with lightly orangey hops, before a dry, hoppy and malty finish.

Major stockist **Marks & Spencer**

Woodforde's ▪ Nelson's Revenge

ABV 4.5%   500 ml   Maris Otter pale malt, crystal malt, Golding and Styrian Golding hops

Nelson's Revenge reflects the famous admiral's associations with Woodforde's county of Norfolk (the hero of Trafalgar was born there, at Burnham Thorpe in 1758). This dark golden ale started life as a house beer for the Limes Hotel at Fakenham.

After an appealing, grapefruit and orange aroma, a fine balance of malty sweetness and juicy grapefruit and tangerines from the hops features in the taste, with a dry, hoppy but only moderately bitter, fruity finish.

Best Bitters

Wye Valley ▪ Butty Bach

ABV 4.5%   500 ml   Maris Otter pale malt, crystal malt, wheat malt, flaked barley, Golding, Fuggle and Bramling Cross hops

Mainly aimed at Welsh customers, 'Little Friend' has been one of Wye Valley's most successful beers, its cask version voted top beer at the Cardiff Beer Festival three years running.

A dark golden ale with a syrupy, floral aroma with a light, sherbety hop note. The taste is floral and sweet, with a gentle hoppy, bitter balance, before a dry, hoppy, bittersweet finish.

Major stockists **Local Sainsbury's, Tesco, Waitrose**

Golden Ales

Golden Ales

Golden Ales are the flavour of the month. No: make that flavour of the decade. The idea of making very pale coloured beers is not new – for instance, some recipes unearthed by brewers for authentic IPAs have turned out remarkably light in colour – but the British ale drinker, until recently, has been generally treated to a diet of various shades of brown. The trend was broken back in the mid-1980s, when a handful of producers started developing beers that were yellow or straw-like in colour. One of these is featured in this section – the award-winning Summer Lightning from Hop Back Brewery.

These new beers not only provided a lighter touch, which was welcome particularly during hot weather, but also appealed to people who normally drank lager, which, in most instances, is the same shiny colour. The beers were sometimes created using lager ingredients, with lager malt employed to match the hue and the delicate palate of a pilsner or a helles beer, and sometimes lager hops such as Hersbrucker and Saaz were imported to make the match even closer. Other brewers stuck firmly to the British ale principle, but made sure that crystal malt did not join pale malt in the mash tun, so the beer was as light in colour as pale ale malt could make it.

Golden ales have become all the rage since. Nearly every brewery now has one. The shade of gold varies from brew to brew, from almost colourless, watery lemon to dark golden, verging on amber, and their strengths cover a wide spectrum (for the purposes of this book, this section tops out at 5%), but they have come to be gathered together as a distinct style, one that is recognized by CAMRA in its Champion Beer of Britain awards.

At a Glance

Strength: ABV 3–5%

Character: Golden in colour, with a sweetish, delicate malt character and good hop profile, often bringing citrus or floral notes to the palate

Serving temperature: Cool (12° C) or, for even more refreshment, slightly colder

Food matches: Seafood, cold meats, chicken, salads

Ballard's ▪ Nyewood Gold

ABV 5%   500 ml   Pearl pale malt, Pilot hops

'Nye', as in the name of this beer, is a collective noun for a group of pheasants, which appear on the label. This beer was first brewed for the 1997 Beauty of Hops competition, where it took top honours in the category for Phoenix hops. The same draught beer then claimed the Best Strong Bitter prize at the Champion Beer of Britain contest in 1999. It was bottled for the first time the same year. Phoenix hops now being scarce, Ballard's has switched the hop to Pilot. The brewery recommends serving Nyewood Gold at a slightly lower temperature than its other beers.

This golden ale has a spicy aroma featuring prominent tart lemon and pineapple notes. Hops and a gentle bitterness overlay smooth, sweet pale malt and light pineapple flavours in the taste, and all this is rounded off by a finish that is dry, hoppy and bitter with yet more tropical fruit character.

Major stockists **Local Asda, Budgens and Waitrose**

Blythe ▪ Bitter

ABV 4%   500 ml   Pale malt, Golding, Fuggle and Cascade hops

Like this Staffordshire brewery, this beer takes its name from the River Blythe that runs at the back of the brewhouse. The cask version was runner-up for West Midlands CAMRA's Beer of the Year award in 2005.

A golden beer with grapefruit and orange notes in the aroma and the crisp, clean, bittersweet taste, rounding off with a dry, bitter, hoppy finish.

Blythe ✳ Ridware Pale

ABV 4.3%   500 ml   Lager malt, Centennial and Cascade hops

Blythe Brewery is located on a farm on the outskirts of the Staffordshire village of Hamstall Ridware, which lends its name to this pale golden beer that was first brewed in 2007.

A refreshing, pale straw-coloured beer with a keenly hoppy aroma, filled with lemon, lime and grapefruit. Lemon and sweet oranges join a piney bitterness in the spritzy, bittersweet taste, all followed by a dry, hoppy, bitter and citrus finish.

Blythe ■ Staffie

ABV 4.4%   500 ml   Pale malt, torrefied wheat, Chinook and Cluster hops

Celebrating the Staffordshire bull terrier, this best bitter has an American accent, thanks to the inclusion of Chinook and Cluster hops.

A golden bitter with a peppery, orange and grapefruit aroma. The crisp taste is filled with orange and lemon notes, and is bittersweet and floral, too, with a good, but unobtrusive malty body. The firmly dry, bitter finish is lipsmackingly hoppy.

Brakspear ■ Oxford Gold

ABV 4.6%   500 ml   Pale malt, crystal malt, Golding and Target hops

As Brakspear Live Organic, this ale won the first ever Organic Beer Challenge, in 2000. It then changed its name to Brakspear Organic Beer, before changing yet again to the current name. The beer now belongs

Golden Ales

to Marston's, following the acquisition of the Wychwood and Brakspear breweries in Witney in 2008, and is brewed at Witney but bottled by Fuller's in London. A non-bottle-conditioned version is produced for sale in Sweden.

A dark golden ale with a malty aroma that has a marmalade-like fruitiness. Malt is paired with vaguely orange and apricot fruit in the bittersweet taste, and features again in the dry, tangy-hoppy, increasingly bitter finish.

Major stockists **Asda, Morrisons, Sainsbury's, Waitrose**

Breconshire ▪ Cribyn

ABV 4.5%   500 ml   Optic low colour malt, Bramling Cross, Northdown and Challenger hops

Named after a Brecon Beacons peak that is known to some climbers as 'the Welsh Matterhorn', this straw-coloured beer was first brewed in 2007, as a replacement for Brecknock Best in the brewery's cask beer range. It was first bottled in November 2008. The brewers suggest trying it with fish, white meats or goat's cheese.

A soft, sweet aroma of lightly peppery lemon and grapefruit leads on to a crisp, firmly hoppy taste of citrus and melon, with a slightly perfumed note to the hop. The finish is dry and notably hoppy, with more fruit. A clean, tasty beer with good body and character.

Breconshire ▪ Golden Valley

ABV 4.2%   500 ml   Optic pale malt, crystal malt, Progress hops

First bottled in 2003, the award-winning Golden Valley was one of this mid-Wales brewery's first ever beers. It was judged Champion Beer of Wales in 2004–5 in its cask-conditioned form. Other awards have ensued. It is 'particularly good with curries and spicy food as well as a BBQ on a warm evening', according to the bottle's back label.

A golden ale with bubblegum and tropical fruit in the nose, with hops slowly adding hints of oranges. The mouthfeel is soft, bringing more estery fruit, oranges and bubblegum, along with a savoury moreishness and a light bitterness. The dry, hoppy, savoury finish is increasingly bitter.

Major stockists **Local Tesco and Thresher**

Cannon Royall ▪ King's Shilling

ABV 3.8%   500 ml   Cocktail and Optic pale malts, wheat malt, Challenger, Golding, Fuggle, Northdown and Cascade hops

This Worcestershire microbrewery adopts military connections as the theme for most of its beers, with this straw-coloured bitter taking its name from the colloquialism 'taking the King's shilling', meaning to join the armed forces. It was first brewed in 2000 and is also available as a draught beer.

A zesty aroma of sherbet lemons and pine, largely from the Cascade hops, leads onto a crisp, dry, bitter taste with yet more pine character and some light lemon sweetness. The finish is dry, hoppy and bitter.

Castle Rock ▪ Elsie Mo

ABV 4.7%   500 ml   Low colour Maris Otter malt, torrefied wheat, Challenger, Styrian Golding and Golding hops

Who, precisely, was Elsie Mo? A pointless question. Despite the blonde bombshell pictured on the label, the name of this Nottinghamshire beer simply comes from the type of malt used: low colour Maris Otter, or LCMO.

A golden ale with pungent lemon and grapefruit in the nose and taste. Lots of zesty citrus hops dominate a clean, smooth malt base, before a dry, bitter finish with lingering citrus fruit.

Major stockist **Local Asda**

Golden Ales

Cheddar ✳ Potholer

ABV 4.5%   500 ml   Maris Otter pale malt, crystal malt, wheat malt, Challenger, First Gold and Styrian Golding hops

When, in 2006, Cheddar Ales opened its doors on the outskirts of the Somerset village of the same name, close to the famous caves that attract thousands of visitors each year, Potholer was its first offering. This refreshing, golden beer has since claimed Society of Independent Brewers (SIBA) regional contest medals.

An appealing, peppery aroma of grapefruit is followed by grapefruit and orange in the crisp taste, before a dry, hoppy, bitter-citrus finish.

Concrete Cow ▪ Midsummer Ale

ABV 3.8 %   500 ml   Pale malt, Pioneer and Styrian Golding hops

Not just a beer for the hottest months or the longest day: the Midsummer in the name of this beer is Midsummer Boulevard, the main street in the brewery's home town of Milton Keynes. The road is so laid out that the sun rises and sets along its path on the summer solstice. The beer is brewed from March to October.

A golden session beer with a clean, lightly hoppy nose that features a twist of lemon. The taste is crisp and falls on the bitter side of bittersweet, with a lemony note from the hops and smooth, delicate pale malt in support. Dry, hoppy finish. A tasty beer for the strength.

Concrete Cow ▪ Watling Gold

ABV 4.5%   500 ml   Pale malt, crystal malt, amber malt, First Gold and Golding hops

Watling Street, the old Roman road that ran from Dover, through London and then across to the Welsh borders, bisects the modern town of Milton

Keynes. The oldest Roman coin to be found in Britain was discovered close to the road and lends its name to this golden ale that is available all year-round. A Roman soldier features on the colourful label.

A deep golden beer with a floral, fruity aroma loaded with peach, elderflower and melon notes. The taste is similarly floral and zesty, with more elderflower and citrus character on a silky, honeyed malt base. The dry finish is floral, hoppy and increasingly bitter. Satisfying and clean.

Conwy ▪ Balchder Cymru/Welsh Pride

ABV 4%   500 ml   Maris Otter pale malt, crystal malt, chocolate malt, torrefied wheat, Cascade, Styrian Golding and Golding hops

Balchder Cymru, or Welsh Pride in English, is Conwy's best-selling cask ale, introduced in bottle for St David's Day, 2007. The red dragon of Wales features prominently on the green label.

A golden bitter with a creamy aroma of nutty malt. The bittersweet taste is also nutty and malty with a light hoppy edge and a gentle citrus note. The finish is dry, nutty and bitter.

Major stockists **Local Co-op and Thresher**

Country Life ▪ Pot Wallop

ABV 4.4%   500 ml   Maris Otter pale malt, Fuggle and Golding hops

First brewed for the Westward Ho! Potwalloping Festival in 2000 and now available all year-round. The festival celebrates the ancient ritual of replacing washed-up pebbles on the town's famous pebble ridge.

A golden ale with a citrus-sharp, hoppy aroma with pear notes. The drying taste falls on the bitter side of bittersweet and features pears, hops and lemon. The dry, bitter finish is fruity and eventually hoppy.

Golden Ales

Cropton ■ Endeavour

ABV 3.6%   500 ml   Pale malt, Challenger and Golding hops

Named after Captain Cook's famous ship, that originally sailed from nearby Whitby, Endeavour is a refreshing, golden bitter aimed at the tourist market in the seaside resort.

Tart fruit – orange, apple and lemon notes – joins hop resins in the aroma, followed by bittersweet oranges in the crisp, dry, tart taste. Juicy oranges then lead into the finish that becomes increasingly dry and bitter.

Dartmoor ■ IPA

ABV 4%   500 ml   Optic pale malt, crystal malt, Challenger, Progress and Perle hops

While there's a decent hop character to this enjoyable, golden ale, it doesn't have the strength to be classed as an authentic IPA, despite its name. The beer joined Jail Ale (see below) in 2008 as Dartmoor's second, regular bottle-conditioned offering.

Floral, honeyed, toffee-like malt features in the aroma. The taste is bittersweet with a tannin-like dryness. Apricot and orange notes come from the floral, fruity hops and malty sweetness lingers in the background. Dry, hoppy finish.

Dartmoor ■ Jail Ale

ABV 4.8%   500 ml   Optic pale malt, crystal malt, wheat malt, Challenger, Progress and Perle hops

Based, as it is, just a short tunnelling distance from the famous prison, what else could this Devon brewery call its well-established, premium cask-conditioned beer? This bottle-conditioned version was winner of the Tucker's Maltings Bottled Beer Competition in 1999.

Toffee-like malt fills the aroma of this golden ale and also the smooth, fairly sweet taste, where it is joined by floral hop notes. The finish is dry, malty and bitter.

Major stockists **Local Tesco and Waitrose**

Deeside ▪ Brude

ABV 3.5%   500 ml   Pale malt, crystal malt, wheat malt, oatmeal, Fuggle, Willamette, Aurora and Bramling Cross hops

In its new home at the Deeside Activity Park, what used to be known as Hillside Brewery now produces three bottle-conditioned beers. Brude is a session ale first brewed in 2006 and presented in a swing-stoppered, screen-printed, classy bottle. It is named after a Pictish king called Brude mac Bili, who defeated the Angles at the Battle of Nechtansmere (or Dunnichen) in the year 685, a victory that helped Scotland establish itself as a nation.

This golden ale has a full, fresh, very fruity aroma, loaded with sweet grapefruit and elderflower notes. The taste is dry and bitter, with a refreshingly sharp, citrus character and grapefruit well to the fore. The finish is very dry, bitter and hoppy.

Deeside ▪ Macbeth

ABV 4.3%   500 ml   Pale malt, crystal malt, wheat malt, Fuggle and Cascade hops

The Scottish king made famous by Shakespeare was killed just over the hill from Deeside Brewery's original home, at the Battle of Lumphanan (1057). This golden beer was designed to commemorate the real Macbeth, rather than the one known from literature. As for Brude (above), the brewery declares it suitable for both vegetarians and vegans.

Soft, melony fruit and smooth malt are obvious first in the aroma, with floral and grapefruit notes then emerging. The taste is very flowery and mostly bitter, with some tart tropical fruit and light background malt, before a dry, bitter, hoppy finish.

Durham ✳ Cloister

ABV 4.5%   500 ml   Maris Otter pale malt, lager malt, crystal malt,
wheat malt, Saaz, Target, Cascade and Columbus hops

All Durham Brewery's beer names have connections with
the spiritual roots of its historic home city and especially the
spellbinding, ancient cathedral – hence the name of this
particular bottled beer that, in its cask form, has a different
identity, being sold as Prior's Gold.

**A full-flavoured, golden bitter with grapefruit in the
sherbety hop aroma. Sharp grapefruit continues in the
clean, hoppy, bittersweet taste, before a dry, bitter,
hoppy finish with more grapefruit.**

Farmer's ▪ Farmer's Golden Boar

ABV 5%   500 ml   Maris Otter and Pearl pale malt, lager malt, caramalt,
Cascade hops

Farmer's Ales brewery stands in former stables
behind the Maldon's Blue Boar Hotel – hence the
name of this straw-coloured ale. Golden Boar was
first brewed in 2006 and has already picked up a
local beer festival award in its cask form. Cascade
is the sole hop, generously added to the copper to
create an American craft-brew experience.

**Juicy, sharp grapefruit and lemon dominate the aroma and taste,
which is also piney and bittersweet. Bitter grapefruit lingers in the
dry, hoppy finish.**

Farmer's ▪ Puck's Folly

ABV 4.2%   500 ml   Lager malt, Golding hops

A local production of *A Midsummer Night's Dream* back in 2003 was the
inspiration for this pale beer from Maldon, Essex. Brewer Nigel Farmer had
been enjoying a pint of Buffy Brewery's Polly's Folly just before watching

the play, and, observing the character of Puck, put the two ideas together to create Puck's Folly.

A pale, green-golden ale with gentle malt and sappy hops in the lightly lemony aroma. Sappy, grassy hops lead over sweet pale malt and gentle lemon in the bittersweet taste, before a dry, hoppy and bitter finish rounds off.

Fox ▪ Branthill Norfolk Nectar

ABV 4.3%   500 ml   Maris Otter pale malt, torrefied wheat, Bramling Cross and Fuggle hops

A fairly sweet beer, hence the name Norfolk Nectar, brewed from barley grown at Branthill Farm, near Wells-next-the-Sea in Norfolk.

A bright golden beer featuring creamy pale malt and lightly fruity hops (tinned peaches and orange zest) in the aroma. The taste is very smooth, with more creamy pale malt, some peachy fruit and also a tea-like bitterness. The drying, hoppy, creamy finish starts bittersweet but becomes gradually more bitter.

Fox ▪ Drop of Real Norfolk

ABV 4.4%   500 ml   Maris Otter pale malt, torrefied wheat, Fuggle and Styrian Golding hops

A pale, citrus bitter, like the above beer brewed from barley grown at Branthill Farm close to Norfolk's north coast and not far away from Fox's home at Heacham.

Tart, fruity hops, with bitter orange and grapefruit flavours, fill the aroma, and sharp grapefruit then continues into the taste, which is mostly bitter and slightly perfumed, with background sweetness from silky pale malt. Sharp, citrus hops feature in the drying finish, with bitterness building.

Golden Ales

Fox ■ Grizzly Beer

ABV 4.8%   500 ml   Lager malt, wheat malt, Cascade hops, honey

'Brewed from a Rocky Mountain recipe', declares the label of this refreshing Norfolk coast beer, which also pictures a ferocious example of the animal from which it takes its name.

A very pale, green-golden beer, with sharp, sherbety, citrus hops in the aroma bringing lemon, grapefruit and sappy, herbal notes. In the crisp taste, delicate pale malt is overlaid with more sharp, refreshing citrus notes, with grapefruit again to the fore, and this carries through into the dry, citrus, hoppy and bitter finish.

Freeminer ✳ Gold Miner

ABV 5%   500 ml   Quench pale malt, pale crystal malt, First Gold hops

Exclusive to the Co-op, Gold Miner was launched in 2003, although the beer had previously enjoyed success as a cask beer called Gold Standard, winner of a Beauty of Hops award. Note the innovative, peel-back label on the new light-weight bottle, giving more information about the provenance of the beer (both the barley and hops are grown locally, the hops solely for Freeminer by a Worcestershire farmer).

A dark golden beer with grapefruit, pineapple and hop resins featuring in the aroma. Sharp, citrus, hoppy notes then fill the mouth, with a touch of pineapple and plenty of sweet malt for support. The finish is dry, full and notably hoppy.

Major stockist **Co-op**

Great Oakley ■ Gobble

ABV 4.5%   500 ml   Pale malt, torrefied wheat, Cascade hops

Ignore the turkey featuring on the label: the name of this beer is actually derived from the initials of Great Oakley Brewery. It was first brewed in

2005 and is available in cask-conditioned form, too. It's a good beer to wash down a curry, according to the brewers.

The aroma is tart, with suggestions of sherbet lemons. More tart fruit – sherbet lemons and pronounced, juicy grapefruit – fills the bittersweet, peppery taste, and grapefruit then runs on into the dry, bitter finish in which the piney nature of the Cascade hops – added at three stages during the copper boil – also shines through.

Great Oakley ▪ Wot's Occurring

ABV 3.9% 500 ml Pale malt, crystal malt, torrefied wheat, Willamette hops

First brewed in 2005, Wot's Occurring is this Northamptonshire brewery's best-selling beer. One to drink with white meats, according to brewer Phil Greenway.

Juicy oranges feature in the lightly spicy aroma of this golden bitter, followed by a crisp, mostly bitter taste balanced by sweet orange flavours. Oranges linger in the drying, hoppy and bitter finish.

Haywood 'Bad Ram' ▪ Dr Samuel Johnson

ABV 4.5% 500 ml Maris Otter pale malt, crystal malt, Challenger hops

Haywood 'Bad Ram' Brewery's home is on a holiday park near Ashbourne, Derbyshire, an area once a favourite of literary giant Dr Johnson. This beer in his honour was developed from a recipe by Steve Wellington, head brewer at the White Shield Brewery, and was first brewed in 2003.

Bitter oranges are the hallmark of this golden ale, from aroma through to finish. Tangy hops also feature in the taste and help dry the aftertaste. Fairly light bodied for the strength.

Hepworth ▪ Marks & Spencer Sussex Bitter

ABV 3.8%   500 ml   Pale malt, crystal malt, aromatic malt, flaked maize, Golding hops

Part of the M&S range of bottle-conditioned beers, Hepworth's Sussex Bitter does more than just hail from Sussex. The pale ale malt is grown in the county, as are the Golding hops that are used three times in the brewing process, including for dry hopping at the end, to create a clean, quaffable bitter.

A golden ale with a spicy aroma of fruity hops (lemon, melon and a hint of pear) and subtle pale malt. The taste is crisp and bitter, with sweet orange and melon flavours, plus a drying, hoppy backnote. Dry, hoppy and bitter finish.

Major stockist **Marks & Spencer**

Hepworth ▪ Prospect

ABV 4.5%   500 ml   Pale malt, crystal malt, Admiral and Golding hops

Brewed using barley grown on the Goodwood estate – pictured artistically on the label – Prospect is described as a 'Sussex organic pale ale'.

A bright golden ale with a soft, floral, honeyed aroma, with a dash of lemon. The taste is also honey-floral and smooth, with initial sweetness soon tempered by a bitter note. The dry, honeyed finish is firmly bitter.

Major stockist **Local Waitrose**

Hobsons ▪ Town Crier

ABV 4.5%   500 ml   Maris Otter pale malt, crystal malt, Progress and Golding hops

Intriguingly described by the brewers as a 'pale Bavarian ale', Town Crier is recommended for drinking younger and cooler than their other bottled

offerings. It was first brewed as a cask beer for a town crier competition in 1994 and is still available in draught form.

A pale yellow beer with sharp lemon notes and delicate pale malt in the nose. The taste is crisply bitter and clean, with a freshening lemony sweetness. Dry, hoppy, bitter finish.
Major stockist **Local Co-op**

Hoggleys ✳ Northamptonshire Bitter

ABV 4%   500 ml   Pale malt, First Gold, Golding and Challenger hops

Hoping to cash in on local allegiances, Hoggleys made Northamptonshire Bitter the first beer they produced for the commercial market. That was back in 2002, and the start of a lot of good things from this small brewery.

Malt leads the way in the aroma of this golden bitter, with a light, citrus-hoppy balance. The taste is fairly crisp, a bittersweet mix of malt and hops with delicate floral and citrus notes from the hops and a touch of honeyed smoothness. There's more honey softness on the swallow, leading to a dry, gently bitter, moreish finish.

Hop Back ✳ Summer Lightning

ABV 5%   500 ml   Maris Otter pale malt, Golding hops

The Summer Lightning story begins in 1988. Hop Back Brewery founder John Gilbert came up with the recipe for this pale, crisp and hoppy, yet strong, beer to contrast with other 5% beers of the time, which were nearly all dark, sweet and sickly. For a name, he stole the title of a PG Wodehouse novel. In cask form the beer has been a trend-setter. Since winning the Best New Brewery Beer award at the Champion Beer of Britain contest in 1989, it has inspired brewers up and down the land to create strong but pale beers which have appeal beyond the traditional ale drinker. The bottle-conditioned version is now a single-hop brew, dropping the Challenger hops it used to include in favour of East Kent Goldings only. The draught version maintains both hops. The brewery recommends serving this and its other bottled beers on the cold side of cool. CAMRA's Best Bottle-Conditioned Beer in 1997.

A pale golden, easy-drinking, strong bitter. Hop resins and a little citrus fruit, along with sweet pale malt, in the aroma lead onto a bittersweet taste of tangy hops, smooth pale malt and hints of pear and lemon. The finish is dry, bitter and malty, with tangy hops.
Major stockists **Booths, Co-op, Majestic, Morrisons, Oddbins, Tesco, Waitrose**

Humpty Dumpty ▪ Cheltenham Flyer

ABV 4.6% 500 ml   Maris Otter pale malt, crystal malt, wheat malt, Challenger and Mount Hood hops

A long-standing Humpty Dumpty beer, this golden ale celebrates the golden age of locomotion in an evocative label that depicts Cheltenham Spa station in its railway pomp, shrouded in steam.

A mellow, honeyed aroma also features light citrus fruit and grassy hop resins. Grassy hops lead the way in the taste, supported by a gentle citrus sharpness and smooth, honeyed malt. Smooth malt lingers in the drying, bitter, hoppy finish.

Humpty Dumpty ▪ Swallowtail

ABV 4% 500 ml   Maris Otter pale malt, caramalt, wheat malt, Willamette, Bramling Cross and Cascade hops

Named after a variety of local butterfly (which features large and colourful on the label), Swallowtail is Humpty Dumpty's biggest selling beer. It predates the change of ownership at the brewery, but the recipe has been revised since the new regime took over. It features Maris Otter barley grown at Branthill Farm in north Norfolk.

A golden ale with light malt joining hop resins and hints of pineapple in the aroma. The taste is peppery, bitter and hoppy with gentle malt support, while the finish is dry, hoppy and full.

Ironbridge ▪ 1779

ABV 4.3%   500 ml   Maris Otter pale malt, crystal malt, torrefied wheat, Pilot, Sovereign and Boadicea hops

'To commemorate the year in which the world's first cast iron bridge was built over the River Severn between Coalbrookdale and Broseley,' reveals the label of this golden bitter, referring to the structure, local to the brewery, that helped trigger the start of the Industrial Revolution.

Malt features in the aroma and provides smoothness to the taste, which is otherwise sharp and tart with hints of grapefruit. The same tart fruit continues into the dry, hoppy, bitter finish.

Ironbridge ▪ Coracle

ABV 3.9%   500 ml   Maris Otter pale malt, caramalt, wheat malt, Boadicea and Golding hops

The small, round boat known as a coracle has long had associations with the River Severn, which runs close to this Shropshire microbrewery. As is stated on the label of this bitter, 'the small craft could easily be carried on a man's back and were used extensively by poachers to transport fish and game back to their homes, usually under the cover of night.'

Light, tart citrus notes and Ovaltine-like malt in the aroma lead to a crisp, bittersweet taste that is spritzy yet malty, with sweet lemon notes from the hops. Dry, increasingly bitter finish with more lemon.

Ironbridge ▪ Gold

ABV 4.6%   500 ml   Maris Otter pale malt, Pilot, Sovereign and Boadicea hops

The brewery's best-selling beer, originally produced for Ironbridge town's Brass Band Festival in 2008 and quickly making itself a permanent fixture.

A bright golden beer with a mellow and soft aroma of honeyed pale malt and just a squeeze of lemon. The firmly bitter taste is also honeyed, with suggestions of tart lemon. In the finish, after a smooth swallow, sappy bitterness really kicks in and lasts well.

Itchen Valley ▪ Pure Gold

ABV 4.8%   500 ml   Maris Otter pale malt, Saaz and Cascade hops

Pure Gold – named after the gold bullion said to be lost with the sinking of HMS Hampshire off the coast of Orkney on 5 June 1916 – is a beer bursting with lively hop flavours. The secret is the addition of Cascade hops in the fermenting vessel and conditioning tank, to complement the gentler Saaz hops which make their presence known in the copper.

A bright golden beer with a fresh, zingy aroma of lemon, orange, grapefruit and pineapple. Zesty citrus notes lead the way in the taste – juicy grapefruit and pineapple flavours – and the same fruitiness continues into the dry, hoppy finish.

Kingstone ▪ Gold

ABV 4%   500 ml   Pale malt, wheat malt, Fuggle and First Gold hops

'What began as a seasonal ale has blossomed into a true all-rounder', declares the label of this golden beer that was first brewed in 2006 and makes the perfect partner to spicy or barbecue food, according to brewer Edward Biggs.

A soft and delicately fruity aroma, with hints of peach and orange, leads on to the same juicy fruit in the mouth, along with floral notes. But there's also a firm bitterness for balance which comes to prominence in the dry, hoppy finish.

Little Valley ▪ Withens IPA

**ABV 3.9%   500 ml   Pale malt, crystal malt, caramalt, wheat malt,
Pacific Gem, Cascade and First Gold hops**

Withens is the name of the reservoir from which this
Yorkshire brewery takes its water. This is an organic,
vegan-acceptable, golden bitter (not an authentic IPA, of
course) that was first brewed in 2005 and goes well with
fish, claims brewer Wim van der Spek.

**Herbal and citrus notes from the hops feature in the
aroma, while the taste is crisp, with a lemony sweetness
and bitter herbal hops. The immediately dry finish is
increasingly bitter and herbal-hoppy.**
Major stockist **Booths**

Loddon ✳ Ferryman's Gold

**ABV 4.8%   500 ml   Maris Otter pale malt, caramalt, wheat malt,
torrefied wheat, Fuggle and Styrian Golding hops**

The flagship golden ale from this expanding brewery on the outskirts of
Reading, Ferryman's had already won beer festival awards as a cask beer
before brewer Chris Hearn decided to bottle it. The beer is brewed to a
higher original gravity than the cask version, but with the fermentation
halted early, to leave plenty of unfermented sugars for bottle conditioning.
It is then drawn off the fermenter without fining or filtration and shipped
down the M4 to Swindon, where Arkell's conditions it for ten days
and then bottles it with a fresh dose of an old Whitbread yeast. With
fermentation resuming in the bottle, the finished product pours at around
4.8% (compared to the cask's 4.4%).

**A golden beer with an aroma packed with sweet tangerine- and
orange-citrus zestiness, backed by hop resins. Sharp, sweet tangerines
and oranges also fill the crisp, refreshing taste, along with a hoppy,
bitter balance. The finish is dry, bitter and hoppy with some lingering
orange notes.**
Major stockists **Asda, Bottoms Up, Budgens, Londis, Tesco, Thresher,
Wine Rack**

Golden Ales

Lymestone ▪ Foundation Stone

ABV 4.5% 500 ml Maris Otter pale malt, dark crystal malt, Pilot, Boadicea and Fuggle hops

All the beers from Lymestone brewery, founded in 2008, have the word 'stone' in their names, as a reference to the Staffordshire town of Stone in which the business is based. Foundation Stone, appropriately, was the first beer brewed by the company.

A golden ale with soft, pale malt and a light lemon freshness in the aroma. The taste is very hoppy and bitter, with sweet lemon notes and light malt behind. Dry, hoppy and firmly bitter finish.

McGivern ▪ Crest Pale

ABV 4.1% 500 ml Pale malt, wheat malt, Bobek and Golding hops

When you're as small a brewery as this North Wales micro, working out of a garden shed and producing only up to about 80 bottles a day, inevitably the strengths and flavours of the beers can vary from batch to batch. But if all the brews are as good as the one tasted of Crest Pale, that shouldn't be a problem. The crest in question is the McGivern family crest and it is shown on the label.

A bright golden beer with a fairly subdued peachy aroma. The taste is also lightly peachy, but crisp, bittersweet and easy drinking. Hops and bitterness build in the dry finish.

O'Hanlon's ▪ Yellow Hammer

ABV 4.2% 500 ml Pale malt, caramalt, First Gold and Cascade hops

A golden beer with a complex hopping regime: First Gold hops are used for bitterness, Cascades are the late hop and then the beer is dry hopped with more First Gold. It's named after the birds that populate the fields around the Devon brewery and the cask version is one of the most demanded golden ales in the South-West.

A yellow golden beer with mellow, honeyed pale malt in the aroma. The taste is sweet and honey-creamy, with tropical fruit and light citrus notes, rounding off dry, bittersweet and fruity, with a faint lemon character. A soft, easy-drinking golden ale.
Major stockists **Local Majestic and Tesco**

Oakleaf ■ Bitter

ABV 3.8%   500 ml   Pale malt, crystal malt, Fuggle, First Gold and Styrian Golding hops

Oakleaf's standard bitter – the first beer produced by the Gosport business when it was founded in 2000 – was introduced in bottled form in 2004.

A golden bitter with juicy oranges and a hint of chocolate in the aroma. The taste is bitter and orange-like from the hops, winding up with a dry, firmly bitter and hoppy finish.

Oakleaf ■ Hole Hearted

ABV 4.7%   500 ml   Pale malt, lager malt, caramalt, torrefied wheat, Cascade hops

This golden ale takes its name from the fact that it was originally brewed for sale at the Hole in the Wall pub in Southsea. The cask version was CAMRA's Champion Beer of Hampshire in 2002 and 2003, while this bottled companion was a SIBA regional champion in 2003.

An explosion of lemon and grapefruit notes awaits you in the aroma and taste, with a light malty sweetness in the background and some floral notes. Bitter, tangy, grapefruit-like hops linger on in the finish.
Major stockists **Asda, Tesco, local Thresher and Waitrose**

Old Chimneys ■ Golden Pheasant

ABV 4.7%   500 ml   Pale malt, caramalt, Challenger and Target hops

Named after the oriental birds that escaped captivity and now live in Thetford Forest, near this East Anglian brewery, Golden Pheasant –

OLD CHIMNEYS BREWERY
MARKET WESTON, DISS, IP22 2NZ

GOLDEN
PHEASANT
PALE DRY BITTER
Alc 4.7% vol   500ml ℮
Bottle conditioned beer - contains live yeast.
Store below 13C to prevent over carbonation.
Brewed from malted barley.
Suitable for vegetarians and vegans.
Lot Number: 165
Best before: 01.08.2010

described as a 'pale dry bitter' – is also sold in cask-conditioned form, and has been bottled since 2002.

A golden ale with juicy citrus-orange notes in evidence in the aroma. More zesty oranges feature in the taste, which is bitter and hoppy with sweet pale malt providing support. Hops then take over in the dry, bitter finish.

Old Luxters ▪ Luxters Gold Ale

ABV 5%   330 ml   Maris Otter pale malt, Fuggle and Golding hops

In 1997, this Buckinghamshire vineyard brewery secured a contract with the Gilbey's wine importer/restaurateur company, to produce Gilbey's Gold, a 'farmhouse ale' in dark green 330 ml bottles. The beer proved so successful that it was added to the permanent range, with the name changed accordingly.

A golden beer with spicy hops edging out malt in the aroma. The taste nicely balances malt and spicy hops, and there is a hint of grapefruit, too. Hoppy, dry finish.

Oldershaw ▪ Caskade

ABV 4.2%   500 ml   Optic pale malt, crystal malt, Cascade hops

The name of this Lincolnshire beer is a play on words, reflecting the choice of American hops for what is primarily a cask-conditioned ale. It is bottled, like Oldershaw's other beers, only when there is spare cask ale available.

A peppery, grapefruit aroma leads to a crisp, spritzy, bitter citrus taste with grapefruit and lime notes, and decent malt support. Dry, bitter, tangy-hoppy finish.

Otley ▪ O1

ABV 4% 500 ml Pale malt, lager malt, torrefied wheat, Celeia and Progress hops

The first beer ever to roll out from this South Wales brewery – hence the name. Since then, O1 has gone on to pick up some illustrious awards in its cask form, including that of Champion Golden Ale in CAMRA's Champion Beer of Britain awards in 2008, which even tops three consecutive Golden Ale first prizes at the Great Welsh Beer and Cider Festival.

A pale yellow beer with zesty, tangerine-like citrus hop notes in the sharp and lively aroma. The bittersweet taste is spritzy and zesty, with more refreshing tangerine and a clean, crisp, hoppy edge, before a dry, bitter, hoppy finish.

Outstanding ▪ Blond

ABV 4.5% 500 ml Low colour pale malt, Pacific Gem and Styrian Golding hops

The unusual hop adding character to this yellow-golden ale from Lancashire is Pacific Gem, from New Zealand. Like all Outstanding's beers, Blond Is declared to be vegan friendly.

A sharp, hoppy, slightly scented aroma leads on to a taste of soft, sweet, pale malt overlaid with tangy, perfumed hop notes which continue into the dry and long-lasting finish.

Pitfield ▪ EKG

ABV 4.2% 500 ml Pale malt, crystal malt, wheat malt, flaked maize, Golding hops

The letters in the name stand for East Kent Goldings. This single-varietal hop beer, featuring the great British aroma hop, grown in the Garden of England, was first produced in 1999. An organic brew, like all Pitfield's beers.

Golden Ales

101

A golden ale with toffee-like malt in the aroma. The taste is also malty and toffee-like, with a dry bitterness coming from the hops and faint notes of almond. The dry, bittersweet finish gradually turns more and more bitter and hoppy, but, overall, hops are rather subdued considering the identity of the beer.

Pitfield ■ Eco Warrior

ABV 4.5%   500 ml   Chariot pale malt, sugar, Hallertau hops

As mentioned in the entry for EKG (above), Pitfield is now an entirely organic brewery and it was this beer, Eco Warrior, which was launched in 1998, that set the organic ball rolling. It quickly found itself a niche and has been stocked by health food shops.

A golden beer with nutty malt prominent in the aroma. Silky, nutty, honeyed malt continues to feature in the bittersweet taste, where it is joined by lightly floral hops. The finish is dry, bitter, malty, hoppy and moreish.

Quantock ■ Quantock Ale

ABV 3.8%   500 ml   Maris Otter pale malt, crystal malt, wheat malt, Challenger and Golding hops

As you'd kind of expect, Quantock Ale was the first beer produced by Quantock Brewery when it opened its Somerset brewhouse in March 2008. This firmly bitter, dry session ale is now brewed every two or three weeks. Like all the brewery's bottled beers, being unfined, it is acceptable to vegetarians and vegans.

A golden bitter, with a grassy, tea-like hop aroma that has a light citrus accent. Bitter, grassy hops also lead in the taste, leaving light citrus-fruity sweetness in the background. The finish is dry, bitter and hoppy.

Quantock ▪ Sunraker

ABV 4.2% 500 ml Lager malt, wheat malt, flaked maize, Perle hops

Quantock's best-selling beer started life as a summer seasonal, but its popularity demanded it became a regular brew and it is now produced every two or three weeks. Lager malt is used in the mash tun to create an extremely pale golden colour.

Grassy hops and sharp lemon feature in the aroma, with sweet lemon and other citrus notes balanced out by drying, bitter hops in the taste, which is light bodied. The finish is dry, bitter and hoppy.

RCH ▪ Pitchfork

ABV 4.3% 500 ml Optic pale malt, Fuggle and Golding hops

First produced in 1993, this beer's name was derived from the unsuccessful Pitchfork Rebellion against King James II by the followers of the Duke of Monmouth. They challenged the King's forces at Sedgemoor (close to the brewery's home near Weston-super-Mare) in July 1685. The beer is also available in cask (Champion Best Bitter at CAMRA's Champion Beer of Britain awards in 1998).

After a mouth-wateringly fruity aroma, this beer is initially soft and fruity to taste, but soon gains a solid, slightly perfumed, orangey hop edge. Hoppy, bitter and dry finish.
Major stockist **Local Thresher**

Ridgeway ✳ High & Mighty
Beer of the Gods

ABV 4.5% 500 ml Dark lager malt or very pale ale malt, caramalt, Perle and Saaz hops

Golden Ales

'Massachusetts USA' says the label. That's the home of the High & Mighty brewery which collaborates with the UK's Ridgeway Brewing in making Beer of the Gods available in Europe. The beer is a curious hybrid of styles, beginning life as a German altbier recipe, then Americanized through a high use of hops and finally top fermented with an English ale yeast. The beer was a finalist in Sainsbury's Beer Competition in 2008. It is brewed by Ridgeway's Peter Scholey at Cotswold Brewing in Foscot, Oxfordshire, where the equipment is geared up for lager production.

Expect some sulphur in the aroma, especially with fresh samples. Beyond this, the lightly floral nose features soft pale malt and sweet lemon. Delicate, silky malt flavours follow in the taste, along with more floral notes and a pleasant, light lemon accent. Initial sweetness is soon balanced by hop bitterness, before a dry, hoppy and increasingly bitter finish.

Ridgeway ■ Oxfordshire Blue

ABV 5%   500 ml   Maris Otter and Optic pale malt, Challenger, Fuggle and Styrian Golding hops

A Tesco Beer Challenge winner for 2005–6, this brew has been designed to be drunk cold, not just lightly chilled. Compare it at both temperatures, says brewer Peter Scholey, and you'll see what he means. Great with barbecues and spicy foods, he says. The beer is now brewed by Peter at Cotswold Brewing Company in Foscot, Oxfordshire, allowing Ridgeway to add 'Oxfordshire' to the name. The beer is then tankered to Hepworth in Sussex for bottling.

A golden ale with an aroma of sherbet lemons and grapefruit. Sharp, sherbety, citrus hops fill the crisp, bittersweet taste, bringing grapefruit and orange peel flavours, while the finish is dry and bitter, with more grapefruit from the hops in evidence.
Major stockist **Tesco**

Ridgeway ▪ ROB (Ridgeway Organic Bitter)

ABV 4.3%   500 ml   Pale malt, pilsner malt, Tradition, Golding and Target hops

Both organic and vegetarian, this beer also appears in draught form occasionally. The ingredients may vary from year to year, according to the availability of organic materials. However, brewer Peter Scholey is confident the flavour will be largely the same. Try it with pizza, pasta or fish, he says.

Tangy, bitter oranges, marmalade notes and hops all feature in the aroma of this golden ale. The taste is crisp, light-bodied and refreshingly clean, with plenty of good, tangy hop flavours, including more bitter orange character that continues into the bitter, hoppy and dry aftertaste.

Spinning Dog ▪ Hereford Organic Bitter

ABV 3.7%   500 ml   Maris Otter pale malt, Spalt hops

In its cask version, this beer from Hereford was the Supreme Champion in the Society of Independent Brewers (SIBA) western region contest for 2005. Note the use of unusual organic German hops.

A golden bitter with a malty, lightly citrus aroma. The taste is clean and well balanced, crisp, bitter and full, with spicy hops to the fore. Dry, hoppy aftertaste.

Suthwyk ▪ Liberation

ABV 4.2%   500 ml   Optic pale malt, crystal malt, Liberty hops

Launched to commemorate the 60th anniversary of D-Day, on 6 June 2004, this beer celebrates the local connections involved in the daring

enterprise. Montgomery and Eisenhower planned Operation Overlord (the D-Day offensive) in Southwick House, a country pile close to the fields where barley for Suthwyk beer is grown. The two men enjoyed refreshments in the local pub after their talks. The label shows the military masterminds examining a bottle of Liberation.

A pale golden beer with a fresh, blackcurrant, hoppy nose, becoming a touch biscuity. The light, bittersweet, slightly perfumed, blackcurrant taste makes it very quaffable. Hoppy, drying finish.

Suthwyk ▪ Skew Sunshine Ale

ABV 4.6%   500 ml   Optic pale malt, Challenger hops

The barley for this premium ale is grown in what is known as Skew Field, on Portsdown Hill, above Portsmouth Harbour. The field faces south and catches the sun – hence the name of the beer. The land is farmed by Martin Bazeley, who hit upon the idea of taking his own barley and having it brewed under contract. Skew was his first beer.

A pale golden ale with a creamy, malty, lightly fruity nose with a hint of sulphur. Light-bodied and fairly spritzy, it tastes citrus-fruity with lightly scented hops crisping up smooth malt. Bitter, fruity, hoppy finish.

Teignworthy ▪ Amy's Ale

ABV 4.8%   500 ml   Pale malt, crystal malt, wheat malt, Bramling Cross and Golding hops

A golden beer named after Teignworthy brewer John Lawton and his wife Rachel's first child, brewed initially in March 1997. It was the first of four ales celebrating the gradual extension of the Lawton family. The labels used to feature drawings made by the children themselves but there's now a new set of smart, themed artwork pulling together the four beers.

A floral, honeyed malt aroma, with earthy hops, leads to a bittersweet taste that is equally flowery and honeyed, with some tart citrus fruit. The finish is firmly bitter, floral and hoppy.

Teme Valley ▪ This

ABV 3.7%   500 ml   Maris Otter pale malt, chocolate malt, wheat malt, Challenger and Golding hops

Teme Valley Brewery is housed behind The Talbot Inn at Knightwick, Worcestershlre. The pub's own wine list has included, since spring 2003, a 'Beer and Food' page, suggesting ideal matches for Teme Valley beers. Here, This – the brewery's session bitter – is recommended as the ideal accompaniment for sandwiches or a ploughman's lunch.

A golden beer with a malty aroma that has hints of chocolate. The taste is bitter, reasonably hoppy and dry, with a buttery malt base. A moreish maltiness lingers in the dry, bitter, lightly hoppy finish.
Major stockist **Local Waitrose**

Golden Ales

Tryst ▪ Carronade IPA

ABV 4.2%   500 ml   Optic pale malt, Cascade and Columbus hops

A beer named after the famous Carron Ironworks, near Falkirk. Carronade cannon, apparently, was used at the Battle of Trafalgar and is said to have revolutionized portable cannon warfare on ships at the time. This best bitter (not strong enough to qualify as a true IPA) was winner of the 2005 Scottish Bottle-Conditioned Beer Championship.

Golden, with lemon and malt in the nose. The taste is bittersweet with citrus notes. Dry, bitter, hoppy finish with lingering sweetness.

Tryst ▪ Stars & Stripes

ABV 4%   500 ml   Pale malt, caramalt, Amarillo, Challenger and Styrian Golding hops

This American-influenced, golden ale – featuring fruity Amarillo hops alongside Challenger and Styrian Goldings – was added to the expanding range of beers from this enterprising Scottish microbrewery in 2007.

A bittersweet beer with a big, juicy citrus aroma, a fruity, sherbety taste that features plenty of grapefruit and melon, and a hoppy, bitter and dry finish.

Vale ▪ Edgars Golden Ale

ABV 4.3%   500 ml   Maris Otter pale malt, Fuggle and Golding hops

Vale Brewery was founded (and is still owned) by brothers Mark and Phil Stevens. Edgar is a Stevens family name, passed down to the first son of the first son over the generations. The trend was broken when Mark was named, so the lads decided to name their first beer Edgar in compensation. It has also been sold at times under the name of Halcyon Daze.

A clean and tasty, pale golden beer with soft melon and peach aromas. The same juicy fruit continues in the mouth, overlaid with a crisp hop bitterness. Dry, bitter, hoppy finish.

Vale ✴ Gravitas

ABV 4.8%   500 ml   Maris Otter pale malt, Perle, Cascade and Centennial hops

Gravitas was first brewed by Vale Brewery in 2007, but it took the winning of a gold award from the Society of Brewers (SIBA) in 2008 to prompt the

brewers to put it into bottle as well. The label describes it as a 'heavily hopped ale', although it's not as demanding in that department as it sounds, and is dangerously refreshing on a hot day.

A pale yellow beer with a fresh, clean aroma of floral and citrus hops, with hints of lemon and grapefruit. The taste is crisp and pleasantly bitter, with a clean grapefruit hop character that lingers on into the dry, bitter finish.

Vale ▪ VPA

ABV 4.2% 500 ml Maris Otter pale malt, crystal malt, Perle, Cascade and Centennial hops

First brewed in 1997 and now a permanent fixture in the portfolio of this Buckinghamshire brewery, VPA (Vale Pale Ale) has picked up beer festival awards in its cask-conditioned form.

A bright golden beer with a fresh aroma of grapefruit and orange zest. The taste is crisp, bittersweet and hoppy, with plenty of zesty citrus fruit. Bitter grapefruit continues in the dry, bitter, hoppy finish.

Wapping ▪ Summer Ale

ABV 4.2% 500 ml Maris Otter pale malt, other ingredients not declared

Before the Wapping Brewery opened up in the cellars of the historic Baltic Fleet pub, opposite Liverpool's Albert Dock, in 2002, this beer was brewed for the pub by the now-closed Passageway Brewery. The recipe has been reviewed and tweaked since production started here (the details remain secret, however) and it's now by far the best-selling beer in the pub.

Golden Ales

A very pale-coloured golden beer with an immediately fruity and floral aroma, featuring elderflower and tart grapefruit. The same floral fruitiness continues in the bittersweet taste, along with a sappy green-hop note. The finish is dry, hoppy-sappy and becomes increasingly bitter.

Wells & Young's ▪ Young's Kew Gold

ABV 4.8%   500 ml   Lager malt, Styrian Golding hops

Some readers may remember a beer called Kew Brew, which was launched by Young's Brewery several years ago and was brewed partly with hops grown at London's famous Kew Gardens. Kew Gold, first released in spring 2008 by the now merged Wells & Young's business, is not the same beer. However, it does support Kew's valuable research work through a financial donation from sales. The beer is also sold at Kew and is available in cask-conditioned form in summer months.

This golden ale is quite light drinking for its strength, floral, spritzy and bittersweet, with elderflower featuring in the aroma, and grapefruit and elderflower flavours, plus a bitter hop note, evident in the taste. The finish is dry, bitter and hoppy.
Major stockists **Budgens, Majestic, Sainsbury's, Tesco, Thresher, Wine Rack**

White ▪ Gold

ABV 4.9%   500 ml   Maris Otter pale malt, wheat malt, Challenger and Golding hops

This beer from East Sussex started life under the name Millennium Madness at the Hastings beer festival in 2000 and is now available all year-round.

Floral, pear drop notes join gentle caramel, hops and malt in the aroma of this golden ale, with estery, pear-like flavours featuring in the bittersweet taste. Dry, fruity, increasingly bitter finish.

Why Not ▪ On the Ball

ABV 4.5%   500 ml   Maris Otter pale malt, crystal malt, Progress and Cascade hops

An easy-drinking golden ale first brewed in 2008 to mark the start of the football season and named after the anthem of Norwich City FC – which probably won't encourage supporters of other teams to try it. Their loss.

A very fruity (peaches and oranges) aroma leads to the same fruit in the bittersweet taste, which is nicely balanced and has a leafy, drying backnote. The finish is dry, fruity and bitter.

Why Not ▪ Wally's Revenge

ABV 4%   500 ml   Maris Otter pale malt, crystal malt, Fuggle and Golding hops

A light ale named in memory of the uncle of Why Not brewer Colin Emms, an ex-naval officer and keen real ale drinker who died at the time Colin was setting up the brewery. His picture used to appear on the label but has now been replaced by a tempting glass of the ale itself.

Orange-golden, with an aroma of malt and floral hops with a hint of orange. The taste is bittersweet, featuring smooth, moreishly savoury malt, topped by floral and citrus hops. The dry, hoppy finish is also moreish and becomes increasingly bitter.

Willoughby ▪ Trust Gold

ABV 3.8%   500 ml   Pale malt, extra pale malt, Pioneer, Fuggle and Bobek hops

This golden session ale comes from a brewery set up in July 2008 on the National Trust estate at Brockhampton, Worcestershire – hence the name of the beer. Pioneer hops provide the backbone of bitterness, while Fuggle and citrus Bobek hops are used late for aroma.

A sharp and hoppy aroma, laced with pithy grapefruit, leads onto a sharp, bittersweet taste that features more grapefruit and zesty lemon from the hops over a clean, delicate pale malt base. The finish is firmly bitter and dry, with lingering zesty citrus fruit.

Windsor Castle ▪ Thin Ice

ABV 4.5%   500 ml   Maris Otter low colour malt, wheat malt, First Gold and Green Bullet hops

First brewed in November 2005, as a Christmas special (at the time it had a penguin on the pump clip), Thin Ice has become this West Midlands brewery's best-selling regular beer. Note the use of Green Bullet hops from New Zealand for aroma.

A pale golden ale with a fresh, lemon-and-grapefruit nose. The taste is also citrus and sherbety, with silky, delicate malt and a leafy, hoppy dryness. The finish is bitter, hoppy and drying, with a pleasant, lingering lemon/fresh root ginger flavour.

Major stockists **Local Thresher and Victoria Wine**

Windsor Castle ▪ Worcester Sorcerer

ABV 4.3%   500 ml   Maris Otter pale malt, crystal malt, wheat malt, Challenger and Golding hops

It took three years for this golden ale to make the transition from cask beer to bottled beer, but it finally arrived in 2008. The name is derived from the name of brewer Chris Sadler's grandfather's boat.

A dark golden ale with a very pleasant mix of caramel-laced malt and orchard fruit in the aroma. The flavour is generally bittersweet, with plenty of ripe, sweet malt and a good bitter edge, as well as tart floral and fruit

notes. Malty sweetness features initially in the drying finish but there's soon a big smack of tangy hops, too.

Major stockists **Local Thresher and Victoria Wine**

Woodforde's ■ Sundew

ABV 4.1%   500 ml   **Maris Otter pale malt, lager malt, Challenger and Styrian Golding hops**

Launched in summer 2006, Sundew is Woodforde's replacement for the beer called Great Eastern in its range of cask and bottled ales. The name is derived from a carnivorous plant that can be found in the marshlands of Norfolk.

A bright golden ale with a floral aroma of light grapefruit and hop resins. Sharp hop resins continue in the taste, which is flowery and has a smooth pale malt base and bitter grapefruit notes. Silky malt lingers in the firmly bitter and dry finish, with lightly floral, leafy hops.

Wye Valley ✳ Dorothy Goodbody's Golden Ale

ABV 4.2%   500 ml   **Maris Otter pale malt, pale crystal malt, wheat malt, Golding and Fuggle hops**

Dorothy Goodbody does not exist, sadly for those red-blooded males who have fallen in love with her computer-generated image on the labels of Wye Valley's ales. Her award-winning Golden Ale, first brewed in 1997, was initially a cask beer for spring and summer, but is now sold all year.

A dark golden ale with tart, marmalade-like fruit and some tea notes in the hoppy aroma. There's more fruit – marmalade oranges – in the hoppy taste, which is mostly bitter but does have a soft, malty sweetness, too. The finish is dry, orange-fruity, hoppy and nicely bitter.

Major stockists **Local Sainsbury's, Tesco and Waitrose**

Golden Ales

Strong Ales

Included in this section are British-style bitters and amber ales that top the nominal 5% ABV limit set here for best bitters, but which are definitely more akin to quaffing beers than to old ales or barley wines. That said, fermentation flavours become more obvious at this level, so expect strong fruit notes in some cases. Also included here are golden ales above 5% ABV. India pale ales, which generally fall into the same alcohol bracket, but have a more pronounced hop character, have their own section, as this is a well-defined style.

At a Glance

Strength: ABV 5.1% upwards (but see also other sections for strong beers of different styles)

Character: Generally full bodied and malty, with good balancing hop character. Sweetness and other flavours, perhaps biscuit, nut and toffee, may come from the malt, while hops may bring fruit, herbal or floral notes, as well as bitterness. Some estery fermentation flavours may be present, ranging from tropical fruit to bubblegum and solvent. Colours range from straw to very dark.

Serving temperature: Cool (12º C)

Food matches: Game, roasted meats, casseroles, curries and other spicy foods, strong cheeses; light-coloured beers also go with seafood and chicken

Atlantic ▪ Fistral Premium

ABV 5.2%   330/500 ml   Pale malt, wheat malt, First Gold hops

Fistral is a famous surfing beach at Newquay, Cornwall. This beer borrows its name to strengthen its appeal to the tourism trade upon which this part of the world relies so heavily. Brewer Stuart Thomson describes it as a 'single hop IPA', but the modest hop character suggests it's actually more of a regular strong ale. It was added to the Atlantic Brewery range in 2005. Like all Atlantic brews, this beer is not only organic but also acceptable to vegans.

A golden-coloured, strong ale with a grassy, hazelnut aroma. The taste is also nutty and oaty-creamy, with sweet pale malt and light hoppy tones. There's more creamy malt in the finish, which is dry and bittersweet at first, but turning more bitter, and leaves a light warming glow.

Barearts ▪ Cascade Beer

ABV 7.3%   500 ml   Lager malt, wheat malt, Cascade hops

This interesting experiment with American hops at West Yorkshire's unusual brewery-cum-nude art gallery involves a typically strong brew. Despite the considerable strength, the malt character is pale and subtle, and generously allows the pungent, citrus Cascade hops to express themselves.

American Cascade hops are immediately evident in the juicy grapefruit and pineapple aroma and then continue boldly in the mouth, joined by slightly earthy, sweet flavours, a bitter balance and suggestions of almonds. The drying finish is a bit thin for the strength but has a nicely-rounded, pleasant bitterness.

Beowulf ▪ Heroes

ABV 5.5%   500 ml   Pale malt, crystal malt, Fuggle and Golding hops

One of the first beers brewer Phil Bennett produced under the Beowulf banner (dating back to 1997), Heroes, being unfined like Phil's other beers, is acceptable to both vegetarians and vegans. It's a good bread and cheese beer, he reckons.

A bright golden ale with sweet mango and lemon in the aroma. The gently warming taste is surprisingly dry, featuring bittersweet tropical fruits, and the finish is even drier, with bitter hops joining the continuing tropical fruit.

Beowulf ▪ Mercian Shine

ABV 5.8%   500 ml   Pale malt, flaked maize, Challenger and Bobek hops

Beowulf's bottles carry the subtitle 'Forest of Mercia', referring to a 92-square mile tract of wilderness, roughly between Lichfield and Wolverhampton, that has been preserved for walks, recreation and education since the 1990s. This is where Beowulf brewery now has its home. The Mercia connection was established much earlier, however, when the brewery was based in a former Co-op store in Yardley, Birmingham, and this beer was first produced.

A pale golden ale with a spicy, slightly perfumed aroma of lemon and grapefruit. The same citrus notes add sharpness to the taste, which is mostly bitter and pepper-spicy, and is crisp for the strength. The finish is also crisp, dry, bitter and hoppy.

Strong Ales

Brakspear ✳ Triple

ABV 7.2%   500 ml   Maris Otter pale malt, crystal malt, black malt, Northdown and Cascade hops

First brewed in March 2005 as a celebratory brew to mark the successful return of Brakspear brewing to Oxfordshire, Triple takes its name from two sources. Firstly, it is hopped three times – twice in the copper (Northdowns

early for bitterness and Cascades late for aroma) and finally in the fermenter with more Cascades after the beer has 'dropped' (Brakspear beers are known for their 'double dropping' system of fermentation, where the beer begins fermenting in an upper tank and then drops through to a second tank, leaving behind tired yeast and unwanted proteins). Secondly, it is thrice fermented – once during primary fermentation, a second time during a long maturation period and finally in the bottle (with the addition of fresh yeast). Triple is brewed at Witney (the brewery is now owned by Marston's) and bottled by Fuller's in London. Each bottle is individually numbered and, if you want to know when it was bottled, you can look it up on the Brakspear website (www.brakspear-beers.co.uk). Like its Belgian namesakes, this English Triple is best served in a chalice-style glass and makes an excellent accompaniment to cheeses, nuts and fruit cake.

Amber, with pineapple, citrus and a hint of liquorice in the full, malty aroma. Rich, malty sweetness is matched by tangy hops and tropical fruit in the taste, backed by butterscotch. Gently warming, hoppy, bittersweet finish, drying all the time, with the malty, slightly salty character of Brakspear's beers in evidence.
Major stockists **Asda, Sainsbury's, Tesco, Waitrose**

Butts ▪ Coper

ABV 6% 500 ml Malts not declared, Fuggle and Golding hops

'A coper is a ship employed in surreptitiously supplying strong drink to deep sea fishermen,' declares the bottle. 'Not a lot of people know that.' The name was suggested by Berkshire brewer Chris Butt's father while he was doing a crossword, so Chris asked him to draw the boat that features on the front of the bottle, too. The beer doubled as the brewery's tenth anniversary ale in 2004.

An amber-red beer with hints of toffee and red berries in the malty, alcoholic aroma. The taste is malty, strong and rather bitter for such a potent beer, with some more toffee and emerging citrus-orange flavours. The finish is dry, bitter and thick, with roasted grain notes.

Church End ▪ Arthur's Wit

ABV 6%   500 ml   Pale malt, torrefied wheat, Mount Hood and Cascade hops

Despite its Belgian-sounding title, Arthur's Wit is not a spiced wheat beer. It is a strong golden ale named after the late Arthur Pampling, a CAMRA activist in the West Midlands. It was bottled for the first time in 2002.

Bitter orange notes from the hops feature in the otherwise floral, alcoholic aroma, leading to more oranges in the strong, bittersweet taste and dry, bitter finish.

Dow Bridge ▪ Conquest

ABV 5.4%   500 ml   Pearl pale malt, crystal malt, chocolate malt, black malt, Fuggle, Challenger and Golding hops

Continuing Dow Bridge's Roman theme, Conquest joined the Leicestershire brewery's bottled beer range in 2008, having previously been sold in cask.

Orange-amber, with a soft aroma of chocolate truffle and nut from the malt. Sweet, nutty malt leads in the taste, which stays sweet despite some toasted grain/coffee-like bitterness emerging. Roasted malt features again in the dry, bittersweet finish that gradually turns bitter.

Freeminer ✳ Morrisons The Best

ABV 6%   500 ml   Pale malt, crystal malt, other malts, First Gold, Golding and Fuggle hops

 After success with Gold Miner for the Co-op (see Golden Ales), Freeminer further mined the own-label sector with this strong ale for Morrisons' The Best range of quality foods and drinks. The beer draws on other Freeminer ales for inspiration. Chiefly, it is modelled on the cask beer called Speculation, but Don Burgess refuses to be drawn on the exact make-up, except to say that it includes six different malts in all.

Amber-red, featuring nutty, treacly malt and spicy hops with grapefruit notes in the aroma. The taste is big, robust

and earthy, loaded with treacly malt and tangy hops. Malt lingers but lipsmacking hops take over in the bitter, slightly warming finish.

Major stockist **Morrisons**

Greene King ✳ Hen's Tooth

ABV 6.5%   500 ml   Tipple pale malt, crystal malt, Challenger, First Gold, Golding, Pilgrim, Admiral and Boadicea hops

Hen's Tooth was launched by Morland Brewery in Abingdon in 1998, its name suggesting a resemblance to the company's celebrated Old Speckled Hen in its make up. The other relevance of the name is to convey how rare it is to find a beer of this strength which is not too heavy or chewy – as rare, as Morland put it at the time, 'as a hen's tooth'. The beer is now brewed and bottled at Bury St Edmunds, following Greene King's take over and closure of the Oxfordshire brewery. The yeast used throughout is the old Morland yeast, but the hops have changed and now include at least the six strains mentioned above.

An amber beer with hints of liquorice, pear drop and banana in the malty aroma. Sweet, ripe malt is joined by liquorice, pear drop, banana, hoppy bitterness and a hint of marzipan in the taste, with malt and a touch more liquorice lingering in the dry, bitter, hoppy finish.

Major stockist **Asda**

Hopdaemon ✳ Leviathan

ABV 6%   500 ml   Pale malt, crystal malt, chocolate malt, caramalt, wheat malt, Golding and Challenger hops

'A beast of a beer', claims Hopdaemon brewer Tonie Prins, referring to the giant sea monster from the pages of the Bible that gives its name to his strong ale. It's great with Stilton, he adds.

Dark amber-red, with faintly toffee-like malt, pineapple and lemon in the nose. The taste is full, sweet and treacle-malty, with

lots of tropical fruit and peppery hops. Dry, nutty malt, with a hint of chocolate, leads in the hoppy, bitter and lightly warming finish.

Humpty Dumpty ▪ Golden Gorse

ABV 5.4%   500 ml   Maris Otter extra pale malt, wheat malt, Challenger, Golding and Cascade hops

Despite its countryside name, Golden Gorse is named, like other beers from this Norfolk brewery, after a steam locomotive that is pictured on the label. The beer has changed quite a bit in recent years, rising from 4.4% to 5.4% and featuring a change of hops, but the pale golden colour and delicate balance of very pale malt and fruit remains similar.

A smooth, malty, lemony aroma, with a touch of pineapple, leads on to a crisp taste of sweet, silky pale malt, lemon, pineapple and pine. The finish is dry, hoppy and bitter, with malt, lemon and pine notes.

Humpty Dumpty ▪ Hop Harvest Gold

ABV 5.2%   500 ml   Maris Otter pale malt and extra pale malt, wheat malt, Golding, Challenger and Perle hops

A golden ale first brewed in 2007 and now repeated once a year, to take advantage of new season hops – hence the name of the beer. The 2008 version (tasted below) was brewed with the first Goldings of the year from Kitchenham Farm, on the Kent and East Sussex border.

2008 version: Soft tropical and citrus fruit joins lightly sappy hops in the modest aroma. The taste is full bodied and bittersweet, with silky pale malt and hints of pineapple and lemon, as well as some alcoholic warmth and perfumed esters. The finish is dry, bitter and sappy-hoppy.

Kingstone ▪ Abbey Ale

ABV 5.1%   500 ml   Pale malt, Challenger and Northern Brewer hops

Just down the hill from Kingstone Brewery's home on Meadow Farm in the Wye Valley stand the ruins of Tintern Abbey, a 12th-century structure

Strong Ales

that was home to the second Cistercian brotherhood in Britain. Even in its latter-century, shell-like, empty-windowed decay, its former grandeur still spoke to William Wordsworth and JMW Turner, both of whom celebrated the abbey in their works. This is precisely what Kingstone has done, too, with this strong ale.

A full-bodied, orange-amber beer with the aroma of a freshly halved orange. The taste also bursts with blood orange fruitiness, but with robust hoppy bitterness and good malt support, too. The dry, bitter finish sees orange flavours linger, but hops last the longest.

Lymestone ■ Stone the Crows

ABV 5.4%   500 ml   Maris Otter pale malt, dark crystal malt, chocolate malt, Pilot, Celeia, Millennium and Fuggle hops

Even the Staffordshire brewers of this complex ale are not sure quite how to categorize it. Is it a porter, an old ale, or just a strong, dark bitter? The last description seems most appropriate, as there is a pronounced hop influence (from four strains of hops) on this robust, ruby-coloured beer.

Juicy berries and bitter oranges join hints of plain chocolate and treacle in the aroma. Zesty oranges, berries and dark, chocolaty malt feature in the slightly perfumed taste, with bitterness coming from both hops and roasted malt, before a dry, bitter, chocolaty finish.

Oakleaf ■ Blake's Gosport Bitter

ABV 5.2%   500 ml   Optic pale malt, crystal malt, chocolate malt, Golding hops

This dark ale commemorates the old Blake's Brewery in Gosport (Oakleaf's home town), which was taken over in 1926 and eventually closed. A beer to go with strong cheeses and chocolate, the brewers suggest.

A ruby-coloured ale with biscuity dark malt and a touch of bubblegum in the aroma. Dark, sweet malt features in the taste, along with bubblegum and pear drops, before a dry, increasingly bitter, hoppy finish in which pear drop, bubblegum and dark malt still feature.
Major stockist **Local Asda**

Old Luxters ▪ Barn Ale

ABV 5.4%   500 ml   Maris Otter pale malt, crystal malt, chocolate malt, Fuggle and Golding hops

Taking its name from this Buckinghamshire vineyard-brewery's rustic location, Barn Ale, first brewed in 1993, is considerably stronger than the cask Barn Ale Special (4.5%) on which it is based.

An amber ale with smooth, nutty malt and floral notes in the aroma. The taste is nutty and sweet, with more floral notes plus a bitter dryness from the hops. Malt continues into the finish, which is also dry, hoppy and bitter.
Major stockist **Local Waitrose**

Oldershaw ▪ Alchemy

ABV 5.3%   500 ml   Optic pale malt, wheat malt, First Gold and Cascade hops

A strong golden ale – a regional champion in its cask-conditioned form in the Society of Independent Brewers (SIBA) awards – deriving its name from the often-overlooked experiments conducted by Sir Isaac Newton into turning dross metals into gold. Newton was born just a few miles away from where Oldershaw Brewery is based.

There's plenty of pale malt to balance the generous, lime-like hop notes in the aroma, before a full-bodied taste of crisp, tangy, citrus hops and smooth malt. Malt gives way to tangy, drying hops in the finish, which also has a bitter marmalade character.

Pen-lon ▪ Gimmers Mischief

ABV 5.2%   500 ml   Pale malt, Pioneer, Pilgrim and First Gold hops

To quote the label, 'a gimmer is a young maiden ewe … like this ale, beautifully bodied, full of life and just that little bit naughty'. Once again,

Pen-lon's farmhouse brewery credentials are pushed well to the fore with this strong golden ale, which brewer Stefan Samociuk describes as 'gently hopped for those who do not like hoppy beers'.

Zesty oranges and hop resins feature along with light, creamy malt in the aroma, followed by a bittersweet, creamy taste of oranges and other citrus fruits. After a sweet swallow, the finish dries as hops emerge more strongly and fruit lingers.

Pen-lon ■ Gimmers Mischief Export

ABV 7%   500 ml   Pale malt, Pioneer and other hops

This stronger version of Pen-lon's Gimmers Mischief (see above) is primarily exported to Denmark. It follows the recipe of its stablemate but, after Pioneer hops have been used for bitterness in the copper, there is an addition of hops grown at Pen-lon itself for aroma (a mixture of Tettnanger, Nugget, Sterling and one as yet unidentified strain).

Zesty orange and melon feature in the spicy aroma. The taste is sweetish and strong, with an underlying warmth, vague tropical fruits and a bitter orange freshness from the hops. The finish is eventually lightly hoppy, with an orange note and a tingly warmth.

Pen-lon ■ Ramnesia

ABV 5.6%   500 ml   Maris Otter pale malt, light crystal malt, Target, Tettnanger and Willamette hops

'It just gets better as it gets older,' says Pen-lon farmer/brewer Stefan Samociuk about this strong ale. Stefan also produces bacon that has been cured in this particular beer.

A reddish-amber ale with juicy oranges and other fruit in the aroma. The taste is full and sweet, with tropical fruit and almond notes from fermentation and gentle hints of toffee from the malt. Dry, softly bitter and fruity finish.

Pitfield ▪ 1830 Amber Ale

ABV 6%   500 ml   Maris Otter pale malt, amber malt, chocolate malt, Fuggle, Golding and Styrian Golding hops

In Victorian times, amber malt was widely used in brewing but it died out in the 20th century. It is now proving popular among brewers keen to resurrect old-fashioned beers, such as Pitfield, which produces this historic, amber-malt-infused ale as part of a series of authentic re-creations of lost beer styles.

Actually ruby in colour, this strong ale has soft, juicy pineapple and malt in the nose. Pineapple again features in the taste, overlaying plenty of malt, with nutty, toasted notes emerging on the swallow. Dry, roasted malt aftertaste.

RCH ▪ Double Header

ABV 5.3%   500 ml   Optic pale malt, Golding hops

The winner of Asda's first bottled beer contest, Double Header is named after a train pulled by two engines (as seen on the label).

Amber, with orange- and resin-like hops in the aroma. Tart oranges continue into the full-bodied, bittersweet taste that has lots of tangy hop. The finish is dry, bitter, lipsmackingly hoppy and tangy.

RCH ▪ Firebox

ABV 6%   500 ml   Optic pale malt, chocolate malt, Progress and Target hops

Firebox: the name reflects the steam-powered nature of RCH's Somerset brewery, plus the fascination with the golden age of railways shared by director Paul Davey and brewer Graham Dunbavan. The beer is imported into the USA by B United.

An orange-amber beer with juicy oranges and light malt in the aroma. Tart hops, bitter oranges and a little dark malt feature in the bitter-sweet taste, which is a touch lighter bodied than expected from the strength. Long, dry, hoppy and bitter finish.

Red Rat ■ Jimmy's Flying Pig

ABV 7%   500 ml   Pale malt, Pioneer and other hops

This Red Rat ale is produced for the Suffolk brewery's neighbour, Jimmy's Farm, the rare breeds farm run by Jimmy Doherty that has featured in its own television series. The first brew rolled out in spring 2007.

An amber beer with gentle caramel, malt, tropical fruit and floral notes in the aroma. Light bodied and easy-drinking for the strength, it tastes bittersweet and malty, with apple and tropical fruit flavours, along with a drying backnote. The finish is dry and bitter, with malt and hops lingering.

Ridgeway ✳ Bad King John

ABV 6%   500 ml   Maris Otter pale malt, crystal malt, chocolate malt, roasted barley, Admiral and Target hops

The 'answer beer' to Ridgeway's Ivanhoe (below), this dark brew is named after John, younger brother of King Richard I, who usurped the throne while Richard was away during the Crusades. John features as an arch-villain in Walter Scott's *Ivanhoe* novel. It's tempting to think of this beer as a stout or a porter, but brewer Peter Scholey is adamant that this should be called a black ale. It's effectively a pale ale with heavily roasted grains added. The mineral composition of the brewing water and the pointed use of late hops ground the beer firmly in the pale ale tradition.

A bright ruby beer, light-bodied for its strength, with winey and citrus fruit in the chocolaty aroma. The taste is crisp and bitter, with juicy,

126

winey and citrus fruit contrasting with the smoky dark flavours and light chocolate characteristics of the malt. Roasted barley dominates the dry finish, bringing bitterness and burnt grain notes.

Ridgeway ▪ Ivanhoe

ABV 5.2% 500 ml Maris Otter pale malt, crystal malt, chocolate malt, Golding and Admiral hops

Ivanhoe was first brewed for the Swedish market and then introduced into the UK and USA (apparently, the film *Ivanhoe* is shown every Christmas on Swedish television and has become closely associated with Englishness and chivalry). The label was designed by a Swedish art student and features Walter Scott's hero, Ivanhoe, fighting King John's knight, Brian de Bois-Guilbert, to save the life of the heroine Rebecca, who is about to be burned at the stake.

An amber ale with a floral, peachy aroma backed with light malt. The smooth, clean, mostly bitter taste is also floral and peachy, with gently nutty malt. Dry, malty, nutty and bitter finish.

Shepherd Neame ▪ 1698

ABV 6.5% 500 ml Pearl pale malt, crystal malt, sugar, Target and Golding hops

1698 was first brewed in 1998, to celebrate Shepherd Neame's 300th birthday. At the time the beer was filtered and pasteurised. This new version, introduced in March 2005, is brewed to the same recipe, except that it is 'thrice hopped'. Target hops go into the copper for bitterness, Goldings are added later for aroma, and yet more Goldings are introduced in the whirlpool, as the beer is being centrifuged to take out unwanted solid matter. The other difference, of course, is in the inclusion of living, fresh bottling yeast, added to the beer after it has been filtered.

A dark golden ale with an aroma of buttery malt, gentle pear drop and slightly grassy hops. The taste is full, smooth and mostly sweet,

with buttery malt, grassy, tangy, scented hops and dried fruit in the background. There's more buttery malt in the dry, hoppy, bitter finish.
Major stockists **Asda, Waitrose**

Teignworthy ▪ Edwin Tucker's Maris Otter

ABV 5.5%   500 ml   Maris Otter pale malt, crystal malt, wheat malt, Willamette, Golding, Bramling Cross and Challenger hops

This amber ale was first produced in 1998, as a tribute to the most highly regarded strain of malting barley ('the master brewer's choice around the world'), and to showcase the work of Tucker's Maltings in Newton Abbot, Devon, where the brewery is located and this beer is sold.

Smooth, toffee-like malt in the aroma is overlaid with tart berries and hints of pear and banana. The taste majors on smooth, sweet malt topped by an earthy, liquorice-like bitterness and a hint of banana. The finish is fairly thick and malty, starting sweet and turning bitter and dry.

Tunnel ▪ Boston Beer Party

ABV 5.6%   500 ml   Maris Otter pale malt, crystal malt, wheat malt, torrefied wheat, Cascade hops

Boston Beer Party, a dark golden, vegan-friendly, American-inspired pale ale (it's Tunnel brewers Mike and Bob's favourite beer style), is matured in casks for two months prior to bottling.

Grapefruit citrus notes feature in the aroma, backed by lightly toffeeish malt. The taste is bittersweet with grapefruit up front and good malt support, while the finish dry with more bitter grapefruit flavour from the hops.
Major stockist **Local Asda**

Wells & Young's ✳ Special London Ale

ABV 6.4 % 500 ml Maris Otter pale malt, crystal malt, Fuggle, Golding and Target hops

Special London Ale is the current name for Young's Export, an originally filtered beer once targeted at the Belgian market and, for a while, brewed under licence in Belgium. This bottle-conditioned version arrived in 1998 and has survived the closure of Young's Brewery in Wandsworth. The beer is now brewed at Wells & Young's in Bedford. It is fermented for seven days and then warm conditioned for up to three weeks over a bed of whole Golding and Target hops. A period of cold stabilization follows before the beer is filtered. The beer is then primed with a hopped wort extract and re-seeded with fresh yeast prior to bottling. CAMRA's Champion Bottle-conditioned Beer 1999.

Orange-golden, with pithy oranges and grapefruit in the aroma. The body is full and smooth, overlaid in the bittersweet taste with zesty, marmalade-like, bitter oranges and other citrus fruits from the generous hopping. Moreish, but delicate, malt flavours are also evident. The long, full finish is dry, bitter and notably hoppy.
Major stockists **Majestic, Sainsbury's, Tesco, Thresher, Waitrose, Wine Rack**

Wye Valley ✳ Dorothy Goodbody's Country Ale

ABV 6% 500 ml Maris Otter pale malt, crystal malt, amber malt, wheat malt, flaked barley, roasted barley, Bramling Cross and Fuggle hops

Wye Valley's Country Ale is a beer with a few identities. It has also been sold in wintertime as Christmas Ale and was first bottled for export to the USA under the name of Our Glass. The brewers advise you to drink it with cheeses or rich puddings but reckon it also matures well in the bottle.

An amber beer with nut and caramel notes from the malt in the aroma. There's a full, luscious malt character to

Strong Ales

the sweet taste, with nut, caramel and treacle all present and some earthy, fruity hops for contrast. Hops eventually take over in the initially bittersweet, malty, treacly finish.

Yates' ■ YSD (Yates' Special Draught)

ABV 5.5%   500 ml   Optic pale malt, crystal malt, Fuggle and Cascade hops

This strong ale replaced a beer of similar potency called Broadway Blitz in the portfolio of this Isle of Wight brewery. 'A drink to be respected', declares the label. Bronze medallist in CAMRA's Champion Bottle-conditioned Beer contest in 2004.

Dark golden in colour, with lots of zesty orange and hop resins in the aroma, this is a fine, hoppy pale ale. There's more zesty fruit and hop resins in the taste, which starts fairly sweet but soon offers a resounding bitter-hop counterbalance. The lasting finish is dry, hoppy and firmly bitter, with more zesty oranges.

India Pale Ales

India Pale Ales

The story of India pale ale has been told time and again, but, to ensure a full understanding of the style, the tale of how beer was shipped out from Britain to India in the 19th century deserves yet another recap.

The essence of a true India pale ale is that it is a strong, pale beer, with plenty of hops. The alcohol and the hops both act as a preservative and so maintained the beer in good condition while it endured a long, arduous sea crossing to refresh the troops and other members of the British Empire in service on the subcontinent. The style is closely associated with Burton-on-Trent, in Staffordshire, where the flinty, mineral-rich waters drew less colour from the malt, but IPA actually has its origins in London, with a brewer named Hodgson, and was adopted by Burton brewers when they saw how successful his trade with India had become.

With the decline of the Empire, IPA began to disappear. By the latter half of the 20th century, with average beer strengths tumbling, authentic IPAs were extremely rare. In their place brewers were sticking the label IPA on beers that were nothing like the genuine article. Some still exist – Greene King IPA, Wadworth's Henry's IPA and Flowers IPA, are three typical examples. But then came a revival, as drinkers clamoured for products with more character and brewers began to unearth old IPA recipes. Just take a glance through the pages of this section to see just how revitalized the IPA sector has become.

At a Glance

Strength: ABV 4.8% upwards

Character: Golden or amber in colour, with a full body and a very pronounced hop accent

Serving temperature: Cool (12° C)

Food matches: Curries and other spicy foods, grilled and roasted meats, mature cheeses

Barearts ▪ India Pale Ale

ABV 7%   500 ml   Maris Otter pale malt, Fuggle hops

A pale golden take on the India pale ale style, a beer that is likely to become more vinous as it ages, according to Barearts brewer Trevor Cook.

Hints of exotic fruit (faint lemon, peach and mango) feature in the aroma, over light, grainy, slightly burnt malt. The taste is full and smooth, with a malty sweetness up front and juicy citrus and tropical fruits following on, but the hop character is a touch low for an IPA. After a sweet swallow, the finish is dry, woody and bitter.

Burton Bridge ▪ Empire Pale Ale

ABV 7.5%   500 ml   Pale malt, invert sugar, Challenger and Styrian Golding hops

Empire Pale Ale was first brewed in 1996 and was voted The Guardian's Best Bottle-Conditioned Beer 1997. It was runner-up in the Joint Guardian/CAMRA competition a year later. It has never been sold in draught form. After primary fermentation, the beer is conditioned in cask for six months and then dry hopped with Styrian Goldings two weeks before being primed and bottled. The days of the Raj are recalled on the label, with its picture of a soldier and a cricketer enjoying a mug of ale. B United is the US distributor.

A dark golden ale with a slightly earthy aroma of sweet pears. The full-bodied taste is also earthy with tangy hops, some bitter oranges and hints of pear, while the thick, tangy, warming aftertaste is dry, bitter and firmly hoppy.

Cheddar ▪ Goat's Leap

ABV 5.7%   500 ml   Maris Otter pale malt, crystal malt, carapils malt, wheat malt, Challenger, Fuggle and Golding hops

India Pale Ales

A new beer for autumn 2008, this golden IPA takes its name from a gorge near Bangalore, India, itself named – legend has it – after an incident where the Hindu god Shiva, in the guise of a goat, bounded across the River Kaveri. Cheddar founder Jem Ham rates it as one of his favourite fishing spots.

Tropical and citrus fruits (oranges) feature in the aroma, with plenty of hops to be enjoyed in the taste, along with more tropical fruit and orange notes, plus a hint of almond. Bitter overall, but with ample background sweetness. The finish is dry, tropical-fruity and bitter, with hops lasting a long time.

Downton ✳ Chimera India Pale Ale

ABV 7%   500 ml   Pale malt, maize, Golding and Pioneer hops

As the label explains, 'the chimera is a mythical beast, a combination of a lion, a goat and a snake'. This strong IPA has won several awards in its draught version since it was introduced in 2004.

A bright yellow IPA with a spicy 'sherbet lemons' aroma. The bittersweet taste is very full, gently warming, mildly perfumed and lemony, with a slightly syrupy texture and suggestions of almond filtering through. The finish is dry, bitter, rather thick but smooth, with a pronounced hop tang.

Durham ▪ St Cuthbert

ABV 6.5%   500 ml   Maris Otter pale malt, crystal malt, wheat malt, Challenger, Target, Columbus, Golding and Saaz hops

St Cuthbert was Durham's first bottle-conditioned beer and was initially called Millennium City – a reference to the fact that Durham was celebrating its 1,000th year as a city at the turn of the millennium. In 2000 Durham re-christened the beer in honour of the saint whose relics were

brought to Durham from Lindisfarne by monks. Inspired by a vision, the monks' decision to settle here heralded the foundation of the city and St Cuthbert still lies in the magnificent cathedral.

A chunky, golden IPA with orange-citrus and resin-like hops initially in the aroma, giving way to nutty malt. The taste is mostly bitter, hoppy and strong, with full malty sweetness in the background bringing a hint of toffee. A little toffee-like malt lingers in the dry, bitter, hoppy, fairly thick finish.

English Wines ✳ Curious Brew Cobb IPA

ABV 5.6% 330 ml Maris Otter pale malt, Cobb hops

The Cobb hop is a rare find these days. It's a form of East Kent Golding that is scarcely grown. English Wines – the company behind Chapel Down Vineyard – still finds good use for them, however, in this fine, traditional IPA brewed for the business by Hepworth in Horsham. The hops, from Kent, are added at four stages during brewing. The beer, formerly filtered for the bottle, is now bottle conditioned.

An amber beer with melon, peach and apricot jam in the aroma. More jammy apricot flavours follow in the full, bittersweet taste, along with smooth malt and firm, fresh hops. Dry, bitter finish of leafy hops.

Fox ▪ IPA

ABV 5.2% 500 ml Maris Otter pale malt, crystal malt, Target and First Gold hops

A traditional IPA, re-created by Fox brewer Mark Bristow from a 150-year-old recipe. It's great with spicy curries, he says.

A golden-coloured India pale ale with spritzy lemon and orange notes in the aroma. The

taste is drying, hoppy and bitter, but with a lively, sweet orange-citrus character, while the finish is dry, bitter and increasingly hoppy.

Haywood 'Bad Ram' ■ Callow Top IPA

ABV 5.2%   500 ml   Maris Otter pale malt, crystal malt, Challenger and Cascade hops

Callow Top is the name of the holiday park in the Derbyshire Peak District where Haywood 'Bad Ram' Brewery is based, hence the name of this India pale ale.

A golden-coloured beer with apple and pears in the aroma and more orchard fruits featuring, along with oranges, in the mostly bitter, hoppy-sharp, drying taste. The finish is dry, bitter and fruity, with hops lasting the longest.

Hopshackle ✳ Double Momentum

ABV 7%   500 ml   Maris Otter pale malt, wheat malt, invert sugar, Challenger and Golding hops

This strong ale is based on an 18th-century recipe, says Hopshackle brewer Nigel Wright, who loves dabbling with old beer styles. When he first attempted this type of beer back in 2008, the taste he created seemed to 'go on and on', which led to the name Momentum. The beer featured here is a more adventurous version of the same brew – broadly in the American style of Imperial IPA – and, as there are twice as many hops used at all stages, it just had to be labelled Double Momentum. Two months' conditioning in cask takes place before the beer is bottled, to allow the intense bitterness of the hops to mellow into other flavours.

Juicy pineapple and melon lead the way in the aroma of this golden-coloured beer, and continue into the clean, powerful taste that also has a pleasant hoppy bite, a big, smooth pale malt presence and a glowing, spicy warmth. Hops slowly build in the drying, sweet and fruity finish. A very enjoyable sipping beer.

King ▪ King's IPA

ABV 5.5%   500 ml   Maris Otter pale malt, crystal malt, wheat malt, Golding and Challenger hops

'A proper one!', declares Sussex brewer Bill King when describing his IPA, with its image of the Taj Mahal on the label. The beer is not fined, making it acceptable to vegetarians.

An amber ale with sweet malt and earthy, fruity hops in the aroma. The bittersweet taste is a little chewy but has a good, tangy hop impact, with zesty orange notes and a hint of roasted grain. The dry finish is hoppy and bitter with a touch more roasted malt.
Major stockist **Local Thresher**

Kingstone ▪ Humpty's Fuddle

ABV 5.8%   500 ml   Pale malt, crystal malt, flaked maize, Fuggle hops

The name Humpty has several historical connections. It was the name of a cannon employed at the Siege of Colchester during the English Civil War; it was bestowed on an egg-like character in Lewis Carroll's *Through the Looking Glass*; and, of course, Humpty is also the star of a nursery rhyme. As Kingstone brewer Edward Biggs explains, in most cases Humpty was left in pieces, which is what may happen if you become 'fuddled' by drinking too much of this genuine IPA, which is also sold in cask form.

An amber ale with apricots and pears dominating the aroma. The taste is also lusciously fruity, with more sweet apricots and pears then a bitter bite from the hops. There's also an oaky tartness before the dry, hoppy, lasting finish in which succulent fruit lingers on.

Lizard ▪ Frenchman's Creek

ABV 4.8%   500 ml   Maris Otter pale malt, crystal malt, Challenger, Fuggle and Styrian Golding hops

Available in bottle since 2006, this beer name checks the unspoilt tributary of the Helford river that divides the Lizard peninsula from the rest of

Cornwall. The beautiful creek also lent its name to the title of a romantic adventure novel by Daphne du Maurier. As IPAs go, this one is on the weaker side.

An orange-golden ale with malt at first in the aroma, then juicy tropical fruit (pineapple) and pink bubblegum. The taste is bittersweet and gently warming, with malt flavour, light varnish notes from the fermentation and a dry hoppiness. The bittersweet, dry finish turns slowly more bitter as hops squeeze through, but there is still a moreish malt character, too.
Major stockist **Local Asda**

Marble ▪ Lagonda IPA

ABV 5%   500 ml   Lager malt, wheat malt, caramalt, Hallertau Aroma, Golding, Admiral, Boadicea and Motueka hops

Originally named after the classic car owned by the proprietor of Manchester's Marble Brewery, Lagonda IPA was first bottled in 2006. Like many of Marble's beers, it is certified organic by the Soil Association and vegetarian by the Vegetarian Society. The unusual hops include Hallertau Aroma and the Saaz-like Motueka, both from New Zealand.

A golden IPA with a spicy aroma of piney, lemony, grapefruit-like hops. The full-bodied taste is crisp, bitter, hoppy and piney with more grapefruit and a little creamy sweet malt behind. Grapefruit continues into the dry, bitter, hoppy finish.

Meantime ✳ India Pale Ale

ABV 7.5%   750 ml   Maris Otter pale malt, crystal malt, Munich malt, Fuggle and Golding hops

First brewed in spring 2005, after lengthy research into the origins of the first India pale ales, this is another painstaking historical re-creation from Meantime Brewing in London. The beer is matured prior to bottling, a dry hopping procedure takes place and then the beer is filled, without re-seeding with new yeast or priming with sugars. You are advised to allow

it to mature awhile in the bottle, but it also drinks very well fresh. The brewers describe it as 'the original curry beer'.

A golden IPA with a malty, hoppy aroma that also features tropical fruit. The smooth taste is full bodied, sweet and hoppy with lots of resins and a citrus sharpness. The finish is dry and loaded with hops, beginning bittersweet and gradually turning bitter.
Major stockist **Sainsbury's**

Molson Coors ✳ Worthington's White Shield

ABV 5.6%   500 ml   Pale malt, crystal malt, Fuggle, Challenger and Northdown hops

For years Worthington's White Shield, along with Guinness Extra Stout, as a rare bottle-conditioned beer, was the welcome standby for beer lovers who found themselves marooned in a keg-only pub. It's the UK's best known IPA, now brewed again in its home town of Burton after being switched by former owner Bass around breweries in Sheffield and Birmingham, and then later farmed out to the now-closed King & Barnes in Horsham. The beer is now brewed three or four times a week at the White Shield Brewery, formerly the microbrewery at the heart of the now-closed Bass Museum/Coors Visitors Centre. After reaching an all-time low of just 300 barrels a year in the mid-1990s, the beer has bounced back, with output now in excess of 1,000 barrels and growing. The one-millionth bottle from the new production line rolled off in 2005. In the copper, Fuggle and Challenger hops provide the bitterness, with Northdowns added for aroma. Following primary fermentation using two strains of yeast, the beer is conditioned for three weeks in tanks, then filtered and re-seeded with new 'sticky' yeast. Primings may be added to ensure fermentability in the bottle. Bottles are then matured for one month before release and should improve with keeping up to the best before date of two years, although

India Pale Ales

White Shield fans often tuck bottles away for much longer. The beer was CAMRA's Champion Bottle-conditioned Beer in 1991, 2000 and 2006.

A light amber beer with a fruity nose, including hints of pineapple and orange. Bitter tropical fruits join lightly nutty malt, hops and almond notes in the taste, before a dry, bitter, hoppy and malty finish.
Major stockists **Booths, Sainsbury's**

North Cotswold ▪ Monarch IPA

ABV 10%   500 ml   Maris Otter pale malt, light crystal malt, wheat malt, Simcoe and Tomahawk hops

Here's a strange one. Most brewers take advantage of Christmas to have at least one day off. North Cotswold Brewery in Shipston-on-Stour, Warwickshire, keeps steaming, however, as this is the day of the year on which Monarch IPA is brewed. The beer is then matured in cask until August, when it is bottled or sold on draught. It is a mighty, powerful beer, packed with American hops and with a whopping 10% ABV – the sort of beer that should indeed withstand a long, turbulent sea voyage out to the distant Indian subcontinent.

An orange-amber beer with zesty oranges and fruit cocktail notes in the aroma. Carbonation fizzes in the mouth with bubbles bouncing around big, powerful, warming flavours of zesty orange and bitter hops. It's mostly sweet but with a slightly earthy backdrop. There are more oranges in the dry, hoppy, bitter finish.

Old Bear ▪ Duke of Bronte Capstan FS

ABV 12.5%   568 ml   Pale malt, torrefied wheat, Pioneer and Golding hops

This beer, first brewed in January 2007 for a Derby beer festival, has a strange double name. One part refers to the literary Brontë family, who lived not far from this Keighley brewery, while the other relates to a strong cigarette. The Duke of Brontë in the title is actually Lord Nelson, from

whom Irishman Patrick Brunty took his new surname of Brontë when he moved to England in the early 1800s. He was later to father the Brontë siblings Emily, Charlotte, Anne and Branwell. The FS in the beer's name refers to Full Strength, the extended name of the cigarette brand Capstan. Some drinkers have identified tobacco in the flavour of the beer, but that may just be fanciful. The beer itself is intended as a take on an imperial IPA, the super-strong, ultra-hoppy beer style that has grown up in the USA.

A very full bodied, gum-tingling, orange-golden beer, with smoky notes, malt sweetness and plenty of tangy, fruity hop resins in the aroma, taste and finish.

Old Chimneys ▪ India Pale Ale

ABV 5.6%   500 ml   Pale malt, amber malt, caramalt, Target and Golding hops

An authentic IPA, known as Lord Kitchener's India Pale Ale, when sold at the Mid-Suffolk Light Railway at Wetheringsett (conveniently, Lord Kitchener opened the old railway line and was Commander-in-Chief in India, 1902–9). Only Target hops are boiled in the copper, but Old Chimneys brewer Alan Thomson allows Golding hops to sit in the hop back as the wort is run off, infusing their own character into the brew and enhancing the aroma. Kitchener still appears on the label, in familiar 'Your country needs you' pose.

A dark golden IPA with orange marmalade in the aroma. The taste is hoppy, bitter and dry with an apricot and orange fruity sweetness and just a hint of pear drop. The dry finish is firmly hoppy and bitter.

Outstanding ✳ Standing Out

ABV 5.5%   500 ml   Maris Otter pale malt, Chinook and Bramling Cross hops

A successful combination of American and British hops in the copper is what gives this yellow-golden Lancashire beer, which is acceptable to vegetarians and vegans, its big, citrus fruit character.

Orange is foremost among the zesty fruit in the aroma. The taste is filled with zesty, bittersweet orange and citrus peel flavours from the generous hopping, and there's a soft warmth in the background. The finish is dry and firmly hoppy with more orange notes.

Pitfield ▪ 1837 India Pale Ale

ABV 7%   500 ml   Maris Otter pale malt, roasted barley, Northdown and Golding hops

A powerful, traditional IPA, part of a series of historic beer style re-creations from this once London-based, now Essex, brewery. All the ingredients are organic, as is the case for all Pitfield's beers.

An amber-coloured beer, with tropical fruits, lemon and hops in the aroma. Estery fruit (pineapple), nutty malt and tangy hops all feature in the full, bittersweet, gently warming taste, with hops taking over in the dry, bitter finish.

Red Squirrel ▪ IPA in the USA

ABV 5.4%   500 ml   Pale malt, pale crystal malt, carapils malt, Munich malt, sugar, Cascade, Chinook and Fuggle hops

An American IPA, these days, is rather different to a British one. It's not just the strains of hops that vary: the quantity of hops is often much greater, too. This Hertford brewery's take on the US IPA style comes from a recipe spotted by Red Squirrel brewer Gary Hayward in an American magazine. It's a perfect companion for spicy foods, he reckons.

A deep golden beer with a zesty aroma of grapefruit and pineapple, backed by hop resins. The taste is keenly hoppy, bringing piney, zesty, grapefruit-like flavours and drying the palate, even though there's initially plenty of sweetness. The full, dry, lasting finish is, as expected, hoppy again, with a tingly zestiness.

Ridgeway ✳ IPA

ABV 5.5%   500 ml   Maris Otter and Optic pale malt, Challenger, Fuggle, Target and Cascade hops

The Society of Independent Brewers' Champion Bottled Beer for the South-East in 2005–6, and southern region Tesco Drinks Awards champion for 2009, is brewed by Ridgeway's Peter Scholey at Cotswold Brewing in Oxfordshire, and is then bottled at Hepworth in Sussex.

A golden IPA with citrus-orange and tinned-peach notes in the hoppy aroma. There's more orange, as well as other citrus fruit, in the full, crisp, bittersweet, hoppy taste, before a dry finish that soon turns hoppy and bitter.

Major stockist **Tesco**

Rodham's ■ IPA

ABV 6.2%   500 ml   Maris Otter pale malt, First Gold hops

Breweries don't come much smaller than Rodham's, set up by Michael Rodham in the cellar of his home in Otley, West Yorkshire. This IPA was originally brewed in 2007, just for the bottle, but it is now occasionally available in cask form, at the slightly lower strength of 5.7% ABV.

A straw-coloured beer with light, sharp lemon and floral notes in the aroma. The taste is mildly earthy, with smooth pale malt, a good bite of hops and more lemon. The finish is dry, hoppy and firmly bitter.

St Austell ✳ Marks & Spencer Cornish IPA

ABV 5%   500 ml   Pale malt, Brewer's Gold, Cascade, Chinook and Willamette hops

This beer, sold exclusively in Marks & Spencer stores, is a lighter version of St Austell's award-winning Proper Job (see below).

A golden beer with sharp, sherbety lemon and grapefruit hop notes in the aroma. Refreshingly sharp hops lead in the crisp, peppery taste, with grapefruit and pine flavours up front and unobtrusive pale malt sweetness in support. The finish is dry, hoppy and clean.

Major stockist **Marks & Spencer**

St Austell ✳ Proper Job

ABV 5.5%   500 ml   Maris Otter pale malt, Brewer's Gold, Cascade, Chinook and Willamette hops

A pale, American-influenced IPA, inspired by an exchange visit St Austell's head brewer Roger Ryman undertook with Bridgeport Brewery in Oregon, whose own IPA has won numerous awards. Proper Job was first brewed in 2005, for the Celtic Beer Festival St Austell hosts every November/December, and first bottled in 2006. A cask version, at the more modest strength of 4.5%, is also brewed. The name refers to the 'proper job' the 32nd (Cornwall) Regiment did in protecting the British residency in Lucknow during the Indian Mutiny of 1857. For their efforts, Queen Victoria upgraded the unit to a light infantry regiment. Winner of the SIBA/Tucker's Maltings bottled beer competition in 2009.

A golden IPA with fresh orange peel, grapefruit and pineapple in the aroma. The same full citrus flavours from the abundant hops continue in the slightly perfumed taste, with just a little restraining malt. There's more grapefruit in the long, drying, hoppy finish.

Major stockist **Local Asda**

Spire ■ Sovereign

ABV 5.2%   500 ml   Pale malt, Vienna malt, wheat malt, Brewers' Gold and Golding hops

To mark its 100th brew, this successful micro-brewery, which was founded in Chesterfield in 2006, decided to re-create an authentic India pale ale and Sovereign was the result. It's a chunky but easy-drinking beer.

An orange-golden beer with an aroma of savoury malt and soft, lightly citrus fruit. The full-bodied taste is bittersweet, with orange notes, while the finish is dry, increasingly bitter and lipsmackingly hoppy.

Teignworthy ✳ Edwin Tucker's East India Pale Ale

ABV 6.5%   500 ml   Lager malt, wheat malt, Bramling Cross and Golding hops

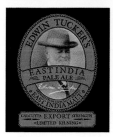

Commissioned from Teignworthy Brewery by Tucker's Maltings, this well-researched replica of a true India pale ale is bursting with hops and packs the alcoholic punch such beers needed in order to cope with the long sea journey to India. The beer is named after Tucker's founder, who started the business by purchasing a malting, seed and agricultural business in 1862.

A golden ale with a tart, zesty aroma of lemon jelly. Tangy, earthy hops dominate the full-bodied taste, bringing more citrus zest, with a malty balance keeping things bittersweet rather than bitter. Bitter citrus fruit continues into the long, dry, lipsmackingly hoppy finish.

Thornbridge ✳ Jaipur IPA

ABV 5.9%   500 ml   Maris Otter pale malt, Chinook and Cascade hops

A traditional IPA with an American accent, Jaipur was first bottled in December 2005, although some bottles have contained filtered beer. A multi-award-winner in its cask form and one of the most highly regarded beers in the country by connoisseurs.

Light tropical fruit and lots of grapefruit from the hops join malt in the aroma of this golden beer. Bitter hops then bring a juicy, citrus sharpness to the palate before a dry, very hoppy and bitter finish.

India Pale Ales

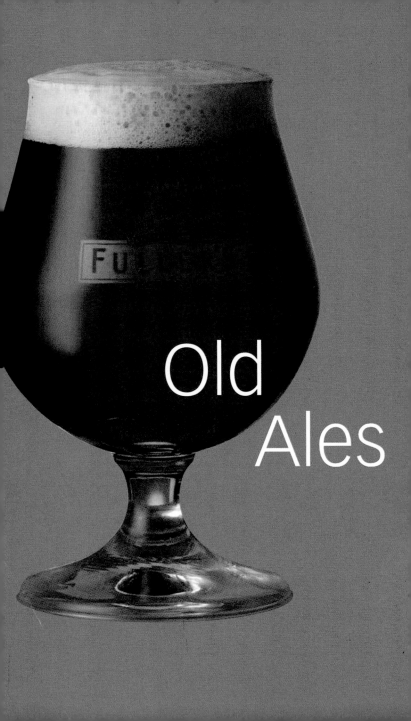

Old

Ales

Old Ales

There is a clue in the name of this beer style. Traditionally, this is a type of beer that was allowed to age before it was consumed. The result was beer that turned sour and was often blended with younger beer for drinkability. The process is best exemplified by the Belgian sour red ales, such as Rodenbach, or even in the rare survivor Greene King Strong Suffolk, which, unfortunately for the purposes of this book, is not bottle conditioned.

The ageing doesn't happen so much these days, but that doesn't stop brewers calling their products old ales. While there is no set standard recipe or flavour, the general characteristics of many such beers are a use of darker malts alongside pale malt and a modest, but balancing, hop input. Many are brewed only for winter, as a dark, warming, nourishing alternative for the colder months. Alongside these, you will also find the likes of Gale's Prize Old Ale (now brewed by Fuller's), which are more authentically aged. These and other strong old ales are well worth tucking away to see how they mature in the bottle.

At a Glance

Strength: ABV 4.5% upwards

Character: Various shades of brown or red in colour, with a full, malty character, often bringing flavours of chocolate and nut. Bitterness is low, but there may be some fruit from fermentation or hops. Truly aged old ales may have a tart, acidic note.

Serving temperature: Cool (12° C) to room temperature

Food matches: Mature cheeses, fruit cake

Adur ■ Merry Andrew

ABV 6.2%   500 ml   Maris Otter pale malt, crystal malt, black malt, torrefied wheat, oats, Sovereign and Perle hops

Brewed once every month, from September to March, this Sussex beer is named after Andrew Boorde, reportedly dubbed the original Merry Andrew. Boorde was a 16th-century physician and traveller. In his eccentric old age, he took to performing comic speeches at country fairs, so giving rise to his cheery nickname. It's also said that he published the first English joke book and – declares the label on the bottle – was eventually arrested for the crime of keeping three loose women in his house.

A ruby-coloured ale with a grassy aroma of light chocolate. The sweet taste features toffee and chocolate from the dark malts, liquorice, floral notes and some apple fruitiness, while the sweet finish is dry and malty with more chocolate, toffee and liquorice.

Ballard's ■ Wassail

ABV 6%   500 ml   Pearl pale malt, crystal malt, Fuggle and Golding hops

Wassail is a drinking salutation, translating as 'Be whole' from Old English. This old ale first appeared in cask in 1980, and in bottle in 1995. The label shows Hengist, the 5th-century leader of the Jutes, toasting Vortigern, King of the Britons. Rowena, Hengist's daughter, who seduced Vortigern, is also depicted on the bottle.

A dark amber-red ale with a creamy, malt and sultana fruit nose. The taste is creamy, rich, sweet and malty, with pronounced toffee notes and a good bitter balance. Toffee and malt fill the finish, along with a firm, drying bitterness from the increasingly forceful hops.

Major stockist **Local Thresher**

Breconshire ▪ Ramblers Ruin

ABV 5%   500 ml   Pale malt, crystal malt, black malt, Golding, Progress and First Gold hops

Ramblers Ruin was first bottled in spring 2005, having been available in cask form since 2003. A beer for bangers and mash or roast beef, says Breconshire brewer Buster Grant.

A substantial amber ale, with tart orange marmalade in the aroma. There's more marmalade in the taste, but also an estery, almost almond-like, note, along with a drying bitterness from the tangy hops. Hints of blackcurrant float around. Fruity hops, with more suggestions of blackcurrant, emerge in the drying finish.

Burton Bridge ▪ Tickle Brain

ABV 8%   500 ml   Pale malt, chocolate malt, Northdown hops

At 8%, this beer – first brewed in 1996, as the intended first of a series of beer style re-creations – more than tickles the brain. However, the brewery gives credit for this euphemism to Shakespeare, from whose writings the name is derived. The ale is an interpretation of an early (16th-century) hopped beer, as might have been produced by brewer monks. Henry VIII, the king who ordered the dissolution of the monasteries, is shown on the label. The beer is aged in casks for at least four months before bottling.

A chestnut-coloured ale with a malty, slightly earthy aroma that has touches of caramel, marzipan, raisin and pear. The taste is sweet, full, alcoholic and warming, with more suggestions of marzipan, along with winey fruit, in the mix of malt and hops. The dry, warming finish begins bittersweet and turns gradually bitter.

Corvedale ▪ Dark & Delicious

ABV 4.6%   500 ml   Maris Otter pale malt, crystal malt, chocolate malt, wheat malt, Pioneer hops

Old Ales

Introduced as a one-off for Christmas 2000, this dark, malty beer is now a regular brew. A winner of numerous medals in the SIBA (Society of Independent Brewers) regional beer contests in both cask and bottled form.

Deep red with an aroma of oranges, juicy berries and chocolate. Smooth, nutty, chocolaty malt, with hints of creamy coffee, features in the bitter-sweet taste, with a hoppy backnote drying the palate and adding a touch of grapefruit. The finish is firmly bitter and dry, with dark chocolate and roasted coffee flavours.

Dare ▪ Old Daredevil

ABV 7.9%   500 ml   Maris Otter pale malt, crystal malt, roasted barley, torrefied wheat, Sovereign hops

A powerful old ale, introduced in winter 2008 by this micro-brewery based at a South Wales valleys pub (The Falcon Inn in Aberdare, hence the bird pictured in full flight on the beer label).

Nutty, chocolaty malt with a hint of marzipan features in the aroma of this ruby beer. The taste is similarly malty, filled with sweet, nutty, chocolaty flavours that contrast with vine fruits, marzipan, alcohol and cough candy sweets. The bittersweet, dry finish is also nutty and malty.

Downton ✳ Chimera Dark Delight

ABV 6%   500 ml   Maris Otter pale malt, chocolate malt, roasted barley, wheat crystal malt, Golding, Pioneer, Challenger and Fuggle hops

This dark old ale from Wiltshire was first brewed in cask form in 2004 and was then a finalist in the Tesco Beer Challenge in 2005. It's the second beer to carry the 'Chimera' name, following on from Chimera IPA.

A deep red beer with creamy coffee, caramel and chocolate in the aroma. The taste is malty sweet, with the contrast of nutty, bitter coffee and chocolate, and suggestions of tropical fruit. Roasted grain features in the dry, bitter, coffee-like finish. It's such a drinkable beer that the strength could easily catch you out.

Durham ✳ Evensong

ABV 5%   500 ml   Maris Otter pale malt, crystal malt, amber malt, Munich malt, wheat malt, Golding, Challenger and Fuggle hops

Introduced in 2001, Evensong is based on a recipe dating from 1937 from the long-defunct Whitaker's Brewery in Halifax. Although the spirit of the original remains, says brewer Steve Gibbs, this is now a wholly Durham creation. CAMRA's Champion Bottle-conditioned Beer of Britain in 2005.

A rich ruby-coloured ale with hints of chocolate and nut from the smooth dark malt in the aroma, along with suggestions of pear and peach. The full-bodied, bittersweet taste majors on smooth roasted malts, balanced by a bitter backnote and some floral and winey fruit notes. The fairly thick finish is dry, malty and bitter with roasted grain.

Fuller's ✳ 1845

ABV 6.3%   500 ml   Pale malt, crystal malt, amber malt, Golding hops

1845 was first brewed in February 1995, with the Prince of Wales doing the honours and adding the hops to the copper. It was a new ale to commemorate the 150th anniversary of the founding of the company and was designed to reflect the type of brew available during the 1840s, hence the use of only Golding hops, the inclusion of amber malt for some biscuity character and the decision to bottle condition it. Its success (twice CAMRA's Champion Bottle-conditioned Beer) has made it a permanent member of the Fuller's range, with brews taking place twice a month. After primary fermentation, the beer enjoys time in conditioning tanks and is then filtered, re-seeded with fresh primary fermentation yeast and bottled, with no primings. More conditioning follows before the bottles are released, allowing Fuller's to boast that the beer is matured for 100 days in all. The best before date is set at two years, but this is a beer that can be appreciated young or old. The beer is imported into the USA through Distinguished Brands International.

A rich, dark amber beer with an aroma of malt, chocolate, light hop resins and hints of oranges and raisins that grow stronger as the beer warms in the glass. The taste is full and rich, yet quaffable, with the malt giving traces of toffee, and a keen bitterness also there for balance. Tangy oranges lurk in the background. The dry, bitter, malty and hoppy finish is full and lasting. Fresh-tasting and classy.
Major stockists **Sainsbury's, Tesco, Waitrose**

Fuller's ✳ Gale's Prize Old Ale

ABV 9%   500 ml   Optic pale malt, crystal malt, chocolate malt, Fuggle and Golding hops

Prize Old Ale was introduced to Gale's brewery in Hampshire in the 1920s, when a new head brewer brought the recipe with him from Yorkshire. The recipe remained largely unchanged in the subsequent 80 years up to the brewery's closure in 2006, except for switching whole hops for pellets and the replacement of wooden hogsheads, which were used for conditioning the beer, with metal tanks. This was where the beer was allowed to mature for 6–12 months. At Gale's, more of the yeast used for primary fermentation was added before bottling, to ensure a secondary fermentation. The last vintage released from Gale's was for 2006, but the brew for 2007 was already maturing in tanks and was transferred to Fuller's in Chiswick where it was eventually bottled for release in early 2008. The end product is noticeably changed from that produced at Gale's, however, in that it now comes in a conventionally crown-capped bottle, instead of a stubby, corked bottle. This allows the higher level of natural carbonation with which it is now bottled to remain in the beer. This seems to accentuate the natural acidity of the beer. It's rather a different beer now, with similarities to the sour red ales of Belgium such as Rodenbach. Some of the original Gale's beer has been held back for blending with future brews, to allow the unique micro flora picked up in the ancient Gale's brewhouse to have its say in any new batches. The beer is imported into the USA through Distinguished Brands International.

2007 vintage: A red/dark amber beer with a spicy, lambic-like aroma of toffee, banana and dried fruits, which leads on to banana toffee and sweet, sharp, winey fruit in the dry, acidic taste. The finish is dry, acidic, bitter and warming, with banana, toffee-like malt, and rapidly fading winey sweetness.

Great Oakley ▪ Delapre Dark

ABV 4.6% 500 ml Pale malt, crystal malt, other dark malts, torrefied wheat, Northdown and Cascade hops

When, in 2006, Northamptonshire CAMRA staged its first beer festival at Delapré Abbey – an imposing, 16th-century structure with Civil War connections – this was the beer that Great Oakley brewed to commemorate the event. It proved so popular that it was added to the brewery's regular range and is now produced weekly.

A near-black ale with a biscuity aroma of dark malt (plain chocolate) and tart berry fruits. The taste is bittersweet and creamy, with more tart, dark malt, plus hints of liquorice and tropical fruits. There are hop notes throughout and it's quite light in body, considering the malt that is involved. Roasted grain flavours emerge in the smooth, drying, increasingly bitter finish.

Hobsons ▪ Old Henry

ABV 5.2% 500 ml Maris Otter pale malt, crystal malt, wheat malt, Challenger and Golding hops

Although largely the same brew as the draught beer of the same name, this Shropshire ale is a touch more heavily hopped for the bottle, to compensate for the absence of dry hops in the cask. The bottle is also available all year-round, unlike the winter-only draught version. The label

describes this amber brew as a beer 'best served with mature Shropshire Blue cheese'.

Orange jelly and gentle pear notes feature in the faintly toffee-like aroma. The taste is sweetish and malty, with more toffee and an apple-orange fruitiness, a smooth body and a drying, bitter backnote. The dry, hoppy finish is increasingly bitter, with a light toffee note and some early fruit quickly fading.

Major stockist **Local Co-op**

Hogs Back ✳ OTT/Old Tongham Tasty

ABV 6%   500 ml   Maris Otter pale malt, crystal malt, chocolate malt, Fuggle hops

Introduced as a cask-conditioned beer in the early 1990s, this dark ruby ale from Surrey was first bottled in 2000 and is now produced monthly. The initials in the name are said to stand for 'Old Tongham Tasty' or 'Over the Top' and the label features pigs flying 'over the top' of the Tongham brewery. A great companion for strong cheese and game, say the brewers.

A ruby ale with biscuity chocolate, treacle, creamy oat notes, some winey fruit and a hint of liquorice in the aroma. Sweet dark malt flavours fill the rich taste, bringing more chocolate and treacle, before a dry, treacle-malty, bittersweet finish.

Major stockists **Budgens, Harrods, Londis, Sainsbury's, Tesco, Waitrose**

King ■ King's Old Ale

ABV 4.5%   500 ml   Maris Otter pale malt, crystal malt, chocolate malt, wheat malt, Whitbread Golding Variety and Challenger hops

A bottled version of this Sussex brewery's award-winning, rich, dark ale that was first brewed in 2002 and is now produced every winter.

Deep ruby, with plenty of toffee and dark chocolate in the nose. The taste is full of luscious toffee and chocolate, on the sweet side but not cloying. Roasted grains are more obvious in the dry, increasingly bitter finish, with more toffee, chocolate and a hint of coffee.

Old Chimneys ✳ Redshank

ABV 8.7%   275 ml   Pale malt, crystal malt, roasted barley, Fuggle and Challenger hops

This strong, fruity ale shares its name with a wading bird and was added to the extensive range of beers from this successful East Anglian brewery in 2000. It is now brewed every three months.

A red beer with raisins and strawberries in the creamy, sweet aroma, along with a pinch of liquorice and toffee-like malt. The taste is ultra smooth, creamy and mostly sweet, with a good malt foundation and lots of strawberry and dried fruit flavours, plus liquorice and warming alcohol. The creamy finish is sweet but with bitterness fighting back as hops come through.

Tipple's ■ Jack's Revenge

ABV 5.8%   500 ml   Pale malt, crystal malt, chocolate malt, Bramling Cross and Golding hops

This dark, strong ale – part of a trio of ghostly beers from Tipple's – recalls the legend of one Jack Ketch, a 17th-century man who was hanged for a murder he didn't commit and who wreaked revenge on the real killer in the afterlife, stabbing him to death on Acle Bridge in Norfolk. Rumour has it that Ketch is still at work because every 7 April fresh blood is discovered on the stonework of the bridge.

A near-black beer with lemon, berries and tropical fruits in the dark malt aroma. The sweetish taste is light-bodied, with more citrus and tropical fruits over smooth, dark malt and an alcoholic buzz. The dry, warming finish is chocolaty and softly bitter.

Tunnel ▪ Nelson's Column

ABV 5.2%   500 ml   Maris Otter pale malt, crystal malt, torrefied wheat, Golding and Cascade hops

An old ale first brewed to commemorate the 200th anniversary of the Battle of Trafalgar in 2005 and now a regular feature of Tunnel's beer list. The labels of Tunnel's nicely-presented bottles feature far-fetched stories about the origins of the beers' names. This one spins a yarn about Nelson's enthusiasm for the iron ore found around the tunnel from which the brewery takes its name, claiming he commissioned cannon balls from it. In 2006, the cask-conditioned version of Nelson's Column was voted CAMRA's Champion Beer of Warwickshire.

A dark amber-red beer with nutty, toasted malt and floral and tropical fruit notes in the aroma. Earthy malt and floral, fruity flavours continue in the sweetish taste, along with orange-citrus, before a dry, bitter, hoppy, spicy, orange-like finish.
Major stockists **Local Asda and Tesco**

White ▪ Chilly Willy

ABV 5.1%   500 ml   Maris Otter pale malt, crystal malt, chocolate malt, wheat malt, Golding and Bramling Cross hops

Chilly Willy is this Sussex microbrewery's best selling bottled beer. It was first brewed in 2003 and – continuing the company's Battle of Hastings theme – is named after the battle's victor, William the Conqueror, who, the label declares, conquered England but not the weather.

This chestnut-coloured beer has a malty aroma suggestive of chocolate digestive biscuits. Chocolate and nut feature prominently in the sweetish, malty taste, along with some tropical fruit and a light, balancing bitterness. The dry finish is also malty, nutty and bitter.

Why Not ▪ Chocolate Nutter

ABV 5.5%   500 ml   Maris Otter pale malt, crystal malt, chocolate malt, Golding and Fuggle hops

This dark ale, first brewed in 2005, is named after the chocolate malt in the recipe, which provides a nuttiness to the flavour. Like most bottled beers from this small Norfolk brewery, it is acceptable to both vegetarians and vegans, as no finings are used to clarify the beer.

Garnet in colour, with creamy, chocolaty, nutty malt in the aroma. The taste is sweet and malty with nut, chocolate and bitter liquorice notes, plus hints of tropical fruit. The finish is dry and bitter with more nut and chocolate.

Yates' ✳ Wight Old Ale

ABV 6%   500 ml   Pale malt, roasted barley, torrefied wheat, Centennial hops

A new strong beer in this Isle of Wight brewer's collection of bottled ales, ruby-red in colour and seasoned with American hops.

A big, winey fruity aroma (red berries and juicy oranges) with dark malt support, leads on to a taste of complex dark malts, zingy oranges and dried winey fruits that has a peppery tingle. The finish is zesty, tingly and dry, with bitter roasted grain flavours.

Barley
Wines

Barley Wines

Barley wine: the name is suggestive of a brewery marketing scheme to prove that British ale is as good as a French Claret. In fact, there is some truth in that, with 19th-century brewers fighting back against the spread of wine consumption in Britain by promoting their strong beers in this way. But the idea of barley wine, a heady brew created from the best new season ingredients and matured for months or even years, dates back centuries. It is said to have been the preserve of the upper classes, who drank it instead of French wine and brandy when duty rates on imports were raised in the 18th century.

With regard to actual recipe guidelines, there are few. This style is about strength more than ingredients, except to point out the obvious that, in order to raise the alcohol level to such heights, there must be a good proportion of malt involved, and then, for balance, a similar level of hopping, with the preservative qualities of the hops joining alcohol in keeping the beer in good shape for its time in the cask or bottle.

As a style, barley wine fell away during the 20th century, to the point where the biggest selling example was a canned product from Whitbread called Gold Label. But, as the microbrewery movement has grown, and customers have become more beer aware, it has made a comeback. Because of its strength, barley wine is not often seen on draught in a pub and it has taken the resurgence of the bottled beer sector to really secure its renaissance. It is one of the best styles of beer with which to experiment. With plenty of alcohol, malt and hops in the mix, these beers mature beautifully, with flavours changing as each month and year passes.

At a Glance

Strength: ABV 7% upwards

Character: Amber-brown in colour, with a full, malty body and a good hop balance. Fruit flavours from both the hops and from fermentation may be present and fortified wine characteristics may develop as the beer ages.

Serving temperature: Cool (12º C) to room temperature

Food matches: Mature cheeses, fruit cakes, Christmas pudding

Ballard's ▪ Birthday Boy

ABV 9.5%   275 ml   Pearl pale malt, Fuggle and Golding hops

Birthday Boy is the latest in the Ballard's series of 'Old Bounder' beers – strong beers in the same style but with different names and strengths. The brewery has been producing these for now for 21 years – hence the name of this particular brew. The first batch of each of new beer rolls out on the first Sunday in December (to tie in with a charity 'beer walk') and the brew is then repeated once or twice during the subsequent year. There is a draught version, too (available over Christmas). Add a little to a Christmas pudding, or treat it like port, says brewery owner Carola Brown. She also suggests you mull it with sugar and spices.

An amber-red-coloured beer with Marmite, malt and vinous dried fruits in the aroma. The taste is sweet and warming, with a hint of toffee in the creamy malt and a complex fruitiness – juicy berries, sultanas and sharp oranges. Dried fruits and tangy hops feature in the sweet, thick, palate-numbing finish, although it is bitterness that has the final word.

Barearts ▪ Dark Barley Wine

ABV 9.6%   500 ml   Maris Otter pale malt, dark crystal malt, Golding hops

Barearts brews two barley wines, and this is the one with the added dark crystal malt for a deeper, rosy-red colour. It's a touch weaker than the Pale Barley Wine (see below), too.

Plenty of toasted malt features in the aroma, along with hints of strawberry and raspberry, plus a little whiff of marzipan. Rich berry fruitiness leads in the taste, along with dried and tropical fruit notes, against a full, malty body, which is sweet and warming, with a creamy texture and an obvious alcoholic strength. The palate-numbing, dry, fruity and sweet finish leaves a satisfying glow.

Barearts ✳ Pale Barley Wine

ABV 9.8%   500 ml   Lager malt, Golding hops

The stronger, paler barley wine from Barearts, with only lager malt providing the cereal base. Nevertheless, this pours a rich amber colour.

Smooth malt, with hints of Ovaltine, leads in the aroma, with faint almond notes and lots of pear and apple. The sweet, pleasantly warming, velvety taste is loaded with fermentation flavours, from pear and tropical fruit to almond and varnish. Deceptively drinkable, with a smooth and warming finish.

Bartrams ■ Mother in Law's Tongue Tied

ABV 9.5%   330 ml   Maris Otter pale malt, dark crystal malt, Galena, Tettnang and Hallertau hops

A copper-coloured barley wine brewed originally at 9% in 2003 to celebrate the 90th birthday of Suffolk brewer Marc Bartram's mother-in-law. With her 95th birthday, the strength was raised to 9.5% (the tasting notes below are based on the 9% version).

Sweet malt in the aroma is joined by pineapple and strawberry as the beer warms. The taste is not as full or rich as expected, hiding the alcohol very well. It's rather bitter for such a strong beer, too, with tangy hops drying the palate and red berry and dried fruit notes also coming through. The finish is dry, hoppy and bitter, with malt lingering.

Chiltern ✳ Bodgers Barley Wine

ABV 8.5%   330 ml   Maris Otter pale malt, Challenger, Fuggle and Golding hops

Brewed first in 1990, to commemorate the tenth anniversary of the founding of this Buckinghamshire brewery, Bodgers recalls the tradition

Barley Wines

of the Chiltern Bodger (a chairmaker who worked in the surrounding beechwoods) in its name, and the year of the brewery's birth in its original gravity (1080). It is a fine accompaniment to the range of beer-related foods sold at the brewery, although the Jenkinson family that runs the business also suggest it could be served lightly chilled as an aperitif or at room temperature instead of a dessert wine. The beer is conditioned in tank for a month, then filtered and re-pitched with new yeast before bottling (off-site, under contract). Bottles are kept at the brewery to mature for four weeks. The sepia-tinged labels picture a bodger at work in 1929.

A golden ale, with a sweet and fruity aroma, featuring succulent mango and zesty orange. The taste is crisp but sweet, with creamy pale malt, light vinous fruit, more zesty oranges and a gentle warmth. The drying, bitter and hoppy finish is smooth, with oranges lingering.

Durham ✳ Bede's Chalice

ABV 9%   500 ml   Maris Otter pale malt, lager malt, Vienna malt, wheat malts, Centennial hops

Originally a Christmas beer, first brewed in 2006 under the name of St Nicholas, Bede's Chalice reflects in its present title the influence of the Benedictine monk the Venerable Bede in North-East England during the seventh and eighth centuries.

A chunky, orange-coloured ale with the zest and pith of bitter oranges in the aroma, along with a suggestion of orchard fruits. There's plenty of carbonation in the mouth, lifting the thick, warming, bittersweet taste that is loaded with more orange character from the hops. The finish is dry, bitter, thick and gum-tingling, with oranges lingering.

Durham ✳ Benedictus

ABV 8.4%   500 ml   Maris Otter pale malt, crystal malt, wheat malt, Golding, Target, Saaz, Styrian Golding and Columbus hops

Based on another bottled beer Durham brews called St Cuthbert (see India Pale Ales), but with a deeper golden colour, Benedictus was added to the brewery's extensive range in 2001.

A golden barley wine with a potent, malty aroma featuring bitter citrus and pine notes from the hops, along with a hint of tropical fruit. The taste is sweet but hoppy, with hops contributing bitterness, earthy resins and juicy citrus and tropical fruit flavours. Earthy resins continue in the dry, hoppy, fruity finish.

Fuller's ✳ Vintage Ale

ABV 8.5% 550 ml   Maris Otter pale malt, crystal malt, Challenger and Northdown hops (2008 vintage)

Fuller's Vintage Ale is usually brewed in a one-off batch (initially 85,000 bottles, but the quantity now varies) in September each year. The packaging is high quality, allowing the brewery to charge around £3.50 per bottle. For that, you get an individually numbered item in a presentation box, with a best before date set three years on. More importantly, you get a rather special beer. Fuller's aficionados will probably gather that the ale is in fact a version of the brewery's excellent Golden Pride barley wine. But, by giving this beer the bottle conditioning treatment (including around eight weeks in conditioning tanks before filtering and re-seeding with fresh Fuller's yeast), the result is a noticeably lighter, fresher beer, quite different from Golden Pride, which is supplied in pasteurised bottles. Some brews have used annual champion strains of barley and hops, although now there has been a return to standard floor-malted barley and regular hops. Fuller's has organized occasional 'vertical tastings' of all Vintage Ales to date, showcasing how the beers have matured and the flavours have ripened over the years.

2006 vintage (tasted young): **Rich malt is joined by a woody, herbal, liquorice-like note in the aroma. The taste is initially sweet and malty, but then balanced by hop-resin bitterness. Citrus orange notes blend with cherry and almonds in the taste, which also offers hints of**

liquorice and aniseed. The drying finish is tangy-hoppy, herbal and warming. Less sweet than some earlier vintages.

2007 vintage (tasted young): **Amber-copper in colour with an instantly fruity aroma (soft tropical fruit, red berries and tart, smoky oranges), with malt, a little chocolate, and hop resins. The generally sweetish taste is notably spicy, with a liquorice-like, tangy bitterness leading the way, then silky malt, marzipan, zesty oranges, vinous raisins and a peppery, tingly warmth emerging. There's a soft, rounded bitterness to the finish, along with mellow citrus fruit and plenty of lingering, tangy hops.**

2008 vintage (tasted young): **A bright amber beer with a fresh, sherbety aroma of citrus hops, smooth malt and sticky orange marmalade. Sharp hop notes lead over deep, ripe malt, with a touch of toffee, light orange notes and a gentle warmth. The drying finish is dominated by tangy hops, leaving a bitter orange accent over the smooth, supportive malt. Fairly light bodied for the strength.**

Major stockist **Waitrose**

Harwich Town ▪ Sint Niklaas

ABV 8%   330 ml   Pale malt, crystal malt, chocolate malt, brown sugar, Golding hops, honey

Brewed in aid of Harwich's St Nicholas church restoration appeal, this is a strong ale in the Belgian style, as the name suggests. Two types of hops are used, regular Goldings and also Goldings that have been allowed to grow old, so that they add bitterness and preservative qualities but little aroma or character. The beer is brewed on a Sunday in October and blessed by a Belgian clergyman. It is then matured for two months before being bottled straight from the cask and made available for sale on St Nicholas's Day (6 December).

A bright red-coloured ale with a leathery, malty aroma that is a little bit cheesy, courtesy of the aged hops. The taste is bitter up front, but there are some sugary notes behind. Toffee-like malt is well evident,

along with dark grain flavours, some winey fruit and a gentle warmth. Roasted malt leads in the dry, bitter finish.

Hogs Back ✳ A over T/Aromas over Tongham

ABV 9%   275 ml   Maris Otter pale malt, crystal malt, chocolate malt, Golding and Bramling Cross hops

One of Hogs Back's earliest brews, A over T (named after its unfortunate side-effect but diplomatically explained as standing for 'Aromas over Tongham') first tempted drinkers in 1993, when it appeared in cask form. In 2006 the draught version was judged CAMRA's Champion Winter Beer of Britain.

A red-coloured beer with winey, tart fruit, malt and tobacco in the aroma. There's lots of flavour on the palate, from sweet, rich, treacly malt to tangy dried and citrus fruits and a good, bitter hop balance. After a warming swallow, the finish is sweet, malty and fruity with a gently increasingly bitterness. A raised carbonation level makes it very easy to drink for the strength and stops it from ever becoming cloying or heavy.

Major stockists **Budgens, Harrods, Londis**

Hogs Back ▪ Brewster's Bundle

ABV 7.4%   275 ml   Maris Otter pale malt, crystal malt, chocolate malt, Golding and Bramling Cross hops

This ale from Surrey was initially produced each February, but is now bottled every month. The 'Bundle' in question is Charley, the first baby daughter of Hogs Back's lady brewer, Maureen Zieher. Charley was born in February 1994 at the weight of 7lb 4oz (hence the 7.4% ABV and the baby and the scales on the label).

A bright amber beer with pineapple, oranges and hints of raspberry in the otherwise floral aroma. Pineapple features strongly in the sweet and warming taste with some tangy hop and smooth, light malt behind. The finish is dry, hoppy and increasingly bitter with malty sweetness and pineapple lingering.

Major stockists **Budgens, Harrods, Londis**

Hogs Back ▪ Wobble in a Bottle/ Santa's Wobble

ABV 7.5% 275 ml   Maris Otter pale malt, crystal malt, chocolate malt, Fuggle and Golding hops

Hogs Back's Christmas cask beer is called Santa's Wobble. It is bottled under that name at Christmas but for the rest of the year it goes by the name of Wobble in a Bottle. It was first produced in 1992.

A copper-amber-coloured beer with a creamy, tangy, vinous aroma with hints of strawberry. Strawberry flavours then continue in the sweet, creamy, malty taste, joined by an oaky dryness and a good hop balance. The finish is dry, bitter and fruity, with malt, hops and an oaky-woody note.

Major stockists **Budgens, Harrods, Londis**

Hopshackle ✳ Restoration

ABV 9% 275 ml   Pilsner malt, Special B malt, chocolate malt, dark candy sugar, Hersbrucker and Mount Hood hops

Hopshackle brewer Nigel Wright's fascination with Belgian brewing continues with this wonderfully balanced barley wine. The ingredients include candy sugar, of which Trappist monasteries make liberal use in their heady brews, and Special B malt, which is a dark crystal malt from Belgium. The hops are a mix of German Hersbrucker and American Mount Hood. After primary fermentation, the beer is aged for six months in a conditioning tank. At the end of this, the beer has dropped bright naturally

and is re-seeded with what Nigel describes as 'an alcohol tolerant yeast strain', re-primed with sugar and bottled. Another four to six weeks is then allowed for a good secondary fermentation before the beer is released. Nigel is looking forward to trying this beer as it ages over the years. A donation of 25 pence from every bottled sold goes to a repair fund for St Guthlac's church in Market Deeping – hence the name of the beer, which was selected through a competition. The vicar blesses each brew while it is in the fermentation vessel. A limited edition beer (around 1,500 bottles only) that is well worth seeking out.

A dark amber-red ale that offers an aroma of creamy malt with traces of treacle, pineapple, berries and a hint of sherry. The taste is sweet and complex, featuring strawberries and other red berries, sultanas and other dried fruits, and a pleasant, peppery warmth. There's a solid malt foundation, a nice tingle on the tongue, more suggestions of sherry and nods towards both cola and Dr Pepper. The finish is not particularly long, but majors on sweet malt and sultanas.

Keltek ▪ Beheaded

ABV 7.6%   500 ml   Maris Otter pale malt, crystal malt, wheat malt, sugar, Fuggle and Cluster hops

Beheaded began life back in 1976, in the 'garden shed' days of Keltek founder Stuart Heath's experiments with commercial brewing. When it first went on sale, 27 years later, it rolled out at a dizzy 10% ABV. The beer is now back to a more manageable 7.6%.

A red-coloured beer featuring an alcoholic, sherry-like aroma, with creamy malt, fruit cake, treacle toffee and liquorice notes. Sherry flavours continue in the taste, which is rather thin bodied for the strength and offers plenty of bitterness to counter the initial sweetness. Dried fruit, creamy malt and a gentle warmth are also evident. The warming finish is dry and bitter, but not heavy, with more dried fruit and malt featuring.

167

O'Hanlon's ✳ Thomas Hardy's Ale

ABV 11.7%   330 ml   **Pale malt, crystal malt, Pilot, Styrian Golding and Golding hops**

Thomas Hardy's Ale was created by Dorchester brewer Eldridge Pope in 1968 to commemorate the 40th anniversary of the death of Wessex writer Thomas Hardy. Its inspiration was a passage in Hardy's novel The Trumpet-Major, which described Dorchester's strong beer thus:

'It was of the most beautiful colour that the eye of an artist in beer could desire; full in body, yet brisk as a volcano; piquant, yet without a twang; luminous as an autumn sunset; free from streakiness of taste but, finally, rather heady.'

This famous quote was recalled on the label of each individually numbered bottle of Hardy's Ale. The beer seemed to be lost forever when Eldridge Pope (now no longer in brewing) lost interest in the beer after the 1999 vintage. However, following an absence of four years, Hardy's was brought back to life by O'Hanlon's in Devon, in conjunction with a company called Phoenix Imports, which bought the brand and saw a future for it in the US. The copper boil lasts about three hours, with fermentation and maturation extending to another six months or so. The beer is then dry hopped with Goldings at a very high rate for two to four months, before being bottled. O'Hanlon's recommends ageing the beer for at least nine months before sampling. Supreme Champion in the International Beer Challenge in 2006.

2006 vintage (tasted after one year)**: Red in colour, with bitter, zesty oranges and vinous dried fruits in the malty aroma. The taste is mostly bitter, with zesty clementine fruitiness, silky malt and a slight woody note. The dry, warming finish is mouth-tingling, featuring sultanas, oranges, hops and some lingering sweetness.**

2008 vintage (tasted young)**: A red-amber beer with plenty of malt and toffee in the aroma that also features sultanas, hop resins and bitter oranges. The taste is bittersweet and fruity, with sultanas and tangerines on top of sugary malt, countered by tangy hops and a spicy warmth. The finish is full and warming, with bitter oranges, dried fruits and sweet, sticky malt before hops take over. Overall, a little sugary and low in carbonation. That should all change with age.**
Major stockists **Booths, Waitrose, local Majestic**

Otley ▪ 08

ABV 8%   500 ml   Pale malt, torrefied wheat, Whitbread Golding Variety and Willamette hops

This powerful ale was brewed in 2005 as an experiment, apparently, and you could say that it's turned out rather well – the draught version was judged Champion Beer of Wales in both 2006 and 2008. The name comes from the strength and from the brewery's distinctive 'O' branding.

An dark golden/amber beer with pineapple and orange in the hoppy aroma. The taste is full, warming, sweet and zesty, with more oranges and estery fruit such as pineapple. Some sweetness lingers in the thick, warming, hoppy, tangy and bitter finish.

Outstanding ▪ Pushing Out

ABV 7.4%   500 ml   Maris Otter pale malt, Chinook and Styrian Golding hops

An orange-golden, vegetarian- and vegan-friendly barley wine from a modestly-named brewery in Lancashire. It's a big-tasting beer, even for its hefty 7.4% ABV level.

Bitter oranges are well to the fore in the aroma, supported by hop resins. The taste is very hoppy, with lots of zesty, bitter oranges. There's plenty of body but malt flavours are very much secondary. Hops linger long in the dry, bitter finish with yet more orange notes.

Pitfield ▪ 1896 XXXX Stock Ale

ABV 10%   375 ml   Maris Otter pale malt, crystal malt, Northdown hops

This authentic re-creation from a former London brewery, now based in Essex, is a beer to lay down and enjoy in a couple of years' time. Stock

ales were designed for such keeping, having plenty of alcohol and body to allow them to mature long after brewing. Pitfield's example is also made from organic ingredients.

2008 vintage (tasted young)**: A golden beer with lots of pineapple and bitter orange in the heady aroma, along with a touch of liquorice. The taste is sweet and alcoholic, with pineapple, pear and tangy, earthy hop notes, before a sweet, thick, warming finish in which hops eventually make their presence known. Should mellow nicely over time.**

Sharp's ✳ Massive Ale

ABV 10%   330/660 ml   Cocktail pale malt, crystal malt, roasted barley, dark candy sugar, Northdown, Northern Brewer and Perle hops

Sharp's may be a major regional brewery these days, but many things at the Cornwall brewhouse still benefit from the hands-on approach, including this potent barley wine, which is completely hand packaged. It was first brewed in 2008 and is given plenty of time to mature before it even goes near any glassware, conditioning in cask for 18 months. After bottling, it is then warm and cold conditioned for six months before going on sale. A massive ale, not only in name.

An amber ale with zesty, bitter oranges and malt in the aroma. Plenty of carbonation means an airy texture in the mouth and light body for the strength, with flavours majoring on sweet malt, sour dried fruits and a hint of orange zest, before a dry, malty, sweet finish featuring hop resins, alcohol and raisin.

Sharp's ✳ St Enodoc Double

ABV 8.5%   500 ml   Cocktail pale malt, crystal malt, roasted barley, dark candy sugar, Northdown, Northern Brewer and Challenger hops

This is Sharp's tribute to the Belgian dubbel style, as brewed by Trappist monks. It has religious connections itself, in being named after the church of St Enodoc, close to the brewery on the North Cornwall coast. The church has origins in the 12th century but was abandoned in later years to the

drifting sands, so that when it was restored in the mid 1800s, it had to be more excavated than renovated. Poet Laureate Sir John Betjeman fell in love with the church and was buried there in 1994, close to members of his family.

This red-coloured ale has a malty, fruity aroma, with sweet red berries and bitter citrus, along with herbal and mildly liquorice-like notes. The taste is drying and malty, but not heavy, with a sweetish character, a spicy warmth and an orange-citrus sharpness, plus more berries. The finish is mildly warming, malty and bittersweet, but fades fairly quickly. Delicate and easy-drinking for the strength.

Woodforde's ■ Headcracker

ABV 7%   500 ml   Maris Otter pale malt, caramalt, Golding and Styrian Golding hops

Barley Wines

This beer from Norfolk, as its graphic name suggests, is not one to treat lightly but it warrants respect not just because of its strength. It has won CAMRA's Best Barley Wine award on no fewer than three occasions (in cask-conditioned form).

A bright amber-coloured beer with tart fruit and barley sugars featuring in the aroma, along with floral and tropical fruit notes. Pineapple and other tropical fruits are then evident in the sweetish taste, which also offers light caramel, bitter citrus and a vinous catch, all underpinned by a firm bitterness from piney hops. The thick, chunky finish is both dry and lipsmackingly hoppy.

Woodforde's ✳ Norfolk Nip

ABV 8%   330 ml   Maris Otter pale malt, crystal malt, chocolate malt, roasted barley, Golding hops

Norfolk Nip closely follows a recipe dating from 1929 for a beer (also called Norfolk Nip) from the much-missed Steward & Patteson brewery in

WOODFORDE'S
Norfolk Ales

Norwich. The original beer was phased out by Watney's in the early 1960s, but the brew was revived by Woodforde's in March 1992 to commemorate the tenth anniversary of the local CAMRA news journal, *Norfolk Nips*. Brewing now takes place annually, on or around St Valentine's Day. The strength and high hop rate should allow this deep ruby-coloured beer to mature well long after it has been bottled.

A vinous aroma of creamy dark malts, treacle, raisins, jammy fruity and Marmite leads on to a vinous and tangy taste that falls on the sweet side of bittersweet, with prune and chocolate flavours. Tangy hops come through again in the dry, chocolaty, coffee-like, bitter finish. A complex and interesting barley wine.

Stouts & Porters

Stouts & Porters

Although stout has come to be considered internationally as an Irish drink, its origins actually lie elsewhere, in the capital city of England. It was in 18th-century London that drinkers first gained a taste for a brown, vinous, aged beer, the origins of which are the subject of much speculation.

The most familiar story has it that the beer was a complex drink made up of three different beers that were blended together at the pub. Called three threads, it was a mix of fresh pale ale, brown beer and aged beer. Eventually, brewers cottoned onto the fact that they could re-create this effect in one brew, producing a brown beer that could be aged for some time before going on sale. They called this entire butt – the entire beer being in one butt, or cask, so to speak – but the populace soon came to know it as porter, possibly after the market porters who drank so much of it. Stronger versions of porter were known as stout porters, later shortened to stout.

Brewing historian Martyn Cornell in his e-book *Amber, Gold & Black* places porter in a different context, as simply a brown beer brewed as an alternative to hoppy ales, a beer that was aged to get rid of the smokiness from the primitive wood-fired malting process of the time and so picked up tart, winey notes along the way. The entire butt, he says, relates to a blending in one finished product of various brews of the beer that had been created from four or five mashings of the same malt.

Whatever the truth, changes to malting technology soon meant that brewers no longer had to rely wholly on brown malts that had a smoky character because they had been cured over wood or direct flames. New pale malt was not only more subtle but also produced more fermentable sugar, making it cheaper. Once brewers had adopted pale malt, to maintain the dark colour of the beer they also added a little of a new black malt that brought more of a roasted flavour to beer. However, porter and stout still didn't quite have that distinctive dryness that stout has become known for today. That's where the Irish came in, when Dublin brewer Arthur Guinness spotted a way of saving money. With malt taxed by the Government, he simply saved money by using a small proportion of untaxed, unmalted roasted barley to darken and flavour his beer instead. This today is the ingredient that contributes much of the dryness and roasted character to an 'Irish-style' stout.

The character of stout and porter has changed, therefore, over the centuries. Today, differences between the two are rather blurred, but as a broad rule of thumb, porters tend to be a little lighter-bodied and a touch sweeter. Both come in various shapes and forms, other than Irish dry. There are still sweet stouts in production, which are low in alcohol and retain a high level of unfermented sugars. Linked to these are milk stouts that include not milk but milk sugar – lactose – that cannot be fermented by brewer's yeast, so the body of the beer is boosted but not the alcohol level. Lactose also adds a sour cream note to the flavour. At the other end of the alcohol spectrum are imperial stouts and Baltic porters, beers that once were shipped from Britain across the icy Baltic to warm the frozen aristocrats of Russia and other Eastern states. It was particularly popular in the Russian court – hence the name imperial stout. To withstand the sea journey, these were both strong and well hopped. They are demanding drinks, with many levels of flavour, and are among the most rewarding of beers to those who understand them.

At a Glance

Strength: ABV 3% upwards; imperial stouts generally start at around 7%

Character: Ruby-red, dark brown or near-black in colour, with a good roasted grain character. Sweet stouts are literally that, and milk stouts have a little sour creaminess. Chocolate and coffee notes are common in both stout and porter, but some – particularly those based on authentic ancient recipes – can be vinous and fruity. Imperial stouts and Baltic porters can be winey, alcoholic, bitter and challenging.

Serving temperature: Cool (12° C) for most stouts and porters; cool to room temperature for the strongest examples

Food matches: Shellfish, barbecues, hams, mature cheeses, chocolate puddings

Acorn ✳ Gorlovka

ABV 6%   500 ml   Maris Otter pale malt, crystal malt, roasted barley, Challenger hops

Gorlovka is Acorn Brewery's only bottle-conditioned beer and is named after the Ukrainian twin town of Barnsley, Acorn's home. Light in strength for an imperial stout, it nonetheless packs all the flavours of the genuine article and was first produced in 2006.

A robust, deep garnet-coloured beer with bitter chocolate and treacle toffee in the aroma. The taste is bitter and peppery, with caramel, dark chocolate, liquorice and tangy hops in the mix. An almost mouth-puckering, leafy bitterness is just about tempered by the sweetness of the malt. Dark chocolate continues in the dry, uncompromisingly bitter finish.

Adur ▪ Black William

ABV 5%   500 ml   Maris Otter pale malt, crystal malt, chocolate malt, black malt, Target hops

Adur's brewery in West Sussex sits on land once owned by a Norman baron named William de Braose. He was born in Brecon and it is said he was not a popular man, especially among his fellow Welsh, who nicknamed him Gwilym Ddu, or Black William. That unflattering title ties in nicely with the colour and dark malt flavours of this sturdy stout, and was an obvious borrow for the name of the beer.

A near black beer with a biscuity, chocolaty aroma with hints of liquorice. Good, complex dark malt flavours fill the mouth – freshly-ground coffee and plain chocolate in particular – although the taste is sweet with an elusive, berry-like fruitiness. The bitter finish is very dry, with well-roasted grains and dark chocolate.

Atlantic ▪ Blue

ABV 4.8% 330/500 ml   Pale malt, crystal malt, chocolate malt, black malt, wheat malt, First Gold and Fuggle hops

This deep ruby beer was first brewed in 2005 and is described by brewer Stuart Thomson as a 'modern porter'. Chocolate malt is roasted at the brewery to create the black malt that adds smoky notes to the recipe. Like other Atlantic beers, Blue is both organic and vegetarian friendly.

Smoky, dark malt, with chocolate and coffee notes, fills the aroma, before a sweet taste of smoky chocolate and nut. Sweet, nutty, dark malt leads in the finish, which becomes slowly more bitter.
Major stockist **Local Asda**

Barearts ▪ Oat Stout

ABV 8.2% 500 ml   Maris Otter pale malt, chocolate malt, oat malt, Fuggle hops

They brew beers with a punch at Barearts, as proved yet again by this ale, which offers a different take on the strong stout concept.

A garnet beer with a creamy aroma that has traces of coffee and melon. The body is light for the strength, but there's an earthy alcoholic note to the taste where dark malt and oats provide a creamy sweetness and melon fermentation flavour is also evident. The sweetish finish is dry, nutty and chocolaty.

Bartrams ▪ Comrade Bill Bartrams Egalitarian Anti Imperialist Soviet Stout

ABV 6.9% 330 ml   Maris Otter pale malt, crystal malt, dark crystal malt, amber malt, chocolate malt, roasted barley, Galena and Golding hops

Stouts & Porters

If there were a prize for the longest beer name in the book (or possibly in the world), this warming stout from a Suffolk micro-brewery would wins hands down. It's already an award-winner for its taste and character. Six cereals enter the mash tun, while Galena hops from the USA are used in the two-hour copper boil, with East Kent Goldings added towards the end. The colourful label pictures brewer Marc Bartram fully prepared for a frosty Russian winter.

A bright ruby-coloured, imperial stout with an appealing, malty aroma featuring plain chocolate with hints of Malteser and tart fruit notes. Bitter, dark chocolate from the roasted grain dominates the taste, which is otherwise peppery and pleasantly warming, and has a mouthfilling, airy texture. Coffee and bitter chocolate both linger in the dry, bitter finish. A bold and tasty beer.

Beachy Head ▪ Parson Darby's Hole

ABV 4% 500 ml Cocktail pale malt, crystal malt, chocolate malt, roasted barley, wheat malt, sugar, Styrian Golding and Challenger hops

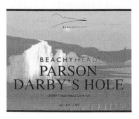

Formidable Beachy Head in East Sussex, from which this microbrewery takes its name, saw many a tragic shipwreck in centuries past. One man who did his bit to save seafarers' lives was the local Parson Darby. In 1680, he used a natural cavern in the rock as the basis for a primitive lighthouse, with excavated rooms above the level of the sea filled with lights to warn ships in danger of hitting land. This beer – a typically dark stout – the Beachy Head brewers considered to be as black as Parson Darby's Hole.

A deep ruby-brown beer with a welcoming aroma of biscuity, dark chocolate, coffee and caramel. Bitter roasted grain features in the

taste, along with some malty sweetness and nut, chocolate and coffee notes, plus a hint of cola. The dry, roasted-grain finish is increasingly bitter. Drinks like a dark mild.

Major stockist **Local Waitrose**

Beowulf ▪ Dragon Smoke Stout

ABV 5.3%   500 ml   Pale malt, black malt, roasted barley, flaked barley, Pilgrim and Golding hops

Dragon Smoke Stout was first produced by this West Midlands brewery back in 1997 and has picked up numerous awards in its draught form. This bottled version is brewed as for the cask equivalent (4.7%), but primed with sugar to ensure a good bottle fermentation. It's therefore a touch stronger and drier.

This near-black, substantial beer has a smoky (but not overbearing), grainy aroma with hints of chocolate and coffee. Dark grains feature again in the mostly bitter, smoky taste along with chocolate notes (good, mouthfilling texture) and then run on into the dry, smoky, bitter finish that is both thick and full.

Beowulf ▪ Finn's Hall Porter

ABV 5.2%   500 ml   Pale malt, crystal malt, black malt, roasted barley, Pilgrim, Fuggle and Golding hops

In the legend of Beowulf, upon which this West Midlands brewery bases its identity, Finn was a Friesian king who fought against the Danes and ended up murdered in his own hall. The beer named in his honour was first brewed in 1998 and (in its cask-conditioned form) was judged West Midlands Beer of the Year in 2006. This bottled version is a touch stronger than the 4.7% draught and, being unfined, is acceptable to both vegetarians and vegans.

A near-black beer with a biscuity, dark chocolate nose. The fairly dry taste is bitter, with more dark chocolate, a light caramel sweetness and a touch of toffee. Bitter, dark chocolate lingers on in the full, dry, roasted grain finish. A big beer, on the bitter side for a porter.

Black Isle ▪ Organic Porter

ABV 4.6%   500 ml   Pale malt, crystal malt, chocolate malt, oats, Challenger and Styrian Golding hops

A Salisbury Beer Festival champion in 2002 under its original cask name of Wagtail, this dark Scottish brew has now been revised in strength, rising from 4.5 to 4.6%.

A dark ruby porter with leather, caramel and smoky dark grains in the biscuity aroma. The taste is creamy and smooth, but light bodied. It falls on the sweet side, despite the dark grain flavours, with a suggestion of leather and some light, hoppy fruit. The finish is gently bitter with plain chocolate notes.

Blythe ▪ Johnson's

ABV 5.2%   500 ml   Pale malt, crystal malt, chocolate malt, black malt, roasted barley, flaked barley, Challenger hops

Now a monthly brew, this porter from Staffordshire was first produced in 2007 and celebrates literary giant Dr Samuel Johnson, who was born in the city of Lichfield (a few miles from Blythe Brewery) in 1709.

A near-black stout with pineapple and smoky dark malt in the aroma with hints of chocolate. Pineapple and brambly fruit feature along with bitter, dark malt and barley in the earthy, gently warming taste, before a full, bitter finish of roasted grain and chocolate.

Breconshire ▪ Night Beacon

ABV 4.5%   500 ml   Pale malt, smoked and dark crystal malts, wheat malt, roasted barley, Progress, Challenger, Golding and Northdown hops

Night Beacon has its origins in a cask stout that was brewed once a year for Bonfire Night. This bottled version is a touch weaker and has a slightly different recipe. It was first bottled in December 2008 and makes a good partner for Welsh black beef stews, according to brewer Buster Grant.

This dark ruby ale has a lightly smoky aroma of biscuity, dark chocolate. There's more dark chocolate in the bittersweet, nutty taste, finishing dry, nutty and bitter with roasted barley notes. Overall, a clean, tasty stout.

Burton Bridge ▪ Burton Porter

ABV 4.5%   500 ml   Pale malt, crystal malt, chocolate malt, Challenger and Target hops

This popular, award-winning porter from the home of pale ale was first brewed back in 1983 and was one of the first beers in the bottle-conditioned beer revival. The simple yellow paint and rubber stamp label that used to adorn bottles has long given way to a more sophisticated paper badge. However, inside the bottle the beer is just the same as before, following the same recipe as draught Burton Porter.

A ruby porter with a biscuity, creamy, grainy aroma. The taste is bittersweet, with smooth, dark malts, hints of liquorice and dry backnotes. There's more liquorice in the dry, bitter, roasted-grain finish.

Butts ✳ Blackguard

ABV 4.5%   500 ml   Ingredients not declared

Blackguard (pronounced 'blaggard') is this Berkshire brewery's porter, introduced as a winter brew but now found all year round. The label features a variation on the brewery's playing card joker logo, showing a 'jester with attitude', as brewer Chris Butt describes it. Ingredients-wise, all Chris will declare is that he uses British malt and British hops.

A deep garnet-coloured beer with a biscuity, dark chocolate aroma. There's more dark chocolate in the bittersweet taste, along with caramel and vanilla notes, before a dry finish of bitter roasted grains.
Major stockist **Local Waitrose**

Cheddar ✳ Totty Pot

ABV 4.7% 500 ml Maris Otter pale malt, crystal malt, chocolate malt, roasted barley, wheat malt, Northdown, Challenger and Golding hops

Named after a cave in the Cheddar complex, Totty Pot is described as a porter, although brewer Jem Ham thinks it falls somewhere between a porter and a stout. It is indeed more bitter than most porters, packed with clean, roasted grain flavours. The beer was first brewed in 2007 and in 2008 claimed first prize in the Tucker's Maltings Bottled Beer Competition.

A deep-garnet beer with a hint of creamy caramel in the biscuity, dark malt aroma. Dark malt flavours – caramel, chocolate and coffee – blend in the bittersweet, light-bodied taste that finishes dry and biscuity with more coffee and chocolate. Well-balanced and easy to drink.

Chiltern ▪ The Lord Lieutenant's Porter

ABV 6% 330 ml Maris Otter pale malt, crystal malt, chocolate malt, Fuggle, Challenger and Golding hops

When Chiltern celebrated its 20th anniversary in 2000, there was a carnival atmosphere at the rural Buckinghamshire brewery. The highlight of the party was the launch of a new beer, a porter, the hops for which had been loaded into the copper by Sir Nigel Mobbs, the Lord Lieutenant of Buckinghamshire, who also mashed in the beer. The Lord Lieutenant's Porter was also made available in bottle, but has only become bottle conditioned in recent years. Chiltern's home also houses an excellent brewery shop, where beer-related foods such as chutneys, cakes and mustards are sold. Here you can find The Lord Lieutenant's Christmas Pudding, which, according to the Jenkinson family who run the business, is a great match for this beer.

A bright ruby beer with an appley, malty aroma with light chocolate traces. The taste is a little earthy, appley and bittersweet, with a touch of liquorice and some smoky dark chocolate, and the texture is light and airy. After a smooth, sweet swallow, bitter, fudgy chocolate and coffee feature in the dry, gently warming finish.

Conwy ▪ Telford Porter

ABV 5.6% 500 ml Maris Otter pale malt, crystal malt, chocolate malt, roasted barley, torrefied wheat, Pioneer, Challenger and Golding hops

Commemorating the opening of Thomas Telford's suspension bridge to the Isle of Anglesey in 1826 (as well as Telford's other achievements in North Wales, including the astonishing Pontcysyllte aqueduct and the River Conwy suspension bridge), this porter was introduced for Conwy's Feast food and drink festival in 2005. Tweaks to the recipe have made the beer darker in colour in recent years.

A dark ruby porter with a biscuity aroma of creamy coffee and chocolate. Light bodied for its strength, this is a lightly nutty beer with smooth dark malt flavours, some chocolate notes and grassy overtones. Roasted grain comes through more strongly in the drying finish, bringing more chocolate. Some sugary sweetness lingers, but ultimately the finish is firmly bitter.

Country Life ▪ Black Boar

ABV 5% 500 ml Maris Otter pale malt, crystal malt, black malt, wheat malt, Golding and Fuggle hops

Available November to June in its cask form, this dark beer is one of Country Life's newest creations. It's described as a Devon porter.

Appley fruit and hints of chocolate and plum feature in the malty aroma of this ruby-red ale, with more apple in the bittersweet, winey taste and dark malt in the background. The finish is dry, with bitter dark malt flavours.

Cropton ▪ Scoresby Stout

ABV 4.2% 500 ml Pale malt, crystal malt, black malt, roasted barley, Fuggle and Challenger hops

This dark brew takes its name from William Scoresby, an 18th-century whaling captain who hailed from Cropton, North Yorkshire. Among his various achievements, Scoresby is said to have invented the crow's nest. He is now commemorated with a plaque at Whitby harbour. The cask equivalent of this beer made its debut in 1988 and this bottled option was first produced in 1996.

A dark ruby beer with grainy dark malts and hints of liquorice and caramel in the aroma. The taste is mostly bitter, featuring dark grains and liquorice, but with a light, malty sweetness. Coffee-like roasted grain features in the very dry, increasingly bitter finish.

Dark Star ▪ Imperial Stout

ABV 10.5% 500 ml Maris Otter pale malt, crystal malt, roasted barley, flaked barley, Target and Golding hops

'Russian export strength', it says on the label, and, at 10.5%, this is certainly a beer to ward off the icy blasts of a Baltic winter. Bottles are vintage dated and are filled for this West Sussex brewery by Branded Drinks in Gloucestershire. A vegan-friendly beer.

2008 vintage: A dark garnet-brown beer with a winey, fruity aroma underpinned by dark malt and laced with a suggestion of sasparilla. The taste awakens the senses: full, alcoholic and warming. Sweet, winey, dried and tropical fruits contrast with tangy hops and liquorice notes, before a dry, numbing, bitter chocolate finish.

Durham ✳ Temptation

ABV 10%   500 ml   Maris Otter pale malt, brown malt, amber malt, roasted barley, wheat malt, Target and Golding hops

We all know the Biblical perils of succumbing to temptation, but many drinkers think it's worth making an exception for this formidable brew from North-East England. The name it was first sold under reveals the style: it was simply called Imperial Russian Stout. The beer has a 'best between' window of six months to five years, but, given the strength and body of this black-as-sin creation, brewer Steve Gibbs reckons it could age well for up to 20 years.

Hints of pear drop and banana enhance biscuity dark malts in the heady, winey aroma. In the mouth, the beer is silky smooth and offers sweet malt flavours ahead of coffee, caramel, liquorice and plain chocolate. Spicy alcohol wafts around the palate and banana is everywhere. Soft liquorice and coffee emerge in the lip-tingling, drying finish.

Elmtree ▪ Dark Horse Stout

ABV 5%   330 ml   Pale malt, roasted malts, Challenger and Golding hops

Like other bottled beers from this micro-brewery, which is located close to the Snetterton racing circuit in Norfolk, Dark Horse Stout is also available in cask-conditioned form and is acceptable to vegans and vegetarians. Good with rich stews, roasts and nut roasts, claim the brewers.

A near-black beer with a biscuity aroma featuring dark malts, light coffee and a hint of liquorice. Coffee and dark chocolate flavours are prominent in the bitter taste, with a touch of winey fruit and some sappy hop notes. Roasted grain and coffee linger in the bitter, dry aftertaste.

Stouts & Porters

English Wines ✳ Curious Brew Admiral Porter

ABV 5% 330 ml   Pale malt, crystal malt, amber malt, chocolate malt, black malt, Admiral and Golding hops

Taking its name from the hop that provides much of the bitterness, this deep ruby-coloured porter also uses Sussex barley and is conditioned with oak. It's part of a small range of bottled beers brewed for the Chapel Down Vineyard in Kent by Hepworth in Horsham. The vineyard folk suggest combining this with their sparkling wine for the perfect black velvet cocktail, but that would be a waste of a very fine porter.

A fleeting snatch of strawberries in the aroma gives way to dark chocolate and creamy oak. The taste is smooth and truffle-like, with creamy, bitter chocolate, nut, an oaky tartness and hints of berries and pears. Solid, dry, bitter finish with lots of roasted grain.

Felstar ▪ Grumpy Rooster

ABV 5.2% 500 ml   Maris Otter pale malt, crystal malt, chocolate malt, black malt, wheat malt, Fuggle, Bramling Cross and Golding hops

There's a domestic fowl theme to many of Felstar Brewery's beers, inspired by the number of hens, geese and other birds that strut around the Essex vineyard where the beers are brewed. Grumpy Rooster is one of the latest additions to the range.

A near-black beer with an aroma of red apples and creamy, grainy malt. The bittersweet taste is also appley and creamy, with dark malt flavours and a hint of liquorice. Roasted grains come through softly in the gently warming, bittersweet finish.

Fox ▪ Cerberus Norfolk Stout

ABV 4.5% 500 ml   Maris Otter pale malt, crystal malt, torrefied wheat, crushed wheat, roasted barley, Fuggle hops

An almost black stout recalling the three-headed dog from mythology who guarded the River Styx to prevent lost souls who had crossed into Hell

from escaping. This Norfolk brew pub also produces a stout that includes samphire seaweed once a year.

Juicy berries and bitter coffee feature in the aroma while, in the thinnish taste, mellow, creamy, dark malts share the honours with a tea-like note and more hints of berry fruits. The finish is very dry and bitter, with coffee in evidence once again.

Harveys ✳ Imperial Extra Double Stout

ABV 9%   275 ml   Maris Otter pale malt, amber malt, brown malt, black malt, Fuggle and Golding hops

An authentic tribute to Albert Le Coq, a Belgian who successfully marketed Barclay Perkins's renowned Imperial Russian Stout to the Baltic region, and particularly the Russian Empire, in the early 1800s. This beer's label re-tells the Le Coq story, including how the brewery his company set up to produce his own powerful beer in Estonia was nationalized by the Bolsheviks in 1917. This beer is inspired by Le Coq's original recipe and was initially bottled with a cork stopper for Harveys by Gale's but, following the closure of Gale's Horndean brewery, future vintages will have a conventional crown cap and a slightly smaller bottle (275 ml instead of 330 ml). The latest vintage was brewed in April 2008 (the first for five years) and conditioned at the brewery for a year, allowing a good secondary fermentation to take place in the tank before the beer was bottled. B United is the US importer.

2003 vintage (tasted after five years): **An intense and challenging beer, from the deep, dark brown colour to the gum-tingling finish. The aroma is smoky with oaky liquorice, polished leather and winey fruit. Smooth malt features in the mostly bitter taste, but with a vinous sharpness at all times. There are suggestions of chocolate in the dark malt at the heart of the beer, but also traces of leather, liquorice and a raspberry-like fruitiness. Tangy hop joins vinous fruit in the gently bitter finish that offers more chocolate, leather and liquorice.**

Harwich Town ▪ Redoubt Stout

ABV 4.2%   500 ml   Pale malt, chocolate malt, roasted barley, torrefied wheat, Pioneer and Pilgrim hops

Brewed first in 2007, this dark ruby stout is named after Harwich's Redoubt Fort, part of the chain of Martello forts built along the English coast in the early 19th century as a defence against Napoleon's navy.

A biscuity, grainy aroma of dark chocolate is echoed in the crisp, biscuity, grainy and drying taste of bitter chocolate in the mouth. There's also a hint of raisin and a good, airy texture. Bitter chocolate lingers in the dry finish. A good, dry stout.

Hoggleys ✳ Solstice Stout

ABV 5%   500 ml   Pale malt, crystal malt, chocolate malt, roasted barley, torrefied wheat, Target, Challenger and Cascade hops

Brewed originally for an annual boating trip Hoggleys brewer Roy Crutchley makes over the winter solstice, this beer from Northamptonshire is now more readily available, by popular demand.

A dark ruby stout with bitter, smoky, roasted malt with traces of coffee and plain chocolate in the aroma, along with a little citrus fruit. The taste is mellow, smoky and a touch milky, with bitter roasted grain for contrast, some more coffee and chocolate, and a hint of tropical fruit. Dry, bitter, roasted grain finish.

Hook Norton ✳ Double Stout

ABV 4.8%   500 ml   Maris Otter pale malt, brown malt, black malt, enzymic malt, Fuggle, Golding and Challenger hops

Brewed to a recipe that is more than 100 years old, Hook Norton's Double Stout is so called because it contains both black and brown malts.

According to the ultra-smart label, the black malt 'enhances the colour and teases the palate', while the brown malt 'gives it a pleasant dryness'. The beer was initially brewed up to the year 1917. It was then resurrected, to great acclaim, in 1996. It is now available in cask-conditioned form in January and February each year, and all year-round in bottle. Only since 2008 has the beer been bottle conditioned, however. It is now brewed at Hook Norton in Oxfordshire and bottled at Thwaites in Lancashire. The beer is imported into the USA via Shelton Brothers.

Near-black, with an inviting aroma of milky coffee and chocolate, with a hint of liquorice and some light, pear-like fruit. Smooth and airy in the mouth, the taste features milk chocolate, bitter coffee and hints of pear. Overall, it's bitter, but not short of background sweetness. Bitter chocolate features in the dry, roasted-grain finish.
Major stockist **Waitrose**

Hop Back ✳ Entire Stout

ABV 4.5%   500 ml   Pale malt, chocolate malt, roasted barley, wheat crystal malt, Pilgrim or Challenger and Golding hops

A cask beer for more than ten years previously, Entire Stout finally made it into bottle in 2001. Both formats have claimed awards. The draught version of this Wiltshire beer was awarded gold in the Stouts & Porters category of CAMRA's Champion Winter Beer of Britain contest in 2008, while this bottled equivalent was winner of the Tucker's Maltings Bottled Beer Competition in 2004 and 2006. Acceptable to vegans.

A dark ruby beer with chocolate and caramel in the full, bitter, roasted grain aroma. Coffee and dark chocolate join malty sweetness and nutty bitterness in the light, airy taste, with more coffee from the roasted grain emerging in the dry, bitter finish.
Major stockists **Tesco, Waitrose**

Hopshackle ✳ Historic Porter

ABV 4.5%   500 ml   Maris Otter pale malt, light crystal malt, chocolate malt, black malt, Fuggle and Golding hops, black treacle

189

First brewed in summer 2007, this surprisingly delicate, light-drinking beer is based on a porter recipe that dates rom the 1750s. It's just one of an impressive range of bottle-conditioned beers from this small brewer situated on the Lincolnshire and Cambridgeshire border.

A bright ruby beer with a biscuity aroma of chocolate, creamy coffee and winey fruit. The bittersweet taste is also biscuity, with more dark malt flavours such as coffee and plain chocolate, as well as dried fruit notes. After a light swallow, roasted grain emerges again in the drying finish, which is not so deep but very pleasant all the same.

Humpty Dumpty ■ Porter

ABV 5.4%   500 ml   Maris Otter pale malt, caramalt, chocolate malt, black malt, Fuggle and Cascade hops

This Norfolk brewery used to produce a beer called Peto's Porter, named in honour of Samuel Peto, a 19th-century local railway pioneer. Peto's departed in 2007 and in its place arrived this near-black ale. The railway theme has been continued, however, with the label of the new beer picturing a railway station porter laden with passengers' luggage.

The aroma is very inviting, packed with caramel, creamy chocolate and honey, reminiscent of Crunchie bars. The taste is bittersweet, creamy and honeyed, with more chocolate and caramel, while the finish is bitter and dry, with caramel and coffee-like roasted grains.

Keystone ■ Porter

ABV 5.5%   500 ml   Maris Otter pale malt, crystal malt, brown malt, black malt, Challenger and Bramling Cross hops

Like all beers from this Wiltshire microbrewery, Keystone's Porter is brewed using only British hops and local barley. In recent years, the barley

has come from fields just a quarter of a mile from the brewery, and has been malted ten miles away, at Warminster's floor maltings. This beer was first brewed in 2007 and is also available in cask form in autumn and winter at the lower strength of 4.5% ABV. Try adding a bottle to a beef or game pot roast, suggests brewer Alasdair Large.

A dark ruby-coloured porter with an aroma of dark chocolate biscuit. Smoky, dark chocolate, tart roasted malt and a touch of caramel feature in the smooth, bittersweet taste, which also has a hint of fruit from the hops. Roasted grain is evident in the dry, increasingly bitter, coffee-accented finish.

Kingstone ▪ No.1

ABV 4.4%   500 ml   Pale malt, flaked barley, roasted barley, Challenger and Target hops

Described on the label as 'premium stout', this uncompromising but quaffable, dark garnet-coloured beer was added to the range of this South Wales brewery in 2007.

An aroma of smoky, biscuity dark grains, with traces of chocolate and caramel, leads on to a dry, bitter taste of dark chocolate, with a suggestion of pear fruitiness. Well-roasted grains feature in the dry, firmly bitter finish.

Marble ✳ Chocolate Marble

ABV 5.5%   500 ml   Pale malt, crystal malt, chocolate malt, roasted barley, wheat malt, Golding hops

Named after the high percentage of chocolate malt used in the mash tun, this Manchester beer was first bottled in 2006. It is also sold as a cask ale. Organically brewed and vegetarian friendly.

A dark ruby-coloured beer with dark chocolate and nut in the slightly winey aroma. Dark chocolate and nut flavours feature again in the firmly bitter taste, with well-roasted grain and more dark chocolate lingering on in the resoundingly bitter finish.

Meantime ✳ London Porter

ABV 6.5%   750 ml   Pale malt, pale crystal malt, Munich malt, brown malt, chocolate malt, black malt, Fuggle hops

Porter, it is claimed, was a blend of three types of beer back in the 18th century (see the introduction to this section of the book). This authentic reproduction from Meantime Brewing in London similarly blends young and aged beer and employs numerous varieties of malt to re-create, using modern materials, a drop of the capital's history. London Porter is packaged in 750 ml Champagne-style bottles, topped with a cork and wire cage.

A deep garnet-coloured porter with a winey aroma of chocolate and caramel. The taste is light bodied, creamy, fresh and easy drinking, with sweet caramel, chocolate and mellow coffee flavours, and light fruity undertones. Coffee and dark chocolate notes linger in the drying, bittersweet finish.

Major stockist **Sainsbury's**

Meantime ▪ London Stout

ABV 4.5%   500 ml   Pale malt, pale crystal malt, Munich malt, brown malt, black malt, Golding hops

Having wowed beer drinkers with their award-winning London Porter, it was time, the Meantime brewers felt, to add London Stout to the range. After all, like porter, stout is a London drink, despite the long association it has with Ireland. This flavour-packed beer arrived in 2008 and immediately started to gather competition medals.

A deep garnet-brown beer with plain chocolate and crumbly biscuit in the slightly tart aroma. The same tartness is evident in the bitter, plain chocolate taste, with roasted grains biting at the palate and overshadowing a light malty sweetness. Good, light texture. The finish is fairly thick, bitter and dry with lots of roasted grain.

Major stockist **Tesco**

North Cotswold ▪ Arctic Global Warmer

ABV 15%   250 ml   Maris Otter pale malt, crystal malt, chocolate malt, roasted barley, wheat malt, Fuggle, Challenger and Golding hops

It's not a misprint. The strength really is 15%, which makes it the strongest beer featured in this book. This Cotswold imperial stout is brewed to a recipe for a beer that was taken on Arctic expeditions.

A deep garnet-brown stout with malt, treacle toffee, smoky dark chocolate and a hint of sherry in the aroma. The taste is both tart and vinous, with dark malt and treacle toffee notes, light sherry and orange-citrus, plus a woody warmth. The finish is warming, dry, malty and oaky, with tart fruit. Not a beer for the faint-hearted.

Old Chimneys ✳ Amber Porter

ABV 4.8%   500 ml   Maris Otter pale malt, amber malt, brown malt, Golding and Pilot hops

Here's a fascinating addition to the Old Chimneys range. It's based on a porter from the old Cobbold's brewery in Ipswich, researched from records dating back to 1785. Brewer Alan Thomson has aimed to be as authentic as possible in re-creating this beer, using traditional floor malt as well as hops grown in the same areas mentioned in the archives, in this case East Kent Goldings and Sussex Pilots (although no mention was made of the varieties of hops in the original recipe). The other key feature is the vigorous secondary fermentation prior to bottling, caused by running the beer into casks after primary fermentation without cooling. Amber malt dominates the flavour, making up one third of the malt grist. Bottles feature Cobbold's 18th-century copper on the label.

Actually ruby in colour, despite its name. The aroma is rich and inviting, full of biscuity malt complemented by milk chocolate and nut. Hazelnuts and milk chocolate characterize the velvety, creamy, generally bitter taste, while the drying finish is nutty, creamy and bitter with hints of coffee and chocolate.

Old Chimneys ■ Black Rat Stout

ABV 4.5%   500 ml   Pale malt, crystal malt, wheat malt, roasted barley, lactose, Fuggle and Challenger hops

A rare example of a milk stout. The key ingredient in this East Anglian beer is lactose (milk sugar). Lactose is not fermentable by standard brewers' yeast and so the sugars remain in the brew adding body but no extra strength. Black Rat is also sold under the name of Leading Porter at the Mid-Suffolk Light Railway in Wetheringsett.

A deep ruby stout with a biscuity, gently tart, bitter chocolate aroma, a chocolaty, bittersweet but slightly sour taste, and a dry, creamy, coffee, chocolate and nut finish.

Oldershaw ■ Grantham Stout

ABV 4.3%   500 ml   Optic pale malt, crystal malt, chocolate malt, roasted barley, wheat malt, First Gold, Willamette and Golding hops

This Grantham brewery's home-town stout is a dry, bitter, ruby-coloured beer first brewed in 1999 and now sold in bottle on an occasional basis (when there's spare cask beer available). In its draught form, it's a SIBA (Society of Independent Brewers) regional gold medallist.

A biscuity, dark chocolate aroma leads to a bitter, dark chocolate taste, with malt adding a touch of sweetness. Dry, bitter, dark chocolate finish with hints of espresso coffee.

Otley ■ Dark O

ABV 4.1%   500 ml   Pale malt, chocolate malt, Fuggle and Golding hops

First produced in 2005, and now a weekly brew, this near-black stout from this successful South Wales family brewery drinks rather like a well-roasted mild. According to the brewers, it's excellent when used in the kitchen, as part of a recipe for gravies and sauces or as a reduction on desserts.

A biscuity aroma of bitter chocolate and coffee leads on to a tart, bitter chocolate taste with some sweeter coffee notes for balance. The finish is dry and biscuity, with more coffee and dark chocolate in evidence.

Outstanding ▪ Stout

ABV 5.5%   500 ml   Pale malt, crystal malt, roasted barley, Pioneer and Bramling Cross hops

A near-black, dry stout that is acceptable to both vegetarians and vegans, like other beers from this Lancashire brewery that first started brewing and bottling in 2008.

Bitter, roasted grains, with hints of smoke, liquorice, chocolate and caramel, feature in the biscuity aroma. The smoky but smooth taste is bittersweet, with more dark malt, chocolate and traces of liquorice. Well-roasted grains linger in the dry, bitter finish.

Pen-lon ▪ Stock Ram

ABV 4.5%   500 ml   Optic pale lager malt, roasted barley, flaked barley, Target, Tettnanger and Nugget hops

A dry and bitter, deep-ruby-coloured stout, brewed for local West Wales preferences, says Pen-lon's farmer/brewer Stefan Samociuk.

Dark malts and biscuity grain feature in the slightly sour, creamy aroma. There's full, smooth malt, with hints of coffee, chocolate and liquorice, in the taste, and also a touch of citrus fruit. Bitterness builds nicely in the drying, biscuity, dark chocolate aftertaste.

Pitfield ▪ 1792 Imperial Stout

ABV 9.3%   330 ml   **Maris Otter pale malt, roasted barley, wheat malt, Northdown hops**

Another beer helping to fill a gap once solely filled by Courage's renowned Imperial Russian Stout (which, regrettably, was last brewed in 1993), this strong, complex, organic ale is typical of the beers that crossed the Baltic to warm the hearts of the imperial Russian court at the turn of the 19th century. It's one of three stouts/porters in the Pitfield portfolio.

This potent dark ruby brew has an inviting, creamy, liqueur-like, chocolaty aroma with a touch of liquorice. Truffle-like chocolate features in the sweet taste, supported by a dry, bitter backnote, but alcohol is the most obvious ingredient. The dry, warming finish is creamy, chocolaty, nutty and bitter.

Pitfield ▪ 1850 London Porter

ABV 5%   500 ml   **Maris Otter pale malt, brown malt, roasted barley, Golding hops**

Pitfield had been producing this porter off and on for a few years before it decided to include it in a new range of beers based on historic beer styles. The recipes for these brews were inspired by the work of the Durden Park Beer Circle, a dedicated and enthusiastic group of private brewers (one reluctantly uses the titles 'amateur' or 'home brewers', such is their proficiency and attention to detail). The Circle goes to extreme lengths to re-create beers that have long ceased to be part of the portfolio of brewers today, unearthing the truth about how beers used to taste.

A deep ruby beer with a coffeeish aroma. The taste is nutty and bittersweet with light roasted notes amidst the malt. Dry, nutty, coffeeish, gently bitter finish.

Pitfield ▪ Shoreditch Stout

ABV 4%   500 ml   Pale malt, roasted barley, flaked barley, Fuggle, Challenger and Target hops

A beer that derives its name from Pitfield Brewery's original location in London, this beer is not as 'stout' as most stouts in this section. It has plenty of roasted grain flavours but the body and strength are on the light side. It was added to Pitfield's range in 1997 and, like all the brewery's beers, is now produced from organic ingredients.

A very dark brown beer with a smoky aroma of coffee and dark chocolate. Coffee and caramel feature in the taste, while the finish is dry and bitter with a coffee-like roasted grain flavour.

Quantock ▪ Stout

ABV 4.5%   500 ml   Maris Otter pale malt, flaked barley, roasted barley, Pilgrim and Golding hops

A stout from deepest Somerset that is also available in cask-conditioned form and was first brewed in summer 2008 (who says stouts are only for winter?). It's now brewed about once every two months.

A near-black stout with a grainy aroma of bitter chocolate, caramel and tobacco. The taste is largely of smoky, bitter, roasted grain, with touches of chocolate, coffee and tobacco, while the finish is dry and bitter with grainy roasted barley.

RCH ▪ Old Slug Porter

ABV 4.5%   500 ml   Optic pale malt, crystal malt, black malt, Fuggle and Golding hops

It's not the most attractive of names for a beer, but there is a reason for this beer's strange title. It's derived from the pesky little creatures that enjoyed the sandy soil around RCH's original brewery at the Royal

Stouts & Porters

Clarence Hotel in Burnham-on-Sea, Somerset. Since the brewery moved to a new, larger home in an old cider works near Weston-super-Mare, the slugs have been a thing of the past, but the beer still has a dedicated following and has picked up awards (winner of the Tucker's Maltings Bottled Beer Competition in 1998). The beer is imported into the USA by B United.

A deep-garnet porter with mellow coffee and creamy, chocolaty dark malt in the aroma. Roasted coffee flavours lead in the mostly bitter taste that has a gentle hop tang and a light, airy body. The dry, bitter, coffee-like finish lasts well.

Major stockist **Local Thresher**

Ridgeway ✳ Foreign Export Stout

ABV 8%   500 ml   Pale malt, pilsner malt, crystal malt, amber malt, black malt, roasted barley, oat malt, Challenger and Styrian Golding hops

There's a strong, dark Christmas offering in the Ridgeway portfolio called Lump of Coal (not bottle conditioned). Foreign Export Stout used to be the same beer but brewer Peter Scholey has now moved to differentiate the two brands, making changes to the malts and hops in the new Foreign Export Stout, which, Peter claims, matures in the bottle like vintage port. The beer is brewed by Peter at either Hepworth in Sussex or Cotswold Brewing in Oxfordshire.

A near-black, strong stout with tangy hops and creamy chocolate and coffee in the aroma. The taste is initially sweet, with creamy, nutty chocolate, gentle caramel and some raisin notes, then there's a hint of tea and some light, tingly warmth. Caramel, dark chocolate and tea feature in the dry, bitter finish that is also filled with hops.

Rodham's ■ Old Albion

ABV 5.5%   500 ml   Maris Otter pale malt, roasted caramalt,
First Gold hops

Albion, an ancient name for Britain, is also the name of the street on
which Rodham's brewery is based in Otley, Yorkshire. Michael Rodham's
porter, which borrows the name but is described on the bottle as a 'black
premium ale', began life as a cask-conditioned beer in 2004 and was first
bottled three years later.

**A dark-garnet-coloured porter, with a creamy, smooth aroma of pears.
The same creamy, smooth pear notes feature, along with subtle
dark malt, in the taste, which is rather bitter and has some peppery,
almond-like alcohol notes. Dark malt is evident in the dry, bitter, fairly
thick finish.**

Salopian ■ Entire Butt

ABV 4.8%   500 ml   Maris Otter pale malt, crystal malt, dark crystal
malt, amber malt, pale chocolate malt, dark chocolate malt, brown
malt, black malt, lager malt, carapils malt, wheat malt, malted
oats, roasted barley, torrefied wheat, Fuggle, Styrian Golding and
Golding hops

As reported in the introduction to this section, in the early 1700s, drinkers
favoured a blend of three beers – pale ale, brown ale and stock ale –
laboriously drawn from three separate casks (or butts). It is said that a
London brewer, Ralph Harwood, hit upon the idea of combining the three
brews in one cask, giving it the name Entire Butt (the brew being entirely
in one butt, so to speak), but some historians suggest different reasons
for the name. Its popularity with local street porters allegedly saw the
new brew re-christened 'porter'. Salopian is a Shropshire brewery but
production of Entire Butt – count the number of malts involved! – is
carried out under contract by Ridgeway Brewing's Peter Scholey, using
equipment at Hepworth in Sussex. The beer is exported to the USA,
Scandinavia and Italy.

**A bright ruby-coloured beer with a biscuity, grainy, milk stout-like
aroma, with chocolate and light winey fruit – rather reminiscent of
rum and raisin ice cream. Milky, creamy notes continue in the taste,**

Stouts & Porters

which is otherwise nutty, chocolaty and coffee-like, with more raisin character. Bitter chocolate and coffee then feature in the drying, creamy aftertaste.

Spinning Dog ▪ Organic Oatmeal Stout

ABV 4.4%   500 ml   Maris Otter pale malt, roasted barley, oats, Hallertau hops

In 2001, Hereford's Spinning Dog Brewery acquired a number of recipes from the closed Flannery's brewery in Aberystwyth. This oatmeal stout was part of the package, a beer that had in fact already claimed the Champion Beer of Wales title. 'A great accompaniment to strong cheese and game casseroles,' according to the label of this very dark red, near-black beer.

Chocolate and coffee feature in the appealing aroma, then bitter dark malts take the lead over a gentle malty sweetness in the mouth, with creamy chocolate in support. Bitter dark chocolate rounds off in the finish.

Spire ▪ Twist & Stout

ABV 4.5%   500 ml   Pale malt, Munich malt, chocolate malt, oat malt, Northern Brewer hops

Twist & Stout is the second stout in the Spire range, following on from the speciality ale called Sgt Pepper Stout, which includes black pepper. This again borrows from a Beatles track for its name (okay, recorded by the Isley Brothers before the Fab Four, if you insist), but it is a completely different beer to Sgt Pepper.

A deep ruby-coloured beer with a big aroma of caramel, toffee and butterscotch, with dark chocolate behind. Butterscotch and toffee lead in the bitter, peppery taste, which also has creamy dark malt flavours and a drying backnote. The biscuity, coffee-like finish becomes increasingly bitter and dry.

Teignworthy ✳ Edwin Tucker's Empress Russian Porter

ABV 10.5%   275 ml   Maris Otter pale malt, chocolate malt, oat malt, roasted barley, Willamette, Golding, Bramling Cross and Challenger hops

This re-creation of the Baltic porter style was inspired in part by the demise of Courage Imperial Russian Stout, once sold in the beer shop at Tucker's Maltings in Devon, where Teignworthy Brewery has its home. It's the sort of strong, warming brew that was shipped to Russia and became known for its medicinal qualities. The beer is not produced every year.

1998 vintage (tasted after one year): **A mellow, dark brown beer with caramel and fruit in the nose. Thick, smooth and sweetish, it has a creamy rum-and-raisin toffee taste with orange-citrus and gentle, roasted, bitter notes. Dry, deep and warming, gently bitter finish, with caramel, toffee and fruit.**

2000 vintage (tasted after six months): **Near-black, with malt, polished leather and coffee in the nose. The taste is sweetish and deep, with strong hops for bitterness, coffee and a little fruit, as well as persistent malt. Sweetish, roasted, hoppy finish.**

2006 vintage (tasted after three years): **Near-black, with an aroma loaded with sweet, smoky malt, polished leather, liquorice, dark chocolate and raisins. The taste is well carbonated, bittersweet and warming, filled with smooth, smoky malt, dark chocolate, caramel, leather and raisin. Bitter chocolate continues into the dry, thick, warming finish.**

Thornbridge ✳ Saint Petersburg

ABV 7.7%   500 ml   Maris Otter pale malt, chocolate malt, roasted barley, Galena and Bramling Cross hops

In 1790, merchant John Morewood bought Thornbridge Hall – which has origins in the 12th century – for the princely sum of £10,000 – money he

had made from selling linen to the city of St Petersburg. What better name then to adopt when the brewery at the impressive Derbyshire country house created this imperial Russian stout in September 2005? The beer is matured for 55 days before bottling and primed with a blend of three sugars.

Deep ruby. The aroma is tropical-fruity at first, then light, biscuity coffee and liquorice emerge. The taste is smooth, with more tropical fruits, lots of sweet malt and a notably bitter, roasted grain element as well as a little liquorice. Intense bitter, roasted, hoppy and dry finish.

Tipple's ■ Topper

ABV 4.5% 500 ml Pale malt, crystal malt, chocolate malt, black malt, Bramling Cross and Golding hops

Topper was one of Tipple's original four beers when this Norfolk Broads brewery was launched in 2004 and it is still a regular product. Imagery relating to these four beers still features on Topper's label, including the monocled gent in the shiny top hat. Try this with some fruit cake, suggests brewer Jason Tipple.

A deep, dark garnet-coloured beer with a biscuity aroma of bitter chocolate and caramel. The taste is bitter and grainy, with creamy, plain chocolate, while the finish is very dry and truffle-like, bringing in coffee to join the chocolate among the dark malt flavours.

Titanic ■ Stout

ABV 4.5% 500 ml Maris Otter pale malt, wheat malt, roasted barley, Cascade, Northdown and Golding hops

Titanic Stout (also sold as a cask-conditioned beer) was the winner of the *Guardian*'s Best Bottle-conditioned Beer in 1994, and then was voted CAMRA/the *Guardian*'s Champion Bottle-conditioned Beer in 2004 (bronze

award also in 2005 and 2006, and joint silver in 2007). The beer is still brewed at Titanic but is now bottled by Hepworth in Horsham. There the beer is filtered and re-seeded with fresh yeast (a different strain to that used for primary fermentation).

Deep ruby with coffee and some liquorice in the biscuity nose. Bitter roasted grain leads in the mouth, but there is a lightly fruity, malty sweetness, too. Smoky coffee, nut and roasted bitterness in the finish.
Major stockists **Local Tesco and Waitrose**

Tryst ▪ Carron Oatmalt Stout

ABV 6.1% 500 ml Pale malt, crystal malt, amber malt, black malt, Challenger, Cascade and Styrian Golding hops

A new beer in 2008, Tryst's Carron Oatmalt Stout was created by brewer John McGarva after researching into Edwardian Scottish recipes.

A ruby-coloured smooth, sweetish and slightly warming stout with a creamy aroma of melon and chocolate. Smoky nut, sweet chocolate and a little cough candy feature in the taste. Chocolate and liquorice feature alongside nut in the dry, bitter finish.

Vale ▪ Black Beauty Porter

ABV 4.3% 500 ml Maris Otter pale malt, deep roasted chocolate malt, Fuggle and Golding hops

A dark horse. Unlike most of the other beers produced by this Buckinghamshire brewery, there are no Saxon or local connections: the name just describes the beer inside, which is rather hoppy for a porter.

A deep ruby beer, which is fruity initially in the aroma (faint peach notes), then becomes biscuity with traces of chocolate in the dark

malt. The body is light, even though there's plenty of smooth dark malt that brings a touch more chocolate to the bittersweet taste to marry with winey fruit. Bitter chocolate and hops feature in the drying finish, with hints of coffee emerging in the roasted grain.

Wapping ▪ Smoked Porter

ABV 5%   500 ml   Pale malt, smoked malt, other ingredients not declared

The world's most famous smoked porter comes from Alaskan Brewing Company in the USA. This Liverpool brew pub's take on the style is somewhat less strong and also less smoky, but is interesting nonetheless. Smoked malt from Bavaria is used in the recipe, but details of other ingredients are kept secret.

A very dark red/brown beer, almost black. The aroma is biscuity and leathery, with hints of berry fruits and a smoked-ham-like smokiness. Juicy berries feature again in the bittersweet taste, which has dark chocolate notes, gentle smoke and a light, warming alcohol character. Bitter chocolate is evident in the dry, smoky finish.

Wapping ▪ Stout

ABV 5%   500 ml   Maris Otter pale malt, other ingredients not declared

The draught version of this dry, near-black stout was a Liverpool Beer Festival winner in 2006. Like all Wapping's bottled beers, it is acceptable to vegans, being unfined.

A biscuity, grainy aroma of plain chocolate leads onto a full flavour of bitter chocolate and juicy berries, with hints of polished leather and a background sweetness. There's more chocolate in the dry, bitter, grainy finish.

Why Not ▪ Roundhead Porter

ABV 4.5% 500 ml Maris Otter pale malt, crystal malt, roasted barley, Fuggle hops

There's a beer in this small Norfolk brewery's portfolio that is called Cavalier Red (actually named after the street on which the brewery is based, but exploited for its Civil War connections). To even things up, Roundhead Porter was added to the range in 2006.

A deep garnet-coloured beer with bitter chocolate character in the aroma. The fairly thin taste is dry and smoky, with more bitter chocolate flavours and some balancing malt. Bitter coffee and chocolate then feature in the drying aftertaste.

Wickwar ▪ Station Porter

ABV 6.1% 500 ml Maris Otter pale malt, crystal malt, black malt, Fuggle hops

An award-winning cask beer (including a gold medal for best Stout and Porter at CAMRA's Great Winter Beer Festival in 2008). This bright ruby beer is named after Wickwar village's long-lost railway halt that was once important to the livelihood of the long-gone Arnold Perrott & Co brewery which operated in this Gloucestershire village. Station Porter was first brewed in 1993 – three years after this new Wickwar Brewery was established in Perrott's former cooperage – and first bottled in 1997.

Winey dried fruit, chocolate and a touch of liquorice feature in the aroma. The taste is fairly sweet and rich in dark malt and grapey, dried fruit flavours, with more hints of liquorice and chocolate. The light, airy body ensures it's not too heavy for the strength. The finish is dry, bitter and chocolaty, with gentle fruit lingering.

Stouts & Porters

Wye Valley ✳ Dorothy Goodbody's Wholesome Stout

ABV 4.6%   500 ml   Maris Otter pale malt, crystal malt, chocolate malt, roasted barley, flaked barley, Northdown hops

The label of this Herefordshire beer claims that the fictional Dorothy Goodbody discovered this recipe in her grandfather's brewing books. The truth is that brewery founder Peter Amor once worked for Guinness and was duly inspired by his experience there to create this award-winning stout. The draught version, launched in 1996, was CAMRA's Champion Winter Beer of Britain in 2002, while this bottled equivalent was judged CAMRA's Champion Bottle-conditioned Beer in 2008 (following on from a joint silver in the same contest a year earlier). The beer is imported into the USA by B United.

A deep garnet stout with a mellow, grainy cappuccino aroma. Creamy coffee joins bitter roasted grains in the full taste, with bitter coffee featuring in the dry finish. A satisfying and interesting stout.

Major stockist **Local Waitrose**

Winter & Christmas Beers

Winter & Christmas Beers

For many years, the only variation most national and regional breweries made to their standard beer list was to add a beer for Christmas. It was normally a bit stronger and a bit darker than their regular offerings and, in those days before monthly specials, seasonal ales and quirky, one-off brews, it gave drinkers a little something special to look forward to.

Winter ales are, by definition, only available in draught form for a month or two of the year but, thanks to the expansion of the bottled beer market, we can now enjoy these beers for a much longer period, and much further from their place of origin. Higher alcohol is still a key feature of most, as is some dark malt, but there is no set style in place as such. Some brewers even try to enhance the festive mood by throwing in a selection of Christmas-cake spices or the odd slice of fruit. But what all the beers in this section have in common is that, collectively, they make the cold days and the long, dark nights all the more bearable.

At a Glance

Strength: ABV 4% upwards

Character: Depends on the individual beer, but generally malty, perhaps with nut and toffee notes, some fruit and a touch of warming alcohol

Serving temperature: Cool (12° C) to room temperature for the strongest examples

Food matches: Again dependent on the individual beer but there should be some good matches for roasted meats, casseroles, fruit cakes and puddings

Ascot ▪ Santa's Reserve

ABV 5.2% 500 ml Maris Otter low colour malt, dark crystal malt, Munich malt, chocolate malt, Cascade, Perle and Amarillo hops, ginger, mixed spices

Known as Winter Reserve in its cask-conditioned form, Ascot's Santa's Reserve is only available in limited quantities every Christmas. This red beer, with its intriguing mix of spices, was first brewed in 2007.

Lightly toffee-like malt is overlaid with Christmas spices (nutmeg to the fore) and a hint of cough candy sweets in the full and inviting aroma. The taste is mostly bitter with plenty of malty body and another suggestion of cough candy, along with gently warming ginger, nutmeg and, possibly, clove spiciness. The finish is dry, warming, spicy, bitter and hoppy. Major stockists **Local Thresher and Wine Rack**

Betwixt ▪ Ice Breaker

ABV 6% 500 ml Maris Otter pale malt, crystal malt, crystal rye, Brewer's Gold hops, mulling spices, port

The inspiration for this spiced winter ale came from the brother of Betwixt brewer Mike McGuigan. Brian McGuigan and his wife, Ann Marie, live and work on historic narrowboats, travelling between the Midlands and North-West England, selling coal, diesel and hand-woven, rope-work fenders. As a thank you for their customers, they asked Mike to brew a Christmas gift beer. The name comes from the fact that the narrowboaters often have to break the ice on the canals in winter. Port, spices and priming sugars are added after the beer has been conditioned in tank at the brewery. Mike offers the choice of drinking the beer cool or mulling with a 'good dollop of honey – to balance out the bitterness of the hops – and a grating of nutmeg'.

Winter & Christmas Beers

An orange-amber beer with winter spices – cinnamon and nutmeg in particular – in the nose, along with zesty peel, hop resins and malt. The taste is mostly sweet and spicy, with citrus peel, light port and a gentle warmth. The port-like, drying finish is sweet, although gradually some bitterness intrudes. Spices linger longest.

Breconshire ■ Winter Beacon

ABV 5.3%   500 ml   Optic pale malt, low colour malt, crystal malt, black malt, wheat malt, First Gold, Fuggle and Golding hops

Best enjoyed after a long walk in the Brecon Beacons, says brewer Buster Grant, and, as if to prove it, there's a picture of a snowy Brecon Beacon peak on the label. This pale winter ale was added to the range in 2003 and, while the cask version remains seasonal, this bottled equivalent is sold all year. A True Taste of Wales award winner.

Amber-orange in colour, this strong ale has a fruity aroma (tropical and sharp citrus fruit) with a hint of bubblegum. There's a savoury maltiness to the sweetish taste with more bubblegum and juicy fruit (suggestions of citrus and blackcurrant). The dry, gently warming finish has a fruity hoppiness and turns slowly but firmly bitter.

Chiltern ✳ Glad Tidings

ABV 4.6%   500 ml   Maris Otter pale malt, chocolate malt, roasted barley, Bramling Cross hops, nutmeg, coriander, orange peel

This Christmas beer from the Jenkinson family in Buckinghamshire was first brewed in 2003. The brewery describes it as a spiced milk stout, and takes pride in using only authentic ingredients – no extracts, oils, juices or flavourings – to create a seasonal accent. The beer is bottled after four weeks' maturation. It is left unfined and unfiltered and then kräusened. Drink it with a winter stew or perhaps some after-dinner chocolates, the family says.

A dark garnet ale with biscuity, dark chocolate overlaid by spices (nutmeg and coriander) and oranges in the nose. The gently warming, bitter taste is also biscuity, with perfumed, earthy spices, dark chocolate and an orange freshness. The dry finish features roasted coffee, earthy spices, a light hop tang and increasing bitterness.

Concrete Cow ▪ Winter Ale

ABV 5%   500 ml   Pale malt, crystal malt, Cascade and Golding hops

This is the beer that illustrates how the brewery came by its name. The typically colourful label features the famous concrete cows of Milton Keynes, a life-size sculpture work by Canadian artist Liz Leyh put in place back in 1978. The cows stand close to the site of the brewhouse and have been various abused, vandalized and dressed up in their three-decade history.

Orange-amber in colour, this seasonal brew features hints of orange over smooth, nutty malt in the nose, followed by a faintly alcoholic, bittersweet taste with more oranges that provide a citrus sharpness over the malty base. Both malt and orange re-emerge in the dry, bitter, hoppy finish.

Fox ▪ Santa's Nuts

ABV 4.8%   500 ml   Maris Otter pale malt, crystal malt, chocolate malt, roasted barley, wheat malt, Target and Challenger hops, hazelnuts

The perfect partner for Christmas pudding, if you ask Fox proprietor Mark Bristow. His festive ale from the Norfolk coast is taken from an American recipe and contains hazelnuts.

A ruby-coloured beer with chocolate, coffee and, of course, nut in the aroma. There's more of the same (plenty of nuts) in the

bittersweet taste, along with smooth malt. The finish is dry and
pleasantly bitter with coffee notes and more nuts. Drinks like a porter.

Hoggleys ✳ Yuletide Ale

**ABV 7.2%   500 ml   Pale malt, crystal malt, black malt, torrefied wheat,
Target and Chinook hops, cinnamon, nutmeg**

It's called Yuletide Ale at present, and only
available at Christmas, but there are plans to
re-name this popular beer and brew it more
frequently. Good thing, too, as the seasonal
spices are subtly used and don't confine its
enjoyment to the festive season.

**An amber-red-coloured ale with a malty nose offering suggestions
of barley sugars and chocolate, along with plummy fruit and gentle
nutmeg and cinnamon. The sweetish taste majors on plummy fruit and
soft spices and is surprisingly light bodied for the strength. Spices run
on gently into the drying, bittersweet finish, along with caramel notes
from the malt. Moreish.**

Hop Back ✳ Pickled Santa

**ABV 6%   500 ml   Pale malt, chocolate malt, wheat malt, wheat crystal
malt, Pioneer and Willamette hops, cinnamon, nutmeg, coriander**

Good with stews, casseroles, Christmas pudding and
chocolate is what the brewers have to say about this festive
ale, and that's pretty much what you'd want from a winter
warmer like this that has the added glow of yuletide spices.
Pickled Santa made its bow as a cask beer in December 2001
and was first bottled two years later.

**This strong, dark copper ale has a perfumed and spicy
aroma, with cinnamon and nutmeg leading the way and
good toasted malt notes in support. Festive spices feature
up front in the taste, with citrus notes from the coriander
and the hops, and smooth toasted malt providing the backdrop.
There's a warming character to the dry, malty, spicy and bitter finish.**

Islay ▪ Nerabus Ale

ABV 4.8%   500 ml   Pale malt, dark crystal malt, caramalt, chocolate malt, wheat malt, Amarillo and Bramling Cross hops

This red-coloured winter ale commemorates the ancient settlement of Nerabus (or Nerabolis) on the Isle of Islay, where various members of the Donald clan, the Lords of the Isles, are buried.

Pineapple, orange and orchard fruits feature in the aroma, along with creamy caramel notes. The smooth, bittersweet taste is creamy, nutty and fruity (oranges and berries), while the finish is dry, malty and bitter, with roasted grains and a lingering suggestion of berries.

Itchen Valley ▪ Father Christmas

ABV 5%   500 ml   Maris Otter pale malt, crystal malt, Whitbread Golding Variety and Golding hops

This beer was first brewed back in 1997 and is available in cask form every December. Not surprisingly, perhaps, the brewers suggest you try it with roast turkey. Given its malty character, that should be a good match.

Amber-red, with a lightly toffee-like aroma of malt with pear notes and a hint of banana. Restrained pear drop and banana flavours feature in the taste, which is sweet, with a moreish, malty backdrop. The finish is a little thin, but otherwise dry, malty, hoppy and bittersweet.

King ▪ Merry Ale

ABV 6.5%   500 ml   Maris Otter pale malt, crystal malt, chocolate malt, enzymic malt, Golding and Whitbread Golding Variety hops

A stronger version of King's Red River, this is the Sussex brewery's Christmas ale in bottle, introduced in 2003. The beer is brewed just once, in November each year, and features a Dickensian carol-singing scene on the label.

Red-amber, with a deeply malty, treacle-toffee aroma. The sweet, full-bodied taste is rich and full of toffee-malt, with a touch of warmth. Bittersweet, toffeeish finish.

Meantime ✳ Winter Time

ABV 5.4%   500 ml   Pale malt, crystal malt, Munich malt, brown malt, black malt, smoked malt, Fuggle hops

Meantime describes this relatively new seasonal beer as a Burton ale – a generally forgotten style of malty beer that has perhaps its best-known living counterpart in Young's Winter Warmer. The complex blend of malts includes smoked malt.

A ruby beer with a lightly smoky, biscuity aroma with traces of caramel and liquorice. The bittersweet, malty, lightly smoky taste features dark chocolate and coffee, with dry, smoky, roasted grains in the moderately bitter finish. Drinks lighter than the strength suggests.
Major stockist **Sainsbury's**

O'Hanlon's ■ Goodwill Bitter

ABV 5%   500 ml   Optic pale malt, crystal malt, torrefied wheat, Challenger, Northdown, Styrian Golding, Golding and Amarillo hops

The Devon brewery's Christmas beer, now also in bottle in and around the festive season. Note the use of American Amarillo hops in the copper.

There's a musty spiciness and some citrus fruit in the smooth, malty aroma of this deep-amber-coloured ale. The same perfumed, spicy quality continues in the gently bitter taste, with juicy, citrus fruit and good malty body. Dry, bitter, spicy, orange-hoppy finish.

Oakleaf ■ Blake's Heaven

ABV 7%   330 ml   Pale malt, crystal malt, chocolate malt, Golding hops

This Gosport brewery's winter ale – playing on the cult BBC sci-fi series *Blake's 7* in its title – is a stronger version of its dark bitter, Blake's Gosport Bitter, which was named after a long-defunct local brewery.

A dark ruby ale with biscuity malt, hints of chocolate and liquorice, and floral notes in the aroma. The taste is soft and sweet, with

bubblegum, almond, chocolate and a light, spicy warmth. Roasted malt emerges more in the dry, thick, nicely bitter finish.

Otley ✳ O-Ho-Ho

ABV 5%   500 ml   Pale malt, crystal malt, Amarillo and Golding hops, blueberries

Otley's Christmas beer offers a rare departure from the brewery's standard black label with large O logo. The O is still there, but the label this time is silver. The beer was first brewed in 2007.

The ingredients list says blueberries but it's tangerines that stand out in the aroma and taste of this light golden beer. After a zesty, Christmassy aroma, the taste is clean, crisp and bittersweet with a malty smoothness beneath the fruit. The drying finish is pleasantly bitter, full and fruity, with gentle but moreish pale malt notes.

Ridgeway ✳ Bad Elf

ABV 4.5%   500 ml   Maris Otter pale malt, Challenger, Fuggle, Cascade and Styrian Golding hops

Ridgeway produces a wide range of interesting Christmas ales, many of them named after various stages of delinquency among Santa's little helpers. Hence, you have Very Bad Elf, Seriously Bad Elf, Criminally Bad Elf and so on. Most of these are not bottle conditioned, because they are exported to the USA (via Shelton Brothers). Bad Elf – the beer that started the series and a pale ale by style – is also not bottle conditioned when sold to America (but this may change). However, there is a 'live' version that is shipped to Europe and may be found on sale in the UK. It is brewed in September or October each year.

A golden ale with zesty, pithy oranges in the aroma, the bittersweet taste and the dry, hoppy finish. Clean, refreshing and not quite what you'd normally expect from a winter beer.

Teignworthy ▪ Christmas Cracker

ABV 6%   500 ml   Maris Otter pale malt, crystal malt, Willamette, Golding, Bramling Cross and Challenger hops

This strong seasonal brew from the Newton Abbot brewery, like its other beers, is also sold in cask-conditioned form. Bottle labels used to be signed by all the brewery staff as a kind of Christmas card for customers.

The colour of cherryade, this strong ale has a complex aroma of chocolaty malt, raisins, red berries, earthy spices and hints of both liquorice and pear drop. The bittersweet, but drying, taste is winey and earthy, with more pear drops and a good, malty body. Bitter pear drops and tangy hops linger in the dry, bitter, malty finish.

Teme Valley ▪ Hearth Warmer

ABV 6%   500 ml   Maris Otter pale malt, crystal malt, chocolate malt, wheat malt, roasted barley, Northdown and Fuggle hops

For Christmas 2002, Teme Valley's Christmas beer, Wass Ale, was made available in bottle, but now this has been renamed Hearth Warmer. It is now brewed every October and is still occasionally sold in cask-conditioned form, too.

A red-amber-coloured beer, with a smoky, malty, lightly toffee-like and vinous aroma that also features hop resins. Raisins, hops and liquorice come through in the taste, together with a hint of pear drops and an earthy bitterness. Roasted grain emerges in the dry, bitter finish, along with a little more liquorice.

Vale ▪ Good King Senseless

ABV 5.2%   500 ml   Maris Otter pale malt, crystal malt, chocolate malt, Fuggle, Pilgrim, Willamette and Mount Hood hops

This winter warmer – a good, lighter alternative to a glass of red wine – is brewed each October and fully matured in time for Christmas. Like all Vale's beers, it carries the slogan 'Brill Beer' – not just because the brewers think their ales are very good, but because the brewery's new home is in the village of Brill in Buckinghamshire.

A dark amber-red beer that features lightly orangey hop notes and smooth dark malt in the aroma. The taste falls on the sweet side, with pineapple and juicy berries on top of smooth, toasted malts. It's a little bit winey, but with a bitter backnote for balance. That bitterness continues into the dry finish, with a little fruit lingering.

Wapping ▪ Winter Ale

ABV 6.5%   500 ml   Maris Otter pale malt, mixed spices, cinnamon, other ingredients not declared

Brewed just once a year, in October, to go on sale in December and January, this notably dark brown ale is enhanced by the addition of mixed spices in the copper boil – one reason why the brewer reckons it's a good match for Christmas pudding and mince pies.

An almost medicinal aroma of dark malt (echoes of cough candy sweets), laced with cinnamon and hints of liquorice, leads on to similar flavours in the sweet taste, along with dark malt bitterness and a hint of port. Cinnamon and dark chocolate feature in the bitter finish.

Pale & Dark Lagers

Pale & Dark Lagers

The British lager market is dominated by international brands. We all know how dull these are and sadly our experience with these has shaped the impression many of us hold of what lager is really like. But, as anyone who has travelled to the Czech Republic or Germany can explain, genuine, well-brewed lagers are anything but bland.

Lager is not really a beer style. It's part of the process used by a number of beer styles. The lagering bit is where the beer is matured for weeks, if not months, at very low temperatures before being released for sale (that's the part that is conveniently omitted for many international brands). This long maturation rounds off the rougher edges and makes for a wonderfully clean, crisp beer. The other thing that lager beers have in common is a low fermentation temperature, using a yeast that largely sinks to the bottom of the beer rather than sitting on the top, as happens in ale fermentation. Otherwise lagers comes in as many shapes and forms as ales, from pale golden beers to impenetrable black beers, and all shades in between. The choice of malts and hops helps brewers to create a rainbow of fascinating styles of beer known as helles, pilsner, Vienna, export, schwarzbier, dunkel, rauchbier, bock and more.

The beers in this section offer an insight into how good British lagers can be. They range in style, from light to dark, and, because most are made in breweries designed for ale production, they are sometimes made in ways that perhaps are not strictly in keeping with all the principles of lager making. But a lager style of one kind or another has been their inspiration, and the brewers have sourced genuine lager beer ingredients to bring them to life.

Bottle conditioning itself is not a common treatment for lager beers. Continental lagers, when bottled, are often filtered, or at least just drawn clear off their yeast. You seldom find sediment in the bottle. But what bottle conditioning does do is to give drinkers a taste for what unpasteurised lager can be like, reflecting the fact that many lagers in Germany and the Czech Republic, for instance, are not pasteurised when they are prepared for sale locally.

At a Glance

Strength: ABV 3% upwards

Character: A crisp, clean pale malt lightness often provides the base for the golden examples, with sometimes the malt having a creamy or buttery nature. Hops on top tend to be rather herbal or floral in character, though some have citrus notes. Dark lagers reflect the malt composition, being either nutty and toasty or, if very dark, full of chocolate and coffee notes, like a stout.

Serving temperature: Cold (8º C)

Food matches: Seafood, chicken, white meats, sausages, spicy foods. Amber lagers go with pizzas and cheese dishes, dark lagers with roasted meats, barbecues, mushrooms and chocolate puddings.

Butts ▪ Le Butts

ABV 5%   500 ml   Pale malt, wheat malt, hops not declared

This beer from West Berkshire is produced with lager yeast and a lager hop. It was originally devised in 2002 to lampoon the booze cruisers who crossed the Channel to pick up car-loads of cheap French lager and, through its name, also poked fun at the Canadian lager giant Labatt, which was doing rather well in the UK at the time.

A dark golden beer with a full, smooth, pale malt aroma topped with floral, herbal hops. Bitter, herbal hops lead in the taste, but with plenty of sweet malt for support. The long finish is dry, bitter and herbal-hoppy. A full-flavoured beer with a lightness of touch.

Cobra ▪ King Cobra

ABV 8%   375/750 ml   Ingredients not declared

Although Cobra is a British company, and therefore warrants a listing in this book, King Cobra is an Indian lager, brewed and bottled in Belgium. When it was launched in 2005, production initially took place in Poland, with the beer then tankered to Rodenbach in Belgium for bottling, but all production now takes place at Rodenbach. King Cobra is brewed to the standard Cobra recipe, but is beefed up for the higher strength. Although the precise ingredients are not disclosed, the recipe contains maize and rice, as well as barley malt, and the hops are German Hallertau (Northern Brewer, Hersbrucker and others). Prior to bottling, the beer is flash pasteurised and re-seeded with fresh yeast, a Belgian ale strain that works well in the bottle. It is bottled flat but warm conditioned for two weeks to start the secondary fermentation. The beer is elegantly packaged in near-black, Champagne-style bottles. It's not cheap, but makes a welcome change from the usual curry beers. A filtered, canned version is packaged at Cains in Liverpool for export.

A golden beer with grainy cereal and a hint of sour lemon that gradually gives way to melon in the nose. Melon juiciness continues

Pale & Dark Lagers

in the mouth, along with grainy cereals and gently spicy, bitter hops. There's some alcoholic warmth, and pleasant, bittersweet fruit at all times. The dry, bitter and fruity aftertaste is a little chewy.

Major stockists **Asda, Sainsbury's, Tesco, Waitrose**

Felstar ▪ Lord Kulmbach

ABV 4.4% 500 ml Maris Otter pale malt, lager malt, crystal malt, black malt, wheat malt, Brewer's Gold and Fuggle hops

Inventive Felstar brewer Franco Davanzo describes this as a bottom-fermented stout, in other words a stout that brewed like a lager. Primary cold fermentation takes ten days, five more days are permitted to allow diacetyl (butterscotch notes) to round out and then the beer is cold-matured for eight weeks.

A near-black beer with light roasted malt and a blackberry fruitiness in the nose. The same fruit emerges in the crisp, clean taste before being passed by roasted malt. The dry finish is also bitter and roasted.

Felstar ▪ Peckin' Order

ABV 5% 500 ml Lager malt, crystal malt, wheat malt, Brewer's Gold and Perle hops

Taking three months from brewing to bottling, Peckin' Order enjoys a primary fermentation with a gradually-reduced temperature and ten days' rest before long cold conditioning.

Malt, fruit and floral hop notes mark the aroma of this dark golden brew. Its taste is lightly fruity, with a buttery maltiness plus lemon notes on the swallow. Creamy malt finish with bitterness and hops.

Hopdaemon ▪ Green Daemon Helles

ABV 5% 500 ml Pale malt, lager malt, Hersbrucker hops

Originally made from organic ingredients, but now employing regular malt and hops, Green Daemon was first brewed in 2000. It now bears the name

extension Helles, after the German pale lager style. The beer is fermented with Hopdaemon's regular ale yeast but at a low temperature, with a period of cold conditioning following at the brewery prior to bottling. Green Daemon is also available cask conditioned in summer.

A shiny golden beer with high carbonation (on this tasting). Sappy hops, lemon and sweet pale malt feature in the aroma, followed in the light-bodied taste by sweet citrus-orange and tangy hop bitterness. The finish is dry and increasingly hoppy and bitter.

Major stockist **Local Tesco**

Jolly Brewer ▪ Benno's

ABV 4%   500 ml   Lager malt, Hallertau hops

A lager brewed for the Wrexham FC Supporters Trust, with 1990s striker Gary Bennett honoured in the name. The town of Wrexham has a distinguished lager-brewing heritage, dating back to the 19th century. This and Tommy's (below) are sold in tall, distinctive, 500 ml bottles.

A golden lager with an aroma of gentle, herbal hops. The taste is a good balance of sweet malt and the same, tangy, herbal hops, rounded off by a dry, herbal hop aftertaste.

Jolly Brewer ▪ Tommy's

ABV 5.5%   500 ml   Maris Otter pale malt, chocolate malt, Hallertau hops

The second Wrexham Supporters Trust beer from this North Wales micro-brewery, a dark lager marking the career of the late Tommy Bamford, the club's greatest ever striker.

A dark red beer with biscuity dark chocolate notes in the aroma. The taste is sweet, with dark malt counter bitterness and more chocolate. The finish is dry, with the bitterness of dark malt taking over.

Old Chimneys ▪ Brimstone

ABV 6.1%   500 ml   Lager malt, wheat malt, Hallertau hops

Named after a yellow butterfly, this East Anglian beer was first brewed as a strong lager in 2000 but the recipe was altered in 2008, reducing the ABV from 6.5% to 6.1% and increasing the volume of wheat malt used in the mash tun to the point where brewer Alan Thomson considers this now to be a hybrid of a wheat beer and a lager. The bottle size was increased from 275 ml to 500 ml at the same time. The label still says 'Pilsener Lager', however, so that's where we'll keep it.

A shiny golden beer with a mellow, nutty-grainy aroma with a little citrus sharpness and fruit salad notes. Soft, creamy nut features in the smooth, sweetish taste, with light tropical fruit and a gentle warmth. Dry, creamy, nutty and mildly bitter finish.

Outstanding ▪ Pilsner

ABV 5%   500 ml   Lager malt, Perle and Saaz hops

Forget the mass-market brews: the taste of a true pilsner is re-created in this vegan-friendly beer from Lancashire.

Delicate, creamy pale malt and clean, herbal hops feature in the aroma, followed by a clean, crisp taste of sweet, but light, pale malt and strong, herbal hops. The finish is dry, hoppy and bitter.

Pen-Ion ▪ Ewes Frolic

ABV 5.2%   500 ml   Optic pale lager malt, light crystal malt, Target, Tettnanger and Sterling hops

Ewes Frolic is a dark golden-coloured, Welsh farmhouse lager, made with floor-malted lager malt and hops that include home-grown Sterling, a hybrid of the famous Czech lager hop, Saaz.

Creamy, nutty malt and grassy hops feature in the aroma with more creamy nut alongside herbal hops in the sweetish taste, which has plenty of smooth, malty body. The finish is dry and herbal hoppy.

Pitfield ✳ Organic Lager

ABV 3.7%   500 ml   Pale malt, Tradition hops

Made from organic pale ale malt and organic German Tradition hops from the Hallertau region, this lager is a relatively new addition to the extensive range of bottle-conditioned beers produced by Pitfield and packs a lot of flavour for the strength.

A pale golden lager with herbal hops, light lemon and delicate, sweet pale malt in the aroma. The taste is sweet, with smooth pale malt again featuring, supported by a lemon sharpness and herbal hops. Dry, bittersweet, hoppy finish.

Teignworthy ✳ Beachcomber

ABV 4.5%   500 ml   Maris Otter pale malt, Willamette, Golding, Bramling Cross and Challenger hops

Described as a lager, and using a bottom-fermenting yeast, Beachcomber was devised as a pale beer for barbecues on summer evenings. It was one of this Devon brewery's first four beers.

A refreshing, golden beer with herbal hops and grapefruit notes in the aroma. The taste is sweet but crisp, with herbal and grapefruit hop character, plus a hint of blackcurrant, before a dry, hoppy, bitter finish.
Major stockists **Local Tesco and Waitrose**

Pale & Dark Lagers

Wheat
Beers

Wheat beer is a type of beer that has come back from the dead. There are two types of wheat beer featured in this book and these are the Belgian witbier and the German weissbier (other wheat styles such as Belgian lambic and German Berlinerweiss have not yet raised their heads in British bottle-conditioned beer circles). The two types are quite different, but share the common distinction of being made with a high proportion (30% or more) of wheat in the cereal grist. Wheat can add a cracker-like dryness to the palate, and makes the beer light and quenching. Beyond this, the beers begin to differ. Belgian witbier is often laced with spices and citrus peel, for a perfumed, citrus character, while German weissbier is fermented with a yeast that creates remarkable fruit flavours, such as banana, pear and apple, and other strange elements such as cloves and bubblegum. Both styles are generally served cloudy, although a filtered version of the German beer is also sold under the name of Kristallweissbier.

Not so long ago, both these classic wheat beer styles were on their last legs. The Belgian style was rescued by a dairyman named Pierre Celis, who founded Hoegaarden brewery to re-create the beer he had enjoyed as a youth but which had all but disappeared. The German style was seen as a drink for old ladies, but has since soared in popularity among young drinkers in particular. The influence of both styles has spread rapidly around the world, and many British brewers now produce their own wheat beers, which may be interpretations of the two styles discussed above, or their own hybrid beer, a sort of British wheat ale.

At a Glance

Strength: ABV 4% upwards

Character: Refreshing, despite a sometimes chewy, bready texture. Fruit from hops, added spices or fermentation is often present.

Serving temperature: Cold (8° C) to cool (12° C)

Food matches: Salads, seafood, chicken, white meats, sausages, spicy foods, goat's cheese. Wheat beers, if not too bitter, also pair well with many desserts.

Black Isle ▪ Organic Wheat Beer

ABV 5%   500 ml   Pale malt, wheat malt, Challenger and Perle hops, orange peel, coriander

Brewed initially in 2001, this Belgian-style wheat beer from the north of Scotland was runner-up in 2002's SIBA Wheat Beer Challenge. Since then it has undergone a change of recipe, with the strength raised from 4.5% to 5%. Brewer David Gladwin suggests that it should be served with fresh Scottish mussels or Black Isle raspberries.

A hazy, yellow beer with lemon jelly and clove-like spice in the perfumed aroma. The taste is sweet and sour, with tart lemon, clove-like bitterness and a peppery warmth, before a chewy, clove-bitter finish.

Cotswold ▪ Wheat

ABV 4.2%   500 ml   Pale malt, wheat malt, Cascade and Hersbrucker hops

Initially, the inspiration for this Oxfordshire beer was said to be the Berliner Weisse style, but it's nowhere near as tart and demanding as that type of wheat beer. It leans more to the Bavarian weissbier model but with a stronger citrus accent. Around 55% of the mash is wheat malt.

A very light, crisp, pale yellow beer with a sharp, wheaty-bready aroma with hints of lemon, grapefruit and tangerine. Grapefruit and tangerine flavours continue in the mostly sweet taste, while bitterness builds in the finish which, as expected, is a little bit chewy.

Little Valley ✳ Hebden's Wheat

ABV 4.5%   500 ml   Pale malt, wheat malt, sugar, Hallertau and Hersbrucker hops, coriander seeds, lemon peel

Little Valley brewer Wim van der Spek's Dutch roots show through in this variation on the theme of a witbier, which is named after the nearby

market town of Hebden Bridge. The grist is half-and-half barley malt and wheat malt. Coriander seeds and lemon peel are added to the brew after it has passed through the whirlpool and before fermentation begins. Organic and vegan friendly.

A refreshing, hazy green-golden beer with tart lemon and soft, sweet, peppery spices in the aroma. Good, sharp lemon notes lead the way in the gently bitter taste, which is mildly warming and slightly perfumed, with peppery spices emerging along with a hint of bubblegum. The dry, lemony finish becomes gradually more bitter.
Major stockist **Booths**

Meantime ✳ Wheat

ABV 5% 330 ml Pale malt, crystal malt, wheat malt, Perle and Northern Brewer hops

Meantime Brewing used to produce an excellent, 5% ABV, Bavarian-style wheat beer for Sainsbury's *Taste the Difference* range of premium products. Meantime's own label wheat beer (then named Wheat Grand Cru) was therefore made a touch stronger, at 6.5%, to differentiate between the two brews. As the Sainsbury's product is no longer available, Meantime's Wheat has been reduced now to the strength normally expected from this style of beer.

Bright golden with banana, bubblegum and vanilla in the aroma. There's more banana in the bittersweet taste, along with pear notes, a light citrus sharpness and creamy, sweet cereals. Clove-like bitterness features in the dry, creamy, chewy finish.
Major stockist **Waitrose**

O'Hanlon's ✳ Goldblade

ABV 4% 500 ml Pale malt, wheat malt, caramalt, Challenger, Pilot and First Gold hops, coriander seeds

A wheat beer in the Belgian style, low on bitterness but laced with aromatic hops and spiced with coriander seeds. Winner of the SIBA

(Society of Independent Brewers) Wheat Beer Challenge 1999 and 2002, hence the beer's earlier name of Double Champion Wheat Beer. Drink with barbecues or pizza, suggest the brewers. Also available in cask form.

A bright golden beer with a clean, peppery, orange aroma. The taste is bittersweet and lightly perfumed with more spice and orange flavours, before a dry, bitter, orange and spice finish.

Major stockists **Local Majestic and Tesco**

Pitfield ✳ N1 Wheat Beer

ABV 5%   330 ml   Pale malt, wheat malt, Hallertau hops, coriander

Brewed with a genuine wheat beer yeast, this is Pitfield's version of a Belgian witbier, complete with coriander spicing. N1 was the brewery's post code when it was based at the famous Beer Shop in Pitfield Street, London (now sadly closed, although internet orders are still taken: see Pitfield's entry in The Breweries section of the book).

A hazy yellow beer with a perfumed aroma of lemons. Sweet lemons lead, along with suggestions of orange squash, in the lightly scented taste that also has plenty of peppery, gently warming coriander character. The finish is dry, spicy and bitter, with more perfumed coriander.

Rebellion ✳ White

ABV 5%   330 ml   Pale malt, wheat malt, First Gold and Cascade hops, coriander, orange peel, lemon peel

This spiced wheat beer from Buckinghamshire was first brewed in 2001 and claimed that year's SIBA (Society of Independent Brewers) Wheat Beer Challenge award for Belgian-style wheats, followed up by a category gold medal in the International Beer Competition in 2002. In 2003 and 2004, it

was voted overall champion in the Wheat Beer Challenge. The beer now rolls out a little stronger than before (was 4.5%) and the bottle size has also changed, down from 500 ml to 330 ml. It's not available on draught and, for bottling, the beer is filtered and re-seeded with fresh yeast.

A hazy yellow beer with lemon-citrus, banana and vanilla in the spicy aroma. The sweet, perfumed taste is full of orange-citrus juiciness with some creamy banana behind, and there's more creamy banana in the orange-like, spicy, bittersweet finish.
Major stockist **Local Waitrose**

St Austell ■ Clouded Yellow

ABV 4.8%   500 ml   Maris Otter pale malt, wheat malt, Willamette hops, vanilla pods, cloves, coriander

St Austell Brewery stages a Celtic Beer Festival in November/December each year, for which it prepared two novel brews in 1999. This beer, known as Hagar the Horrible at the time, was one. Brewer Roger Ryman popped down to his local supermarket to pick up the ingredients to make his vision of a German-style wheat beer become reality. He didn't want foreign yeast strains in his brewhouse, where there might be a chance of St Austell's own prized yeast becoming contaminated, and so set about re-creating weissbier flavours artificially, by adding spices to the beer after the boil, as it strained through the hops in the hop back. Vanilla pods, whole cloves and coriander seeds were the key flavourings and they blended together so well that Roger decided to submit the beer for the Tesco Beer Challenge, which it duly won. In 2003, the beer was re-vamped. The strength was dropped to 4.8% from 5%, the clove content was reduced and a touch more vanilla (four pods per barrel) completed the update, which was packaged in a new, slender green bottle. The name is shared with a rare butterfly, which, just like German wheat beers, is a popular continental visitor to Britain in summer. Drink with lightly spiced foods such as Thai curry, Roger suggests.

A hazy golden beer, with cloves, vanilla, dried coriander and banana in the nose. Banana and creamy vanilla feature in the crisp taste, along with a lemony coriander note and some cloves, with vanilla, clove, banana and coriander-citrus in the bready, sweet, creamy finish.

Major stockist **Local Tesco**

Sharp's ▪ Honey Spice Wheat Beer

ABV 6.4%   330 ml   Cocktail pale malt, wheat malt, candy sugar, Golding and Bobek hops, honey, ground ginger, coriander, cinnamon, nutmeg

First brewed in 2008 and judged the top wheat beer in the International Beer Challenge the same year, this innovative beer was also a finalist in the Sainsbury's Beer Competition. A slightly weaker (6%) version, bottled at Hepworth in Sussex, was available for a while but the brewery has now reverted to the full, 6.4% beer, bottled by hand in house.

A golden yellow-coloured beer with pineapple and grapefruit leading in the aroma. The taste is complex, bittersweet and clean, combining tropical fruit, citrus zest, a honeyed smoothness, perfumed spice and a pinch of cinnamon, while the finish is dry, bitter, spicy and lightly perfumed.

Suthwyk ▪ Palmerston's Folly

ABV 5%   500 ml   Optic pale malt, wheat malt, Saaz and Styrian Golding hops

This wheat beer, with 40% of the cereal grist made up of malted wheat, is the latest offering from Suthwyk Ales, the farm-based business that has grain grown on its land malted and turned into beer for it by Hepworth in Horsham and Oakleaf in Gosport. The name refers to the forts along Portsdown Hill, close to the farm. These forts were constructed to defend Portsmouth harbour against a French invasion but, by the time that they were finished, it was obvious that France had no intention of attacking Britain, hence the nickname given to the scheme of Palmerston's Folly, after the Prime Minister who commissioned the work.

A straw-coloured beer with a lightly perfumed aroma of lemon and sweet cereals. The taste is crisp, clean, bitter, spicy and light textured, with a lemon sharpness and gentle floral notes. The finish is slow to build but winds up dry, bitter and perfumed.

White ▪ Weissbier

ABV 4%   500 ml   Pale malt, wheat malt, Pioneer and Boadicea hops

First brewed in 2008, as an experiment in step mashing (where the temperature of the mash tun is gradually raised to new temperatures – historically for a better extract from less amenable malt), this Bavarian-style wheat beer from Sussex is now brewed in the summer and autumn each year. It's a little lightweight for a weissbier but the flavours are authentic.

A very pale, green-golden beer with a soft, spicy aroma featuring banana, lemon, vanilla and clove. Sharp lemon, creamy cereals and hints of banana and clove feature in the bittersweet, but quite thin, taste, rounding off with a dry, chewy, mildly bitter finish that has a gentle lemon sharpness to the end.

Wheat Beers

Speciality Beers

Speciality Beers

This is the section of the book where anything goes. It's reserved for brewers who have pushed the boat out and tried to do something different. That generally means the inclusion of some interesting ingredients, over and above the standard barley malt, water, hops and yeast, or twists to the brewing process. Here you will find honey beers, fruit beers, smoked beers, chocolate beers, coffee beers, ginger and spiced beers, beers made with green hops, beers aged in wood (possibly the industry's most intriguing trend in recent years) and more – evidence yet again that the world of brewing never stands still.

At a Glance

Strength and character: All beers are different, so no universal characteristics apply

Serving temperature: Again varies, but most should be served cool (12º C), with lagers and some wheat types served cold (8º C). Stronger ales may work well without chilling.

Food matches: See individual beers for ideas

Atlantic ■ Black

ABV 5.5%   330 ml   Pale malt, crystal malt, chocolate malt, black malt, wheat malt, Fuggle and First Gold hops, molasses, blackcurrants

The subtitle of this Cornish beer – Organic Dining Ale – reveals its purpose in life. In 2008, Atlantic Brewery was approached by Michelin-starred chef Nathan Outlaw to create a beer specifically to accompany food and to provide an alternative to wine. Discussions followed about styles of beer and Nathan's style of cooking, which is dominated by rich, dark meats such as beef and venison, often accompanied by a red-fruit-based sauce. The resultant beer is a dark porter, fortified by blackcurrants and molasses, which are added during fermentation. It is now sold in Nathan's restaurant in Fowey.

A near-black beer with an aroma loaded with juicy blackcurrants and light chocolate. Juicy, luscious blackcurrants dominate the bitter, full-bodied taste, leaving dark malts as a second feature. The same fruit runs on into the dry finish, which turns firmly bitter as hops and roasted grains come in.

Atlantic ■ Gold

ABV 4.6%   330/500 ml   Pale malt, wheat malt, Fuggle and First Gold hops, root ginger

Gold Organic Premium Ale, to give it its full title, but it's not just organic: it's also acceptable to vegans. For a spicy kick, only organic root ginger is used (added to the copper boil), with no extracts or powders. The crisp, clean palate and ginger accent ensure it goes well with spicy foods and barbecue dishes, according to Atlantic brewer Stuart Thomson. Like other beers from this Cornwall brewery, it is presented in a clear-glass bottle.

A golden-coloured beer with an unusual, gingery, minty, grassy aroma. Delicate, sweet pale malt provides the foundation of the taste with lightly perfumed ginger and some grassy notes set on top. The softly warming finish is then dry and bittersweet with a pleasant ginger flavour lingering.

Major stockist **Local Asda**

Conwy ▪ Cwrw Mêl/Honey Fayre

ABV 4.5%   500 ml   Maris Otter pale malt, crystal malt, torrefied wheat, Challenger and Pioneer hops, honey

Welsh honey is added to this brew after the copper boil but before fermentation begins, the aim being to create a dry-tasting beer with honeyed aromas. It's named after Conwy's Honey Fayre, a street market dating back to medieval times that gave Welsh people the right to sell local produce inside the English walled town. Brewer Gwynne Thomas recommends drinking the beer with Conwy mussels and oriental cuisine.

A fine, pale straw-coloured beer with a modest aroma of soft honey. The taste is bittersweet, clean and crisp, with most of the body seeming to come from the honey, which is not at all perfumed or floral. The malt behind is very delicate and there are some light, spritzy citrus notes. The finish is gently bitter and quite thin, with a honeyed softness.

Major stockists **Local Co-op and Thresher**

Conwy ▪ Marks & Spencer Welsh Honey Bitter

ABV 4.5%   500 ml   Maris Otter pale malt, crystal malt, torrefied wheat, Challenger and Pioneer hops, honey

If you're wondering what the difference is between Conwy's Honey Fayre and this own-label brew for Marks & Spencer, the answer lies primarily in the honey. Whereas Honey Fayre uses a mix of two-thirds standard blended honey and one-third Welsh honey from Newquay, this M&S brew features 100% Newquay honey. There are also some subtle differences in the ingredients mix. The beer was added to the M&S bottle-conditioned beer range in the summer of 2008.

A bright golden beer with a mellow, softly honeyed aroma with a hint of lemon. The bittersweet, perfumed taste is crisp, but with a full, honeyed softness and a light squeeze of lemon. Honey lingers in the otherwise, dry, hoppy, bitter finish, providing a silky moreish note.

Corvedale ▪ Green Hop

ABV 4.5%   500 ml   Maris Otter pale malt, crystal malt, wheat malt, Fuggle hops

Green Fuggle hops, fresh and undried from a Shropshire farm, add the novelty to this best bitter. The beer was first produced in 2004 but only two brews are produced each year, one on the first day of hop cutting and one on the last. It's a substantial, robust brew in which the green hops, which can be strident, do not dominate.

An amber ale with nutty, chocolaty, toasted malt and light, sappy hops in the aroma. The same nutty, toasted malt continues in the mostly bitter taste, more than balancing out the powerful green hop notes. The dry finish is firmly hoppy, tangy and bitter with more nutty malt.

Cropton ▪ Honey Gold

ABV 4.2%   500 ml   Pale malt, crystal malt, caramalt, Fuggle hops, honey

This beer (for a time known as Honey Farm Bitter) was introduced in cask form for Cropton's first beer festival in 1998. It is a single-varietal hop brew, using only Fuggle, along with a dose of local Yorkshire honey.

A shiny golden ale with a subtle aroma of faint honey, soft malt and gentle citrus fruit. The taste is bittersweet, with an orange-citrus sparkle and a smoothness from the delicate honey. The honey is a little more obvious in the dry, bitter, moreish finish.

Downton ▪ Honey Blonde

ABV 4.3%   500 ml   Maris Otter pale malt, maize, Golding, Pioneer and Tettnang hops, honey

This very pale golden beer is Downton's latest offering in bottle, added to the range in 2009, having first been brewed as a cask beer in May 2008 and immediately claiming a 'Beer of the Festival' award in Hampshire. The recipe has been tweaked for bottling

but involves Mexican honey being added as a priming. The beer is then cold filtered and re-seeded with fresh yeast ready for the bottle.

Delicate, smooth pale malt, honey and gentle citrus notes feature in the aroma, leading on to a crisp, moderately bitter taste with a good, developing hop note and a smooth, perfumed, well-judged honey background. The finish – dry, bitter, honeyed and hoppy – lasts well.

Farmer's ▪ A Drop of Nelson's Blood

ABV 3.8%   500 ml   Maris Otter pale malt, crystal malt, black malt, Cascade and First Gold hops, brandy

There's a shot of brandy in every cask of this beer from Maldon, Essex – a reference to the fact that Nelson's body was brought back to Britain in a cask of brandy, which the sailors reportedly drank on their return. The red-amber ale was first brewed for Trafalgar Day a number of years ago.

Chocolaty malt features in the slightly vinous aroma and continues into the bittersweet taste that is also lightly fruity. The finish is dry, bitter and malty. Brandy contributes to the taste but is not obvious t any stage.

Felstar ▪ Howlin' Hen

ABV 6.5%   330 ml   Maris Otter and Pearl pale malt, chocolate malt, wheat malt, roasted barley, Golding, Galena and Hersbrucker hops

Brewed in September, ideally for drinking at Christmas the following year, this rich beer is conditioned in oak casks for a vanilla accent, making it, says Felstar brewer Franco Davanzo, 'justifiably expensive'. He also claims it goes excellently with fruit cakes and puddings.

A very deep ruby-coloured stout with a moussey brown foam. Light fruit notes give way to mellow, creamy, sweet coffee in the aroma, while the creamy, sweetish, coffeeish taste has a warmth that indicates its strength. Strong, bitter coffee finish.

Fox ▪ Da Crai

ABV 3.9 %   500 ml   Lager malt, wheat malt, Cascade, Pilot and First Gold hops, lemongrass

Designed for drinking with curries and other spicy foods, this very pale golden beer from Norfolk takes its name from the Thai for lemongrass, which is the unusual ingredient in the brew.

Sweet and tart citrus notes lead in the lightly spicy aroma, followed in the crisp, dry taste by tart lemon, a mild, perfumed spiciness and a gentle warmth. There's more tart lemon in the dry, hoppy, gently spicy, bitter finish.

Fox ▪ Nelson's Blood

ABV 5.1%   500 ml   Maris Otter pale malt, crystal malt, chocolate malt, black malt, Fuggle, Cascade and Bramling Cross hops, cloves, Nelson's Blood rum

First brewed for the 200th anniversary of the Battle of Trafalgar, this commemorative brew contains a shot of Nelson's Blood rum. This rum is exclusive to The Lord Nelson pub in Nelson's home village of Burnham Thorpe and has been produced since Trafalgar time. About 150 ml is added to every nine-gallon cask prior to bottling. Earlier, the beer is seasoned with cloves, which are added to the copper boil. CAMRA Champion Bottled Beer of East Anglia in 2008.

This red beer is unusual and not for all tastes. The aroma opens up with winey fruit, cloves, light chocolate and a Belgian wild yeast note that continues into the mostly bitter taste, where it is joined again by cloves and red-wine fruitiness. Cloves feature in the finish, too, which is moderately dry, winey-fruity and increasingly bitter.

Fuller's ✳ Brewer's Reserve

ABV 7.7%   500 ml   Ingredients vary

Fuller's early experiments with wood-maturing beer were hampered by a dispute with Customs & Excise about the duty payable on beers that are aged in casks that had previously contained whisky for 30 years. The matter was finally resolved, however, after the beer had been quietly maturing in oak for more than 500 days. There were, in fact, three beers involved, the company's 1845, ESB and Golden Pride, and the first ever Brewer's Reserve that finally emerged was a blend of all three. Future editions may well be different. Each bottle is individually numbered and sold in a smart presentation box, mostly through Fuller's own brewery shop in Chiswick, London.

A dark amber beer with creamy oak and zesty oranges in the aroma. There's more of the same in the gently warming taste, along with smooth malt and a hint of whisky. The finish is a little slow to build but ends up dry, with bitter oranges, soft oak and hops.

Great Gable ▪ Yewbarrow

ABV 5.5%   500 ml   Pale malt, crystal malt, amber malt, chocolate malt, wheat malt, oat malt, Northdown hops, honey, fruit syrup

First brewed at Christmas 2002 under the title of Yulebarrow – a pun on the name of Yewbarrow, the Cumbrian fell on which Great Gable Brewery's spring is located – this strong mild with a twist proved so popular that it was kept on in the brewery's range and is now sold under the simpler Yewbarrow name. While vegetarians will have no qualms about drinking this beer, as there are no finings used, vegans should note that there is some honey in the recipe.

A dark ruby beer with creamy coffee and chocolate biscuits in the aroma. The taste is a nicely balanced combination of biscuity malt, coffee, bitter chocolate, berry fruits and malty sweetness, while bitter chocolate leads in the light finish.

Hobsons ✳ Postman's Knock

ABV 4.8% 500 ml Maris Otter pale malt, dark crystal malt, pale chocolate malt, Fuggle and Golding hops, vanilla pods

This strong mild laced with vanilla is named in honour of writer Simon Evans, who settled in Hobsons' home village of Cleobury Mortimer, Shropshire, to improve his health after gas poisoning in World War I. He took a job as a postman, walking 18 miles a day in the country air, picking up snippets of information and meeting characters he would use to populate his short stories in the 1920s and 1930s. Five pence for every bottle sold is given to the Acorn Hospice that cares for sick children and their families in the Midlands.

A dark-amber/red-coloured ale with chocolate, coffee, nut and treacle in the aroma. The taste, falling just the bitter side of bittersweet, is also nutty and chocolaty, with freshly-ground coffee notes and a full, rich body. The dry, nutty, coffee-like finish is pleasantly bitter.

Major stockist **Local Co-op**

Hop Back ▪ Crop Circle

ABV 4.2% 500 ml Pale malt, flaked maize, wheat malt, Golding, Pioneer, Saaz and Tettnang hops, coriander

A winner in the Spring/Summer 2000 Tesco Beer Challenge, Crop Circle was designed as a light beer for the warmer months, with bitterness playing second fiddle to aroma when it came to the choice of hops. Goldings and Pioneer do most of the hop work, with Saaz and Tettnang (plus more Pioneer) added late in the copper. Coriander is added at this stage, too.

A watery-golden-coloured beer with a crisp, spicy, peppery aroma of lemon-citrus. The taste is clean, bittersweet, peppery and lightly perfumed, with orange and lemon notes. The finish is dry, bitter and hoppy with a lemon sharpness and earthy coriander spice. A delicate, refreshing beer.

Major stockists **Morrisons, Tesco**

Hop Back ▪ Spring Zing

ABV 4.2% 500 ml   Pale malt, wheat malt, flaked maize, Golding, Pioneer, Styrian Golding, Tettnang and Pioneer hops, coriander, lemongrass

Hop Back's Taiphoon (see below) put lemongrass into beer more than ten years ago. Spring Zing is a subtle variation on the theme, very similar to Taiphoon but with Styrian Golding hops replacing Saaz in the copper and less lemongrass in the mix. A Tesco Drinks Awards champion.

A pale green-golden beer with a lightly perfumed, gently earthy, peppery aroma. There's a bitter lemon tartness to the taste, which is crisp, peppery and gently perfumed-hoppy, with a coriander earthiness. The finish is dry, hoppy, perfumed, peppery and bitter.

Hop Back ▪ Taiphoon

ABV 4.2% 500 ml   Pale malt, wheat malt, flaked maize, Golding, Pioneer, Saaz, Tettnang and Pioneer hops, coriander, lemongrass

Introduced in 1999, this Wiltshire beer is designed as a partner for Asian cuisine (the key ingredient, lemongrass, also features widely in oriental, particularly Thai, cooking). But it's an enjoyable, refreshing drink on its own, too.

A pale green-golden beer with a mix of sweet malt and light, peppery, earthy spices in the aroma, along with a squeeze of lemon and a whiff of perfume. The crisp taste is perfumed and peppery, with bitter lemon and earthy coriander, while the finish is dry, hoppy, perfumed and bitter.

Hopshackle ▪ Hop and Spicey

ABV 4.5% 500 ml   Maris Otter pale malt, light crystal malt, black malt, Fuggle and Mount Hood hops, honey, cinnamon, root ginger, orange peel

The recipe for Hop and Spicey was one that Hopshackle founder Nigel Wright practised many times as a home brewer before he turned

243

professional. As the name implies, it offers hop bitterness and then plenty of spice. The honey in the ingredients list goes in early in the boil, to ensure sterility, then the other exotic contributions are added toward the end of the beer's time in the copper. It's generally brewed only in autumn and winter, but, being bottled, can be found at other times of the year.

An amber-red ale with a complex aroma featuring malt, toffee, fruit cake spices and a dash of cola. The taste is bittersweet and malty (more faint toffee), with a notable spice character – perfumed, mildly warming and earthy, suggestive of ginger and lavender. A light gingery burn on the swallow leads to a dry, bitter, scented finish with malt lingering.

Humpty Dumpty ▪ Norfolk Nectar

ABV 4.6%   500 ml   Maris Otter pale malt, crystal malt, wheat malt, Challenger and Mount Hood hops, honey

Humpty Dumpty's honey beer makes the most of local produce. The malt comes from Branthill Farm, on Norfolk's coast, and the honey is sourced from the Broadland town of Reedham where the brewery is based.

A golden ale with traces of melon in the lightly fruity aroma, along with a honeyed softness. The big, mostly bitter taste blends well-restrained honey with a citrus sharpness from the hops, while the firmly bitter and hoppy finish also has a honeyed smoothness.

Itchen Valley ▪ Hambledon Bitter

ABV 4.5%   500 ml   Maris Otter pale malt, roasted barley, Galena and Saaz hops, honey, elderflower

A beer first brewed in 2000 to celebrate the village that is recognized as the home of cricket. Hambledon, with its famous Bat & Ball pub, and cricket club established in 1760, is just 15 miles from the brewery. Honey and elderflower spice up the finished beer before it heads for bottling.

A bright golden ale with balanced honey and sappy elderflower along with malt in the aroma. Perfumed honey and floral, fruity elderflower

flavours, along with sharp grapefruit notes, feature in the taste, which falls on the bitter side of bittersweet. Dry, bitter, hoppy finish.

Itchen Valley ■ Treacle Stout

ABV 4.4% 500 ml Maris Otter pale malt, crystal malt, chocolate malt, roasted barley, Progress hops, treacle, liquorice

This Hampshire beer is unusually flavoured. Liquorice is added to the copper boil, while treacle primes the finished beer before it is bottled. It was first brewed in 1999 and is also sold in cask form.

A ruby/brown beer with a creamy collar. Coffeeish dark malt and treacle feature in the aroma before more dark malts, treacle and light liquorice combine in the smooth taste. The same flavours lead in the mostly bitter finish, with liquorice more pronounced.

Keystone ✳ Gold Spice

ABV 4% 500 ml Maris Otter pale malt, amber malt, wheat malt, Boadicea hops, root ginger

The spice referred to in the name of this straw-coloured ale from Wiltshire is ginger, which is added in root form to the cask in which the beer is matured prior to bottling. Gold Spice started life as a winter warmer, but its refreshing character soon ensured it was brewed at other times of the year, too.

Fresh root ginger colours the aroma, bringing lemony, spicy notes. Warming ginger is also very evident in the crisp, bittersweet taste, along with earthy, lemony flavours, and it lingers in the delicate finish, too.

King ■ Cereal Thriller

ABV 6.3% 500 ml Maris Otter pale malt, enzymic malt, flaked maize, Whitbread Golding Variety hops

When King founder Bill King was managing director of the King & Barnes brewery, the company produced a beer with a high percentage of maize

in the mash tun. They called it Cornucopia. He has revived the idea at his Horsham microbrewery, with the name this time chosen via a local competition. It's now an occasional brew.

A golden beer with sweet cereals, light oranges and floral notes in the aroma. The taste is smooth, full-bodied, mostly sweet and gently warming, with tropical fruit notes and a pleasant bitter balance. The drying finish is still sweet at first, but eventually turns bitter as hops push through.

Little Valley ✳ Ginger Pale Ale

ABV 4%   500 ml   Pale malt, crystal malt, caramalt, sugar, Pacific Gem and Cascade hops, ginger

A new beer in spring 2008, Little Valley's Ginger Pale Ale features Fairtrade Ginger, along with the Fairtrade sugar that features in the recipes of this Yorkshire brewery's other beers. Like those beers, it is also organic and vegan friendly.

A shiny golden ale with an aroma of fresh ginger. The taste is bittersweet and spritzy, with a pleasantly warming ginger bite and good body for the strength. There's more gingery warmth in the dry, bitter finish. If you like ginger, you'll love this refreshing beer.

Major stockist **Booths**

Lizard ▪ An Gof

ABV 5.2%   500 ml   Maris Otter pale malt, crystal malt, chocolate malt, smoked malt, Golding and Challenger hops

The special twist in this red-amber-coloured Cornish beer comes through the inclusion of wood-smoked malts in the mash tun. It is named after Mychel Josef, a blacksmith from St Keverne ('an Gof' is Cornish for blacksmith) who led a Cornish rebellion against unfair taxes imposed by King Henry VII in 1497. He was defeated in London and brutally executed at Tyburn. The beer has been available in bottle since 2005.

Biscuity, smoked malt, with light toffee and chocolate, features in the aroma. Smokiness in the sweetish taste is restrained, leaving toffee, chocolate and nut to lead, along with an almost banana-like fruit note. The dry, malty, nutty and smoky finish becomes increasingly bitter.

Major stockist **Local Asda**

Marble ■ Ginger 6

ABV 6%   500 ml   Pale malt, crystal malt, wheat malt, Boadicea hops, ginger

Originally brewed for the wedding of Marble brewer James Campbell in 2006, this is a stronger version of Marble's cask Ginger (4.5%). The beer is aged for a minimum of three weeks with a generous addition of fresh and dried ginger prior to bottling.

An orange-golden beer with ginger toffee and a lemony freshness in the aroma. The taste is mostly bitter but with a real spicy kick and a fiery ginger burn. The same spicy warmth features in the dry, hoppy and bitter finish. A muscular ginger beer: don't expect subtlety.

Meantime ✳ Chocolate

ABV 6.5%   330 ml   Pale malt, crystal malt, Munich malt, brown malt, chocolate malt, black malt, Fuggle hops, chocolate

A rich beer containing real chocolate, to enhance and complement the dark malty flavours of the mash. Introduced in 2005, it has since claimed various awards, including the title of World's Best Chocolate Beer in the 2007 World Beer Awards, run by Beers of the World magazine. Like other Meantime beers, this is acceptable to vegetarians.

A dark claret-coloured beer with a fudgy aroma of chocolate and vanilla. The taste is fudgy, rich and sweet, with chocolate leading the way and raisin flavours in support. Big, mouth-filling texture. Chocolate features in the bittersweet finish, but with roasted grains fighting back.

Meantime ✳ Coffee Porter

ABV 6%   330 ml   Pale malt, crystal malt, Munich malt, brown malt, chocolate malt, black malt, Fuggle hops, coffee

Meantime founder Alastair Hook conceived this beer while attending the World Beer Cup in the USA. He was judging the category for coffee beers and realized that most beers added coffee to a stout base, whereas, in his mind, a softer, less astringent porter base would be more compatible. Initially brewed to only 4%, Meantime's Coffee Beer has now been boosted to 6% and brought things back full circle when it won the gold medal itself in the World Beer Cup in 2006 (just one of the many awards it has so far claimed). To create this distinctive beer, Fairtrade arabica bourbon coffee from Rwanda is added to the base porter. Try it instead of coffee after a meal, but bear in mind that it does contain caffeine.

A deep garnet-coloured beer with a fabulous aroma of freshly-milled coffee beans and chocolate-vanilla ice cream. Fresh roasted coffee flavours dominate the taste, but without overwhelming the creamy vanilla notes and the fine balance of bitterness and sweetness. Coffee fills the dry, bitter finish, too.

Major stockist **Local Waitrose**

Meantime ✳ Raspberry Grand Cru

ABV 6.5%   330 ml   Pale malt, wheat malt, raspberry fruit extract, Perle and Northern Brewer hops

Fruit beers can often be either very sweet and commercial or very dry, tart and demanding. Meantime's Raspberry Grand Cru, happily, falls nicely in the middle of this range, offering good, sharp fruit flavours that are neither too cloying nor too shrill. The raspberries are added during a period of maturation at the brewery. A great beer to try with chocolate desserts.

Gold with a blush of red. Raspberries dominate the nose, taste and finish, with tart, sharp and acidic notes nicely balanced by sweetness. Bitterness builds in the dry finish.

Major stockist **Local Waitrose**

O'Hanlon's ✳ Original Port Stout

ABV 4.8%   500 ml   Optic pale malt, crystal malt, caramalt, roasted barley, flaked barley, Pilot and Styrian Golding hops, port

A 'corpse reviver', in the Irish tradition of hangover cures, this dry stout is enhanced by the addition of Ferreira port prior to bottling, at a ratio of two bottles per brewer's barrel (36 gallons), which raises the strength from 4.6 to 4.8%. The draught version was one of O'Hanlon's earliest beers – the port was added to mark out the cask beer from a popular keg stout also sold in the London pub run by brewer John O'Hanlon – and it claimed the top stout prize in CAMRA's Champion Winter Beer of Britain awards for 2002. This bottled version was CAMRA's Champion Bottle-conditioned Beer in 2003 and 2007.

A ruby-brown beer with fruit in the biscuity, roasted barley nose. This is a classic, dry, bitter stout in the mouth, with more than a trace of winey fruit. Dry, roasted, bitter finish.
Major stockists **Thresher, Wine Rack, local Sainsbury's, Tesco and Waitrose**

Old Chimneys ✳ Good King Henry Special Reserve

ABV 11%   275 ml   Pale malt, crystal malt, wheat malt, roasted barley, Fuggle and Challenger hops

Good King Henry was an imperial Russian stout, brewed to 9.6% ABV. In 2005, however, Old Chimneys celebrated its tenth anniversary with a stronger version, stored in cask with oak granules for six months. The beer was then given a further 18 months to mature in the bottle before going on sale. This new Special Reserve has now taken over entirely, and the original Good King Henry has been usurped. However, contrary to first impressions, this beer takes its name not from a

Speciality Beers

249

monarch but from a rarely-grown vegetable. Only limited numbers of each vintage are available, but they are well worth seeking out.

2005 vintage (tasted after four years)**: A tarry brown beer with a creamy, oaky aroma with hints of raisins, chocolate and treacle. The taste is smooth and syrupy, oaky and creamy, sweet and oily, with dried fruits and suggestions of leather, citrus and port. The thick, sweet finish is ultra smooth, with more creamy oak and a pleasant warmth.**

Old Chimneys ▪ Hairy Canary

ABV 4.2%   500 ml   Lager malt, wheat malt, Hallertau hops, sugar, lactose, stem ginger, lemon

Old Chimneys' fruit beer is designed as a thirst quencher for hot days. Wort is drawn from a brew of Brimstone (see Pale & Dark Lagers) 24 hours into fermentation and mixed with sucrose, lactose, stem ginger and lemon. The name is borrowed from a rare yellow fly.

A golden beer with sweet and sharp lemon and ginger in the aroma. The spritzy taste is also sweet and sharp, with an earthy ginger warmth and the zingy, sourness of lemon juice. Bitter lemons and gingery warmth provide the finish.

Old Chimneys ▪ Red Clover

ABV 6.2%   500 ml   Pale malt, crystal malt, wheat malt, roasted barley, Challenger and Fuggle hops, cloves

Red Clover is a blended old ale, with cloves added to the green beer after fermentation. It's brewed two or three times a year but is mostly sold during the festive season (try it with Christmas pudding).

The colour of cherryade, this innovative beer has a full clove and malt aroma, with some winey fruit. The taste is sweet but not cloying, with

clove aromatics, bitterness and warmth on top of creamy, velvet malt, plus more winey fruit. The finish is dry, thick, bittersweet and warming, with cloves lasting to the end. Light drinking on the whole for its strength.

Otley ▪ O-Garden

ABV 4.8%   500 ml   Pale malt, torrefied wheat, Amarillo and Celeia hops, roasted orange peel, coriander, cloves

It's a cheeky name, but this spice-and-citrus-laden beer is nothing like the famous Belgian witbier brewed by InBev. It's not even a wheat beer and, with Otley's now well-known, striking black-and-white labels, there can be no confusing it with its mass market namesake. In its cask-conditioned form, O-Garden claimed the gold medal for Speciality Beers at CAMRA's Champion Beer of Britain contest in 2008.

A light golden ale with spicy coriander and orange notes in the aroma. The taste is crisp and fairly bitter, with perfumed, peppery coriander and tart, tangy oranges. Dry, peppery, bitter finish with more oranges and coriander.

Outstanding ▪ Ginger

ABV 4.5%   500 ml   Pale malt, crystal malt, Chinook and Styrian Golding hops, ginger

This copper-coloured ale is not one of the most subtle of ginger beers. But, if you like a good kick of spice, you won't be disappointed with this vegan-friendly offering from Lancashire.

An aroma reminiscent of ginger ale mixer drinks leads on to a full, slightly bitter flavour of perfumed, earthy, rooty ginger, with light toasted malt support. There's a good spicy glow throughout and, after a burning swallow, it's ginger all the way in the finish, which is moderately bitter.

Speciality Beers

Outstanding ▪ Smoked Out

ABV 4.5%   500 ml   Pale malt, smoked malt, roasted barley, Pilgrim and Saaz hops

This deep-amber beer that echoes the Franconian tradition of using smoked malts in beer is not for all tastes but the smokiness is well handled nonetheless.

Smoked malt dominates the aroma. The bittersweet taste is also very smoky with a hickory smoke character, but hidden beneath are sweet citrus notes and tangy hops. Hops fight back in the dry, smoky, increasingly bitter finish.

Pen-Ion ▪ Chocolate Stout

ABV 4.5%   500 ml   Pale malt, roasted barley, flaked barley, Target and Pilgrim hops, dark chocolate

Yes, this stout does include real chocolate, and it was first brewed for a chocolate manufacturer, but it was never intended to be a particularly chocolaty drink – which is perhaps why brewer Stefan Samociuk recommends serving it with a rich beef stew.

A deep garnet-coloured stout with a thick head that just allows chocolate, juicy berries and liquorice to emerge in the aroma. The taste is mostly sweet, with plain chocolate and hops adding some bitterness to the mix. Juicy berries, too. The dark malt finish starts bittersweet and becomes more bitter, developing a chocolaty thickness.

Pen-Ion ▪ Heather Honey Ale

ABV 4.2%   500 ml   Pale malt, Target hops, honey

Originally brewed for a bee-keeper who keeps hives on the Brecon Beacon mountain range, where the bees work the ling heather flowers to create

distinctive heather honey, this golden-coloured beer is a perfect partner to a plate of roast pork, according to Pen-lon farmer/brewer Stefan Samociuk.

As expected, lightly perfumed honey features in the otherwise peppery aroma, along with light tropical fruit. Smooth, moreish honey leads in the sweet taste, bringing soft floral notes but, thankfully, the honey is not overpowering. It then adds a pleasant softness to the drying, floral, increasingly bitter finish.

Pen-lon ▪ Torddu

ABV 4.2%   500 ml   Pale malt, crystal malt, First Gold hops, fruit

As with Torwen (below), local, seasonal fruits are a feature of this light-coloured beer, first brewed in 2008. As the label reveals, Torddu is a breed of Welsh sheep distinguished by a black band that runs around the body.

Golden-amber, with soft berry fruits featuring in the aroma, along with gentle malt and a hint of bubblegum. The chewy taste is soft, sweet and berry-fruity, rounding off with a subtle, dry, fruity finish.

Pen-lon ✳ Torwen

ABV 4.5%   500 ml   Pale malt, roasted barley, flaked barley, Target hops, local fruits

Described as a 'dark fruit beer', Torwen was first brewed in 2008 to take advantage of the local fruit harvest. The fruits included now change according to the season, and the tasting notes below were based on a brew featuring 'summer fruits'. Torwen is a breed of sheep that grazes the mountains of Wales, the name literally translating as 'white belly'.

A deep garnet beer with biscuity dark grain, chocolate, caramel and juicy berries in the aroma. The sweetish taste features smooth, dark grain, faint chocolate and juicy blackberries. Dry, fruity, biscuity, dark grain finish.

RCH ▪ Ale Mary

ABV 6%   500 ml   Optic pale malt, chocolate malt, Progress and Target hops, ginger, cloves, cinnamon, coriander, nutmeg, pimento

Ale Mary is RCH's Firebox (see Strong Ales), but with spice oils and essences added prior to bottling. It was first 'created' for Christmas 1998 and has remained a festive favourite. It was judged CAMRA's Champion Bottle-conditioned Beer in 2001.

Oranges overlaid with exotic, peppery spice dominate the perfumed nose of this strong amber beer. The spices impart an unusual taste, with the bitter citrus qualities of Firebox exaggerated by the coriander in particular, and the other flavourings providing a peppery, gingery warmth. Dry, scented, bitter orange finish with a light ginger burn.

Sharp's ▪ Chalky's Bark

ABV 4.5%   330 ml   Tipple pale malt, wheat malt, candy sugar, glucose, Northdown, Brewer's Gold, Bobek and Cascade hops, ground ginger

Buoyed by the success of Chalky's Bite (see below), Cornish brewery Sharp's joined forces again with TV chef Rick Stein in 2009 to launch this interesting ginger beer. Dried ground ginger is stewed with glucose and then added to the beer before fermentation. The beer is brewed at Sharp's, but bottled by Hepworth in Sussex. 'I'm damned chuffed with it!,' says Rick.

A golden-coloured beer with lemon and soft ginger in the spicy, perfumed aroma. The taste is crisp, with gentle, tea-like hops, lemon and a light gingery burn. The drying, mildly bitter finish offers more tea-like hops and a subtle gingery warmth.

Major stockist **Waitrose**

Sharp's ▪ Chalky's Bite

ABV 6.8%   330 ml   Maris Otter pale malt, wheat malt, candy sugar, glucose, Northdown, Golding, Styrian Golding and Saaz hops, wild Cornish fennel

Designed in conjunction with TV chef Rick Stein, whose establishments in Padstow lie just across the estuary from Sharp's Cornish brewery, this beer has seafood in its sights. Wild Cornish fennel is the bridging ingredient between the beer and the fruits of the ocean, bringing a light aniseed flavour to the palate. The fennel is added during a two-month maturation period at 0° C, while the beer sits on fresh hops. After the beer is sterile filtered, a Belgian yeast strain is added ready for bottling and the bottled beer is warm and cold conditioned for three months before going on sale. The name, of course, refers to Rick Stein's pet Jack Russell terrier, who accompanied him on his culinary adventures but died a few years ago.

A golden ale with a complex aroma combining piney, aniseed notes with oranges and tangerines. Sharp, sweet orange leads on the palate, balanced by gentle aniseed, bitter hops, a spicy warmth and a touch of bubblegum. The finish is very dry, featuring orange and aniseed again. Clean-tasting and pleasant.
Major stockists **Sainsbury's, Waitrose**

Samuel Smith ✳ Yorkshire Stingo

ABV 8%   550 ml   Ingredients not declared

Samuel Smith, in Tadcaster, North Yorkshire, is one of the few remaining British breweries to still use oak casks and to maintain a cooper to look after them. As other breweries began to experiment with ageing beer in wood, it made sense for Sam's to have a go, too, considering the number of seasoned casks it has on site. The result is a powerful, complex ale matured for more than a year in well-used oak. While the precise ingredients remain undeclared (in typical Sam's very private fashion), the bottle label does reveal that cane sugar joins water, malted barley, hops and yeast in the brew. Yorkshire Stingo – named after a local term for a type of barley wine – is Sam's only bottle-conditioned beer. It was first issued in 2008, is vegan friendly and is imported into the USA through Merchant du Vin.

The colour of cherryade, this substantial beer has plenty of toffee-like malt and creamy oak in the fresh aroma, along with liquorice and

red berries. Buttery oak adds dryness and tannin notes to the mostly bitter, treacly malt taste, which also features raisins and red berries and is gently warming. The bitter, hoppy finish is also dry, creamy, oaky and smooth, with hints of cherry and raisins.

Spire ▪ Sgt Pepper Stout

ABV 5.5%   500 ml   Maris Otter pale malt, amber malt, pale chocolate malt, Northern Brewer and Fuggle hops, black pepper

Some people like to add black pepper to strawberries, believing that it enhances the taste. Spire Brewery adds it to a stout and, in doing so, it has created a beer that has certainly turned a few heads. Such has been the interest in this Beatle-inspired creation that the brewery is actively seeking a patent for the recipe and brewing process. In its cask-conditioned form, Sgt Pepper claimed a bronze medal at CAMRA's Winter Beer of Britain contest in 2009. It's good with seafood, steak and ale pie, and sausages, claim the brewers, but here's another suggestion: strawberries?

A near-black stout with a biscuity aroma of crisp, freshly-roasted coffee and dark chocolate. Bitter chocolate leads in the taste, but spicy, aromatic black pepper really does come through and runs on into the dry, bitter chocolate finish that lasts well.

Teme Valley ▪ The Hop Nouvelle

ABV 4.1%   500 ml   Maris Otter pale malt, wheat malt, green hops

Brewed once a year, during the hop harvest, this is an ale equivalent to wine's Beaujolais Nouveau. The hops (whichever variety is available) are plucked from bines less than half a mile from the Worcestershire brewery and, within the hour, without kilning, are cast green into the copper, delivering a sappier, more resin-like flavour to the beer than standard dried hops. The beer then takes its place at a green-hop beer festival held every October at The Talbot Inn, the pub that is home to the brewery.

2008 version (featuring green First Gold hops)**: A pale yellow beer with an aroma of sappy, lemony hops. Sappy, tart, peppery hop notes lead in the taste, along with a citrus sharpness. There's a pleasant sweetness behind, but this is a predominantly bitter beer. The finish is very dry, firmly bitter, sappy and hoppy.**

Thornbridge ✳ Bracia

ABV 9%   500 ml   Maris Otter pale malt, dark crystal malt, brown malt, chocolate malt, Munich malt, black malt, peated malt, roasted barley, Target, Pioneer, Northern Brewer and Sorachi Ace hops, chestnut honey

They're nothing but adventurous at Thornbridge. This stately home brewery is responsible for some of the most intriguing and successful beers in Britain today and Bracia is no exception. Even if you overlook the number of malts in the mash tun, or the intriguing blend of hops – including the rare Sorachi Ace from Japan – or even the fact that the yeast in the bottle is Champagne yeast (added after three months of cold maturation), there is still something that catches the eye and that's chestnut honey, sourced from a beekeeper in North-East Italy. The beer is loosely based on a beverage called Bracia that is named on a Roman inscription at Haddon Hall, near Thornbridge, in Derbyshire. It is said to be a drink of Iron Age origin, given its name by the Celts. As the Thornbridge brewers admit, information beyond this is scarce, except that the brew would have been high in alcohol and contained honey. The honey Thornbridge has selected has a rich and pungent flavour, gleaned as the bees are buzzing around sweet chestnut trees.

An near-black beer with a deeply complex aroma that is suggestive of creamy coffee, polished leather, honey, cedar, little bursts of orange and, as the label declares, white chocolate. The gently warming taste is thick and ultra-smooth, with a luxurious, fondant texture. Sweet, perfumed honey is well in evidence, as you'd expect, balanced by creamy, bitter chocolate and nut. More bitter chocolate then joins espresso coffee in the thick, dry, nutty finish that also features a little citrus zest and a honeyed, scented accent.

Thornbridge ✳ Halcyon

ABV 7.7%   500 ml   Maris Otter pale malt, Fuggle and Target hops

'At Thornbridge we like to do things a little differently …', says the blurb on this intriguing beer. The difference this time lies in the use of 'a massive amount' of green hops, fresh from the bine, that are added to this India pale ale as it is maturing at the brewery. Freshly picked Target hops from Herefordshire share the honours with 'home-grown' Fuggles from Derbyshire. Apart from huge, tangy hop flavours, these may be responsible for a natural haze in the glass. To add to the quirkiness, the yeast chosen to go into the bottle is a saison yeast from Belgium. 'Can you capture the essence of fresh hops in a bottle?', asks the label. The answer is yes, but don't expect to be able to taste anything else after!

A cloudy golden-amber beer with an instant hit of pungent, sappy hops that are almost menthol in their cleanness, with an orange jelly note for contrast. The hop notes in the taste are sappy and shrill, tangy and peppery, piney and cleansing, just about leaving room for an orange jelly sweetness. Hops continue thick and fast in the finish, burning the throat and drying the palate.

Tipple's ▪ Crackle

ABV 4%   500 ml   Pale malt, crystal malt, chocolate malt, Golding and Atlas hops, spices, citrus fruit, treacle

Test-brewed during the first snows of winter 2005, this ruby-coloured, spiced beer from Norfolk then became a regular seasonal offering in 2006, when it was given the name Crackle to evoke the idea of a drink to enjoy before a roaring log fire. A good partner for a mince pie.

A smoky, spicy aroma, with cinnamon to the fore and cough candy notes leads to a smoky, spicy taste of smooth,

dark malt, bitter cloves and cinnamon, with little bursts of orange. The bittersweet, drying finish has a chocolaty maltiness and yet more spices.

Tipple's ■ Ginger

ABV 3.8%   500 ml   Maris Otter pale malt, crystal malt, Atlas hops, root ginger

This delicately-hopped ale is enhanced by the addition of fresh root ginger towards the end of the copper boil. It was planned only as a summer refresher, but is now brewed all year-round. The brewers have composed a poem for the label that revolves around a World War I flying ace named Ginger. Try the beer with apple pie, they say.

A golden-coloured ale with a ginger beer aroma. It's a light-drinking beer with a bittersweet taste and good, fresh ginger-citrus flavours. The dry finish is mildly bitter with a soft, gingery burn.

Traditional Scottish Ales ■ Ginger Explosion

ABV 5%   500 ml   Maris Otter pale malt, torrefied wheat, Hallertau and First Gold hops, root ginger

Root ginger in the mash tun, and yet more root ginger added to the bottle, are what provide a generous kick of spice to this warming, golden-coloured beer that was voted CAMRA's Champion Bottle-conditioned Beer of Scotland in 2007.

The aroma is initially reminiscent of home-made ginger beer – fiery and earthy – then, as biscuity malt shows through, a ginger snaps character emerges. The taste is sweet and earthy with lots of fresh ginger and light, balancing hop, and there's also a ginger burn to the sweet, but increasingly hoppy and bitter, finish.

Speciality Beers

259

Traditional Scottish Ales ✳ Brig o' Allan

ABV 4%   500 ml   Maris Otter pale malt, crystal malt, chocolate malt, torrefied wheat, Fuggle and First Gold hops, black treacle

Originally brewed in 2001 by Bridge of Allan Brewery, which is now part of Traditional Scottish Ales, this traditional 80/- ale is laced with a little black treacle. CAMRA's Champion Bottle-conditioned Beer of Scotland in 2005.

A wonderfully-balanced, ruby beer with a richly malty, welcoming aroma of chocolate and toffee. The taste is enjoyably full and malty, with more chocolate and toffee, plus raisin notes. Toffee and chocolate run on into the drying, bittersweet finish.

Tryst ▪ Blàthan

ABV 4%   500 ml   Pale malt, caramalt, Challenger hops, elderflower

Taking its name from the Gaelic for 'little blossom', Tryst's elderflower-infused beer was added to the Scottish brewery's range in 2008.

A yellow-golden ale with a floral, grapefruit-like aroma and a dry, hoppy, fruity, bittersweet taste, combining tart grapefruit with elderflower and a sappy leafiness. The same flavours continue in the dry, bitter finish.

Why Not ▪ Norfolk Honey Ale

ABV 3.8%   500 ml   Maris Otter pale malt, crystal malt, Fuggle hops, honey

A local award-winner, this orange-golden beer was first brewed in 2006 and is now produced every other month. The key feature is Norfolk honey, which certainly has an impact on the flavour. There are no finings used to clear the beer, which makes it acceptable to vegetarians, but vegans, of course, should be wary of the inclusion of honey.

A highly perfumed, lavender-like aroma leads on to more lavender and a honeyed smoothness in the bittersweet taste, rounding off with a dry, smooth, bitter but honey-scented finish.

Windsor Castle ▪ Mud City Stout

ABV 6.6%   500 ml   Maris Otter pale malt, crystal malt, chocolate malt, roasted barley, wheat malt, oats, Golding and Northern Brewer hops, vanilla pods, raw cocoa

The Mud City in question is the town of Lye, near Stourbridge in the West Midlands, where Windsor Castle brews its Sadler's 'incomparable' Ales. Lye was once famous for its houses made of mud. This stout, laced with both vanilla and cocoa, was first brewed in November 2007 and has quickly established itself as a regular, year-round beer in the Sadler's range.

A deep ruby stout with an aroma of Ovaltine and chocolate, plus a touch of toffee. The bittersweet taste is chocolaty, with caramel notes and a light, airy texture, followed by a dry, thick, bittersweet finish with dark chocolate and toffee.

Major stockists **Local Thresher and Victoria Wine**

Yates' ▪ Holy Joe

ABV 4.9%   500 ml   Optic pale malt, crystal malt, torrefied wheat, Cascade hops, coriander

The ingredients list suggests that this is going to be a citrus beer, with the zesty inclusion of American Cascade hops and powdered coriander added late into the copper. The taste backs this up. The beer is named after a local character from the 1850s who roamed the Isle of Wight highways abusing sinners.

A bright amber-coloured beer with toasted malt, tart fruit and spicy, peppery notes in the aroma. There's more toasted malt, plus earthy spice, tangy hop and orange-citrus notes, in the mostly bitter taste, while the finish is bitter, tangy and hoppy, with, again, toasted malt and earthy coriander flavours.

The Breweries

In this section of the *Good Bottled Beer Guide* you'll find a comprehensive listing of UK breweries that produce bottle-conditioned beer.

The rosette symbol against a brewery's name highlights those breweries that produce consistently good bottle-conditioned beers. This, of course, does not mean that all other breweries are bad, just that breweries awarded rosettes set a very high standard. Hopefully, we can award even more rosettes in future editions.

Breweries are arranged alphabetically, with full contact details and a brief description of the business. Included here also is information about how the brewery bottles its beer. A full list of bottle-conditioned beers follows, arranged in increasing strength order, together with the alcohol by volume figure (ABV) and a short description of the beer style, except where this is already clear from the name of the beer itself.

Note: in some instances a brewery may call a beer 'Best Bitter' or 'IPA', for instance, but stylistically the beer may fall into another category. The more accurate category is what is used here.

Acorn

Acorn Brewery of Barnsley Ltd, Unit 3, Aldham Industrial Estate, Wombwell, Barnsley, South Yorkshire S73 8HA
☎ (01226) 270734
@ sales@acorn-brewery.co.uk
🌐 www.acorn-brewery.co.uk
Mail order service

◼ Acorn Brewery was only founded in 2003 but has doubled its capacity already to meet demand for its beers. The one bottle-conditioned beer it produces is matured for a month before and after bottling, which takes place at Hambleton Brewery.

Gorlovka (6%, imperial stout)

Adur

Adur Brewery Ltd, Little High Street, Shoreham by Sea, West Sussex BN43 5EG
☎ (01273) 467527
@ info@adurbrewery.com
🌐 www.adurbrewery.com

◼ This small brewery in the Adur Valley of Sussex now produces three regular bottle-conditioned beers, all brewed and bottled on site.

Velocity (4.4%, best bitter)
Black William (5%, stout)
Merry Andrew (6.2%, old ale)

Ales of Scilly

Ales of Scilly, Higher Trenoweth, St Mary's, Isles of Scilly TR21 0NS
☎ (01720) 422419
@ mark@alesofscilly.co.uk

◼ Opened in 2001 and expanded to a five-barrel plant in 2004, Ales of Scilly is the most south-westerly brewery in the UK. The single bottle-conditioned beer listed below is bottled by hand on site during winter and matured for two or three months at the brewery before going on sale.

Scuppered (4.6%, best bitter)

Amber

Amber Ales Ltd, PO Box 7277, Ripley, Derbyshire DE5 4AP
☎ (01773) 512864
@ info@amberales.co.uk
🌐 www.amberales.co.uk

◼ Amber Ales opened in 2006 on a Derbyshire business park. The beers below are bottled straight from the fermentation vessel, with sugar for priming.

Blond (3.9%, summer golden ale)
Original Stout (4%)
Pale (4.4%, best bitter)
Winter Ruby (5.1%, winter ale)
Organic Pale Ale (5.2%, strong ale)
Saison (6%, spring spiced ale)
Imperial IPA (6.5%)

Anglo Dutch

The Anglo Dutch Brewery, Unit 12, Saville Bridge Mill, Mill Street East, Dewsbury, West Yorkshire WF12 9AF
☎ (01924) 457772
@ anglodutchbrew@yahoo.co.uk
🌐 www.anglo-dutch-brewery.co.uk

◼ Brewery formed in 2000 by Dutchman Paul Klos and Englishman Mike Field. There are plans to bottle condition the entire beer range but initially there is just one offering, which is bottled in house direct from casks.

Raspberry Beer (4.2%)

Appleford
Appleford Brewery Co. Ltd, Unit 14, Highlands Farm, High Road, Brightwell-cum-Sotwell, Wallingford, Oxfordshire OX10 0QX
☎ (01235) 848055
@ sales@applefordbrewery.co.uk
🌐 www.applefordbrewery.co.uk
■ Former Morland Brewery accountant Andrew Torrance opened this farm-based brewery in 2006. Bottling started in autumn 2008, with beers filled straight from the cask without primings or re-seeding of yeast.

Brightwell Gold (4%, golden ale)
Power Station (4.2%, best bitter)

Ascot
Ascot Ales Ltd, Unit 5, Compton Place, Surrey Avenue, Camberley, Surrey GU15 3DX
☎ (01276) 686696
@ info@ascot-ales.co.uk
🌐 www.ascot-ales.co.uk
■ Brewery founded in 2007. The bottled beers are hand filled from the cask and primed with sugar.

Posh Pooch (4.2%, best bitter)
Alligator Ale (4.6%, pale ale)
Anastasia's Exile Stout (5%)
Santa's Reserve (5.2%, spiced winter ale)

Atlantic
Atlantic Brewery, Treisaac Farm, Treisaac, Newquay, Cornwall TR8 4DX
☎ (01637) 880326
@ stuart@atlanticbrewery.com
🌐 www.atlanticbrewery.com
Mail order service
■ This small, farm-based brewery began production in 2005 and so far has concentrated on bottled beers. The beers are all Soil Association-accredited organic and are left unfined (thus acceptable to vegans). They are filled directly on site from the conditioning tank and are allowed three months to mature in bottle before going on sale.

Gold Organic Premium Ale (4.6%, ginger-spiced beer)
Blue Organic Premium Ale (4.8%, porter)
Red Organic Premium Ale (5%, red ale)
Fistral Premium (5.2%, strong ale)
Black Organic Dining Ale (5.5%, blackcurrant porter)

Ballard's
Ballard's Brewery Ltd, The Old Sawmill, Nyewood, Petersfield, Hampshire GU31 5HA
☎ (01730) 821301
@ info@ballardsbrewery.org.uk
🌐 www.ballardsbrewery.org.uk
Mail order service
■ Founded in 1980 at Cumbers Farm, Trotton, Ballard's has been trading at Nyewood in West Sussex (despite the Hampshire postal address) since 1988 and bottle conditioning for a number of years. All the beers are fined in a conditioning tank, sterile filtered and re-seeded with dried yeast before bottling.

Breweries

Best Bitter (4.2%)
Nyewood Gold (5%, golden ale)
Wassail (6%, old ale)
Old Bounder series (names vary: 9.5%, barley wine)

Bank Top
Bank Top Brewery Ltd,
The Pavilion, Ashworth Lane,
Bolton BL1 8RA
- (01204) 595800
- @ dave@banktopbrewery.com
- www.banktopbrewery.com
- ■ Founded in 1995, Bank Top now operates out of a former tennis pavilion in Bolton. The bottle-conditioned beers are filled straight from casks.

Dark Mild (4%)
Flat Cap (4%, golden ale)
Volunteer Bitter (4.2%, golden ale)
Pavilion Pale Ale (4.5%, golden ale)
Port 'o' Call (5%, port-laced mild)
Santa's Claws (5%, Christmas best bitter)
Leprechaun Stout (6%, spring)

Barearts
Barearts Brewery Studio Bar, 108–110 Rochdale Road, Todmorden, Lancashire OL14 7LP
- (01706) 839305
- @ trev@barearts.com
- www.barearts.com
- Mail order service
- ■ A small craft brewery owned by people who run a nude art gallery. The beers are not sold in cask form or sold to pubs, but are available to drink in or take-away from the gallery. There are around 30 bottle-conditioned beers produced at Barearts,

with high strength the common factor. The beers listed below are representative of the range. All beers are chilled and fined in a three-stage process prior to bottling with a small amount of priming sugar added. There are no labels on the bottles, only neck ties, to make recycling easier at the brewery.

Brown Ale (5.2%)
India Pale Ale (7%)
Cascade Beer (7.3%, strong ale)
Oat Stout (8.2%)
Dark Barley Wine (9.6%)
Pale Barley Wine (9.8%)

Bartrams
Bartrams Brewery, Rougham Estate, Ipswich Road, Rougham, Suffolk IP30 9LZ
- (01449) 737655
- @ marc@bartramsbrewery.co.uk
- www.bartramsbrewery.co.uk
- Mail order service
- ■ Marc Bartram set up his own brewery in 1999 and moved into new premises, on an old airfield, in 2004. An earlier Bartrams Brewery operated in Tonbridge, Kent, between 1894 and 1920. It was run by Captain Bill Bartram, whose image Marc wanted to use on his beer labels and pump clips. No photograph was found, however, so Marc grew a beard, became Captain Bill and now features on all his beers. Each beer is filtered and re-seeded with fresh yeast prior to bottling. The bottles are mostly sold in local farmers' markets.

Marld (3.4%, mild)
Rougham Ready (3.6%, bitter)

Premier Bitter (3.7%)
Little Green Man (3.8%, golden ale)
Red Queen (3.9%, bitter)
Cats Whiskers (4%, spiced fruit beer)
Green Man (4%, golden ale)
Grozet (4%, gooseberry beer)
Headway (4%, bitter)
Pierrot (4%, golden ale)
The Bee's Knees (4.2%, honey beer)
Megalithic Ale (4.2%, best bitter)
Catherine Bartram's IPA (4.3%, best bitter)
Mother McCleary's Milk Stout (4.3%)
Jester Quick One (4.4%, best bitter)
Beltane Braces (4.5%, best bitter)
Coal Porter (4.5%)
Stingo (4.5%, honey beer)
Captain Bill Bartram's Best Bitter (4.8%)
The Captain's Cherry Stout (4.8%)
Captain's Stout (4.8%)
Damson Stout (4.8%)
Beer Elsie Bub (4.8%, honey beer)
Darkside (5%, dark wheat beer)
Suffolk 'n' Strong (5%, best bitter)
Xmas Holly Daze (5%, best bitter)
New Year Daze (5.2%, strong ale)
The Venerable Reed (5.6%, nettle ale)
AH 64 Specale (6.4%, IPA)
Comrade Bill Bartrams Egalitarian Anti Imperialist Soviet Stout (6.9%)
September Ale (7%, barley wine)
Mother in Law's Tongue Tied (9.5%, barley wine)
Alder Carr Farm 10th Anniversary (10%, old ale)

Battlefield
See **Tunnel**

Beachy Head
Beachy Head Brewery,
Gilbert Estate Office, Upper Street, East Dean, East Sussex BN20 0BS
☎ (01323) 423906
@ info@beachyhead.org.uk
🌐 www.beachyhead.org.uk
■ Small brewery established behind the Seven Sisters Sheep Centre in 2006, majoring on bottle-conditioned beers, which are matured at the brewery for two months before going on sale.

Parson Darby's Hole (4%, stout)
Original Ale (4.5%, best bitter)
Legless Rambler (5%, best bitter)

Bees
Bees Brewery, c/o Branston's, 1487 Melton Road, Queniborough, Leicester LE7 3FP
☎ (07971) 577526
@ bees-brewery@hotmail.co.uk
■ Brewery opened in early 2008, brewing four regular bottle-conditioned beers, plus a range of short-run beers based on flowers, herbs and spices. All are kräusened and filled directly from the fermentation vessel.

Amber (3.8%, bitter)
Navigator (4.5%, best bitter)
Stripey Jack (4.6%, black bitter)
Wobble (5%, stout)

Beeston
Beeston Brewery Ltd,
Fransham Road Farm, Beeston, Norfolk PE32 2LZ
☎ (01328) 700844

info@beestonbrewery.co.uk
www.beestonbrewery.com

■ Set up in an old farm building, Beeston opened for business in 2007. The beers below are fined and kräusened prior to bottling from tanks in house.

Afternoon Delight (3.7%, golden ale)
Worth the Wait (4.2%, golden ale)
On the Huh (5%, best bitter)
Norfolk Black (6%, stout)

Belvoir

Belvoir Brewery Ltd, Crown Park, Station Road, Old Dalby, Leicestershire LE14 3NQ
☎ (01664) 823455
colin@belvoirbrewery.co.uk
www.belvoirbrewery.co.uk

■ Established in 1995 by Colin Brown, who used to brew with both Shipstone's and Theakston, this brewery sits in the Vale of Belvoir (pronounced 'beaver'). The brewery has been greatly enlarged and now houses a visitor centre. As well as cask ales, three bottle-conditioned beers are now in production, with primary yeast sedimented out and fresh yeast re-seeded prior to bottling, which is handled by Branded Drinks in Gloucestershire. The stout, however, retains primary yeast and is not re-seeded.

Beaver (4.3%, best bitter)
Melton Mowbray Oatmeal Stout (4.3%)
Peacock's Glory (4.7%, best bitter)

Beowulf

The Beowulf Brewing Company, Craft Units 3 & 4, Chasewater Country Park, Pool Road, Brownhills, Staffordshire WS8 7NL
☎ (01543) 454067
beowulfbrewing@yahoo.co.uk
www.beowulfbrewery.co.uk

■ Beowulf was founded in a converted shop in Birmingham in 1997. In 2003 owner Philip Bennett moved the business to new premises at a country park. His range of bottled beers are conditioned in cellar tanks prior to bottling, without being filtered or re-seeded with yeast, but with some sugar added as a priming. Bottles are then kept at the brewery for at least two months before release.

Finn's Hall Porter (5.2%)
Dragon Smoke Stout (5.3%)
Heroes (5.5%, strong ale)
Mercian Shine (5.8%, strong ale)

Best Mates

Best Mates Brewery, Sheephouse Farm, Ardington, Wantage, Oxfordshire OX12 8QB
☎ (01235) 835684
bestmatesbrewery@btconnect.com
www.bestmatesbrewery.co.uk

■ Brewery founded in 2007 by two best mates, close to the racing stables that was once home to three-times Cheltenham Gold Cup winner Best Mate. The bottled beers are filled directly from casks after a minimum of two weeks' maturation at the brewery.

Scutchammers Knob (3.6%, bitter)
Vicar's Daughter (3.7%, golden ale)
Alfie's (4.4%, coriander-spiced ale)
Satan's Sister (4.5%, best bitter)

Betwixt

Betwixt Beer Co. Ltd, The Brewery, 8 Pool Street, Birkenhead, Wirral, Merseyside CH41 3NL
☎ (0151) 647 7688
@ brewer@betwixtbeer.co.uk
🌐 www.betwixtbeer.co.uk
◾ Taking its name from its location, 'betwixt the Mersey and the Dee', this Wirral-based business is run by brewer Mike McGuigan. Bottled beer for sale in local pubs and at farmers' markets includes this one bottle-conditioned offering, which remains unfiltered and is not re-seeded with fresh yeast.

Ice Breaker (6%, spiced winter ale)

Bewdley

Bewdley Brewery Ltd, Unit 7, Bewdley Craft Centre, Lax Lane, Bewdley, Worcestershire DY12 2DZ
☎ (01299) 405148
@ bewdleybrewery@hotmail.co.uk
🌐 www.bewdleybrewery.co.uk
◾ Bewdley opened for business in an old schoolhouse in 2007. The beers are bottled straight from casks that have been primed with sugar. They are then warm conditioned for three weeks before release.

Junior School (3.4%, golden ale)
Old School (3.8%, bitter)

Senior School (4.1%, bitter)
Bah Humbug (4.6%, Christmas old ale)

Black Isle

Black Isle Brewery Ltd, Old Allangrange, Munlochy, Highland IV8 8NZ
☎ (01463) 811871
@ greatbeers@blackislebrewery. com
🌐 www.blackislebrewery.com
Mail order service
◾ Converted farm buildings in the Highlands of Scotland provide a home for Black Isle Brewery, which was set up 1998. The Black Isle itself is a peninsula across the Moray Firth from Inverness, with an ancient history of barley production and a spectacular coastline. The following Soil Association-accredited organic beers are also sanctioned by the Vegetarian Society. The Porter and the Wheat Beer are kräusened with one- or two-day old fermenting wort in a conditioning tank prior to bottling, but the other beers listed are filtered, re-seeded with fresh yeast and primed with sucrose.

Porter (4.6%)
Wheat Beer (5%)
Goldeneye Pale Ale (5.6%, IPA)
Scotch Ale (6.4%, strong ale)
Export Oatmeal Stout (7.2%)

Blackawton

Blackawton Brewery, Unit 7, Peninsula Park, Moorlands Trading Estate, Saltash, Cornwall PL12 6LX
☎ (01752) 848777

Breweries

@ enquiries@blackawtonbrewery.
eclipse.co.uk

🌐 www.blackawtonbrewery.com

◼ Blackawton Brewery was set up
in 1977, one of the first of the
new wave of microbreweries
founded after the early
successes of CAMRA. Until 2001
it was the longest established
brewery in Devon, but then it
was sold and the new owners
moved it across the River Tamar
to Cornwall. The brewery moved
yet again in 2003, but this time
just around the corner to larger
premises. In March 2009, the
company changed hands again.
The bottle-conditioned beers
are brewed at Blackawton but
bottled by other brewers.

Winter Fuel (5%, spiced winter
ale)
Head Strong (5.2%, strong ale)

Blackfriars

Blackfriars Brewery, The
Courtyard, Main Cross Road, Great
Yarmouth, Norfolk NR30 3NZ

☎ (01493) 850578

@ pints@blackfriars-brewery.co.uk

🌐 www.blackfriars-brewery.co.uk

Mail order service

◼ Brewery founded by former
teacher and schools inspector
Bill Russell in 2004. The beers
are fined (not with isinglass, so
they are vegetarian friendly)
before bottling, then warm
conditioned for two weeks
before release. They are
available in both 500-ml and
2-litre bottles.

Mild (3.4%)
Yarmouth Bitter (3.8%)

Charter Ale (4%, orange fruit
beer)
Harbour Lights (4%, bitter)
Mitre Gold (4%, golden ale)
Time and Tide (4%, stout)
Volunteer (4%, orange fruit beer)
Spring Tide (4.2%, best bitter)
Whyte Angel (4.5%, wheat beer)
St George's Honey Ale (4.7%,
honey beer)
Maritime (5%, best bitter)
Old Habit (5.6%, old ale)
Audit Ale (8%, barley wine)

Blue Anchor

Blue Anchor Inn Brewery,
50 Coinagehall Street, Helston,
Cornwall TR13 8EL

☎ (01326) 562821

@ theblueanchor@btconnect.com

🌐 www.spingoales.com

◼ Famous as one of the handful
of home-brew houses still in
operation when CAMRA took
up the challenge of preserving
British brewing heritage in
1971, The Blue Anchor is one
of the UK's classic pubs. The
thatched building began life as a
monks' resting place in the 15th
century. Its brewery – noted
for its 'Spingo' ales – has been
refurbished in recent years.
Bottling takes place in house.

Spingo Middle (5%, best bitter)
Spingo Special (6.6%, strong ale)
**Christmas Special/Easter
Special/Extra Special** (7.8%,
barley wine)

Blue Bear

Blue Bear Brewery Ltd, Unit
1, Open Barn Farm, Kempsey,
Worcester WR5 3LW

☎ (01905) 828258

@ info@bluebearbrewery.co.uk
🌐 www.bluebearbrewery.co.uk
■ Family-run brewery set up in 2005 in an old potato barn. The beers are bottled in house from conditioning tanks, having been allowed to settle for two weeks and then fined.

Roar Spirit (4.2%, best bitter)
White Boar (4.5%, golden ale)

Blythe

Blythe Brewery, Blythe House Farm, Lichfield Road, Hamstall Ridware, Staffordshire WS15 3QQ
☎ (07773) 747724
@ info@blythebrewery.plus.com
🌐 www.blythebrewery.co.uk
■ After working for 27 years in the fluorochemical industry, Robert Greenway began brewing in 2003, using two-and-a-half-barrel equipment in a converted barn on a Staffordshire farm. His vegan-friendly bottled beers – conditioned first in cask, racked bright then kräusened using the same yeast as used in the primary fermentation – are sold at local farmers' markets.

Bitter (4%, golden ale)
Ridware Pale (4.3%, golden ale)
Chase Bitter (4.4%, best bitter)
Staffie (4.4%, golden ale)
Palmer's Poison (4.5%, best bitter)
Old Horny (4.6%, best bitter)
Johnson's (5.2%, porter)

Boggart

Boggart Hole Clough Brewery, Unit 13, Brookside Works, Clough Road, Moston, Manchester M9 4FP
☎ (0161) 277 9666
@ boggartoffice@btconnect.com
🌐 www.boggart-brewery.co.uk
■ Brewery founded in 2001 next to Boggart Hole Clough Park. The beers below are bottled directly from casks.

Brew (4.4%, red ale)
IPA (4.7%, best bitter)
Rum Porter (4.7%, rum-laced porter)
Sundial (4.8%, golden ale)
Waterloo Sunset (5.1%, porter)

Bowman

Bowman Ales Ltd, Wallops Wood, Sheardley Lane, Droxford, Hampshire SO32 3QY
☎ (01489) 878110
@ info@bowman-ales.com
🌐 www.bowman-ales.com
Mail order service
■ Brewery established in converted farm buildings in 2006 by two former brewers from the Cheriton Brewhouse. The beers below are bottled for them at Oakleaf Brewery, where yeast is allowed to drop out and fresh primary fermentation yeast is added before filling.

Quiver Bitter (4.5%, golden ale)
Nutz (5%, chestnut beer)

Bradfield

Bradfield Brewery, Watt House Farm, High Bradfield, Sheffield, South Yorkshire S6 6LG
☎ (0114) 285 1118
@ info@bradfieldbrewery.com
🌐 www.bradfieldbrewery.com
■ Bradfield Brewery was set up in 2005 on a working dairy farm in the Peak District, and uses

Breweries

the farm's own bore-hole water supply. The beers are bottled direct from conditioning tanks, but filtered versions also exist.

Farmers Stout (4.5%)
Farmers Pale Ale (5%)
Farmers Sixer (6%, strong ale)

Brakspear
The Brakspear Brewing Co., Eagle Maltings, The Crofts, Witney, Oxfordshire OX28 4DP
☎ (01993) 890800
@ info@brakspear-beers.co.uk
🌐 www.wychwood.co.uk
Mail order service

■ Following the closure of Brakspear's brewery in Henley-on-Thames, brewing of the Brakspear brands finally settled at Wychwood Brewery in Witney when a new brewhouse was constructed to house brewing vessels from the old Henley site. The whole enterprise was bought by Marston's in 2008, but two bottle-conditioned beers continue in the portfolio. Both are brewed at Witney but are bottled by Fuller's.

Oxford Gold (4.6%, golden ale)
Triple (7.2%, strong ale)

Brandon
The Brandon Brewery, 76 High Street, Brandon, Suffolk IP27 0AU
☎ (01842) 878496
@ enquiries@brandonbrewery. co.uk
🌐 www.brandonbrewery.co.uk
■ This Suffolk market town brewery opened in 2005. The beers are all bottled in house.

Beer in casks drops bright and is then kräusened before filling.

Breckland Gold (3.8%, golden ale)
Old Rodney (4%, bitter)
Saxon Gold (4%, golden ale)
Molly's Secret (4.1%, honey beer)
Norfolk Poacher (4.1%, bitter)
Royal Ginger (4.1%, ginger-spiced beer)
Gun Flint (4.2%, best bitter)
Wee Drop of Mischief (4.2%, best bitter)
Waxie's Dargle (4.3%, best bitter)
Rusty Bucket (4.4%, best bitter)
Hum Dinger (4.5%, best bitter)
Slippery Jack (4.5%, stout)
Grumpy Bastard (5%, orange fruit beer)
Napper Tandy (5%, best bitter)

Branscombe Vale
Branscombe Vale Brewery, Branscombe, Devon EX12 3DP
☎ (01297) 680511
@ branscombebrewery@yahoo. co.uk
■ It was in 1992 that Branscombe Vale set up home in an old farm that is now owned by the National Trust. In 2002, it made the move into regular bottle-conditioned beer production, with beer brewed at Branscombe and bottled by neighbour O'Hanlon's, without filtration or re-seeding of yeast.

Draymans Best Bitter (4.2%)

Breconshire
The Breconshire Brewery Ltd, Ffrwdgrech Industrial Estate, Brecon, Powys LD3 8LA
☎ (01874) 623731

@ sales@breconshirebrewery.com
🌐 www.breconshirebrewery.com
Mail order service
■ Breconshire was opened in 2002 to expand the business of CH Marlow, a beer wholesaler which has supplied pubs in South, Mid and West Wales for more than 30 years. The bottled beers are now bottled in house. They are sterile filtered and re-seeded with fresh yeast.

Golden Valley (4.2%, golden ale)
Cribyn (4.5%, golden ale)
Night Beacon (4.5%, stout)
Red Dragon (4.7%, red ale)
Ramblers Ruin (5%, old ale)
Winter Beacon (5.3%, winter ale)

Brown Cow
Brown Cow Brewery, Brown Cow Road, Barlow, Selby, North Yorkshire YO8 8EH
☎ (01757) 618947
@ susansimpson@ browncowbrewery.co.uk
🌐 www.browncowbrewery.co.uk
■ Brewery founded in 1997 and gradually expanded. The two beers below are bottled for Brown Cow by Hambleton Ales.

Captain Oates (4.5%, mild)
Celebration Ale (5.1%, strong ale)

Buckle Street
Buckle Street Brewery, Unit 11, Two Shires Industrial Estate, Buckle Street, Honeybourne, Worcestershire WR11 7QF
☎ (01386) 831173
@ info@bucklestreetbrewery.co.uk
■ Brewery founded at the end of 2008 on a former air force base

and named after a local Roman road. The beers are bottled in house with primings, straight from casks.

No.1 (4% golden ale)
Dog in the Fog (4.5%, best bitter)

Buffy's
Buffy's Brewery Ltd, Rectory Road, Tivetshall St Mary, Norwich, Norfolk NR15 2DD
☎ (01379) 676523
@ buffysbrewery@gmail.com
🌐 www.buffys.co.uk
Mail order service
■ Brewery founded in 1993 at Norfolk's 15th-century Mardle Hall. It has expanded considerably since those early days. All beer is brewed and bottled on site, filled from the cask.

Polly's Folly (4.3%, golden ale)
Norwegian Blue (4.9%, best bitter)
Buffy's Ale (5.5%, old ale)
9X (9%, barley wine)

Burton Bridge
Burton Bridge Brewery, 24 Bridge Street, Burton upon Trent, Staffordshire DE14 1SY
☎ (01283) 510573
@ bbb@burtonbridgebrewery. fsnet.co.uk
🌐 www.burtonbridgebrewery. co.uk
■ Burton Bridge Brewery, a microbrewery in the pale ale capital, was established in 1982 by former Allied Breweries employees Bruce Wilkinson and Geoff Mumford. They began bottling in the same year and

Breweries

were one of the pioneers of the bottle-conditioned beer revolution. The beers are filled from casks and are not re-seeded with yeast or primed.

Burton Porter (4.5%)
Bramble Stout (5%, blackberry stout)
Empire Pale Ale (7.5%, IPA)
Tickle Brain (8%, old ale)

Butts

Butts Brewery Ltd, Northfield Farm, Great Shefford, Hungerford, Berkshire RG17 7BY

☎ (01488) 648133
@ enquiries@buttsbrewery.com
🌐 www.buttsbrewery.com
◼ Butts Brewery was established in 1994 in converted farm buildings by Chris Butt. All his beers are Soil Association-accredited organic. Two bottled beers, Barbus Barbus and Blackguard, were introduced in 1999, and three more have followed since. Each beer is primed, filtered and then re-seeded with Butts's own yeast prior to bottling on site. The beers are then conditioned in the bottle for at least a month before they are released.

Blackguard (4.5%, porter)
Barbus Barbus (4.6%, best bitter)
Golden Brown (5%, brown ale)
Le Butts (5%, pale lager)
Coper (6%, strong ale)

Cambridge Moonshine
Moonshine Brewery, Hill Farm, Shelford Road, Fulbourn, Cambridge CB21 5EQ

☎ (01223) 514366
@ mark@moonshinebrewery.co.uk
🌐 www.moonshinebrewery.co.uk
◼ Cambridge Moonshine was founded in 2004 but moved in autumn 2008 to new, larger premises just outside the city of Cambridge. The beers are kräusened for bottling, filled in house from casks and warm conditioned before release.

Sparkling Moon (3.6%, golden ale)
Harvest Moon Mild (3.9%)
Barton Bitter (4%)
CB1 (4.2%, best bitter)
Red Watch (4.2%, summer blueberry beer)
Pigs Ear Porter (4.5%)
Minion of the Moon (4.6%, best bitter)
Black Hole Stout (5%)
Chocolate Orange Stout (6.7%)

Cannon Royall
Cannon Royall Brewery Ltd, Rear Fruiterers Arms, Uphampton Lane, Ombersley, Worcestershire WR9 0JW

☎ (01905) 621161
@ info@cannonroyall.co.uk
🌐 www.cannonroyall.co.uk
◼ Brewery founded in 1993 in a converted cider house behind the Fruiterers Arms pub in Ombersley. The following beers are all matured before and after filling at the brewery and are hand-bottled from casks with the addition of sugar syrup for priming.

Fruiterers Mild (3.7%)
King's Shilling (3.8%, golden ale)
Arrowhead Bitter (3.9%)

Muzzle Loader (4.2%, best bitter)
Arrowhead Extra (4.3%, best
bitter)

Castle

Castle Brewery, Unit 9a-7,
Restormel Industrial Estate,
Lostwithiel, Cornwall PL22 0HG
- (01726) 871133
- @ castlebrewery@aol.com
- ■ Brewery founded in 2007 by
  Andy White, previously brewer
  at Keltek Brewery when it was
  based in Lostwithlel. Andy had
  developed some Castle Brewery
  brands during his time there.
  He bottles the beers, which are
  vegetarian friendly, himself on
  site.

Moat Mild (4.4%)
Battle Stout (4.6%)
Once a Knight (5%, best bitter)
Lostwithiale (7%, barley wine)
Hung Drawn and Slaughtered
(10%, barley wine)

Castle Rock
Castle Rock Brewery,
Queensbridge Road, Nottingham,
Nottinghamshire NG2 1NB
- (0115) 985 1615
- @ admin@castlerockbrewery.
  co.uk
- ⊕ www.castlerockbrewery.co.uk
- ■ Founded as Bramcote Brewery
  in 1996, Castle Rock moved
  to new premises next to
  Nottingham's Vat & Fiddle pub
  in 1998 (when the new name
  was adopted), and was then
  taken over by the Tynemill pub
  company in 2001. Considerable
  expansion has since taken
  place. For the bottle, the beer
  is fined, re-seeded with special

bottling yeast and primed with
sugars. Bottling takes place at
an unnamed outside contractor.

Elsie Mo (4.7%, golden ale)

Cheddar
Cheddar Ales, Winchester
Farm, Draycott Road, Cheddar,
Somerset BS27 3RP
- (01934) 744193
- @ brewery@cheddarales.co.uk
- ⊕ www.cheddarales.co.uk
- Mail order service
- ■ Brewery founded on the fringe
  of the village of Cheddar in 2006
  by former Butcombe brewer
  Jem Ham. The beers are bottled
  on site, having been filtered and
  re-seeded with the same yeast
  used for primary fermentation
  and primed with sugar. They are
  matured at the brewery for at
  least a month before release.

Gorge Best (4.2%, best bitter)
Potholer (4.5%, golden ale)
Totty Pot (4.7%, porter)
Goat's Leap (5.7%, IPA)

Cherwell Valley
Cherwell Valley Brewery Ltd,
Unit 2, St David's Court,
Top Station Road, Brackley,
Northamptonshire NN13 7UG
- (01280) 706888
- ⊕ www.cherwellvalley.co.uk
- Mail order service
- ■ Small brewery that opened in
  January 2008. The beers are
  bottled from casks, usually
  without priming or kräusening.

Kineton Fight (3.6%, bitter)
Duke of Cumberland's Head
(4%, bitter)

Cropredy Bridge 1644 (4.2%, best bitter)
Lark Rise (4%, summer golden ale)
Old Noll (4.9%, winter old ale)

Chiltern
The Chiltern Brewery, Nash Lee Road, Terrick, Aylesbury, Buckinghamshire HP17 0TQ
📞 (01296) 613647
@ info@chilternbrewery.co.uk
🌐 www.chilternbrewery.co.uk
Mail order service
■ Chiltern Brewery was set up in 1980 on a small farm and is the oldest brewery in the Chilterns. The Jenkinson family who run it specialize in beer-related foods (cheeses, sausages, mustards, etc.), as well as traditional ales. On site is a well-stocked visitors' centre-cum-shop. While the winter beer, Glad Tidings, is both brewed and bottled on site, bottling for the other two beers is handled by an outside party.

Glad Tidings (4.6%, spiced winter stout)
The Lord Lieutenant's Porter (6%)
Bodgers Barley Wine (8.5%)

Church End
Church End Brewery, Ridge Lane, Nuneaton, Warwickshire CV10 0RD
📞 (01827) 713080
🌐 www.churchendbrewery.co.uk
■ Church End Brewery was founded in 1994, in an old coffin workshop next to The Griffin Inn in Shustoke, Warwickshire. In 2001 it moved to new premises,

in Ridge Lane, near Atherstone. Bottling now takes place at Bicester Brewery in Oxfordshire, where the beer is filtered and re-seeded with fresh yeast.

Nuns Ale (4.5%, golden ale)
Rugby Ale (5%, best bitter)
Arthur's Wit (6%, strong ale)

Clearwater
Clearwater Brewery, 2–4 Devon Units, Hatchmoor Industrial Estate, Devon EX38 7HP
📞 (01805) 625242
@ brian@clearwaterbrewery.co.uk
■ Devon brewery, founded in 1999 and offering close links to the English Civil War in its beer names. The bottle-conditioned beers are now brewed and bottled on site, filled from the cask with no fresh yeast or sugar primings added.

Cavalier (4%, bitter)
1646 (5.2%, strong ale)
Oliver's Nectar (5.2%, strong ale)

Coastal
Coastal Brewery, Unit 9b, Cardrew Industrial Estate, Redruth, Cornwall TR15 1SS
📞 (07875) 405407
@ coastalbrewery@tiscali.co.uk
🌐 www.coastalbrewery.co.uk
■ Coastal Brewery was set up by former publican Alan Hinde in 2006, after moving to Cornwall from Cheshire. His range of bottle-conditioned beers was launched in 2009 and is likely to expand. Bottles are filled from conditioning tanks in which beer has been chilled and allowed to drop clear (although some beers

are aged in casks instead and bottled from these). No finings or extra yeasts are used.

Golden Sands (6%, strong ale)
St Piran's Porter (6%)
Erosion (8%, barley wine)

Cobra
Cobra Beer, Alexander House, 14–16 Peterborough Road, London SW6 3BN
☎ (020) 7731 6200
@ cobrabeer@cobrabeer.com
🌐 www.cobrabeer.com
■ Cobra as a curry lager brand seems to have been around for decades. The truth is it was only set up in 1989 when Karan (now Lord) Bilimoria, son of an Indian Army general, spotted a gap in the market for what he described as a less bloating beer for drinking with curry. With the help of a Czech brewer, Karan devised a beer that was initially brewed for him in India. Later, he switched production to Charles Wells in Bedford. The original Cobra lager is still brewed there, as well as in India again. In 2005, Cobra introduced the unusual, bottle-conditioned King Cobra, which is now produced in Belgium.

King Cobra (8%, pale lager)

College Green
See **Hilden**

Combe Martin
Combe Martin Brewery,
4 Springfield Terrace, High Street, Combe Martin, Devon EX34 0EE
☎ (01271) 883507

■ This tiny brewery produces bottled beer in small quantities for the North Devon tourist trade. The therefore largely seasonal beers are matured in casks and then bottled with a small amount of priming sugar.

Past-Times (3.9%, bitter)
Hangman's (4.5%, best bitter)
Shamwick Ale (6.2%, old ale)

Concrete Cow
Concrete Cow Brewery,
Unit 59, Alston Drive,
Milton Keynes MK13 9HB
☎ (01908) 316794
🌐 www.concretecowbrewery.co.uk
■ This small brewery opened in 2007 and now produces a range of bottled beers as well as cask ales. Bottles are filled straight from fermenting vessels, with no fining, filtration, priming or re-seeding of yeast, and are matured at the brewery for up to six weeks before release.

Ironbridge Brew (3.7%, bitter)
Midsummer Ale (3.8%, golden ale)
Cock n Bull Story (4.1%, bitter)
Fenny Popper (4.1%, bitter)
Watling Gold (4.5%, golden ale)
Old Bloomer (4.7%, best bitter)
Winter Ale (5%)

Coniston
Coniston Brewing Co. Ltd,
Coppermines Road, Coniston, Cumbria LA21 8HL
☎ (01539 4) 41133
@ beer@conistonbrewery.com
🌐 www.conistonbrewery.com
Mail order service

This little brewery was set up in 1994 behind Coniston's Black Bull pub and achieved a minor miracle in turning out CAMRA's Champion Beer of Britain in 1998 with Bluebird Bitter. With orders flooding in, and capacity way surpassed by demand, Coniston contracted out the brewing of a bottled version to Brakspear. Since the demise of the Henley brewery, the contract to brew Coniston beers for the bottle has stayed with former Brakspear head brewer Peter Scholey. He now produces the beers himself, using equipment at Hepworth & Co. in Horsham. Coniston also has a small range of other bottled beers, bottled without yeast close to the brewery.

Bluebird Bitter (4.2%, best bitter)
Bluebird XB (4.4%, best bitter)
Old Man Ale (4.8%, best bitter)

Conwy
Conwy Brewery Ltd, Unit 3, Parc Caer Seion, Conwy LL32 8FA
☎ (01492) 585287
@ enquiries@conwybrewery.co.uk
🌐 www.conwybrewery.co.uk
■ Small brewery set up in autumn 2003 after two years of planning. The beers below – which are sold under both Welsh and English names – are bottled in house after filtration and re-seeding with new yeast, and the addition of a small amount of sugar primings.

Mulberry Dark (3.8%, mild)
Balchder Cymru/Welsh Pride (4%, golden ale)

Cwrw Gwledd/Celebration Ale (4.2%, best bitter)
Cwrw Mêl/Honey Fayre (4.5%, honey beer)
Marks & Spencer Welsh Honey Bitter (4.5%, honey beer)
Telford Porter (5.6%)

Corvedale
Corvedale Brewery, The Sun Inn, Corfton, Craven Arms, Shropshire SY7 9DF
☎ (01584) 861239
@ normanspride@aol.com
🌐 www.corvedalebrewery.co.uk
■ Publican Norman Pearce is the brewer in the tiny brewery housed behind The Sun Inn in rural Shropshire. Norman bottles the beers himself, filling glassware with unfiltered, unfined beer from a cask. The beers are therefore vegetarian friendly.

Katie's Pride (4.3%, mild)
Norman's Pride (4.3%, best bitter)
Farmer Rays Ale (4.5%, best bitter)
Green Hop (4.5%, green hop beer)
Dark & Delicious (4.6%, old ale)

Cotleigh
Cotleigh Brewery Ltd, Ford Road, Wiveliscombe, Somerset TA4 2RE
☎ (01984) 624086
@ sales@cotleighbrewery.com
🌐 www.cotleighbrewery.co.uk
Mail order service
■ Cotleigh was founded way back in 1979 and has moved home a number of times as trade has developed. New owners took over in 2003 and two regular

bottled real ales have been introduced. These are brewed at Cotleigh and bottled by O'Hanlon's in Devon, keeping the same yeast used in the primary fermentation.

Buzzard (4.8%, best bitter)
Peregrine Porter (5%)

Cotswold
Cotswold Brewing Co. Ltd, Foxholes Lane, Foscot, Oxfordshire OX7 6RL
- (01608) 659631
- @ lager@cotswoldbrewing company.com
- www.cotswoldbrewing company.com
- Brewery established in 2005 by former Archers head brewer Richard Keene and his wife, Emma. It specializes in quality lagers but also offers the following beer in bottle-conditioned form. This is brewed at Cotswold and packaged at Bath Ales, without filtration or the re-seeding of yeast.

Wheat (4.2%)

Country Life
Country Life Brewery, The Big Sheep, Abbotsham, Bideford, Devon EX39 5AP
- (01237) 420808
- @ info@countrylifebrewery.com
- www.countrylifebrewery.com
- This small brewery was acquired from Lundy Island in 1999 and set up at the Pig on the Hill pub, near Westward Ho! The plant was then moved in 2002 to The Big Sheep farm attraction, where the beers are offered

in daily tastings to visitors and brewery tours are available in summer. The beers are transferred to a bottling tank from the fermenter, allowed to settle and then bottled in house. All are said to be acceptable to vegetarians. Monthly special cask brews may also find their way into bottles from time to time.

Old Appledore (3.7%, bitter)
Baa Tenders Best (4.2%, best bitter)
Pot Wallop (4.4%, golden ale)
Golden Pig (4.7%, golden ale)
Black Boar (5%, porter)
Country Bumpkin (6%, strong ale)
Devonshire 10'der' (10%, barley wine)

Cox & Holbrook
Cox & Holbrook, Manor Farm, Brettenham Road, Buxhall, Suffolk IP14 3DY
- (01449) 736323
- Accountant David Cox set up this brewery in Great Finborough in 1997 but moved to farm premises in 2003. The beers below have been produced on a short-run basis in recent times but new bottling equipment is due to come on stream and this will increase availability and allow the range to be expanded. The beers are primed with a little cane sugar and filled from conditioning tanks.

Albion (4.2%, golden ale)
Stormwatch (5%, best bitter)
Stowmarket Porter (5%)

Cropton

Cropton Brewery & The New Inn, Cropton, Near Pickering, North Yorkshire YO18 8HH
☎ (01751) 417330
@ info@croptonbrewery.com
🌐 www.croptonbrewery.com
Mail order service

■ Cropton Brewery was set up in 1984 in the cellar of the New Inn, initially just to supply that pub. By 1994 it had outgrown the cellar and a purpose-built brewery was installed behind the pub. The bottled beers are Vegetarian Society accredited. They are matured in conditioning tanks, filtered and then seeded with fresh yeast and priming sugar ready for filling.

Endeavour (3.6%, bitter)
King Billy Bitter (3.6%)
Two Pints Bitter (4%)
Honey Gold (4.2%, honey beer)
Scoresby Stout (4.2%)
Balmy Mild (4.4%)
Yorkshire Warrior (4.4%, best bitter)
Rudolph's Revenge (4.6%, Christmas ale)
Yorkshire Moors/Marks & Spencer Yorkshire Bitter (4.6%, best bitter)
Blackout (5%, porter)
Monkman's Slaughter (6%, strong ale)
Old Goat Strong Bitter (8%, barley wine)

Crown

Crown Brewery, Hillsborough Hotel, 54–58 Langsett Road, Sheffield, South Yorkshire S6 2UB
☎ (0114) 232 2100

■ Hotel cellar brewery, established in 2001. The following beers were added to the range in 2007 and are bottled in house from tanks, without primings or the re-seeding of yeast.

Wheetie-Bits (4%, wheat beer)
Wheat Stout (6.6%)
Ring of Fire (10.3%, chili beer)

Dare

Dare Brewery Ltd, Falcon Inn, 1 Incline Row, Godreaman, Aberdare, Rhondda Cynon Taff CF44 6LU
☎ (07812) 366369
@ info@darebrewery.co.uk
🌐 www.darebrewery.co.uk
■ Brewery opened in a refurbished barn at The Falcon Inn (a separate business) in Aberdare. The beers below are bottled from matured casks and primed with unrefined sugar.

Valley Dark (4%, mild)
Dat Dare (4.1%, bitter)
Elwyn Samuel's Beer (4.8%, best bitter)
Falcon Flyer (5.2%, strong ale)
Old Daredevil (7.9%, old ale)

Dark Star

Dark Star Brewing Company Ltd, Moonhill Farm, Burgess Hill Road, Ansty, Haywards Heath, West Sussex RH17 5AH
☎ (01444) 412311
@ info@darkstarbrewing.co.uk
🌐 www.darkstarbrewing.co.uk
■ Originally Brighton based, Dark Star now resides in the Sussex countryside. Just the one bottle-conditioned beer is currently available, bottled for

Dark Star by Branded Drinks in Gloucestershire.

Imperial Stout (10.5%)

Dartmoor
Dartmoor Brewery Ltd,
The Brewery, Station Road,
Princetown, Devon PL20 6QX
☎ (01822) 890789
@ ale@dartmoorbrewery.co.uk
🖰 www.dartmoorbrewery.co.uk
■ Princetown Brewery was established in 1994 by former Gibbs Mew and Hop Back brewer Simon Loveless. The brewery moved to a new site, a few hundred yards from its original base, in 2004, and the name was changed to Dartmoor Brewery in 2008. The beers for bottling are fined and racked bright before being re-seeded with fresh primary fermentation yeast.

IPA (4%, golden ale)
Jail Ale (4.8%, golden ale)

Dartmouth
Dartmouth Brewery,
63 East Street, Newton Abbot,
Devon TQ12 2JP
☎ (07969) 860184
@ joelane11@hotmail.com
■ Small brewery established in autumn 2007. The beers below are bottled straight from the fermentation vessel and conditioned in bottle before going on sale.

Ranger (4.2%, best bitter)
Golden Showers (4.5%, golden ale)
Big 5 (5%, best bitter)

Summer Solstice Special (8%, barley wine)

Darwin
Darwin Brewery Ltd,
63 Back Tatham Street,
Sunderland, Tyne & Wear SR1 3SD
☎ (0191) 514 4746
@ info@darwinbrewery.com
🖰 www.darwinbrewery.com
■ Darwin Brewery was founded in 1994 as a research facility for students at the University of Sunderland's Brewlab. In 1997, its directors took over the nearby Hodge's Brewery and the whole business was relocated to a new site in Sunderland in 2002. One of the brewery's specialities is the re-creation of historic beer styles. The bottled beers are filled directly from conditioning tank and are kräusened, if that is required to ensure a good secondary fermentation.

Imperial Ale (7.2%, old ale)
Extinction Ale (8.3%, old ale)

Deeside
Deeside Brewery, Deeside Activity Park, Dess, Aboyne, Aberdeenshire AB34 5BD
☎ (07966) 033451
@ info@deesidebrewery.co.uk
🖰 www.deesidebrewery.co.uk
Mail order service
■ Deeside is the new name for Hillside Brewery, following its move to the Deeside Activity Park in 2008. The business was founded by former archaeologist Rob James in 2006. The beer is allowed a couple of weeks' conditioning after fermentation

Breweries

281

and then bottled. It is then matured in the bottle for a month before release.

Brude (3.5%, golden ale)
Lulach (4%, golden ale)
Macbeth (4.3%, golden ale)

Dorset Piddle
Dorset Piddle Brewery, Unit 7, Enterprise Park, Piddlehinton, Dorchester DT2 7UA
☎ (01305) 849336
🌐 www.dorsetpiddlebrewery. co.uk
■ Brewery opened by two publicans in 2007, with bottling commencing a year later. The beers are primed with sugar and filled from casks.

Jimmy Riddle (3.9%, bitter)
Piddle (4.3%, best bitter)
Silent Slasher (5.3%, strong ale)

Dow Bridge
Dow Bridge Brewery, 2–3 Rugby Road, Catthorpe, Leicestershire LE17 6DA
☎ (01788) 869121
@ dowbridge.brewery@virgin.net
🌐 www.dowbridgebrewery.co.uk
■ Dow Bridge Brewery was founded in 2002 by Russell Webb and has already extended its capacity. Bottled beers were added in 2006. These are filled from conditioning tanks, without primings, and matured after bottling.

Acris (4%, bitter)
Centurion (4.3%, best bitter)
Ratae'd (4.5%, best bitter)
Fosse (5%, best bitter)
Conquest (5.4%, strong ale)

Downton
The Downton Brewery Co., Unit 11, Batten Road, Downton Industrial Estate, Downton, Wiltshire SP5 3HU
☎ (01725) 513313
@ martins@downtonbrewery.com
🌐 www.downtonbrewery.com
■ Downton Brewery was founded in 2003, with equipment leased from near-neighbour Hop Back Brewery. A close relationship continues between the two breweries, with Hop Back bottling Downton beers and also offering Downton beers as part of its mail order service. The beers are chilled, kräusened (or primed with honey in the case of Honey Blonde), filtered and then re-seeded with new yeast ready for bottling.

Honey Blonde (4.3%, honey beer)
Chimera Dark Delight (6%, old ale)
Chimera India Pale Ale (7%)

Dunham Massey
Dunham Massey Brewing Company, 100 Oldfield Lane, Dunham Massey, Altrincham, Trafford WA14 4PE
☎ (0161) 929 0663
@ info@dunhammasseybrewing. co.uk
🌐 www.dunhammasseybrewing. co.uk
■ Former Tetley Walker brewer John Costello founded this brewery in a restored barn on National Trust land in 2007. The beers are bottled on site.

Little Bollington Bitter (3.7%)
Chocolate Cherry Mild (3.8%)

Dunham Dark (3.8%, mild)
Dunham Light (3.8%, mild)
Big Tree Bitter (3.9%, golden ale)
Dunham Milk Stout (4%)
Treacle Treat (4.1%, autumn treacle bitter)
Dunham Stout (4.2%)
Stamford Bitter (4.2%, golden ale)
Deer Beer (4.5%, best bitter)
Cheshire IPA (4.7%, best bitter)
Dunham Porter (5%)
Winter Warmer (6.6%, winter ale)

Durham

The Durham Brewery, Unit 5a, Bowburn North Industrial Estate, Bowburn, Co. Durham DH6 5PF
☎ (0191) 377 1991
@ gibbs@durham-brewery.co.uk
🌐 www.durham-brewery.co.uk
Mail order service

■ Durham Brewery was set up by former music teachers Steve and Christine Gibbs in 1994 and the brewery now produces a wide range of cask beers and several highly-regarded bottle-conditioned beers, including a past CAMRA Champion Bottle-conditioned Beer (Evensong). All are brewed and bottled on site, with beers passing from fermenters into conditioning tanks, where gravity is allowed to drop out most of the yeast. This ensures that all the bottled beers are acceptable to vegetarians and vegans. There is no filtration and primings are added only if deemed necessary. Steve is no advocate of filtering beer for bottling and re-pitching with new yeast. 'Our only application of modern methods is in scrupulous hygiene and cleanliness,' declares the brewery's literature.

Cloister (4.5%, golden ale)
Evensong (5%, old ale)
St Cuthbert (6.5%, IPA)
Benedictus (8.4%, barley wine)
Bede's Chalice (9%, barley wine)
Temptation (10%, imperial stout)

Earl Soham

Earl Soham Brewery, The Street, Earl Soham, Woodbridge, Suffolk IP13 7RT
☎ (01728) 684097
@ info@earlsohambrewery.co.uk
🌐 www.earlsohambrewery.co.uk
■ Founded behind The Victoria pub in the village of Earl Soham in 1984, this brewery moved along the road to larger premises in a converted garage in 2001. Next door stands Eat Anglia, a well-stocked post-office/delicatessen that sells Earl Soham's beers. The beers are bottled according to demand and are hand-filled direct from casks.

Gannet Mild (3.3%)
Victoria Bitter (3.6%)
Sir Roger's Porter (4%)
Albert Ale (4.4%, best bitter)
Brandeston Gold (4.5%, golden ale)

Elmtree

Elmtree Beers, Snetterton Brewery, Oakwood Industrial Estate, Harling Road, Snetterton, Norfolk NR16 2JU
☎ (01953) 887065
@ sales@elmtreebeers.co.uk
🌐 www.elmtreebeers.co.uk
Mail order service

Small brewery founded in 2007 close to the Snetterton motor racing circuit. The bottled beers are matured for a week before bottling (after re-seeding with fresh primary fermentation yeast) and then condition for eight weeks before being released. They are all vegan friendly.

Bitter (4.2%, best bitter)
Dark Horse Stout (5%)
Golden Pale Ale (5%, golden ale)
Nightlight Mild (5.7%)

Elveden

Elveden Ales, by Walled Garden, Elveden Courtyard, Elveden, Thetford, Norfolk IP24 3TQ
☎ (01842) 878922

■ Small brewery opened in 2004 by Iceni Brewery's Brendan Moore and his daughter, Frances. It is housed on the Elveden estate, the home of the Guinness family, who encourage the production and sale of local crafts and food and drink on the site. The Elveden Ale and Stout below are packaged in stoneware bottles as well as conventional glass.

Stout (5%)
Elveden Ale (5.2%)
Men of Suffolk (6.1%, strong ale)
Arctic Ale (10%, barley wine)

English Wines

English Wines Group, Chapel Down Winery, Tenterden Vineyard, Small Hythe, Tenterden, Kent TN30 7NG
☎ (01580) 763033

@ sales@englishwinesgroup.com
🌐 www.englishwinesgroup.com
Mail order service

■ This Kent vineyard, whose wines are sold under the Chapel Down label, entered the world of beer in late 2005, joining forces with Hepworth & Co. in Horsham, which brews and bottles the beer. There are three beers in the range, two of which are now bottle conditioned (the other is a premium lager). All are sold under the Curious Brew name.

Curious Brew Admiral Porter (5%)
Curious Brew Cobb IPA (5.6%)

Exe Valley

Exe Valley Brewery, Silverton, Exeter, Devon EX5 4HF
☎ (01392) 860406
@ exevalley@supanet.com

■ Exe Valley Brewery, formerly known as Barron's Brewery, moved into bottled beer production in 2001, and now uses Country Life Brewery for bottling. Green beer is racked into casks ready for filling, then the bottled beer is allowed to mature at the brewery before going on sale.

Devon Glory (4.7%, best bitter)

Fallen Angel

Fallen Angel Microbrewery, PO Box 95, Battle, East Sussex TN33 0XF
☎ (01424) 777867
@ custservice@ fallenangelbrewery.com
🌐 www.fallenangelbrewery.com
Mail order service

■ Small, family brewery that only rarely produces draught beer, with most of the emphasis placed on bottle-conditioned ales. The distinguishing feature of the packaging is original artwork, drawn by erotic artist Lynn Paula Russell. No finings are used, thus making all beers acceptable to vegetarians.

St Patrick's Irish Stout (3.1%)
Fire in the Hole Chili Beer (3.3%)
Cowgirl Lite (3.7%, golden ale)
Gamekeepers Bitter (3.9%, bitter)
Shepherdess Draught (3.9%, bitter)
Kama Sumatra (4%, coffee porter)
Hickory Switch Porter (4.3%, smoked honey beer)
Howlin' Red Ale (4.4%, honey beer)
Lemon Weissbier (4.5%)
Angry Ox Bitter (4.8%, best bitter)
Black Cat Ale (4.8%, honey stout)

Farmer's

Farmer's Ales, Maldon Brewing Co. Ltd, The Stable Brewery, The Blue Boar Stable Yard, Silver Street, Maldon, Essex CM9 4QE
✆ (01621) 851000
@ info@maldonbrewing.co.uk
⊕ www.maldonbrewing.co.uk
■ Maldon Brewing Co. was set up in 2002 by Nigel and Christine Farmer and now trades as Farmer's Ales. It is based in the courtyard of the historic Blue Boar Hotel in Maldon, which takes a selection of the brewery's beers.

A Drop of Nelson's Blood (3.8%, brandy-laced bitter)
The Hotel Porter (4.1%)
Puck's Folly (4.2%, golden ale)
Captain Ann (4.5%, best bitter)
Edward Bright's Stout (4.5%)
Farmer's Golden Boar (5%, golden ale)
Dark Horse (6.6%, strong ale)

Fat Cat

The Fat Cat Brewing Company Ltd, 98–100 Lawson Road, Norwich, Norfolk NR3 4LF
✆ (01603) 788508
⊕ www.fatcatbrewery.co.uk
■ Brewery opened in 2005 by the owner of Norwich's Fat Cat free house (CAMRA national Pub of the Year in 1998 and 2004). Bottled beers for sale in the pub were added to the range in summer 2007 and are filled for Fat Cat by Tipple's Brewery, where primed beer is bottled from casks.

Honey Ale (4.3%, honey beer)
Stout Cat (4.6%)
Marmalade Cat (5.5%, strong ale)
Dark Ol' Puss (6%, spiced old ale)
IPA (7%)

Felstar

The Felstar Brewery, Felsted Vineyard, Crix Green, Felsted, Essex CM6 3JT
✆ (01245) 361504
@ sales@felstarbrewery.co.uk
⊕ www.felstarbrewery.co.uk
Mail order service
■ Felstar Brewery was built in 2001 in the old bonded stores of Felsted Vineyard, the first commercial vineyard in East Anglia. Production of its own

beers neatly filled a space in the site's own shop, between English wines and ciders. The brewery is run by former graphic designer Marcello Davanzo (known to everyone as Franco), who has chosen the rooster as his brewery logo. If you ever call into Franco's shop, you'll know why. Try driving out again without running over one of his free-ranging poultry stock. His beers are bottled on site, being racked bright after conditioning in the cask and seeded with the same yeast as used in primary fermentation. Bottom-fermenting beers are kräusened and/or primed with unrefined molasses. Franco is one of the most inventive brewers around, tearing up the rulebooks and mixing and matching ale recipes with lager production methods, which makes categorising the beers a little difficult!

Crix Gold (4%, golden ale)
Chick Chat (4.1%, bitter)
Lord Kulmbach (4.4%, dark lager)
Hoppin' Hen (4.5%, best bitter)
Old Crix (4.5%, best bitter)
Wheat (4.8%)
Good Knight (5%, porter)
Peckin' Order (5%, pilsner)
Grumpy Rooster (5.2%, porter)
Lord Essex (5.4%, strong ale)
Howlin' Hen (6.5%, wood-aged beer)
Back Stabber (10%, imperial stout)

Ffos y Ffin
Ffos y Ffin Brewery, Ffos Y Ffin Fawr, Capel Dewi, Carmarthenshire SA32 8AG

☎ (07838) 384868
@ info@ffosyffinbrewery.co.uk
🌐 www.ffosyffinbrewery.co.uk
◼ Brewery founded in 2006 and housed on a working dairy farm in West Wales, using water from a well on the site. The beers are kräusened and fined before bottling.

Merlins Brew (3.6%, bitter)
Cothi Gold (3.9%, golden ale)
Cwrw Caredig (4.1%, golden ale)
Poets Choice (4.4%, best bitter)
Paxtons Pride (5.5%, old ale)
Towy Ale (5.5%, strong ale)
Guili Warmer (6.7%, strong ale)

Forgotten Corner
Forgotten Corner Brewery, 64 West Street, Millbrook, Cornwall PL10 1AE
☎ (01752) 829363
◼ Brewery opened in June 2008 by former home brewer Beverley Gibson at Maker Barracks on Cornwall's Rame Peninsula (the address above is for postal services and other contact). The beers are bottled straight from casks, without priming or re-seeding with yeast.

JP (3.7%, golden ale)
Trust Ale (4%, bitter)
Hunter's Porter (5.5%)

Fox
Fox Brewery, 22 Station Road, Heacham, Norfolk PE31 7EX
☎ (01485) 570345
@ info@foxbrewery.co.uk
🌐 www.foxbrewery.com
Mail order service
◼ This pub brewery opened in 2002 and brews not just for

the pub but other outlets, too. Sales of bottles (added in 2003) have really taken off. Both pub and brewery have been extended as a result. The beers are kräusened with fresh wort before being bottled.

Branthill Best (3.8%, bitter)
Da Crai (3.9%, lemongrass-spiced beer)
Heacham Gold (3.9%, golden ale)
Nina's Mild (3.9%, spring)
Red Admiral (4.2%, best bitter)
Branthill Norfolk Nectar (4.3%, golden ale)
Drop of Real Norfolk (4.4%, golden ale)
Cerberus Norfolk Stout (4.5%)
Samphire Stout (4.5%, seaweed stout)
Grizzly Beer (4.8%, golden ale)
Santa's Nuts (4.8%, Christmas ale)
Nelson's Blood (5.1%, rum-laced old ale)
IPA (5.2%)
Punt Gun (5.9%, winter porter)

Freeminer
Freeminer Ltd, Whimsey Road, Steam Mills, Cinderford, Gloucestershire GL16 8DN
(01594) 827989
@ sales@freeminer.co.uk
■ Established in 1992, the only brewery in the Royal Forest of Dean moved to new, larger premises in 2002. Bottling on a major scale resumed in 2003, with the launch of the Co-op own-label beer, Gold Miner, and continued with the introduction of The Best for Morrisons. Bottling is now handled by Meantime Brewing. Green beer

is trucked from Freeminer to Greenwich, where it is sterile filtered and then re-pitched with a special bottling yeast ready for filling. New, light-weight, eco-friendlier bottles are now employed.

Gold Miner (5%, golden ale)
Morrisons The Best (6%, strong ale)

Frog Island
Frog Island Brewery, The Maltings, Westbridge, St James Road, Northampton NN5 5HS
(01604) 587772
@ beer@frogislandbrewery.co.uk
@ www.frogislandbrewery.co.uk
Mail order service
■ Taking its name from an area of Northampton that is prone to flooding, Frog Island hopped into the brewing world in 1994. It set up shop in an old malthouse once owned by the Thomas Manning brewery. The beers are bottled on site, unprimed, from casks.

Natterjack (4.8%, best bitter)
Fire Bellied Toad (5%, best bitter)
Croak and Stagger (5.6%, strong ale)

Front Street
Front Street Brewery, 45 Front Street, Binham, Fakenham, Norfolk NR21 0AL
(01328) 830297
@ steve@binhamchequers.co.uk
@ www.binhamchequers.co.uk
■ Small brewery opened at The Chequers Inn in the Norfolk village of Binham in 2005. The beers below are bottled directly

from casks. Extra seasonal beers may also be available.

Callum's Ale (4.3%, best bitter)
Ebony Stout (4.5%, autumn/winter)
Swoopy's Song (4.9%, spring/summer liquorice-spiced golden ale)
China Gold (5%, spring spiced golden ale)
Unity Strong (5%, best bitter)
Old Sid (10.2%, winter barley wine)

Fuller's
Fuller, Smith and Turner PLC, Griffin Brewery, Chiswick Lane South, London W4 2QB

☏ (020) 8996 2000
@ fullers@fullers.co.uk
🌐 www.fullers.co.uk

■ Fuller's operates on a site linked to beer production for more than 325 years. Messrs Fuller, Smith and Turner came together in 1845 and descendants of the founders are still on the board today, running a highly successful business with countless brewing awards to its name. In 2005 Fuller's took over Gale's of Horndean, closing that brewery in March 2006. Some Gale's beers are now produced at Chiswick, but sadly only Prize Old Ale survives from the Gale's range of bottle-conditioned ales. Fuller's has an off-licence at the brewery for bottled beer sales.

1845 (6.3%, old ale)
Brewer's Reserve (7.7%, wood-aged beer)
Vintage Ale (8.5%, barley wine)
Gale's Prize Old Ale (9%, old ale)

Fulstow
Fulstow Brewery, 6 Northway, Fulstow, Louth, Lincolnshire LN11 0XH

☏ (01507) 363642
@ fulstow.brewery@virgin.net
🌐 www.fulstowbrewery.co.uk
Mail order service

■ This small Lincolnshire brewery was set up in 2004. Its beers also carry the name Fugelestou Ales, after the ancient name of its home village. In preparation for bottling, the beer is dropped bright, primed with dried malt extract and re-seeded with fresh yeast.

Fulstow Common (3.8%, bitter)
Marsh Mild (3.8%)
Village Life (4%, bitter)
Northway IPA (4.2%, golden ale)
Pride of Fulstow (4.5%, best bitter)
Sledge Hammer Stout (8%, imperial stout)

Fun Fair
Fun Fair Brewing Company, 34 Spinney Road, Ilkeston, Derbyshire DE7 4LH

☏ (07971) 540186
@ sales@funfairbrewingcompany.co.uk
🌐 www.funfairbrewingcompany.co.uk

■ Brewery opened in 2004 and now in its third home. Bottled beers were introduced to the range in 2008. They are filled straight from bottling tanks with no primings or re-seeding of yeast.

Dive Bomber (4.6%, golden ale)
Cake Walk (6%, fruit beer)

Glenfinnan

Glenfinnan Brewery Co. Ltd,
Glenfinnan, Highland PH37 4LT
- (07999) 261010
- info@glenfinnanbrewery.co.uk
- www.glenfinnanbrewery.co.uk
- Small Highland brewery opened in 2007, some 15 miles from Fort William. The 'gold' in the beer name below reflects not just the colour of the beer but also the £4,000 of gold (worth millions in today's money) that is said to have gone astray in the area during the Jacobite rebellion of 1745–6.

Gold (4%, golden ale)

Grainstore

Davis'es Brewing Co. Ltd,
Grainstore Brewery, Station Approach, Oakham, Rutland LE15 6RE
- (01572) 770065
- grainstorebry@aol.com
- Rutland beers were once famous, thanks to the presence of Ruddles Brewery, long sadly defunct (Ruddles brands are now brewed by Greene King). Rutland beers live on, however, chiefly through this brewery established in an old railway grainstore. Three bottle-conditioned beers are now produced (although John Clare is only occasional). Prior to bottling, these are re-seeded with primary fermentation yeast and then filled by hand from casks.

Rutland Panther (3.4%, mild)
John Clare (4.3%, golden ale)
Ten Fifty (5%, best bitter)

Great Gable

**Great Gable Brewing Co.
Ltd**, Wasdale Head Inn, Wasdale, Cumbria CA20 1EX
- (01946 7) 26229
- wasdaleheadinn@msn.com
- www.greatgablebrewing.com
- The Wasdale Head Inn stands remote and welcoming at the heart of Lakeland climbing and walking country. Since 2002, it has been home to the Great Gable microbrewery. Spring water from the fellside is used in each brew. There are plans to bottle most of the brewery's regular ales and bottling now takes place in house, direct from the fermentation vessel, with bottles matured for at least three weeks before release.

Wasd'ale (4.4%, best bitter)
Brown Tongue (5.2%, brown ale)
Yewbarrow (5.5%, honey mild)

Great Oakley

Great Oakley Brewery,
Bridge Farm, 11 Brooke Road, Great Oakley, Northamptonshire NN18 8HG
- (01536) 744888
- tailshaker@tiscali.co.uk
- www.greatoakleybrewer.co.uk
- Brewery established in 2005 in converted stables on a former working farm. The beers overleaf are brewed at Great Oakley but packaged at Milestone Brewery in Nottinghamshire, where bottles are filled directly from casks and primed.

Wot's Occurring (3.9%, bitter)
Gobble (4.5%, golden ale)
Delapre Dark (4.6%, old ale)

Green Tye

Green Tye Brewery,
Green Tye, Much Hadham,
Hertfordshire SG10 6JP
☎ (01279) 841041
@ info@gtbrewery.co.uk
Mail order service

■ Set up in 1999, Green Tye
turns out a wide range of
cask ales, many of which find
their way into bottle. Brewer
William Compton allows beer
to drop bright in casks and then
kräusens it before filling.

Union Jack (3.6%, bitter)
Mustang Mild (3.7%)
Snowdrop (3.9%, spring golden
ale)
Field Marshall (4%, bitter)
Hadham Gold (4%, golden ale)
Hertfordshire Hedgehog (4%,
bitter)
Smile for the Camera! (4%,
summer honey and elderflower
beer)
Jack Frost (4.1%, golden ale)
Autumn Rose (4.2%, autumn best
bitter)
East Anglian Gold (4.2%, golden
ale)
Green Tiger (4.2%, summer best
bitter)
Mad Morris (4.2%, spring golden
ale)
Wheelbarrow (4.3%, best bitter)
Coal Porter (4.5%)
Conkerer (4.7%, autumn best
bitter)

Greene King

Greene King PLC, Westgate
Brewery, Westgate Street,
Bury St Edmunds, Suffolk IP33 1QT
☎ (01284) 763222
@ www.greeneking.co.uk

■ Founded in 1799, Greene King
is now one of Britain's national
breweries, having expanded by
acquiring pub groups and other
breweries in recent years. From
Morland (now closed), Greene
King acquired its only bottle-
conditioned ale (although it does
produce a range of pasteurised
beers, including the notable
Strong Suffolk, a complex blend
of matured and young ales).

Hen's Tooth (6.5%, strong ale)

Hammerpot

Hammerpot Brewery Ltd,
Unit 30, The Vinery, Arundel Road,
Poling, West Sussex BN18 9PY
☎ (01903) 883338
@ sales@hammerpot-brewery.
co.uk
@ www.hammerpot-brewery.
co.uk

■ This tiny brewery opened in
2005, near Hammerpot village,
West Sussex. Bottling followed
soon after.

White Wing (4%, bitter)
Red Hunter (4.3%, best bitter)
Woodcote Bitter (4.5%, best
bitter)
Bottle Wreck Porter (4.7%)
Madgwick Gold (5%, golden ale)

Harveys

**Harvey and Son (Lewes)
Ltd**, The Bridge Wharf
Brewery, 6 Cliffe High Street,
Lewes, East Sussex BN7 2AH
☎ (01273) 480209
@ maj@harveys.org.uk
@ www.harveys.org.uk

■ This popular, family-run brewery,
established in the 18th century,

took the bold step of introducing the intriguing bottled beer mentioned below in 2000. The good news is that a new vintage has just been released, brewed and bottled in house.

Imperial Extra Double Stout (9%)

Harwich Town
Harwich Town Brewing Co., Station Approach, Harwich, Essex CO12 3NA
- (01255) 551155
- @ info@harwichtown.co.uk
- www.harwichtown.co.uk
- ■ Small brewery founded in 2007 by a former customs officer, with many beers named after local landmarks. The beers below are bottled direct from conditioning tanks, with no primings.

Hoppy Poppy (3.6%, golden ale)
Leading Lights (3.8%, bitter)
Redoubt Stout (4.2%)
Parkeston Porter (4.5%)
Lighthouse (4.8%, best bitter)
Sint Niklaas (8%, Belgian-style barley wine)

Haywood 'Bad Ram'
Haywood 'Bad Ram' Brewery, Sandybrook, Ashbourne, Derbyshire DE6 2AQ
- (01335) 344884
- @ acphaywood@aol.com
- www.callowtop.co.uk
- ■ Unusual brewery housed in a converted barn on a holiday park in the Derbyshire Peak District. The beers, re-seeded with fresh yeast and primed, are filled from casks.

Dr Samuel Johnson (4.5%, best bitter)
Callow Top IPA (5.2%)

Heart of Wales
Neuadd Arms Brewing Co., Heart of Wales Brewery, Zion Street, Llanwrtyd Wells, Powys LD5 4RD
- (01591) 610236
- @ lindsay@heartofwalesbrewery.co.uk
- www.heartofwalesbrewery.co.uk
- ■ Small brewery set up in converted stables at a popular Mid-Wales pub in 2004. Bottled beers are filled straight from the fermentation vessel with nothing added.

Irfon Valley Bitter (3.6%)
Aur Cymru (3.8%, golden ale)
Wheel Ale (3.9%, bitter)
D'rovers Return (4%, bitter)
Bitter (4.1%)
Shake, Ramble & Roll (4.2%, best bitter)
Horse Play (4.3%, best bitter)
Welsh Black (4.4%, stout)
Boggled (4.5%, best bitter)
Noble Eden Ale (4.6%, porter)
Charioteer (4.8%, best bitter)
Folk 'n' Ale (5.3%, brown ale)
Inn Stable (6.8%, strong ale)
High as a Kite (10.5%, barley wine)

Hepworth
Hepworth & Company Brewers Ltd, The Beer Station, The Railway Yard, Horsham, West Sussex RH12 2NW
- (01403) 269696
- @ mail@hepworthbrewery.co.uk
- www.hepworthbrewery.co.uk

■ Brewery founded in an old railway halt in Horsham in 2000, by Andy Hepworth, former head brewer of the local King & Barnes brewery, and colleagues. The two beers below are brewed and bottled on site. Hepworth also bottles for a number of other breweries.

Marks & Spencer Sussex Bitter (3.8%, golden ale)
Prospect (4.5%, golden ale)

Hesket Newmarket
Hesket Newmarket Brewery Ltd, Old Crown Barn, Back Green, Hesket Newmarket, Cumbria CA7 8JG
🕿 (01697) 478066
@ sales@hesketbrewery.co.uk
🌐 www.hesketbrewery.co.uk
■ Brewery founded at the Old Crown pub in the northern Lake District in 1988 and taken into ownership by a village co-operative in 1999. The beers below are filtered, re-seeded with fresh yeast and primed before bottling in house.

Haystacks (3.7%, golden ale)
High Pike (4.2%, best bitter)
Doris's 90th Birthday Ale (4.3%, best bitter)
Scafell Blonde (4.3%, golden ale)
Catbells (5%, golden ale)
Old Carrock (6%, old ale)

Hilden
Hilden Brewing Co., Grand Street, Hilden, Lisburn, Co. Antrim BT27 4TY
🕿 (028 92) 660800
@ irishbeers@hildenbrewery.co.uk
🌐 www.hildenbrewery.co.uk

■ Hilden, founded in 1981, was, for some years, the only cask ale brewery in Northern Ireland, albeit a very small one with limited outlets. Access to the beers is still difficult, but the installation of a bottling line in 1999 now allows more people to sample Hilden's ales. The beer below carries the College Green Brewery name (after Hilden's small brewery in Belfast that is sometimes used) but is brewed and bottled at Hilden. It is filled from a conditioning tank without filtration or the re-seeding of yeast.

Molly's Chocolate Stout (4.2%)

Hobsons
Hobsons Brewery & Co. Ltd, Newhouse Farm, Tenbury Road, Cleobury Mortimer, Shropshire DY14 8RD
🕿 (01299) 270837
@ beer@hobsons-brewery.co.uk
🌐 www.hobsons-brewery.co.uk
Mail order service
■ This family-run brewery was set up in 1993 but moved to its current premises (an attractive old farm building) in 1996. An extension to the property in 2001 provided space for a bottling plant. The beers are chilled, sterile filtered and re-seeded with fresh yeast, ready for bottling, and all are declared acceptable to vegetarians.

Manor Ale (4.2%, best bitter)
Town Crier (4.5%, golden ale)
Postman's Knock (4.8%, vanilla-laced mild)
Old Henry (5.2%, old ale)

Hoggleys

Hoggleys Brewery, Unit 12, Litchborough Industrial Estate, Northampton Road, Litchborough, Northamptonshire NN12 8JB

📞 (01604) 831762

@ hoggleys@hotmail.com

🌐 www.hoggleys.co.uk

■ Starting tiny, as a part-time operation in 2003, Hoggleys is now a full-time business operating from a new, bigger site. The company name is drawn from a merger of the surnames of the two founders, Julie Hogg and Roy Crutchley. The beers are not fined, making them acceptable to vegetarians. They are filled directly from a fermentation vessel and matured in the bottle before release.

Kislingbury Bitter (4%)
Mill Lane Mild (4%)
Northamptonshire Bitter (4%, golden ale)
Reservoir Hogs (4.3%, best bitter)
Pump Fiction (4.5%, best bitter)
Solstice Stout (5%)
Yuletide Ale (7.2%, Christmas porter)

Hogs Back

Hogs Back Brewery Ltd, Manor Farm, The Street, Tongham, Surrey GU10 1DE

📞 (01252) 783000

@ info@hogsback.co.uk

🌐 www.hogsback.co.uk

Mail order service

■ This purpose-built brewery was set up in restored farm buildings (circa 1768) in 1992. All the brewery's bottled beers are handled in house. The brews are filtered and then injected with fresh yeast prior to filling, with priming sugars occasionally added to ensure a good fermentation in the bottle. The elaborate, gold-embossed labels are the work of brewery partner Tony Stanton-Precious, a former draughtsman. Hogs Back also has a fine shop/off-licence on site, offering a wide range of bottled beers from other breweries.

TEA/Traditional English Ale (4.2%, best bitter)
BSA/Burma Star Ale (4.5%, best bitter)
OTT/Old Tongham Tasty (6%, old ale)
Brewster's Bundle (7.4%, barley wine)
Wobble in a Bottle/Santa's Wobble (7.5%, barley wine)
A over T/Aromas over Tongham (9%, barley wine)

Hook Norton

Hook Norton Brewery Co. Ltd, The Brewery, Hook Norton, Banbury, Oxfordshire OX15 5NY

📞 (01608) 737210

🌐 www.hooky.co.uk

Mail order service

■ Classic Victorian brewery still steaming away in the Oxfordshire countryside. There's now one bottle-conditioned beer in the range (brewed at Hook Norton and bottled at Thwaites), with the possibility of more to follow.

Double Stout (4.8%)

Hop Back

Hop Back Brewery PLC, Units 22–24, Batten Road, Downton Business Centre, Downton, Wiltshire SP5 3HU

☏ (01725) 510986
@ info@hopback.co.uk
🌐 www.hopback.co.uk
Mail order service (01725) 511331

■ Originally based at a Salisbury brew pub, The Wyndham Arms, Hop Back was set up in 1986. It moved to an industrial unit at Downton in 1992 and stepped up bottled beer production in 1997 with the installation of a new bottling line. All beers are cold conditioned, kräusened, filtered and re-seeded with fresh yeast prior to bottling.

Crop Circle (4.2%, coriander-spiced ale)
Spring Zing (4.2%, lemongrass-spiced beer)
Taiphoon (4.2%, lemongrass-spiced beer)
Entire Stout (4.5%)
Summer Lightning (5%, golden ale)
Pickled Santa (6%, spiced Christmas ale)

Hopdaemon

Hopdaemon Brewery Co. Ltd, Unit 1, Seed Road, Newnham, Kent ME9 0NA

☏ (01795) 892078
@ info@hopdaemon.com
🌐 www.hopdaemon.com
Mail order service

■ New Zealander Tonie Prins founded Hopdaemon on the edge of Canterbury in 2001. However, demand for his beers led to a move to new premises in Newnham in 2005. Tonie describes his beers as 'traditional ales with a slight New World twist' and, to market them, has combined the medieval traditions of Canterbury and its cathedral with a sprinkling of legend and a touch of home-spun folklore based around the local hopgardens. He bottles the beers by hand himself, chilling them for up to a week before filling to allow proteins to drop out and then re-seeding with dried bottling yeast.

Skrimshander IPA (4.5%, best bitter)
Green Daemon Helles (5%, pale lager)
Leviathan (6%, strong ale)

Hopshackle

Hopshackle Brewery Ltd, Unit F, Bentley Business Park, Northfields Industrial Estate, Market Deeping, Lincolnshire PE6 8LD

☏ (01778) 348542
@ nigel@hopshacklebrewery.co.uk
🌐 www.hopshacklebrewery.co.uk
Mail order service

■ Small brewery set up in 2006 by experienced former home brewer Nigel Wright. The beers all have their own production quirks, but essentially, for bottling, they are primed and re-seeded with fresh yeast.

Hop and Spicey (4.5%, spiced ale)
Historic Porter (4.8%)
Double Momentum (7%, IPA)
Restoration (9%, barley wine)

Humpty Dumpty

Humpty Dumpty Brewery, Church Road, Reedham, Norfolk NR13 3TZ

☎ (01493) 701818

@ info@humptydumptybrewery.co.uk

🌐 www.humptydumptybrewery.co.uk

■ Opened in 1998 next to The Railway Tavern pub in Reedham, Humpty Dumpty moved in 2001 to a new site alongside Pettitts Animal Park (a popular family attraction) in the same picturesque riverside village. In May 2006, the brewery changed hands but continues to produce a wide variety of ales, including new beers and seasonal lines.

Little Sharpie (3.8%, golden ale)
Lemon & Ginger (4%, spiced fruit beer)
Swallowtail (4%, golden ale)
Humpty Dumpty Ale (4.1%, bitter)
Broadland Sunrise (4.2%, golden ale)
Reedcutter (4.4%, golden ale)
Cheltenham Flyer (4.6%, golden ale)
Norfolk Nectar (4.6%, golden ale)
Railway Sleeper (5%, best bitter)
Hop Harvest Gold (5.2%, strong ale)
Golden Gorse (5.4%, strong ale)
Porter (5.4%)

Iceni

The Iceni Brewery, 3 Foulden Road, Ickburgh, Mundford, Norfolk IP26 5BJ

☎ (01842) 878922

■ Iceni was founded by Ulsterman Brendan Moore in 1995 and some of his beers are named after Celtic queens and/or the Iceni tribe, which once inhabited this part of England. The beers below, left to drop bright, are then kräusened before bottling direct from casks. Brendan – a driving force in the local microbrewing movement – is also a partner with his daughter, Frances, in Elveden Ales (see entry).

Honey Mild (3.6%, honey beer)
Thetford Forest Mild (3.6%)
Boadicea Chariot Ale (3.8%, bitter)
Elveden Forest Gold (3.9%, golden ale)
Celtic Queen (4%, bitter)
Fine Soft Day (4%, bitter)
Lovely Day (4%, bitter)
Swaffham Pride (4%, bitter)
Cranberry Wheat (4.1%, fruit wheat beer)
Snowdrop (4.1%, golden ale)
Fen Tiger (4.2%, coriander-spiced ale)
Thomas Paine Porter (4.2%)
Honey Stout (4.3%, honey beer)
Deirdre of the Sorrows (4.4%, best bitter)
Ported Porter (4.4%, port-laced porter)
Roísín Dubh (4.4%, best bitter)
Good Night Out (4.5%, best bitter)
It's a Grand Day (4.5%, ginger-spiced beer)
Norfolk Gold (5%, golden ale)
Norfolk Lager (5%, pale lager)
Raspberry Wheat (5%, fruit wheat beer)
Swaffham Gold (5%, golden ale)
Winter Lightning (5%, golden ale)
Men of Norfolk (6.2%, strong ale)

Breweries

Ironbridge

Ironbridge Brewery Ltd,
7 Merrythought Village, Ironbridge,
Telford TF8 7NJ
- (01952) 433910
- @ david@ironbridgebrewery.co.uk
- www.ironbridgebrewery.co.uk
- Brewery founded in 2008 in a Victorian foundry. For bottling, the unfiltered beers are filled from casks and re-seeded with fresh lager yeast.

Coracle (3.9%, golden ale)
1779 (4.3%, golden ale)
Gold (4.6%, golden ale)

Islay

Islay Ales Company Ltd,
The Brewery, Islay House
Square, Bridgend, Isle of Islay
PA44 7NZ
- (01496) 810014
- @ info@islayales.com
- www.islayales.com
- Mail order service
- Using the slogan 'Ales from the Isle of Malts', Islay Ales was founded in 2003, at last offering a little variation on a Scottish island that had seven, world-famous whisky distilleries, but no brewery. The beers featured below are all bottled by hand after the beer has been kräusened. They are also sold in cask-conditioned form.

Finlaggan Ale (3.7%, bitter)
Black Rock Ale (4.2%, best bitter)
Dun Hogs Head Ale (4.4%, stout)
Saligo Ale (4.4%, golden ale)
Angus Og Ale (4.5%, best bitter)
Ardnave Ale (4.6%, golden ale)
Nerabus Ale (4.8%, winter ale)
Single Malt Ale (5%, golden ale)

Isle of Purbeck

Isle of Purbeck Brewery,
Bankes Arms Hotel, Manor Road,
Studland, Swanage, Dorset
BH19 3AU
- (01929) 450227
- www.bankesarms.com/micro.html
- Small brewery that has been operating from the Bankes Arms Hotel since 2003. The bottled beers are filled from tanks for the brewery by Branded Drinks in Gloucestershire.

Fossil Fuel (4.1%, bitter)
Solar Power (4.3%, pale lager)
Studland Bay Wrecked (4.5%, best bitter)
IPA (4.8%)

Itchen Valley

Itchen Valley Brewery Ltd,
Prospect Commercial Park,
Prospect Road, New Alresford,
Hampshire SO24 9QF
- (01962) 735111
- @ info@itchenvalley.com
- www.itchenvalley.com
- Mail order service
- Itchen Valley Brewery was founded in 1997 but changed hands a year later. The new owners launched into bottle-conditioned beers in a big way and bottling now accounts for a major chunk of the business. All the beers are brewed at Itchen Valley but are bottled elsewhere under contract. They are filtered and fresh yeast is added prior to bottling. Itchen Valley's parent company specializes in pub signage, hence the colourful bottle labels. Many bottles are sold at farmers' markets.

A move to new, larger premises, close to the original site, took place in June 2006.

Godfathers (3.8%, bitter)
Fagins (4.1%, bitter)
Hampshire Rose (4.2%, best bitter)
Wykehams Glory (4.3%, best bitter)
1644 Battle of Cheriton (4.4%, golden ale)
Treacle Stout (4.4%, liquorice- and treacle-laced stout)
Hambledon Bitter (4.5%, honey and elderflower beer)
Pure Gold (4.8%, golden ale)
Father Christmas (5%, Christmas old ale)
Wat Tyler (5%, best bitter)

Jarrow
Jarrow Brewery, The Robin Hood, Primrose Hill, Jarrow, Tyne & Wear NE32 5UB
☏ (0191) 483 6792
@ jarrowbrewery@btconnect.com
🌐 www.jarrowbrewery.co.uk
■ Brewery opened by Jess and Alison McConnell at their Robin Hood pub in 2002. The beers below are bottled for Jarrow by Hambleton Ales.

Rivet Catcher (4%, golden ale)
Red Ellen (4.4%, winter ale)
Venerable Bede (4.5%, golden ale)
McConnells Irish Stout (4.6%)
Westoe IPA (4.6%, wheat beer)

Jolly Brewer
Jolly Brewer, Kingston Villa, 27 Poplar Road, Wrexham LL13 7DG
☏ (01978) 261884
@ pene@jollybrewer.co.uk
🌐 www.jollybrewer.co.uk
Mail order service
■ Since 2000, Penelope Coles has branched out from the off-licence and craft brewing shop she runs in Wrexham and opened her own commercial brewery, building on 25 years of brewing experience. The beers are bottled straight after fermentation and primed with sucrose. No finings are used in the beers, making them acceptable to vegans.

Benno's (4%, pale lager)
Chwerw Cymreig (4%, bitter)
Druid's Ale (4%, golden ale)
Festival Ale (4%, bitter)
Suzanne's Stout (4%)
Cwrw Du (4.2%, brown ale)
Taid's Garden (4.2%, best bitter)
Betton Bitter (4.3%, best bitter)
Lucinda's Lager (4.5% pale lager)
Porter (4.5%)
Taffy's Tipple (4.5%, best bitter)
Y Ddraig Goch (4.5%, stout)
Dynes Dywyll (5%, best bitter)
Cwrw Carrog (5.5%, strong ale)
Tommy's (5.5%, dark lager)

Kelham Island
Kelham Island Brewery Ltd, 23 Alma Street, Sheffield, South Yorkshire S3 8SA
☏ (0114) 249 4804
@ sales@kelhambrewery.co.uk
🌐 www.kelhambrewery.co.uk
■ Successful, expanded brewery that opened in 1990 at Sheffield's Fat Cat pub and moved into new premises next door nine years later. As well as offering a range of filtered bottled beers, Kelham also hand

bottles the following bottle-conditioned beers, straight from casks with sugar primings.

Night Rider (5.2%, autumn stout)
Pale Rider (5.2%, strong ale)
Brooklyn Smoked Porter (6.5%)
Grande Pale (6.6%, strong ale)

Keltek
Keltek Brewery, Candela House, Cardrew Way, Redruth, Cornwall TR15 1SS
☎ (01209) 313620
@ sales@keltekbrewery.co.uk
🌐 www.keltekbrewery.co.uk
Mail order service
■ Founded in Tregony in 1997, to supply beers to the Roseland peninsula of Cornwall, Keltek was later moved to Lostwithiel. It has since been moved, yet again, to new premises in Redruth. The beers are bottled in house from either casks or conditioning tanks, without sugar priming.

Magik (4%, bitter)
King (5.1%, strong ale)
Beheaded (7.6%, barley wine)

Keystone
Keystone Brewery, Old Carpenter's Workshop, Berwick St Leonard, Salisbury, Wiltshire SP3 5SN
☎ (01747) 820426
@ alasdair@keystonebrewery.co.uk
🌐 www.keystonebrewery.co.uk
Mail order service
■ Brewery founded in July 2006 by former army man Alasdair Large and his wife, Charlotte. For bottling, the beers are matured

and fined bright. They are then kräusened with fresh, day-old wort before filling.

Gold Spice (4%, ginger-spiced ale)
Large One (4.2%, best bitter)
Porter (5.5%)

King
WJ King & Co., 3–5 Jubilee Estate, Foundry Lane, Horsham, West Sussex RH13 5UE
☎ (01403) 272102
@ sales@kingbeer.co.uk
🌐 www.kingbeer.co.uk
Mail order service
■ Bill King, latterly managing director of King & Barnes, returned to brewing on a much smaller scale in 2001. Setting up this small brewery in the same town of Horsham, Bill was swiftly brewing up to capacity and bottled beers were soon added to the cask range. All beers are filled directly from the fermentation vessel, with a small amount of priming sugar added but without filtering or the use of isinglass finings, which makes them acceptable to vegetarians.

Horsham Best Bitter (3.8%, bitter)
Winters T'Ale (4.1%, winter golden ale)
Birthday Beer (4.4%, golden ale)
Five Generations (4.4%, best bitter)
King's Old Ale (4.5%)
Mallard Ale (5%, golden ale)
Red River Ale (5%, best bitter)
King's IPA (5.5%, IPA)
Cereal Thriller (6.3%, maize beer)
Merry Ale (6.5%, winter ale)

Kingstone

Kingstone Brewery,
Tintern, Monmouthshire
NP16 7NX
📞 (01291) 680111
@ info@kingstonebrewery.co.uk
🌐 www.kingstonebrewery.co.uk
Mail order service

■ This small brewery opened on a Monmouthshire farm in 2005 and changed hands in 2007, when production was moved to a new site, adjacent to a farm shop, just outside Tintern. The shop stocks bottled beers from all over Wales. Kingstone beers are filled directly from the fermenter, without filtration or priming. All are declared vegan friendly.

Tewdric's Tipple (3.8%, bitter)
Challenger (4%, bitter)
Gold (4%, golden ale)
No.1 (4.4%, stout)
Classic Bitter (4.5%, best bitter)
1503 (4.8%, old ale)
Abbey Ale (5.1%, strong ale)
Humpty's Fuddle (5.8%, IPA)

Langton

Langton Brewery, Grange Farm, Welham Road, Thorpe Langton, Leicestershire LE16 7TU
📞 (07840) 532826

■ Small brewery founded behind a pub in 1999 and re-locating to a converted barn in 2005. Bottled beers were introduced in 2007 and are filled in house, straight from the fermenting vessel, without finings, primings or re-seeding of yeast. In addition to the beers shown below, a few 'own-label' bottles are produced for individual local customers.

Caudle Bitter (3.9%)
Inclined Plane Bitter (4.2%, golden ale)
Bowler Strong Ale (4.8%, best bitter)
Welland Poacher (7.5%, barley wine)

Laverstoke Park

Laverstoke Park Produce LLP,
Laverstoke Park Farm, Overton, Hampshire RG25 3DR
📞 (01256) 772813
@ office@laverstokepark.co.uk
🌐 www.laverstokepark.co.uk

■ Organic farm enterprise founded by former Formula 1 driver Jody Scheckter. It commissioned its first bottled beers in 2008, using malt and hops organically grown on site. These are brewed under contract at Hepworth in Sussex, with fresh yeast added to the beer before bottling.

Organic Real Lager (4.5%, pale lager)
Organic Real Ale (5%, best bitter)

Leatherbritches

Leatherbritches Brewery,
Green Man & Blacks Head Royal Hotel, St John Street, Ashbourne, Derbyshire DE6 1GH
📞 (07976) 279253
@ leatherbritches@btconnect.com

■ Former pub brewery in the Derbyshire Peak District that moved to a bigger site in Ashbourne in 2008.

Hairy Helmet (4.9%, golden ale)
Bespoke (5.2%, strong ale)
Porter (5.4%)
Scary Hairy (5.9%, strong ale)
Blue (9%, fruit and spice beer)

Breweries

Leek

Staffordshire Brewery Ltd
(t/a Leek Brewery & Staffordshire
Cheese Company), Unit 12,
Churnet Side, Cheddleton,
Staffordshire ST13 7EF
☎ (01538) 361919
@ leekbrewery@hotmail.com
🌐 www.beersandcheese.co.uk
▦ Brewery established in 2002
that moved to a new home in
summer 2004. In addition to
being part of a business that
produces hand-made cheeses,
Leek turns out a wide range
of bottled beers, which are
declared to be safe for vegans
as they contain no finings. A
selection of fruit beers is also
produced.

Staffordshire Gold (3.8%, golden
ale)
Danebridge IPA (4.1%, golden
ale)
Staffordshire Bitter (4.2%, best
bitter)
Black Grouse (4.5%, stout)
Hen Cloud (4.5%, golden ale)
St Edward's (4.7%, best bitter)
Rudyard Ruby (4.8%, best bitter)
Leekenbrau (5%, pale lager)
Double Sunset (5%, golden ale)
Cheddleton Steamer (6.5%,
wheat beer)
Dark Peak Extra Strong (8%,
imperial stout)
White Peak Extra Strong (8%,
barley wine)

Lion's Tale

Lion's Tale Brewery, Red
Lion, High Street, Cheswardine,
Shropshire TF9 2RS
☎ (01630) 661234
@ cheslion96@yahoo.co.uk

▦ Brewery added to the Red Lion
pub in 2005. The bottled beers
listed below are filled directly
from casks.

Blooming Blonde (4.1%, golden
ale)
Lion Bru (4.1%, bitter)
Chesbrewnette (4.5%, stout)
Chesmasbells (5.2%, Christmas
old ale)

Little Valley

Little Valley Brewery Ltd,
Turkey Lodge, New Road, Cragg
Vale, West Yorkshire HX7 5TT
☎ (01422) 883888
@ info@littlevalleybrewery.co.uk
🌐 www.littlevalleybrewery.co.uk
Mail order service
▦ Little Valley was opened in
2005 by Dutch brewer Wim
van der Spek, previously
of Black Isle Brewery and
breweries in Germany and The
Netherlands. His beers are all
organic and approved by the
Soil Association, as well as
vegan, backed by Vegan Society
accreditation. Prior to bottling,
the beers spend at least four
weeks in conditioning tanks
and are then primed with sugar
and a bottling yeast. Bottles
condition for two weeks before
leaving the brewery.

Withens IPA (3.9%, golden ale)
Ginger Pale Ale (4%, ginger-
spiced beer)
Cragg Vale Bitter (4.2%, best
bitter)
Hebden's Wheat (4.5%)
Stoodley Stout (4.8%)
Tod's Blonde (5%, golden ale)
Moor Ale (5.5%, strong ale)

Lizard

Lizard Ales, The Old Nuclear
Bunker, Pednavounder, Coverack,
Cornwall TR12 6SE
☎ (01326) 281135
@ lizardales@msn.com
🌐 www.lizardales.co.uk
Mail order service
■ Small brewery which opened on
the Lizard peninsula in 2004 and
is run by former lawyer Mark
Nattrass. His beers are matured
in conditioning tanks and
kräusened before bottling. They
are then matured in the bottle
for at least three months before
going on sale.

Kernow Gold (3.7%, golden ale)
Bitter (4.2%, best bitter)
Frenchman's Creek (4.8%, IPA)
An Gof (5.2%, smoked beer)

Loddon

The Loddon Brewery Ltd,
Dunsden Green Farm, Church
Lane, Dunsden, Oxfordshire
RG4 9QD
☎ (0118) 948 1111
@ sales@loddonbrewery.com
🌐 www.loddonbrewery.com
■ A 240-year-old brick and
flint barn between Reading
and Henley-on-Thames was
extensively renovated to house
Loddon Brewery when it was
established in 2003. Chris
and Vanessa Hearn run the
business, Chris using the sales
skills he previously exercised at
Batemans, Morrells and other
companies. The brewery is large
by microbrewing standards, with
a capacity of 90 barrels. Its first
bottle-conditioned beer arrived
in 2005 (bottled for Loddon

by Arkell's) and now there
are plans to bottle two more
draught brews: the sweet, nutty
Hullabaloo and the chocolaty
old ale, Hocus Pocus.

Ferryman's Gold (4.8%, golden
ale)

Lymestone

Lymestone Brewery Ltd,
The Old Brewery, Mount Road,
Stone, Staffordshire ST15 8LL
☎ (01785) 817796
@ enquiries@lymestonebrewery.
co.uk
🌐 www.lymestonebrewery.co.uk
Mail order service
■ Brewery opened in 2008 by Ian
Bradford, former head brewer
at Titanic, and colleague Ron
Makins. The bottled beers are
kräusened and filled from casks
in house.

Foundation Stone (4.5%, golden
ale)
Stone the Crows (5.4%, strong
ale)

McGivern

McGivern Ales, 17 Salisbury
Road, Wrexham LL13 7AS
☎ (01978) 354232
@ mcgivernmatt@hotmail.com
■ Tiny brewery established in early
2008, brewing just one cask a
day, and hand bottling up to 80
beers at a time. The ABVs of the
beers below may vary.

Crest Bitter (3.9%, golden ale)
Amber Ale (4%, bitter)
Crest Pale (4.1%, golden ale)
Kune Kune Ale (4.1%, bitter)
Wheat Beer (4.1%)

Pale Ale (4.2%)
Stout (4.2%)
No.17 Pale (4.3%, pale ale)
Porter (4.4%)
No.17 Bitter (4.8%, best bitter)

Marble
Marble Brewery,
73 Rochdale Road,
Manchester M4 4HY
☎ (0161) 819 2694
@ thebrewers_marblebeers@msn.com
🌐 www.marblebeers.com
■ Brewery established at Manchester's Marble Arch pub in 1997, specialising in organic beers. The bottled ales are kräusened, racked bright and re-seeded with fresh primary fermentation yeast, before bottling by hand from casks.

Chocolate Marble (5.5%, stout)
Lagonda IPA (5%)
Tawny No.3 (5.7%, strong ale)
Ginger 6 (6%, ginger-spiced beer)

Marston's
See **Brakspear**

Mayfields
Mayfields Brewery, No. 8 Croft Business Park, Leominster, Herefordshire HR6 0QF
☎ (01568) 611197
@ info@mayfieldsbrewery.co.uk
■ Brewery opened in 2005 and making full use of the local hop gardens. It even brews with hops grown on the farm where the business was founded. The beers for bottling are all vegan friendly and are allowed to drop mostly bright in conditioning tanks before filling, without any primings or the re-seeding of yeast.

Ryeland Gold (3.8%, golden ale)
Naughty Nell's (4.2%, best bitter)
Auntie Myrtle's (4.5%, best bitter)

Meantime
Meantime Brewing Co. Ltd, The Greenwich Brewery, 2 Penhall Road, London SE7 8RX
☎ (020) 8293 1111
@ info@meantimebrewing.com
🌐 www.meantimebrewing.com
■ Meantime Brewing was set up by continental beer specialist Alastair Hook, who re-creates classic European beer styles (Belgian ales, kölsch, Viennese lagers, wheat beers, etc.) at his Greenwich base. The bottle-conditioned beers are matured at the brewery before filling. Imports to the USA are through Artisanal Imports. In addition to the beers listed below, Meantime has launched an annual programme of limited-edition beers based on classic beer styles from Belgium and Germany. Some of these are made available in bottle-conditioned format.

London Pale Ale (4.3%)
London Stout (4.5%)
Wheat (5%)
Winter Time (5.4%, winter ale)
Coffee Porter (6%)
Chocolate (6.5%, chocolate porter)
London Porter (6.5%)
Raspberry Grand Cru (6.5%, fruit wheat beer)
India Pale Ale (7.5%)

Mersea Island

Mersea Island Brewery,
Rewsalls Lane, East Mersea,
Colchester, Essex CO5 8SX
- ☎ (01206) 381830
- @ beers@merseawine.com
- 🌐 www.merseawine.com
- ■ This brewery was set up on a family-owned vineyard in 2005. They also offer bed & breakfast accommodation and holiday lets, if you fancy learning more about the beers and wines while exploring the Essex coast. All the beers are sterile filtered, primed with sugar syrup and re-seeded with fresh, bottom-fermenting yeast for bottling.

Island Yo Boy (3.9%, bitter)
Island Gold (4.5%, golden ale)
Island Monkeys (4.5%, stout)
Island Stout (5%)

Milestone

Milestone Brewing Co. Ltd,
Great North Road, Cromwell,
Newark, Nottinghamshire
NG23 6JE
- ☎ (01636) 822255
- @ info@milestonebrewery.co.uk
- 🌐 www.milestonebrewery.co.uk
- Mail order service
- ■ Nottinghamshire brewery established in 2005. The beers below are filled on site from conditioning tanks and primed with sugar.

Lion's Pride (3.8%, bitter)
Vixen (3.8%, spiced winter ale)
Loxley Ale (4.2%, golden ale)
Black Pearl (4.3%, stout)
Comet (4.3%, best bitter)
Crusader (4.4%, golden ale)
Cupid (4.4%, winter golden ale)

Dasher the Flasher (4.5%, winter ale)
Imperial Pale Ale (4.9%, IPA)
Olde Home Wrecker (4.9%, old ale)
Prancer (4.9%, spiced winter ale)
Donner Blitzed (5.4%, treacle- and rum-flavoured winter ale)
Raspberry Wheat Beer (5.6%)

Molson Coors

The White Shield Brewery,
Horninglow Street, Burton-on-Trent, Staffordshire DE14 1NG
- ☎ (01283) 511000 Ext 3507
- @ steve.wellington@coorsbrewers.com
- ■ Proof that large-scale brewing is now an international affair was provided by the sale of Bass. The historic brewer was purchased in 2000 by Interbrew, which, because it also owned Whitbread, was then forced to sell off part of its new acquisition. In stepped Coors (now Molson Coors), one of America's major brewers, to take over most of the Bass breweries and some of its brands, including the Worthington's range. Thus a high-tech Colorado company became owners of the Bass Museum, a shrine to the halcyon days of traditional ale production, and with it its vibrant Museum Brewing Company. This was later re-named Coors Visitor Centre, but has since closed. The Museum brewery is still working, however, using the name of The White Shield Brewery. It began life as a static display but became fully

Breweries

operational in 1994. A new bottling line, capable of filling 900 bottles per hour, was later introduced to cope with demand for Worthington's White Shield, which was acquired following the closure of King & Barnes in Horsham. Other bottle-conditioned beers may occasionally be available.

Worthington's White Shield (5.6%, IPA)

Moor

Moor Beer Company, Chapel Court, Pitney, Somerset TA10 9AE
- ☎ (07887) 556521
- @ justin@moorbeer.co.uk
- 🌐 www.moorbeer.co.uk
- ■ Moor Beer Company was founded on a dairy farm (now a pig farm) by Arthur Frampton in 1996. Brewing ceased temporarily in 2005 when the equipment was sold to the Otley Brewery in South Wales, which produced Moor's beers for a while. A new brewery was then installed at Moor and a change of brewer ensued. The following beers are hand bottled.

Somerland Gold (5%, golden ale)
Old Freddy Walker (7.3%, old ale)
JJJ IPA (9%)

Moulin

Moulin Brewery, 2 Baledmund Road, Moulin, by Pitlochry, Perthshire & Kinross PH16 5EW
- ☎ (01796) 472196
- @ enquiries@moulinhotel.co.uk
- 🌐 www.moulinhotel.co.uk
- ■ Moulin Brewery was opened in 1995 at the Moulin Hotel in Pitlochry, during celebrations for the hotel's 300th anniversary (the hotel housed a brewery when it opened in 1695, so it was deemed fitting to recommence brewing on the site). Brewing has been relocated since to the Old Coach House opposite the main building. The one bottled beer is settled in tank, with more yeast and sugar added before filling.

Ale of Atholl (4.5%, best bitter)

Nailsworth

Nailsworth Brewery Ltd, The Village Inn, The Cross, Bath Road, Nailsworth, Gloucestershire GL6 0HH
- ☎ (07878) 448377
- @ jonk@nailsworth-brewery.co.uk
- 🌐 www.nailsworth-brewery.co.uk
- ■ Pub brewery founded in 2004, bottling two beers on site direct from casks, after priming.

The Large Blue (4.1%, bitter)
The Mayor's Bitter (4.2%, best bitter)

Naylor's

Naylor's Brewery, Midland Mills, Station Road, Crosshills, Keighley, West Yorkshire BD20 7DT
- ☎ (01535) 637451
- @ naylorsbrewery@btconnect.com
- 🌐 www.naylorsbrewery.com
- ■ Brewery founded in 2005 at the Old White Bear pub in Crosshills, but moving in 2006 to larger premises in the same village. A sizeable, regular range of bottle-conditioned beers was produced for a while, but this was

discontinued in favour of filtered bottles in 2009, leaving only occasional bottle-conditioned beers available (details vary).

Nelson

Nelson Brewery, Unit 2, Building 64, Historic Dockyard, Chatham, Kent ME4 4TE
- (01634) 832828
- @ sales@nelsonbrewingcompany.co.uk
- www.nelsonbrewingcompany.co.uk

Mail order service

■ Brewery established in Chatham's historic dockyard in 1995 as Flagship Brewery, but changing its name in 2004 and gaining new ownership in 2006. The bottle-conditioned beers are re-seeded with the same yeast as used in primary fermentation and primed with sugar.

Press Gang Pale Ale (4.3%, golden ale)
Friggin in the Riggin (4.7%, best bitter)

Nethergate

Nethergate Growler Brewery, The Street, Pentlow, Essex CO10 7JJ
- (01787) 283220
- @ orders@nethergate.co.uk
- www.nethergate.co.uk

Mail order service

■ Nethergate was founded in Clare, Suffolk, in 1985 and is one of the most successful breweries in East Anglia, so much so that it needed to find a new, bigger home in 2005. There's one regular bottle-conditioned beer in the range, but almost every Nethergate cask beer is also bottled at some time or other.

Augustinian (4.5%, best bitter)

Norfolk Square

Norfolk Square Brewery, Unit 7, Estcourt Road, Great Yarmouth, Norfolk NR30 4JQ
- (01493) 854484
- @ beer@norfolksquarebrewery.co.uk
- www.norfolksquarebrewery.co.uk

■ Small brewery established in 2008 and adding bottles to the range the same year. Primed beer is bottled directly from casks.

Pi (3.8%, bitter)
Square Miled (4%, spring mild)
Scroby (4.2%, best bitter)
Stiletto (4.5%, golden ale)
Winklepicker (5%, winter porter)
Sunshiny (5.5%, summer strong ale)

North Cotswold

North Cotswold Brewery, Unit 3, Ditchford Farm, Campden Road, Shipston-on-Stour, Warwickshire GL56 9RD
- (01608) 663947
- @ ncb@pillingweb.co.uk
- www.northcotswoldbrewery.co.uk

Mail order service

■ North Cotswold Brewery was founded in 1999 but was taken over by former Firkin brewer Jon Pilling in 2005. His ten-barrel brewkit turns out cask beers for the local trade, as well as the bottle-conditioned beers featured below, which are filtered and re-seeded with fresh yeast prior to bottling.

Pig Brook (3.8%, golden ale)
Smoked Maple Porter (5%)
Monarch IPA (10%)
Arctic Global Warmer (15%, imperial stout)

North Curry

The North Curry Brewery Co., Gwyon House, Church Road, North Curry, Taunton, Somerset TA3 6LH
🕿 (07928) 815053
@ thenorthcurrybreweryco@ hotmail.co.uk
🌐 www. thenorthcurrybrewerycouk.com
Mail order service
■ Reviving brewing in North Curry village after an absence of more than 100 years, this business was founded in summer 2006. Bottling started the same year, with primed beer bottled in house straight from casks.

Church Ale (3.9%, bitter)
Red Heron Ale (4.3%, best bitter)
The Withyman Ale (4.6%, best bitter)
Level Headed Ale (4.7%, old ale)

North Wales

North Wales Brewery, Ty Tan-y-Mynydd, Moelfre, Abergele, Conwy LL22 9RF
🕿 (0800) 083 4100
@ northwalesbrewery@uwclub. net
🌐 www.northwalesbrewery.net
■ Previously known as Paradise Brewery, this business moved from Cheshire to North Wales and re-commenced production in 2008. Bottling resumed at the same time, with beers filled in house straight from the fermenting vessel.

Bodelwyddan Bitter (4%, bitter)
Feffryn y Ffarmwr (4%, bitter)
Welsh Stout (4.4%)
Llew Aur (4.5%, golden ale)
Abergele Ale (5%, best bitter)
Dragon's Wheat (5%, summer wheat beer)

North Yorkshire

North Yorkshire Brewing Company Ltd, Pinchinthorpe Hall, Guisborough, North Yorkshire TS14 8HG
🕿 (01287) 630200
@ sales@nybrewery.co.uk
🌐 www.nybrewery.co.uk
Mail order service
■ Brewery founded in 1989 in Middlesbrough and moved in 1998 to Pinchinthorpe Hall, a moated, listed house that was home to the Lee family and their descendants for centuries until 1957. The house now also includes a hotel and restaurant, and its own spring water is used for brewing. All the beers are registered as organic. In addition to the beers below, other draught beers are also bottled at times. They are all filled on site, direct from casks.

Best Bitter (3.6%, golden ale)
Prior's Ale (3.6%, golden ale)
Archbishop Lee's Ruby Ale (4%, bitter)
Boro Best (4%, bitter)
Cereal Killer (4.5%, wheat beer)
Fools Gold (4.6%, golden ale)
Golden Ale (4.6%)

Flying Herbert (4.7%, best bitter)
Lord Lee's (4.7%, best bitter)
Dizzy Dick (4.8%, best bitter)

Nutbrook

Nutbrook Brewery Ltd,
6 Hallam Way, West Hallam,
Derby DE7 6LA
- (0800) 458 2460
- chris@nutbrookbrewery.com
- www.nutbrookbrewery.com
- ■ Small, family-run brewery established in 2007. Bottling began a year later, with beers primed with a sugar solution and bottled from casks.

Or8 (3.8%, bitter)
Bitlyke (4.2%, best bitter)
Responsibly (4.4%, best bitter)
Banter (4.5%, golden ale)
Mongrel (4.5%, old ale)
Midnight (4.7%, stout)
More (4.8%, mild)

O'Hanlon's

**O'Hanlon's Brewing Co.
Ltd**, Great Barton Farm,
Whimple, Devon EX5 2NY
- (01404) 822412
- info@ohanlonsbrewery.com
- ■ O'Hanlon's was set up in 1996 to serve John O'Hanlon's pub in Clerkenwell, London, but quickly expanded to supply other outlets. In 2000, he sold the pub and moved the brewery to Devon. O'Hanlon's is now a major bottler and has secured the contract to brew and market the revered Thomas Hardy's Ale, as well as its old stablemate, Royal Oak. Generally, the beers are bottled, unfiltered, direct from conditioning tanks, although the process for

Thomas Hardy's Ale is a little more complicated. Beers are imported into the US by Phoenix Imports.

Goldblade (4%, wheat beer)
Yellow Hammer (4.2%, golden ale)
Original Port Stout (4.8%, port-laced stout)
Goodwill Bitter (5%, Christmas ale)
Royal Oak (5%, best bitter)
Thomas Hardy's Ale (11.7%, barley wine)

Oakleaf

The Oakleaf Brewing Co. Ltd,
Unit 7, Clarence Wharf Industrial Estate, Mumby Road, Gosport, Hampshire PO12 1AJ
- (023 92) 513222
- info@oakleafbrewing.co.uk
- www.oakleafbrewing.co.uk
- ■ Ed Anderson, a former Firkin brew pub brewer, set up Oakleaf with his father-in-law, Dave Pickersgill, in 2000. Their industrial unit home stands on the side of Gosport harbour. They brew and bottle the following beers in house, with each beer chilled, filtered and re-seeded with fresh yeast.

Bitter (3.8%, golden ale)
Maypole Mild (3.8%)
Nuptu'ale (4.2%, golden ale)
Heart of Oak (4.5%, best bitter)
Pompey Royal (4.5%, best bitter)
Hole Hearted (4.7%, golden ale)
I Can't Believe It's Not Bitter (4.9%, pale lager)
Blake's Gosport Bitter (5.2%, strong ale)
Blake's Heaven (7%, winter ale)

Breweries

Offa's Dyke

Offa's Dyke Brewery, Chapel Lane, Trefonen, Oswestry, Shropshire SY10 9DX
- (01691) 656889
- @ derekcjones@hotmail.co.uk
- www.offasdykebrewery.com
- ■ Brewery opened in 2003 at The Barley Mow pub, which sits astride Offa's Dyke, on the Wales-England border. Bottling commenced in 2008. The beers are fined, primed with a little sugar and then allowed ten days to warm-condition after filling.

Barley Gold (3.8%, golden ale)
Thirst Brew (4.2%, best bitter)
Grim Reaper (5%, porter)

Old Bear

Old Bear Brewery, Unit 4b, Atlas Works, Pitt Street, Keighley, West Yorkshire BD21 4YL
- (01535) 601222
- @ sales@oldbearbrewery.co.uk
- www.oldbearbrewery.co.uk
- Mail order service
- ■ Small brewery founded in 1993 as Old White Bear Brewery, and later undergoing a change of ownership as well as name. A move to new, custom-designed premises took place in 2004. The beers below are now bottled (in recycled pint glassware) by hand, in house, and then matured before going on sale.

Bruin (3.5%, mild)
Estivator (3.8%, golden ale)
Original (3.9%, bitter)
Black Mari'a (4.2%, stout)
Honeypot (4.4%, honey beer)
Goldilocks (4.5%, golden ale)
Hibernator (5%, best bitter)

Duke of Bronte Capstan FS (12.5%, IPA)

Old Chimneys

Old Chimneys Brewery, Hopton End Farm, Church Road, Market Weston, Diss, Norfolk IP22 2NX
- (01359) 221411
- www.oldchimneysbrewery.com
- Mail order service
- ■ Suffolk brewery, despite the postal address, founded by former Greene King and Broughton brewer Alan Thomson in 1995. His first bottles came out in autumn 2000, majoring on strong beers for sipping, but more quaffable brews have found their way into bottle in recent years. All the beers are matured in cask, and sometimes kräusened or primed, prior to bottling. Bottles are then given three weeks' secondary fermentation at the brewery before they go on sale. All beers are declared suitable for vegetarians, but Black Rat and Hairy Canary, with their milk-derived lactose, do not conform to vegan standards.

Meadow Brown (3.4%, mild)
Great Raft Bitter (4.1%, bitter)
Hairy Canary (4.2%, lemon- and ginger-spiced beer)
Black Rat Stout (4.5%, milk stout)
Golden Pheasant (4.7%, golden ale)
Amber Porter (4.8%)
India Pale Ale (5.6%)
Brimstone (6.1%, pale lager)
Red Clover (6.2%, clove-spiced ale)
Redshank (8.7%, old ale)

Good King Henry Special Reserve (11%, wood-aged imperial stout)

Old Luxters

Old Luxters Farm Brewery, Old Luxters Vineyard, Hambleden, Henley-on-Thames, Oxfordshire RG9 6JW

☎ (01491) 638330

@ enquiries@chilternvalley.co.uk

🌐 www.chilternvalley.co.uk

Mail order service

◾ Old Luxters was set up in 1990 in a 17th-century barn by David Ealand, owner of Chiltern Valley Wines. A new bottling line was installed in spring 1998. In total, conditioning and maturation for bottled beers at the brewery take five weeks, with beers filtered and re-seeded with primary fermentation yeast. The brewery also holds a warrant as a supplier to The Queen.

Old Windsor Gold Ale (4.5%, golden ale)
Dark Roast (5%, best bitter)
Luxters Gold Ale (5%, golden ale)
Old Windsor Dark Ale (5%, best bitter)
Barn Ale (5.4%, strong ale)
Damson Ale (7%, fruit beer)

Olde Swan

Olde Swan Brewery, 89 Halesowen Road, Netherton, Dudley DY2 9PY

☎ (01384) 253075

◾ Famous old brew pub, known familiarly as Ma Pardoe's after the long-serving landlady who once ran the place. Brewing ceased for a number of years but resumed in 2001. The beers below are bottled locally (although not in house) from casks that are allowed to settle and are then re-seeded with fresh yeast.

Entire (4.4%, best bitter)
Bumblehole (5.2%, strong ale)
Black Widow (7.2%, winter ale)

Oldershaw

Oldershaw Brewery, 12 Harrowby Hall Estate, Harrowby, Grantham, Lincolnshire NG31 9HB

☎ (01476) 572135

@ info@oldershawbrewery.com

🌐 www.oldershawbrewery.com

◾ Brewery founded by Gary and Diane Oldershaw next to the family home in 1997, the first brewery in Grantham for 30 years. The bottled beers are produced very much on an ad hoc basis, to use up surplus beer after all required casks have been filled. Any of the Oldershaw range may therefore be bottled, although the ones below are the most likely to be found. They may not all be available at any one time. The process involves racking the beer from casks and kräusening.

Caskade (4.2%, golden ale)
Grantham Stout (4.3%)
Regal Blonde (4.4%, pale lager)
Old Boy (4.8%, best bitter)
Yuletide (5.2%, Christmas ale)
Alchemy (5.3%, strong ale)

Organic

The Organic Brewhouse, Unit 1, Higher Bochym, Cury Cross Lanes, Helston, Cornwall TR12 7AZ

☎ (01326) 241555

@ orgbrewandy@tiscali.co.uk

🌐 www.theorganicbrewhouse.com

■ This entirely organic brewery was set up by Andy Hamer in 2000 in a former slaughterhouse in the shadow of Goonhilly Downs radio station in Cornwall. It is the southernmost brewery in mainland Britain. The first bottle-conditioned beer was brewed in 2001. The vegan-friendly beers are filled from a cask or conditioning tank and may be kräusened if necessary.

Lizard Point (4%, bitter)
Serpentine (4.5%, mild)
Black Rock Stout (4.7%)
Wolf Rock (5%, best bitter)

Otley

Otley Brewing Co. Ltd, Unit 42, Albion Industrial Estate, Pontypridd, Rhondda Cynon Taff CF37 4NX

📞 (01443) 480555

@ info@otleybrewing.co.uk

🌐 www.otleybrewing.co.uk

Mail order service

■ Family business (uncles, nephews, brothers) set up in 2005, building on a long tradition of running pubs in the Pontypridd area of South Wales. The bottles are filled from casks, carrying over primary fermentation yeast, and then conditioned at the brewery for two weeks before going on sale.

O1 (4%, golden ale)
Dark O (4.1%, stout)
O-Garden (4.8%, spiced ale)
O-Ho-Ho (5%, Christmas ale)
O8 (8%, barley wine)

Outstanding

Outstanding Brewing Co. Ltd, Unit 4b, Britannia Mill, Cobden Street, Bury BL9 6AW

📞 (0161) 764 7723

@ info@outstandingbeers.co.uk

🌐 www.outstandingbeers.com

■ Business established in 2008 by brewer and equipment supplier David Porter and two colleagues. The beers are bottled direct from casks or conditioning tanks and are primed.

Blond (4.5%, golden ale)
Ginger (4.5%, ginger-spiced beer)
OSB (4.4%, best bitter)
SOS (4.5%, best bitter)
Pilsner (5%)
Smoked Out (5%, smoked malt beer)
Standing Out (5.5%, strong ale)
Stout (5.5%)
Pushing Out (7.4%, barley wine)

Parish

Parish Brewery, 6 Main Street, Burrough-on-the-Hill, Leicestershire LE14 2JQ

📞 (01664) 454801

■ Parish Brewery is one of the great survivors among Britain's microbreweries, founded way back in 1983. Owner Barrie Parish produces three bottled beers, all filled in house from casks that are allowed to settle naturally, without finings. Primary fermentation yeast is thus carried over into the bottles.

Bitter (4%)
Borough Bitter (4.7%, best bitter)
Baz's Bonce Blower (12%, barley wine)

Pen-lon

Pen-lon Cottage Brewery,
Penlon Cottage Trading Ltd,
Penlon Farm, Pencae, Llanarth,
Ceredigion SA47 0QN

- ☎ (01545) 580022
- @ beer@penlon.biz
- 🌐 www.penlon.biz
- ■ Sheep are the inspiration at this small West Wales producer, 'where hand-crafted brewing complements the natural farm cycle'. To this end they even grow some of their own hops, and feed the spent malt grains to their own pigs. The first beers arrived in shops in 2004, with attractive labels drawn by Penny Samociuk who runs the brewery with husband Stefan. The beers are bottled straight from the fermenter, with a small amount of priming sugar added. No cask ales are currently produced.

Lambs Gold (3.2%, bitter)
Tipsy Tup (3.8%, bitter)
Heather Honey Ale (4.2%, honey beer)
Torddu (4.2%, fruit beer)
Chocolate Stout (4.5%)
Stock Ram (4.5%, stout)
Torwen (4.5%, fruit beer)
Twin Ram (4.8%, best bitter)
Ewes Frolic (5.2%, pale lager)
Gimmers Mischief (5.2%, strong ale)
Ramnesia (5.6%, strong ale)
Gimmers Mischief Export (7%, strong ale)

Penpont

Penpont Brewery, Inner
Trenarrett, Altarnun, Cornwall,
PL15 7SY

- ☎ (01566) 86069
- @ info@penpontbrewery.co.uk
- 🌐 www.penpontbrewery.co.uk
- ■ Penpont Brewery opened its doors in autumn 2008 in a converted milking parlour on the northern edge of Bodmin Moor. The beers are bottled directly from the fermentation vessel.

St Nonna's (3.7%, bitter)
Cornish Arvor (4%, golden ale)
Roughtor (4.7%, best bitter)

Pitfield

Pitfield Brewery, Ashlyns
Farm, Epping Road, North
Weald, Epping, Essex CM16 6RZ

- ☎ (0845) 833 1492
- @ sales@pitfieldbeershop.co.uk
- 🌐 www.pitfieldbeershop.co.uk
- Mail order service
- ■ Pitfield was founded in 1981 and, after several years out of production, was revived in 1996, next to Hoxton's well-known Beer Shop. The shop closed, after more than 20 years, in 2006, but the business goes on as a mail order operation. Pitfield Brewery then re-located to a garden/craft centre in Essex, but moved again in 2008, to an organic farm closer to London (the brewery has Soil Association accreditation). The beers are matured in cask for two to three weeks before being racked mostly bright. New yeast is added as required, with maltose syrup primings used to encourage a good secondary fermentation. The bottles are then kept at the brewery for at least two weeks before release. Because finings have been omitted, the beers hold no fears

311

for vegetarians or vegans, but they may be a little hazy as a result. Special one-off brews are occasionally produced.

Organic Lager (3.7%, pale lager)
Bitter (3.7%, bitter)
Shoreditch Stout (4%)
EKG (4.2%, golden ale)
Eco Warrior (4.5% golden ale)
Red Ale (4.8%, best bitter)
N1 Wheat Beer (5%)
1850 London Porter (5%)
1830 Amber Ale (6%, strong ale)
1824 Mild Ale (6.5%)
1837 India Pale Ale (7%)
1792 Imperial Stout (9.3%)
1896 XXXX Stock Ale (10%, barley wine)

Poachers

Poachers Brewery, 439 Newark Road, North Hykeham, Lincolnshire LN6 9SP
☎ (01522) 807404
🌐 www.poachersbrewery.co.uk
■ Poachers was opened in May 2001 and is run by ex-RAF man George Batterbee, who now brews in a converted barn behind his house. The range of bottled beers are all matured in cask before being racked bright and kräusened for bottling.

Trembling Rabbit Mild (3.4%)
Shy Talk Bitter (3.7%, golden ale)
Pride (4%, bitter)
Bog Trotter (4.2%, best bitter)
Billy Boy (4.4%, best bitter)
Black Crow Stout (4.5%)
Hykeham Gold (4.5%, golden ale)
Monkey Hanger (4.5%, best bitter)
Jock's Trap (5%, best bitter)
Trout Tickler (5.5%, strong ale)

Potbelly

Potbelly Brewery, 25–31 Durban Road, Kettering, Northamptonshire NN16 0JA
☎ (01536) 410818
@ toni@potbelly-brewery.co.uk
🌐 www.potbelly-brewery.co.uk
■ Brewery founded in February 2005. The beers mentioned below are bottled in house. They are conditioned in a tank for a week, then kräusened prior to filling.

Wicksteed Heritage (4.2%, best bitter)
Beijing Black (4.4%, mild)
Pigs Do Fly (4.4%, golden ale)
Inner Daze (4.6%, golden ale)
Redwing (4.8%, best bitter)
Captain Pigwash (5%, porter)
Jingle Bellies (5%, Christmas ale)
Yeller Belly (5.2%, strong ale)
Crazy Daze (5.5% strong ale)

Potton

The Potton Brewery Co., 10 Shannon Place, Potton, Bedfordshire SG19 2SP
☎ (01767) 261042
@ info@potton-brewery.co.uk
🌐 www.potton-brewery.co.uk
■ Reviving the Potton Brewery Co. name, after it disappeared following a take-over in 1922, this business was set up in 1999, by two former Greene King employees. The one bottle-conditioned beer is brewed for Wimpole Hall, a National Trust property in Cambridgeshire. It is conditioned first in cask, decanted, kräusened and then bottled.

Butlers' Ale (4.3%, best bitter)

Prospect

Prospect Brewery, 120 Wigan Road, Standish, Wigan WN6 0AY

- (01257) 421329
- @ sales@prospectbrewery.com
- www.prospectbrewery.org.uk
- Founded in August 2007, Prospect Brewery is run by former child care professional Patsy Slavin from her home. The beers are bottled directly from casks by Patsy herself, using equipment at Bank Top Brewery, where she learned her brewing skills.

Silver Tally (3.7%, golden ale)
Nutty Slack (3.9%, mild)
Pioneer (4%, bitter)
Blinding Light (4.2%, golden ale)
Gold Rush (4.5%, golden ale)
Clementine (5%, Christmas spiced fruit beer)
Pickaxe (5%, porter)
Big Adventure (5.5%, strong ale)

Quantock

Quantock Brewery, Unit E, Monument View, Chelston Business Park, Wellington, Somerset TA21 9ND

- (01823) 662669
- @ rob@quantockbrewery.co.uk
- www.quantockbrewery.co.uk
- Small Somerset brewery that started operation at the end of 2007. The beers are bottled from casks and primed with sugar. No finings are added, which makes them safe for vegans.

Quantock Ale (3.8%, bitter)
Sunraker (4.2%, golden ale)
Stout (4.5%)
White Hind (4.5%, best bitter)
Royal Stag IPA (6%)

Ramsgate

Ramsgate Brewery Ltd, 1 Hornet Close, Pyson's Road Industrial Estate, Broadstairs, Kent CT10 2YD

- (01843) 868453
- @ info@ramsgatebrewery.co.uk
- www.ramsgatebrewery.co.uk
- Brewery opened in 2002 on Ramsgate seafront but moved to a new, larger location in 2006. The bottled beers are filled from tanks, having been allowed to drop bright, primed and re-seeded with fresh yeast.

No.3 (5%, golden ale)
Dogbolter (5.6%, porter)
Exodus (6.2%, stout)
India Ale (8.3%, IPA)
Ancestors (9%, wood-aged beer)

RCH

RCH Brewery, West Hewish, Weston-super-Mare, Somerset BS24 6RR

- (01934) 834447
- @ rchbrew@aol.com
- www.rchbrewery.com
- This brewery was originally installed behind the Royal Clarence Hotel at Burnham-on-Sea in the early 1980s (hence the name), but since 1993 brewing has taken place on a rural site, a couple of fields away from the rumble of the M5 motorway. The beers are shipped in conditioning tanks to Branded Drinks in Gloucestershire for bottling. They are distributed in the USA by B United.

PG Steam (4%, bitter)
Pitchfork (4.3%, golden ale)

Old Slug Porter (4.5%)
Double Header (5.3%, strong ale)
Ale Mary (6%, spiced beer)
Firebox (6%, strong ale)

Rebellion

Rebellion Beer Co.,
Bencombe Farm, Marlow
Bottom, Buckinghamshire SL7 3LT
☎ (01628) 476594
@ info@rebellionbeer.co.uk
🌐 www.rebellionbeer.co.uk
Mail order service
▦ Rebellion was the company
that brought brewing back to
Marlow, following the closure of
Wethered by Whitbread. Opened
in 1993, the brewery has since
moved locally and expanded,
serving a sizeable pub trade. A
new bottling line allows the one
bottle-conditioned beer, and
other bottled beers, to be filled
on site.

White (5%, wheat beer)

Red Rat

Red Rat Craft Brewery,
12 Broadmere Cottages, Truston,
Bury St Edmunds, Suffolk IP31 1EH
☎ (01359) 269742
@ sales@redratcraftbrewery.co.uk
🌐 www.redratcraftbrewery.co.uk
▦ Brewery set up in summer 2007
by ex-soldier Kevin McHenry.
The Hadley in the beer name is
Tony Hadley, former front man
of Spandau Ballet, who is a
shareholder in the business. The
beers are bottled on site from
a tank after they have dropped
bright and are kräusened.

Hadley's (4%, golden ale)
Waterloo (4.2%, wheat beer)

Jimmy's Same Again (5.2%,
strong ale)
Crazy Dog Stout (6%)
Jimmy's Flying Pig (6%, strong
ale)

Red Rock

Red Rock Brewery, Higher
Humber Farm, Bishopsteignton,
Devon TQ14 9TD
☎ (01626) 879738
@ john@redrockbrewery.co.uk
🌐 www.redrockbrewery.co.uk
▦ Family-run brewery based in a
renovated barn on a working
farm.

Humber Down (3.6%, brown ale)
Back Beach (3.8%, golden ale)
Red Rock (4.2%, best bitter)
Drift Wood (4.3%, best bitter)
Rushy Mede (4.4%, organic
golden ale)
Dark Ness (4.5%, porter)
Break Water (4.6%, best bitter)

Red Squirrel

Red Squirrel Brewery,
14b Mimram Road, Hertford
SG14 1NN
☎ (01992) 501100
@ gary@redsquirrelbrewery.co.uk
🌐 www.redsquirrelbrewery.co.uk
Mail order service
▦ Hertford brewery founded in
2004, taking its name from the
endangered British squirrel
species. Brewer Gary Hayward
supports the red squirrel's
fight for survival through
small donations from sales of
Conservation Bitter.

RSB (3.9%, golden ale)
Conservation Bitter (4.1%)
IPA in the USA (5.4%)

Reepham

Reepham Brewery, Unit 1, Collers Way, Reepham, Norfolk NR10 4SW

☎ (01603) 871091

■ Reepham is one of the longest established breweries in Norfolk, founded in 1983. Its contribution to the bottle-conditioned beer scene is not entirely conventional, as the beer mentioned is packaged only in 2-litre PET bottles for sale in some local off-licences, with a best before date set at just six weeks after filling.

Rapier Pale Ale (4.3%, best bitter)

Rhymney

Rhymney Brewery Ltd, Unit A2, Valley Enterprise Centre, Dowlais, Merthyr Tydfil CF48 2SR

☎ (01685) 722253

@ enquiries@rhymneybreweryltd.com

🌐 www.rhymneybreweryltd.com

■ Rhymney Brewery, established in 2005, produces a range of filtered beers for the bottle, but also bottle conditions beer on request for other businesses, such as the CAMRA Beer Club, for which its Dark (4%) has been made available in 'real' form.

Ridgeway

Ridgeway Brewing, Beer Counter Ltd, South Stoke, Oxfordshire RG8 0JW

☎ (01491) 873474

@ peter.scholey@beercounter.co.uk

■ Ridgeway Brewing is run by Peter Scholey, former head brewer at Brakspear, who, in addition to brewing bottle-conditioned beers for other brewers, also brews for his own business, using equipment at Hepworth & Co. in Horsham and other venues. The Ridgeway long-distance footpath passes just a few hundred yards from Peter's front door in South Oxfordshire – hence the brewery name. The beers are sterile filtered before being re-seeded with fresh yeast for bottling.

Bitter (4%)
ROB (Ridgeway Organic Bitter) (4.3%, golden ale)
Bad Elf (4.5%, Christmas ale)
High & Mighty Beer of the Gods (4.5%, golden ale)
Oxfordshire Blue (5%, golden ale)
Ivanhoe (5.2%, strong ale)
IPA (5.5%)
Bad King John (6%, strong ale)
Foreign Export Stout (8%)

Ringmore

Ringmore Craft Brewery, Higher Ringmore Road, Shaldon, Devon TQ14 0HG

☎ (01626) 873114

@ geoff@ringmorecraftbrewery.co.uk

■ Brewery set up in 2007 by two former deputy headteachers. It started as a hobby and has grown beyond expectations. The beers are fined using auxiliary finings, rather than isinglass (making them vegan friendly), then racked into a new cask ready for bottling.

Holly Boo Ale (4%, raspberry beer)
Secret Santa (4%, winter cinnamon-spiced ale)

Rollocks (4.5%, golden ale)
Oarsome Ale (4.6%, best bitter)
Belles (5%, winter golden ale)
Whistling Bridge (5%, curaçao-spiced ale)
Atmospheric Ale (5.7%, old ale)
Santa's Little Helper (5.7%, winter spiced old ale)

Rodham's
Rodham's Brewery,
74 Albion Street, Otley,
West Yorkshire LS21 1BZ
☎ (01943) 464530
■ Brewery established by Michael Rodham in the cellar of his house in 2005 and expanded a little since. The beers for bottling are settled naturally (no finings) in casks for three weeks before being re-seeded with fresh primary fermentation yeast and primed with dried malt extract. Bottles are then matured at the brewery for at least four weeks before going on sale.

Wheat Beer (4.6%)
Old Albion (5.5%, porter)
IPA (6.2%)

Rooster's
Rooster's Brewing Company Ltd, Unit 3, Grimbald Park, Wetherby Road, Knaresborough, North Yorkshire HG5 8LJ
☎ (01423) 865959
@ sean@roosters.co.uk
🌐 www.roosters.co.uk
■ Brewery opened in 1993 by Sean Franklin, a former wine student and previously owner of Franklin's Brewery. New premises were acquired in 2001. Bottle-conditioned beer was introduced in 2009, through a series of hand-crafted beers sold in 750-ml bottles. Each is casked from the fermentation vessel, primed and re-seeded with fresh primary fermentation yeast before bottling. After filling, beers are allowed at least three months to condition before release.

Wild Mule (3.9%, golden ale)
Leghorn (4.3%, golden ale)
Yankee (4.3%, golden ale)
Nector (5%, Christmas ale)

Sadler's
See **Windsor Castle**

Saffron
Saffron Brewery, The Cartshed, Parsonage Farm, Henham, Bishop's Stortford, Hertfordshire CM22 6AN
☎ (01279) 850923
@ tb@saffronbrewery.co.uk
🌐 www.saffronbrewery.co.uk
Mail order service
■ Brewery founded in 2005 and moved to a new, larger location, in a converted barn, in 2008. The beers below were added to the range in 2006. They are bottled in house, kräusened and filled from casks. Imperial Ale is a limited-edition brew in 750-ml bottles. It contains real saffron and is therefore sold at a premium price.

Ramblers Tipple (3.9%, bitter)
Brewhouse Bell (4%, golden ale)
Squires Gamble (4.3%, best bitter)
Blonde (4.3%, golden ale)
Imperial Ale (4.3%, saffron beer)
Flying Serpent (4.5%, brown ale)

Henham Honey (4.6%, honey beer)
Chestnut Grove (4.8%, best bitter)
Tiddly Vicar (5.1%, strong ale)
Silent Night (5.2%, porter)

St Austell
St Austell Brewery Co. Ltd, 63 Trevarthian Road, St Austell, Cornwall PL25 4BY

- (01726) 74444
- @ info@staustellbrewery.co.uk
- www.staustellbrewery.co.uk

Mail order service

- St Austell joined the band of bottle-conditioned beer brewers in spring 2000, when it won the Tesco Beer Challenge with Clouded Yellow. Further bottle-conditioned ales have been added in the years since. These have been brewed at St Austell and packaged under contract, by Thwaites In Blackburn, but a new bottling hall at St Austell means that the multi-award-winning range will be handled in house from now on. The beers are sterile filtered and re-seeded with the original yeast strain prior to bottling.

Clouded Yellow (4.8%, wheat beer)
Admiral's Ale (5%, best bitter)
Marks & Spencer Cornish IPA (5%)
Proper Job (5.5%, IPA)

St Jude's
St Jude's Brewery, 2 Cardigan Street, Ipswich, Suffolk IP1 3PF

- (01473) 413334
- @ gt6xxx@yahoo.co.uk
- www.stjudesbrewery.co.uk

- Brewery established in an 18th-century coach house in 2007. The beers below are fined, then filled from casks, but Pagan Path and St Francis remain unfined, making them vegan friendly.

Pagan Path (4%, vanilla-laced wheat beer)
Royal Tudor Honey Ale (4%, summer honey beer)
St Francis (4%, bitter)
Gypeswic Bitter (4.4%, best bitter)
Ipswich Bright IPA (4.4%, best bitter)
Coachman's Whip (5.2%, strong ale)
Devereaux's Dark Porter (5.5%)
John Orford's Strong Brown Ale (5.5%)
St Gabriel's Christmas Ale (6%)
St Mary's Stout (6%)
Wolsey's Winter Warmer (6.2%, winter ale)

Salopian
Salopian Brewing Co., Ltd, The Brewery, 67 Mytton Oak Road, Shrewsbury, Shropshire SY3 8UQ

- (01743) 248414
- @ enquiries@salopianbrewery. co.uk
- www.salopianbrewery.co.uk

- Salopian was founded in 1995 and changed hands two years later. Bottle-conditioned beers were introduced in 1996 but the wide range once produced has now dwindled to just one. This is brewed for Salopian by Peter Scholey of Ridgeway Brewing at Hepworth & Co. in Horsham.

Entire Butt (4.8%, porter)

- Three Horse Shoes landlord Frank Goodwin had been a home brewer long before deciding to brew for his own pub. His bottle-conditioned ales are sold in tiny numbers (no wholesaler calls, please!), with the most famous, Farrier's, among the strongest beers around (the strength varies from brew to brew). All beers are produced with malt extract, rather than from a full mash and are bottled in house with the addition of a little priming sugar.

Norton Ale (3.6%, bitter)
Canon Bitter (4.2%, best bitter)
Peploe's Tipple (6%, strong ale)
Farrier's Beer (14.7%, barley wine)

Samuel Smith
Samuel Smith Old Brewery (Tadcaster), High Street, Tadcaster, North Yorkshire LS24 9SB
- (01937) 832225
- Fine, traditional brewery, housed in Tadcaster's Old Brewery, vacated by John Smith's when it moved next door in 1884. The very private company has long produced a range of interesting bottled beers, but the only bottle-conditioned beer did not arrive until 2008.

Yorkshire Stingo (8%, wood-aged barley wine)

South Hams
South Hams Brewery Co. Ltd, Stokeley Barton, Stokenham, Kingsbridge, Devon TQ7 2SE
- (01548) 581151

- @ info@southhamsbrewery.co.uk
- www.southhamsbrewery.co.uk
- South Hams opened in Plymouth in 1993 as Sutton Brewery. In 2004 the brewery moved to Stokenham and the name was changed. The beers are brewed here but bottled by Country Life Brewery direct from casks.

Devon Pride (3.8%, bitter)
XSB (4.2%, best bitter)
Wild Blonde (4.4%, spring/ summer golden ale)
Sutton Comfort (4.5%, mild)
Eddystone (4.8%, IPA)
Devon Porter (5%, winter porter)

Spectrum
Spectrum Brewery, Unit 11, Wellington Road, Tharston, Norwich, Norfolk NR15 2PE
- (07949) 254383
- @ info@spectrumbrewery.co.uk
- www.spectrumbrewery.co.uk
- Brewery founded in 2002, which became registered organic in 2007. The beers below are filled from tank and are fined and primed if necessary. The finings are not isinglass, so the beers are all vegan friendly.

Light Fantastic (3.7%, golden ale)
Dark Fantastic (3.8%, mild)
Bezants (4%, golden ale)
42 (4.2%, best bitter)
Black Bottle (4.5%, stout)
Capt. Scarlet (4.5%, autumn best bitter)
Spring Promise (4.5%, spring best bitter)
Wizzard (4.9%, best bitter)
Old Stoatwobbler (6%, old ale)
Trip Hazard (6.5%, strong ale)
Yule Fuel (7%, Christmas ale)

Spinning Dog

Spinning Dog Brewery,
88 St Owen Street, Hereford
HR1 2QD
☎ (01432) 342125
@ jfkenyon@aol.com
🌐 www.spinningdogbrewery.co.uk
Mail order service
■ Small, family-run brewery
established in 2000 and based
at Hereford's Victory pub. It
was expanded in 2002 to meet
demand for its popular beers.
The bottled beers are filtered
and re-seeded with fresh yeast
prior to filling and then matured
for at least a month in the bottle
before going on sale.

Hereford Organic Bitter (3.7%,
golden ale)
Gamekeeper's Bitter (4.2%, best
bitter)
Hereford Best Bitter (4.2%)
Organic Oatmeal Stout (4.4%)
Mutley's Revenge (4.8%, best
bitter)

Spire

Spire Brewery Ltd, Units 2–3,
Gisborne Close, Ireland Business
Park, Staveley, Chesterfield,
Derbyshire S43 3JT
☎ (01246) 476005
@ info@spirebrewery.co.uk
🌐 www.spirebrewery.co.uk
■ Brewery founded by former
teacher and Scots Guards
bandsman David McLaren in
2006. Music plays a major role
in the names of his beers, which
are bottled direct from casks
and primed with malt extract.
The bottles are then both warm-
and cold-conditioned at the
brewery before release.

Overture (3.9%, bitter)
Whiter Shade of Pale (4%,
golden ale)
80 Shilling Ale (4.3%)
Dark Side of the Moon (4.3%,
mild)
Chesterfield Best Bitter (4.5%)
Twist & Stout (4.5%, stout)
Sovereign (5.2%, IPA)
Sgt Pepper Stout (5.5%, pepper-
spiced stout)
Winter Wonderland (6.1%,
winter old ale)
Britannia Cream Ale (6.4%,
strong ale)

Spitting Feathers

Spitting Feathers Brewery,
Common Farm, Waverton,
Chester CH3 7QT
☎ (01244) 332052
@ info@spittingfeathers.org
🌐 www.spittingfeathers.org
■ Farm-based brewery set up in
2005. Bottled beers are available
only in small quantities, filled
in house from cask beer that is
allowed to drop mostly bright.

Farmhouse Ale (3.6%, bitter)
Thirstquencher (3.9%, golden
ale)
Special Ale (4.2%, best bitter)
Old Wavertonian (4.4%, stout)
Basketcase (4.8%, best bitter)

Stationhouse

**Stationhouse at Frodsham
Brewery**, Lady Heyes Craft
Centre, Kingsley Road, Frodsham,
Cheshire WA6 6SU
☎ (01928) 787917
@ enquire@stationhousebrewery.
co.uk
🌐 www.stationhousebrewery.
co.uk

321

Isambard Kingdom Brunel 1859
(4.7%, best bitter)
Turkey's Delight (5.1%,
Christmas ale)

Suthwyk

Suthwyk Ales, Offwell
Farm, Southwick, Fareham,
Hampshire PO17 6DX
☎ (023 92) 325252
@ mjbazeley@suthwykales.com
🌐 www.suthwykales.com
Mail order service

■ Suthwyk Ales does not brew
it self. It is run by barley farmer
Martin Bazeley, who decided to
go the whole hog and complete
the 'field to table' cycle by
commissioning a beer brewed
from malt kilned by Warminster
Maltings from his own Optic
barley. Produced by Hop Back
Brewery, Skew Sunshine Ale
proved to be a hit and was
followed up by a second
offering, Bloomfields, and then
a third, Liberation. The beers
are now mostly brewed and
bottled for Martin by Hepworth
& Co. in Horsham (the cask-
conditioned versions, and some
bottled beers, are brewed at
Oakleaf Brewery in Gosport).
Martin is also a partner in
Southwick Brewhouse, a bottled
beer shop housed in the old
Hunt's brewery in Southwick,
Hampshire (the brewery is still
intact and can be toured).

Bloomfields (3.8%, golden ale)
Liberation (4.2%, golden ale)
Skew Sunshine Ale (4.6%,
golden ale)
Palmerston's Folly (5%, wheat
beer)

Swaton

Swaton Brewery Ltd,
North End Farm, Swaton, Sleaford,
Lincolnshire NG34 0JP
☎ (01529) 421241
@ swatonbrewery@hotmail.co.uk
🌐 www.swatonbrewery.com
■ Brewery opened in 2007 in the
outbuildings of the owner's
working farm. A visitor centre/
shop/café now stands alongside.
Beers are bottled in house, with
fresh yeast added before filling.

Happy Jack (4.2%, golden ale)
Dozy Bull (4.5%, best bitter)
Three Degrees (4.7%, best bitter)

Teignworthy

Teignworthy Brewery Ltd,
The Maltings, Teign Road,
Newton Abbot, Devon TQ12 4AA
☎ (01626) 332066
@ sales@teignworthybreweryLtd.
co.uk
🌐 www.teignworthybrewery.com
Mail order service (via Tucker's
Maltings)
■ Teignworthy was founded in
1994 by former Oakhill and
Ringwood brewer John Lawton,
using part of the Victorian
malthouse of Edward Tucker &
Sons. (Tucker's Maltings is now
a fascinating tourist attraction.)
The bottled beers are the same
as John's cask beers, except
that usually they are filtered and
re-pitched with new yeast.

**Reel Ale/Edwin Tucker's
Devonshire Prize Ale**
(4%, bitter)
Spring Tide (4.3%, best bitter)
Old Moggie (4.4%, best bitter)
Beachcomber (4.5%, pale lager)

Harvey's Special Brew (4.6%, golden ale)
Pippa's Pint (4.7%, best bitter)
Amy's Ale (4.8%, golden ale)
Maltster's Ale (5%, best bitter)
Martha's Mild (5.3%)
Edwin Tucker's Maris Otter (5.5%, strong ale)
Christmas Cracker (6%, Christmas ale)
Edwin Tucker's Choice Old Walnut Brown Ale (6%)
Edwin Tucker's East India Pale Ale (6.5%)
Edwin Tucker's Empress Russian Porter (10.5%, imperial porter)

Teme Valley
Teme Valley Brewery,
The Talbot, Knightwick, Worcestershire WR6 5PH
🕿 (01886) 821235
@ chris@temevalleybrewery.co.uk
🌐 www.temevalleybrewery.co.uk
◼ The Talbot Inn at Knightwick is owned by the Clift family, who farmed hops locally from the 19th century up to the year 2000. The hops they cultivated are still used in the pub's brewery, which was set up in 1997. Brewer Chris Gooch produces a range of cask and bottled beers to the same recipes, with the beers below bottled, without fining or filtration, by Branded Drinks in Gloucestershire.

This (3.7%, bitter)
The Hop Nouvelle (4.1%, green hop bitter)
That (4.1%, bitter)
Wotever Next? (5%, best bitter)
Hearth Warmer (6%, winter ale)

Thornbridge
Thornbridge Brewery,
Thornbridge Hall, Ashford-in-the-Water, Derbyshire DE45 1NZ
🕿 (01629) 641000
@ info@thornbridgebrewery.co.uk
🌐 www.thornbridgebrewery.co.uk
◼ Thornbridge opened in October 2004, brewing in the former joiner's and stonemason's workshop in the grounds of Thornbridge Hall, near Bakewell in the Peak District. Plans are in hand to re-locate and expand the brewery, which has an excellent reputation for innovative, quality beers.

Jaipur IPA (5.9%)
Halcyon (7.7%, green hop IPA)
Saint Petersburg (7.7%, imperial stout)
Bracia (9%, chestnut honey beer)

Three B's
Three B's Brewery,
Laneside Works, Stockclough Lane, Feniscowles, Blackburn, Lancashire BB2 5JR
🕿 (01254) 207686
@ info@threebsbrewery.co.uk
🌐 www.threebsbrewery.co.uk
◼ After more than 20 years of making beer, Robert Bell founded Three B's Brewery in 2001 and now turns out a range of cask beers, plus the four following bottled brands. The beers – which take their names from aspects of the mill trade that once dominated the brewery's home town of Blackburn – are matured in conditioning tanks or casks then filled directly, keeping the same primary fermentation yeast.

and re-seeded with fresh yeast
ready for the bottle.

Brig o'Allan (4%, 80/-)
Ginger Explosion (5%, ginger-
spiced beer)

Tryst
Tryst Brewery, Lorne Road,
Larbert, Falkirk FK5 4AT
☎ (01324) 554000
@ john@trystbrewery.co.uk
🌐 www.trystbrewery.co.uk
Mail order service
■ Small brewery founded by
experienced brewer John
McGarva in 2003, in an industrial
unit close to the station in the
town of Larbert. His bottled
beers followed soon after.
The bottles are filled in house
from prepared casks, the same
primary fermentation yeast
carrying over to the bottle.

Brockville Dark (3.8%, mild)
Brockville Pale (3.8%, golden ale)
Blàthan (4%, elderflower beer)
Drovers 80/- (4%)
Stars & Stripes (4%, golden ale)
Carronade IPA (4.2%, golden ale)
Carron Oatmalt Stout (6.1%)

Tunnel
Tunnel Brewery Ltd, c/o Lord
Nelson Inn, Birmingham Road,
Ansley, Warwickshire CV10 9RX
☎ (02476) 394888
@ info@tunnelbrewery.co.uk
🌐 www.tunnelbrewery.co.uk
■ Brewery set up in 2005 and
taking its name from the
five-mile railway tunnel that
passes beneath the village of
Ansley. The pub mentioned
in the address is a separate

business, but does sell Tunnel's
beers. Bottled beers arrived in
2006. Before filling, the beers
are generally held in casks
for a month and then lightly
kräusened. All are declared
vegan friendly. The back labels
of most bottles carry lengthy,
light-hearted 'Rumour has it...'
stories about the beer's name.

Golden Samurai (3.7%, golden
ale)
Linda Lear Beer (3.7%, bitter)
Late OTT (4%, bitter)
Meadowland (4%, golden ale)
Roger the Goblin (4%, Christmas
ale)
Legend (4.3%, best bitter)
Czech Style Black Lager (4.4%)
Trade Winds (4.6%, best bitter)
Parish Ale (4.7%, best bitter)
Shadow Weaver (4.7%, stout)
Fields of Gold (5%, golden ale)
Jean Cloudy Van Damme (5%,
wheat beer)
Stranger in the Mist (5%, wheat
beer)
Munich Style Lager (5.2%, pale
lager)
Nelson's Column (5.2%, old ale)
Vienna Style Lager (5.2%)
Boston Beer Party (5.6%, strong
ale)
Northern Lights (6.1%, strong
ale)
Quill (7%, strong ale)

Under *Battlefield Brewery* name
(originally for Battlefield Heritage
Centre, Bosworth):
Let Battle Commence (3.8%,
bitter)
Richard III Plantagenet (4.2%,
golden ale)
Henry Tudor (5%, old ale)

Uncle Stuart's

Uncle Stuart's Brewery and Shop, Wroxham Barns, Tunstead Road, Hoveton, Norwich, Norfolk NR12 8QU

☎ (01603) 783888

@ stuartsbrewery@aol.com

■ Stuart Evans started out brewing bottled beers in very small quantities at his home in rural Norfolk in spring 2002. He later opened The Little Beer Shop in Blofield, selling his own and other bottled beers, but this has now closed as Stuart has relocated both shop and brewery to the Wroxham Barns craft and tourist centre.

North Norfolk Beauty (3.8%, golden ale)
Pack Lane Mild (4%)
Excelsior (4.5%, best bitter)
Local Hero (4.7%, best bitter)
Norwich Castle (5%, golden ale)
Buckenham Woods (5.6%, strong ale)
Strumpshaw Fen (5.7%, strong ale)
Norwich Cathedral (6.5%, strong ale)
Christmas Ale/Winter Ale (7%)

Vale

Vale Brewery Company, Tramway Business Park, Ludgershall Road, Brill, Buckinghamshire HP18 9TY

☎ (01844) 239237

@ info@valebrewery.co.uk

🌐 www.valebrewery.co.uk

■ Vale Brewery was opened in 1995 by brothers Mark and Phil Stevens. Their brewery was originally housed in an industrial unit on the fringe of Haddenham, but in 2007 they moved to Brill, another picturesque village nine miles away. Bottling dates from 1997. All the beers are matured in casks, sterile filtered, primed with sweet wort and re-seeded with fresh yeast.

Black Swan (3.9%, mild)
Wychert (3.9%, bitter)
VPA (4.2%, golden ale)
Black Beauty Porter (4.3%)
Edgar's Golden Ale (4.3%)
Grumpling (4.6%, best bitter)
Marks & Spencer Buckinghamshire Ale (4.6%, best bitter)
Gravitas (4.8%, golden ale)
Good King Senseless (5.2%, Christmas ale)

Vale of Glamorgan

Vale of Glamorgan Brewery Ltd, Unit 8a, Atlantic Trading Estate, Barry, Vale of Glamorgan CF63 3RF

☎ (01446) 730757

@ info@vogbrewery.co.uk

🌐 www.vogbrewery.co.uk

■ Brewery opened in 2005 and moving into bottling in summer 2008. Bottles are conditioned for three weeks before going on sale.

Bitter Than Ever (4.3%, best bitter)
Grog y VoG (4.3%, golden ale)
Wheats Occurrin? (5%, wheat beer)

Wagtail

Wagtail Brewery, Old Buckenham, Norfolk NR17 1PF

☎ (01953) 887133

@ wagtailbrewery@btinternet.com

🌐 www.wagtailbrewery.com

■ Small East Anglian brewery established in 2006 and specialising in bottle-conditioned beers, all of which are declared to be acceptable to vegans.

Best Bittern (4%, bitter)
Goldrush (4%, golden ale)
King Tut (4%, golden ale)
Plan B (4%, bitter)
English Ale (4.2%, best bitter)
Black Beauty (4.5%, porter)
Black Shuck (4.5%, stout)
Hornblower (4.5%, best bitter)
ESB (5.2%, strong ale)
Jumping Jericho (5.2%, Christmas ale)

Wapping
Wapping Beers Ltd,
The Baltic Fleet, 33a Wapping, Liverpool L1 8DQ

☎ (0151) 709 3116

@ siholt@wappingbeers.co.uk

🌐 www.wappingbeers.co.uk

■ Brewery established in 2002 in the historic Baltic Fleet pub, directly across the road from Liverpool's famous Albert Dock. Bottles are filled in house from casks of beer that has been racked from the fermenting vessel. Warm and cold conditioning follows before the beers are released.

Baltic Gold (3.9%, golden ale)
Zebu Bitter (4%, golden ale)
Summer Ale (4.2%, golden ale)
Smoked Porter (5%)
Stout (5%)
Winter Ale (6.5%, spiced winter ale)

Warcop
Warcop Brewery, 9 Nellive Park, St Brides Wentlooge, Newport NP10 8SE

☎ (01633) 680058

@ william.picton@tesco.net

🌐 www.warcopales.com

■ Brewery established in 1998 by chemist and experienced home brewer Bill Picton, in a former milking parlour between Newport and Cardiff. The above address is his home/office: the brewery is a few miles away. Bill produces an enormous range of bottle-conditioned beers, with names often connected to the heavy industries of South Wales. Not all are available at all times, however, so a listing here would not be very useful (the Warcop website is a better bet). The beers are filled directly from casks. They are primed with a sugar syrup and are matured both before and after bottling.

Warwickshire
Warwickshire Beer Co. Ltd,
Queen Street, Cubbington, Warwickshire CV32 7NA

☎ (01926) 450747

@ info@warwickshirebeer.co.uk

🌐 www.warwickshirebeer.co.uk

Mail order service

■ Warwickshire was set up in 1998 in a former village bakery (an earlier Warwickshire Brewery ran for a couple of years in the mid-1990s producing some beers of the same name). Seven bottle-conditioned beers are now available, filled in-house from matured casks primed with sugar. Snipe Ale is a dry-hopped version of Best Bitter.

Best Bitter (3.9%, bitter)
Snipe Ale (3.9%, bitter)
Lady Godiva (4.2%, golden ale)
Churchyard Bob (4.9%, best bitter)
Warwick Market Ale (4.9%, best bitter)
Jolly Green Giant (5%, green hop beer)
Kingmaker (5.5%, strong ale)

Wells & Young's
Wells & Young's Brewing Co., Havelock Street, Bedford MK40 4LU
- (01234) 272625
- @ sales@charleswells.co.uk
- www.wellsandyoungs.co.uk
- ■ This major new name in British brewing came into effect in autumn 2006, with the merger of the brewing interests of Charles Wells and Young's. In addition to the bottle-conditioned beers below, which are filtered and re-seeded with fresh yeast for bottling, the brewery also offers an excellent take-home alternative in the form of mini-casks of fresh, live Bombardier bitter.

Young's Bitter (4.5%, best bitter)
Young's Kew Gold (4.8%, golden ale)
Young's Special London Ale (6.4%, strong ale)

Welton's
Welton's Brewery Ltd,
1 Mulberry Trading Estate, Foundry Lane, Horsham, West Sussex RH13 5PX
- (01403) 242901
- @ sales@weltons.co.uk
- www.weltonsbeer.com

■ Welton's Brewery opened in an old milking parlour near Dorking, Surrey, in 1995 and re-located to Horsham, West Sussex, in 2003. Many of the brewery's cask ales find their way into bottle, but here are listed the regular bottled offerings. These are filled in house, direct from casks. No finings are used, making them vegan friendly.

Pride 'n' Joy (2.8%, bitter)
Sussex Pride (4%, bitter)
Old Cocky (4.3%, golden ale)
Horsham Old (4.5%, winter old ale)
Export Stout (4.7%)
Red Cross Mild (5.1%, spring mild)
Old Harry (5.2%, strong ale)
Clipper (6.1%, summer/autumn IPA)

Westerham
Westerham Brewery Co. Ltd, Grange Farm, Pootings Road, Crockham Hill, Edenbridge, Kent TN8 6SA
- (01732) 864427
- @ info@westerhambrewery.co.uk
- www.westerhambrewery.co.uk
- Mail order service
- ■ Westerham Brewery was set up in 2004 on a National Trust farm close to Sir Winston Churchill's country retreat, Chartwell, with founder Robert Wicks, an ex-City financier, reviving brewing in the area after a gap of nearly 40 years. Yeast strains preserved from Westerham's last operating brewery, Black Eagle, are used to ferment the beers, which are sterile filtered and then re-seeded with fresh yeast in

preparation for bottling, which takes place at Thames Distillers in London.

British Bulldog (4.3%, best bitter)
William Wilberforce Freedom Ale (4.8%, best bitter)

White
White Brewing Co.,
Pebsham Farm Business Park, Pebsham Lane, Bexhill on Sea, East Sussex TN40 2RZ
🕿 (01424) 731066
@ whitebrewing@btconnect.com
🌐 www.white-brewing.co.uk
Mail order service
■ Family brewery established in 1995 in a coastal Sussex farm building, bringing Battle of Hastings connections into some of its beer names. Beer for bottling is kräusened daily during fermentation and then drawn from the top of the fermenting vessel, without filtration or re-seeding of yeast. Bottles are warm conditioned for two weeks and cold conditioned for a week before going on sale.

1066 Country Bitter (4%)
Blonde (4%, golden ale)
Weissbier (4%, wheat beer)
Bottle of Hastings (4.5%, best bitter)
Grumpy Guvnor (4.5%, best bitter)
Maiden Bexhill Ale (4.5%, best bitter)
Gold (4.9%, golden ale)
Chilly Willy (5.1%, old ale)

White Shield
See **Molson Coors**

Whittingtons
Whittingtons Brewery,
Three Choirs Vineyard, Newent, Gloucestershire GL18 1LS
🕿 (01531) 890555
@ brewery@threechoirs.com
🌐 www.whittingtonsbrewery. co.uk
Mail order service
■ Whittingtons Brewery was founded in spring 2003 on the Three Choirs Vineyard. It takes as its theme the character of Dick Whittington, who was born in the area, and his cat: hence the brewery's slogan, 'Purveyors of the purrfect pint'. Bottle-conditioned beer that is bought from the brewery and local shops and supermarkets is bottled in house, direct from the tank, with no filtration or re-seeding of yeast. Cats Whiskers sold in Sainsbury's and Tesco is bottled by Branded Drinks in Gloucestershire. Some filtered bottled beers are also available but one of these, Nine Lives, may soon be offered bottle conditioned.

Cats Whiskers (4.5%, best bitter)
A Winter's Tail (5.1%, winter ale)

Why Not
The Why Not Brewery,
17 Cavalier Close, Thorpe St Andrew, Norwich, Norfolk NR7 0TE
🕿 (01603) 300786
@ colin@thewhynotbrewery.co.uk
🌐 www.thewhynotbrewery.co.uk
■ This tiny brewery was set up in 2005 by keen brewer Colin Emms, in a purpose-built shed at the rear of his house. He only regularly brewed bottled beers

at the outset, but now also supplies cask ale. Bottled beers are filled from conditioning tanks and are not filtered or fined, making them acceptable to vegans (apart from the honey beer, which is only vegetarian friendly). The bottle labels carry the slogan: 'Fancy a beer? Why not!'.

Wally's Revenge (4%, golden ale)
On the Ball (4.5%, bitter)
Roundhead Porter (4.5%)
Cavalier Red (4.7%, red ale)
Norfolk Honey Ale (5%, honey beer)
Chocolate Nutter (5.5%, old ale)

Wibblers
Wibblers Brewery Ltd,
c/o 11 Orchard Drive, Mayland, Essex CM3 6EP
☎ (01621) 789003
@ Info@wibblers.com
🌐 www.wibblers.com
■ Brewery established in summer 2007. The vegetarian-friendly beers are bottled, unfined, from the cask, with no primings, to keep carbonation more akin to the cask versions.

Apprentice (3.9%, golden ale)
Hoppy Helper (4%, golden ale)
Hop Harvest (4.1%, golden ale)
Santa's Night Off (4.2%, Christmas ale)
Darker Mild (4.3%)

Wicked Hathern
Wicked Hathern Brewery Ltd, 17 Nixon Walk, East Leake, Loughborough, Leicestershire LE12 6HL
☎ (01509) 842585

@ john@theworsfolds.fsnet.co.uk
🌐 www.wicked-hathern.co.uk
■ It was the Reverend Edward Thomas March Phillips, apparently, who declared that the Leicestershire village of Hathern was 'Wicked'. The 19th-century cleric despaired at the drunken brawls and the cockfighting that were common in the village, not least between the gravestones of his churchyard, and after his condemnation of public standards the local nickname of Wicked Hathern stuck. This brewery opened in the village in 2000 but has already closed. Its beers are now brewed at Leek Brewery, filled from casks and primed with sugar.

Doble's Dog (3.8%, mild)
Burly Court Jester (4%, bitter)
Hathern Cross (4%, golden ale)
WHB (Wicked Hathern Bitter) (4.1%)
Albion Special (4.3%, best bitter)
Cockfighter (4.5%, best bitter)
Hawthorn Gold (4.8%, golden ale)
Derby Porter (5%)
Swift 'Un (5%, golden ale)
Soar Head (5.1%, strong ale)
Gladstone Tidings (5.4%, Christmas ale)

Wickwar
Wickwar Brewing Co.,
The Old Brewery, Station Road, Wickwar, Gloucestershire GL12 8NB
☎ (0870) 777 5671
@ brewcrew@wickwarbrewing.com
🌐 www.wickwarbrewing.co.uk
Mail order service

Breweries

■ Wickwar was launched in 1990 in the cooperage of the long-gone Arnold, Perrett & Co. brewery. By 2004, however, the brewery had outgrown these limited premises and moved across the road into the main buildings, expanding capacity at the same time. The beers featured here are brewed at Wickwar and bottled in house, without being filtered, simply emulating the cask products.

BOB (4%, bitter)
Old Arnold (4.8%, best bitter)
Station Porter (6.1%)

Willoughby
Willoughby Brewing Co.,
Brockhampton Brewery,
Whitbourne, Herefordshire
WR6 5SH
☎ (01885) 482359
■ Brewery opened in July 2008 on a National Trust estate in the Herefordshire countryside. It was soon into bottling, filling beer directly from the fermentation vessel and conditioning bottles at the brewery before release.

Trust Gold (3.8%, golden ale)

Windsor Castle
Windsor Castle Brewery Ltd
t/a Sadler's Ales, 7 Stourbridge Road, Lye, Stourbridge, Dudley DY9 7DG
☎ (01384) 895230
@ enquiries@ windsorcastlebrewery.com
🌐 www.windsorcastlebrewery. com
Mail order service

■ Picking up a family brewing tradition that ended with the closure of Thomas Sadler's brewery, adjacent to the Windsor Castle Inn at Oldbury, in 1927, this new business was opened in 2004 by fourth-generation brewers John and Chris Sadler. A new Windsor Castle Inn has been built next to the site of the current brewery, in the town of Lye. The bottled beers are hand filled from casks or fermenting vessels.

Worcester Sorcerer (4.3%, golden ale)
Thin Ice (4.5%, golden ale)
Stumbling Badger (4.9%, best bitter)
Mud City Stout (6.6%, cocoa- and vanilla-laced stout)

Wissey Valley
Wissey Valley Brewery,
The Hop & Hog, 1 High Street, Downham Market, Norfolk PE38 9DA
☎ (01366) 386658
@ info@wisseyvalleybrewery.com
🌐 www.wisseyvalleybrewery.com
■ Brewery set up in 2002 and moving location a few times already. The latest venue is a beer shop-cum-hog roast retailer that also sells brewing supplies. The beers featured below – sold under the Cap'n Grumpy banner (the original name of the brewery) – are bottled from the cask and are primed with sugar or wort.

Wild Widow Mild (3.6%)
Best Bitter (3.9%, bitter)
Busted Flush (4.5%, best bitter)

Golden Rivet (5%, golden ale)
Cherry Pickers (6%, cherry stout)
Khaki Sergeant Strong Stout
(6%)

Wizard

Wizard Ales, Unit 4, Lundy View,
Mullacott Cross Industrial Estate,
Ilfracombe, Devon EX34 8PY
- (01271) 865350
- @ mike@wizardales.co.uk
- www.wizardales.co.uk
- ■ Founded in Warwickshire in
  2003, Wizard Ales packed its
  bags and headed for a new
  home in Devon in 2007. The
  beers listed here are bottled on
  site from the fermenting vessel,
  with fresh wort added as a
  priming.

Lundy Gold (4.1%, golden ale)
Druid's Fluid (5%, best bitter)

Woodforde's
Woodforde's Norfolk Ales
(Woodforde's Ltd), Broadland
Brewery, Woodbastwick,
Norwich, Norfolk NR13 6SW
- (01603) 720353
- @ info@woodfordes.co.uk
- www.woodfordes.co.uk
- Mail order service
- ■ Woodforde's was founded
  in 1981 in Drayton, near
  Norwich, and moved to a
  converted farm complex in the
  picturesque Broadland village
  of Woodbastwick in 1989. It
  brews a wide range of award-
  winning beers (including two
  former CAMRA Champion Beers
  of Britain), many of which are
  now also bottled, with primary
  fermentation yeast allowed to
  sediment out and the beers

re-seeded with fresh yeast.
Wherry, however, is bottled
under contract at Hepworth
in Sussex, where the beer is
filtered and re-seeded.

Wherry (3.8%, bitter)
Sundew (4.1%, golden ale)
**Marks & Spencer Norfolk
Bitter** (4.5%, best bitter)
Nelson's Revenge (4.5%, best
bitter)
Norfolk Nog (4.6%, mild)
Admiral's Reserve (5%, best
bitter)
Headcracker (7%, barley wine)
Norfolk Nip (8%, barley wine)

Woodlands
Woodlands Brewing Company,
Unit 3, Meadow Lane Farm,
London Road, Stapeley, Nantwich,
Cheshire CW5 7JU
- (01270) 620101
- @ woodlandsbrewery@btconnect.
  com
- www.woodlandsbrewery.co.uk
- Mail order service
- ■ Woodlands opened in autumn
  2004, using equipment
  purchased from the closed
  Khean Brewery, and
  moved to new premises in
  winter 2007/2008. Adding
  distinctiveness to the beer
  range is the brewery's water
  source, a spring that bubbles up
  through local peat fields. Bottling
  commenced in 2006 and the
  bottles are all filled directly from
  fermenting vessels, without
  fining, filtration or priming. They
  are then allowed four weeks
  of warm conditioning before
  leaving the brewery. All these
  beers are also sold on draught.

Breweries

Mild (3.5%)
Drummer (3.9%, bitter)
Light Oak (4%, golden ale)
Oak Beauty (4.2%, best bitter)
Woodcutter (4.3%, golden ale)
Bitter (4.4%, best bitter)
Midnight Stout (4.4%)
Bees Knees (4.5%, honey beer)
Redwood (4.9%, best bitter)
General's Tipple (5.5%, strong ale)

Worthington
See **Molson Coors**

Wye Valley
Wye Valley Brewery, Stoke Lacy, Herefordshire HR7 4HG
☎ (01885) 490505
@ sales@wyevalleybrewery.co.uk
🌐 www.wyevalleybrewery.co.uk
Mail order service

■ Wye Valley began production in 1985 and, growing substantially, has since moved premises twice, taking up residence in Stoke Lacy in 2002. Wye Valley seasonal cask beers all roll out under the 'Dorothy Goodbody' title. There is not, and never has been, a real Dorothy: she is just a figment of the brewery's fertile imagination, a computer-generated 1950s blonde bomb-shell dreamt up to market the range. Three of these beers are regularly available in bottle-conditioned form, complete with a picture of the seductive Miss Goodbody on the front. Bottling now takes place in house, having been matured, filtered, re-seeded with fresh bottling yeast and kräusened to ensure good natural carbonation. The US importer is B United.

Dorothy Goodbody's Golden Ale (4.2%)
Butty Bach (4.5%, best bitter)
Dorothy Goodbody's Wholesome Stout (4.6%)
Dorothy Goodbody's Country Ale (6%, strong ale)

Yates'
Yates' Brewery Ltd, Unit 6, Dean Farm, Whitwell Road, Whitwell, Ventnor, Isle of Wight PO38 2AB
☎ (01983) 731731
@ info@yates-brewery.co.uk
🌐 www.yates-brewery.co.uk
Mail order service

■ Dave Yates used to work for Burts Brewery on the Isle of Wight and also joined the short-lived Island Brewery. Since 2000, he's been brewing on his own, with a five-barrel plant overlooking the sea at The Inn at St Lawrence pub, near Ventnor (the above address is the office and distribution centre). Bottled beers were launched in 2003 and are filled from a cask after being kräusened.

Undercliff Experience (4.1%, bitter)
Blonde Ale (4.5%, golden ale)
Holy Joe (4.9%, coriander-spiced beer)
Wight Winter (5%, winter ale)
YSD (Yates' Special Draught) (5.5%, strong ale)
Wight Old Ale (6%)
Yule Be Sorry (7.6%, barley wine)

Yetman's
Yetman's Brewery, Bayfield Farm Barns, Bayfield Brecks, Holt, Norfolk NR25 7DZ

☏ (07774) 809016
@ sales@yetmans.net
🌐 www.yetmans.net
Mail order service
■ Brewery initially established to serve the owners' restaurant, but now brewing in its own right and based in 200-year-old barn. Three of the beers are available in bottle-conditioned format. These are fined in tank and then re-seeded with fresh yeast ready for bottling.

Orange (4.2%, best bitter)
Stout (4.2%)
Green (4.8%, best bitter)

Yorkshire Dales
Yorkshire Dales Brewing Co. Ltd, Seata Barn, Elm Hill, Askrigg, North Yorkshire DL8 3HG
☏ (01969) 622027
@ info@yorkshiredalesbrewery. com
■ Small brewery opened in 2005. The beers for bottling are chilled, racked into casks and primed with sugar before filling by hand. Two or three weeks of warm conditioning follow before the beers go on sale. Being unfined, they are acceptable to vegetarians and vegans.

Butter Tubs (3.7%, golden ale)
Buckden Pike (3.9%, golden ale)
Askrigg Ale (4.3%, golden ale)
Garsdale Smokebox (5.6%, smoked porter)

Internationa
Selection

There's never been a better time to drink bottle-conditioned beers. As the previous pages show, the number being produced in the UK is increasing all the time and these beers are rubbing shoulders on the shelves of off-licences with an ever-expanding range of bottle-conditioned beers from overseas. The following list features a selection of the best available in the UK today. Some of these may only be found in specialist beer shops or via internet mail order companies that stock a huge range of beers.

The Americas

American craft brewers are now well known for their quality beers and their never-satiated desire to experiment and push the boundaries of beer creation. But there's similar thinking all across the American continent now, from Canada in the north, through the USA, right down to South America, where Brazil, in particular, is developing an interesting craft brewing sector.

Alaskan Smoked Porter 6.5%, **Alaskan**
- Smoky, bittersweet, roasted porter with just a trace of fruit behind.

Belgian Ale 8.5%, **Dado**
- A sweet, creamy, orange-golden ale from Brazil, with gentle banana and toffee notes.

Bigfoot Barleywine Style Ale 9.6%, **Sierra Nevada**
- Copper-red, Californian winter classic, loaded with sweet malt and fruit but with a big hoppy finish.

Blanche de Chambly 5%, **Unibroue**
- Canadian white beer in the Belgian style, with lemon sharpness and malty-toffee undertones.

Black Butte Porter 5.2%, **Deschutes**
- A smooth, sweetish porter with chocolate, vanilla and nut flavours.

Celebration Ale 6.8%, **Sierra Nevada**
- Pungent citrus hoppiness dominates this festive offering from northern California.

Dead Guy Ale 6%, **Rogue Ales**
- Sharp citrus notes feature in this bronze ale that drinks lighter than its strength. *Note: none of Rogue's beers are pasteurised and most contain yeast sediment, although they are not officially declared bottle conditioned.*

Eau Bénite 7.7%, **Unibroue**
- A warming, zesty tripel from Canada.

Golden Monkey 9.5%, **Victory**
- A Belgium-influenced, perfumed ale from Pennsylvania, incorporating spices for further mystery.

Goose Island India Pale Ale 5.9%, **Goose Island**
- Glorious Chicago-brewed hopfest, filled with juicy fruit.

Honker's Ale 5%, **Goose Island**
- A fresh, full-tasting ale with loads of hop-pocket character.

Ilex 7%, **Dado**
- A creamy, malty beer from Brazil, with herbal-spicy notes from the infusion of a South American species of holly.

Imperial Stout 10.4%, **Left Hand**
- A fruity, sweet but dangerously drinkable, dark ruby beer from Colorado.

Imperial Stout 11%, **Rogue Ales**
- A stunning recreation of the imperial Russian stout style, full-

International Selection

flavoured and complex, mixing roasted grain and liquorice with sweeter malt and hoppy fruit.

La Fin du Monde 9%, Unibroue
■ Canadian 'tripel' blond, described as the 'beginning of paradise': orange-hoppy and pleasingly acidic.

Local 1 9%, Brooklyn
■ A golden, full-bodied, zesty, Belgian-style tripel from the brewers of Brooklyn Lager.

Matilda 7%, Goose Island
■ A beer built in the Orval mould with plenty of hops and a deliberate wild yeast note.

Mocha Porter 5.2%, Rogue Ales
■ A bittersweet, chocolaty dark beer with a nutty, coffee finish.

Obsidian Stout 6.4%, Deschutes
■ A big, satisfying stout with roasted bitterness, creamy malt and chocolate in the taste.

Raftman 5.5%, Unibroue
■ Whisky malt beer from Quebec, bittersweet, malty and lightly smoky, with a pleasant lemon-hop overlay.

Sierra Nevada Pale Ale 5.6%, Sierra Nevada
■ A crisp, refreshing Californian classic, marrying malt and bitterness with a dry, citrus hop bite.

Shakespeare Stout 6.3%, Rogue Ales
■ Despite the strength, not too heavy, with crisp roasted grain flavours.

World Wide Stout 18%, Dogfish Head
■ A seriously big, peppery, cola-like, alcoholic stout with sherry notes., from a Delaware brewery known for pushing the envelope.

Australia

Home of the Amber Nectar, but don't let that put you off. Australia is building an interesting reputation for quality beers, spearheaded by the long-established Coopers brewery in Adelaide.

Coopers Stout 6.3%, Coopers
■ Crisp, clean and lightly bitter stout with roast grain character, although a touch thin for its strength.

Gentlemen's Pale Ale 4.8%, Gentlemen's
■ Easy-drinking, but tasty, amber ale with floral and orange notes on top of clean malt.

Little Creatures Pale Ale 5.2%, Little Creatures
■ Tangy, peppery hops and full citrus fruit feature in this golden ale.

Original Pale Ale 4.5%, Coopers
■ A crisp, lagerish beer with light pear fruit and hops in the taste and an increasingly bitter aftertaste.

Sparkling Ale 5.8%, Coopers
■ A classic, with a sweetish, fruity flavour, rounded off by a drying, bittersweet finish.

Vintage Ale 7.8%, Coopers
■ A full-bodied, fruity barley wine that is vintage stamped, so you can compare it from year to year.

Belgium

The Belgians have honed bottle conditioning down to a fine art. Many of their best-known beers enjoy a secondary fermentation in the bottle, from the powerful, nourishing ales created by monks in Trappist monasteries to the fresh, spicy and citrus notes of the *witbier*, the country's wheat beer style.

Abbaye des Rocs 9%, Abbaye des Rocs
■ Not from an abbey, but from a modern brewery set up in the 1980s close to the French border. Rich, fruity and spicy.

Abt 12 10.5%, St Bernardus
■ A full-bodied, complex abbey beer, fruity and smooth.

Achel Blonde 8%, Achel
■ The newest of the Trappist breweries, on the Dutch border. The Blonde is peppery, bittersweet and dryish. Look out, too, for the maltier Brune.

Affligem Blonde 6.8%, Affligem
■ Soft, sweetish, spicy ale from an abbey-beer producer owned by Heineken.

Augustijn Grand Cru 9%, Van Steenberge
■ A bittersweet, powerful, golden ale with a tropical fruit character.

Barbãr 8%, Lefèbvre
■ A honey beer that manages to remain bitter rather than sweet, with heavy fruit and malt flavours.

Beersel 7%, Drie Fonteinen
■ A bittersweet, easy-drinking, citrus blond containing wheat.

Bersalis 9.5%, Oud Beersel
■ Pineapple and pear drops in a full-on, golden tripel.

Black Albert 13%, Struise Brouwers
■ Deceptively powerfully, hugely complex, bittersweet, spicy imperial stout from some seriously inventive brewers.

Blanche de Bruxelles 4.5%, Lefèbvre
■ Lightly toffeeish, spiced, fruity witbier from the makers of Barbãr.

Blanche des Honnelles 6%, Abbaye des Rocs
■ A strong wheat beer with citrus notes.

Bon Secours Bière Vivante!! Blonde 8%, Caulier
■ A sweet, warming, slightly earthy, fruity golden beer.

Bon Secours Bière Vivante!! Brune 8%, Caulier
■ Spicy, malty and warming, with more than a suggestion of chocolate orange about it.

Brigand 9%, Van Honsebrouck
■ Strong blond ale, akin to Duvel, sweetish, perfumed, peppery and warming.

Bruegel 5.2%, Van Steenberge
■ A malty amber ale with a floral bitterness.

Chimay Blanche/Cinq Cents 8%, Chimay

■ Hoppy, bitter orange- and apricot-accented, zesty beer, from a Trappist monastery near the French border. The white cap marks it out from other Chimay beers.

Chimay Bleue/Grand Réserve 9%, Chimay

■ Blue-capped biggest of the Chimay brothers: full, smooth and malty with fruit notes and a renowned port-like finish.

Chimay Rouge/Première 7%, Chimay

■ Sweetish, malty, spicy, weaker stablemate of Blanche and Bleue, this time with a red cap.

Corsendonk Agnus 7.5%, Bocq

■ Commissioned brew for a wholesaler, using a defunct abbey name; classy, refreshing, bittersweet and lemony.

Corsendonk Pater 7.5%, Van Steenberge

■ A sweet, dark beer with a hint of raisin.

Cuvée René 5%, Lindemans

■ A gueuze lambic, typically demanding, sour and acidic, with an earthy, cidery character.

Daas Witte 5%, Daas

■ Thinnish witbier, with an orange-squash-like fruitiness and some perfumed coriander.

Delirium Tremens 9%, Huyghe

■ Jokey-named beer served in a stone-effect bottle but far from gimmicky in its mouth-numbing mix of fruit and hop flavours.

De Verboden Vrucht/Le Fruit Défendu 8.5%, InBev

■ A spiced, malty, fruity beer with a drying, hoppy finish. The name translates as Forbidden Fruit.

Duvel 8.5%, Duvel Moortgat

■ The famous 'Devil beer', deceptive in its blond looks. Full zesty bitterness, subtle pear fruit and surprisingly light body for its strength.

Gouden Carolus Classic 8.5%, Het Anker

■ Mellow, toffeeish beer from 'The Anchor' brewery, based in Mechelen.

Gouden Carolus Hopsinjoor 8%, Het Anker

■ A hoppy tripel, full of bitter pear and citrus fruit notes, with a dry, warming finish.

Grottenbier 6.5%, St Bernardus

■ A malty, spiced brown ale, devised by Pierre Celis of original Hoegaarden fame, and aged in caves.

Hoegaarden 4.9%, InBev

■ Bittersweet, easy-drinking, fruity wheat beer, flavoured with coriander and curaçao. The style's market leader, with a gently peppery, bitter orange and stewed apple character.

Hoegaarden Grand Cru 8.5%, InBev

■ Strong, flowery, spicy, bittersweet strong beer, with hints of mango and orange and a suggestion of whisky.

Kasteelbier Blonde 11%, Van Honsebrouck

■ A big, alcoholic, almondy beer with a sweetish finish.

La Chouffe 8%, Achouffe

■ A coriandered blond with bitter fruit notes.

Leffe Tripel 8.4%, InBev

■ Leffe is the market leader in Abbey ales, but only this Tripel, a decent example of the style, is bottle conditioned.

Leute Bokbier 7.5%, Van Steenberge
- A chestnut beer with dark malt and raisin flavours and a dry, bitter finish.

McChouffe 8.5%, Achouffe
- Ruby-coloured, malty merger of Belgian and Scottish styles.

Orval 6.2%, Orval
- World classic ale from a Trappist monastery: bitter, dry and fruitily acidic.

Pater 6 6.7%, St Bernardus
- A full-flavoured, chestnut-coloured, fruity dubbel.

Piraat 9%/10.5%, Van Steenberge
- A big, strong blond in the Duvel fashion, with a sweet, perfumed, citrus, hoppy flavour. Two strengths are available.

Poperings Hommel Beer 7.5%, Van Eecke
- The Belgian hopgardens distilled in one glass. A full-flavoured onslaught of sappy hops well balanced by sweetness, fruit and spice notes.

Prior 8 8%, St Bernardus
- A sweet, dark ale with a dried fruit character.

Reinaert Grand Cru 9.5%, Proef
- Dry-finishing, burnished-copper brew, nicely balancing malty sweetness and light fruit, with pear in the aroma.

Reinaert Tripel 9%, Proef
- A malty, bittersweet, pleasant tripel with a light raisin-like character.

Rochefort 6 7.5%, Rochefort
- Rarely seen away from its Ardennes Trappist homeland, but an amazing malty, spicy confection.

Rochefort 8 9.2%, Rochefort
- Light-drinking for its strength, spicy, peppery and fruity.

Rochefort 10 11.3%, Rochefort
- Dreamy, peppery and dry, with background fruit. The top-of-the-range offering from this brewery.

Silly Saison 5%, Silly
- No-joke beer from Silly town, drinking sweet and light despite its deep raisiny, figgy fruit flavours and plenty of malt.

St Bernardus Tripel 7.5%, St Bernardus
- Widely acclaimed, golden tripel with a delicate bitterness.

Spéciale Noël 9%, Abbaye des Rocs
- A mostly sweet, red Christmas ale with complex floral and fruity flavours.

Stille Nacht 12%, de Dolle Brouwers
- A golden Christmas beer from the 'Mad Brewers', brim-full of orange zestiness.

Tripel Karmeliet 8%, Bosteels
- Abbey beer from a brewery better known for its 8% beer, Kwak. Sweet malt, strong toffee, hints of lemon, an oaty creaminess and spicy hops.

Urthel Parlus Magnificum 7.5%, Leyerth
- Attention-grabbing, red-orange ale with chocolate and herbal hops in the bitter taste and finish.

Val-Dieu Blonde 6%, Val-Dieu
- A slightly chewy, lemon-accented, sweetish blonde.

Val-Dieu Brune 8%, Val-Dieu
- A winey, sweet and malty, red-brown beer with soft chocolate flavours.

Val-Dieu Triple 9%, Val-Dieu

- Golden, with jammy apricots and oranges featuring in the sweet taste.

Vicardin Tripel-Gueuze 7%, Vicaris

- Strange hybrid of gueuze and tripel, featuring toffee-like malt and a tart acidity.

Vieille Provision 6.5%, Dupont

- Crisp, herbal and gently bitter, with an orange acidity: a leading exponent of the saison style of quenching summer beers.

Westmalle Dubbel 7%, Westmalle

- Complex, sweetish brown beer from the largest Trappist brewery. Spice, dark malt, rum and raisin.

Westmalle Tripel 9.5%, Westmalle

- A pale, aromatic, classic tripel, with an enjoyable fruit and honey character.

Westvleteren 8 8%, Westvleteren

- A melon-, almond- and liquorice-accented, slightly acidic ruby beer from a Trappist brewery near the Belgian hop fields, close to France.

Westvleteren 12 10.2%, Westvleteren

- A hearty, spicy, sweetish ale with a herbal-like bitterness. The monks' most celestial beer: once voted the best in the world by internet beer fans.

Westvleteren Blonde 5.8%, Westvleteren

- A full-flavoured blond. All Westvleteren beers are strictly rationed and are very hard to get hold of.

France

The brewers of France face a tough battle with the wine industry but they are making a mark. Many come from the north, but there are microbreweries all over the country today, many producing interesting bottle-conditioned beers. Note, however, that some of the best-known French beers in the local *bière de garde* (aged beer) style – Jenlain, Ch'ti, Trois Monts, for instance – are conditioned and matured at the brewery before bottling, rather than in the bottle itself, and are filtered, so they don't feature in this list.

Blonde du Mont Blanc 5.8%, Mont Blanc

- Sweet and lemony, golden beer from the Alps with herbal notes.

Britt Blanche 4.8%, Britt

- Spicy, Breton wheat beer, fruity and peppery.

Coreff Ambrée 5%, Deux Rivières

- An amber Breton ale with a reasonable hop presence.

Duchesse Anne 6.5%, Lancelot

- A strong blonde ale from Brittany.

Etoile du Nort 5.5%, Thiriez

- A firmly hoppy, tangy and dry beer from northern France.

Gavroche 8.5%, St-Sylvestre
- A malty, herbal, fruity brew from close to the Belgian frontier.

La Lutine Bière Ambrée 5.5%, La Lutine
- A nutty, hoppy amber ale from a Dordogne microbrewery.

La Lutine Bière Blanche 5%, La Lutine
- A bitter witbier with a citrus zing.

La Lutine Bière Blonde 6.5%, La Lutine
- A zesty, orange-accented golden ale, with a mild, dry finish.

La Lutine Bière Brune 5%, La Lutine
- Tasty, mostly sweet brown ale with toffee and chocolate notes.

La Maline 5.8%, Thiriez
- A red beer from Flanders, with sweet, earthy, dark malt flavours.

Lancelot 6%, Lancelot
- A Breton brew, featuring biscuity malt and tropical fruit.

Germany and Czech Republic

Germany's brewing industry has a well-deserved reputation for excellence. The range of beer styles is extensive, from hell, export, pils, bocks and alts to Kölsch from Cologne, smoked rauchbier from Bamberg and tart wheat beers from Berlin. However, for the bottle, most of these tend to be filtered and usually pasteurised. The best-known examples of bottle-conditioned beers in Germany are weissbiers, the Bavarian-style wheat beers that are served cloudy, with yeast deliberately in suspension. Not all weissbiers are bottle conditioned, though. Many of the biggest names are pasteurised, even though there's plenty of yeast in the bottle. This section also features a fascinating beer from the Czech Republic. Most of the country's outstanding lagers are filtered and, again, often pasteurised for the bottle, so this beer, from the Bernard brewery in the town of Humpolec, is quite a discovery.

Aventinus 8%, Schneider
- Amazingly complex welzenbock with a full, smooth, fairly sweet and malty taste, well supported by bananas, marzipan and spice.

Erdinger Weissbier 5.3%, Erdinger
- From the world's largest wheat beer brewery, just outside Munich: a mellow, quaffable, mildly clove-spiced, fruity brew.

Erdinger Weissbier Dunkel 5.6%, Erdinger
- An easy-drinking, dark wheat beer, a sweet mix of mild clove, chocolate and a hint of liquorice.

König Ludwig Weissbier Dunkel 5.5%, Kaltenberg
- A dark wheat beer combining chocolate, vanilla and banana flavours.

König Ludwig Weissbier Hell
5.5%, Kaltenberg
- ■ Castle-brewed, bittersweet, Bavarian favourite, imported by Thwaites.

Maisel's Weisse 5.7%, Maisel's
- ■ Easy-drinking, apple- and orange-fruity weissbier with warming hints of liquorice and spicy clove.

Pikantus 7.3%, Erdinger
- ■ Complex, strong wheat beer with sweet, mildly spicy, almond and raisin flavours.

Pinkus Hefe Weizen 5%, Pinkus
- ■ An organic wheat beer with sharp lemon and banana notes in the taste.

Prinz Luitpold Weizenbock 8%, Kaltenberg
- ■ A rich and smooth, fruity, strong wheat beer with a dry but sweet finish.

Riegele's Weisse 5%, Riegele
- ■ An enjoyably tart and challenging weissbier from a family-owned brewery in Augsburg. Imported by Pilgrim Brewery.

Schneider Weisse 5.4%, Schneider
- ■ Highly-rated Bavarian wheat beer from just north of Munich: spicy, dry and fruity (banana), with a touch of sourness.

Schneider Weisse Weizen Hell 5.2%, Schneider
- ■ A blond variation on Schneider's wheat beer, appley and sweet.

Svatecni Lezak 5%, Bernard
- ■ A bottle-conditioned Czech lager with a full buttery maltiness and tangy, herbal hops for balance. The beer is sold in a tall, swing-stoppered bottle. Bernard's Cerné Pivo, a finely filtered dark lager, is also left unpasteurised.

The Netherlands

It may be best known for Heineken and other sweetish lager beers, but the Netherlands has much in common with its near neighbour, Belgium, when it comes to good, bottle-conditioned beers, although the selection is understandably smaller.

Christoffel Bier 6%, Christoffel
- ■ A characterful pilsner loaded with tangy hops. It has also been sold as Christoffel Blond.

Christoffel Bok 7.8%, Christoffel
- ■ Chocolate and dried fruit notes in a full-bodied red beer, lagered for 12 weeks or more.

Columbus 9%, IJ
- ■ A dark golden beer with a dry, herbal hop accent.

Hertog Jan Double 7.3%, Hertog Jan
- ■ A Dutch dubbel with tart fruit, dark malts and warming alcohol throughout.

Korenwolf 5%, Gulpener
- ■ Named after the Dutch for a hamster (literally 'corn wolf'): a spiced beer in the Hoegaarden mould, brewed with four different cereals.

La Trappe Blonde 6.5%, Schaapskooi

■ A fruity blonde from a Trappist monastery near Tilburg.

La Trappe Dubbel 6.5%, Schaapskooi

■ A sweet, malty, spicy and nourishing dubbel with pear and raisin notes.

La Trappe Quadrupel 10%, Schaapskooi

■ Sweetish, spicy, malty and warming, with marzipan undertones.

La Trappe Tripel 8%, Schaapskooi

■ A well-regarded, bittersweet, fruity tripel.

La Trappe Witte 5.5%, Schaapskooi

■ Witbier with a tart apple and lemon, spicy taste. Not too sweet.

Robertus 6%, Christoffel

■ Unusual dark lager in the Munich style with roasted malt flavours.

Zatte Tripel 8%, IJ

■ A tasty, fruity (bitter orange) tripel with a gently bitter aftertaste.

Scandinavia

With the craft brewing movement taking off in Norway, Sweden and Denmark, we are likely to see more and more interesting beers heading our way from Scandinavia. This trio of beers from Norway hints at what the future may hold.

Ardenne Blond 7.5%, Haand Bryggeriet

■ Sweet, strong and full-bodied, with orange-citrus notes.

Norwegian Wood 6.5%, Haand Bryggeriet

■ Smoked, coffee-accented beer laced with juniper berries.

Odin's Tipple 10.9%, Haand Bryggeriet

■ A take-no-prisoners dark beer with dried fruit, liquorice, pear and chocolate in the taste.

Africa

All the beers in this section come from a brewery in South Africa, which offers a range of bottle-conditioned ales.

Robson's Durban Pale Ale 5.7%, Shongweni

■ A golden ale with pineapple and orange notes.

Robson's East Coast Ale 4%, Shongweni

■ A bittersweet, creamy, golden ale resembling a weissbier.

Robson's Mango Fruit Beer 5%, Shongweni

■ One of a series of Robson's fruit beers, but the best by some way, with the mango not too dominant.

Robson's Wheat Beer 5%, Shongweni

■ Tropical fruits and perfumed coriander feature in this hazy yellow wheat beer.

Shopping
Around

The Real Ale Shop on Branthil Farm, near Wells-next-the-Sea

Teddy Maufe in his bottle-conditioned beer shop

Teddy Maufe plucks an earful of barley from his Norfolk field and barely conceals his annoyance. 'We've had people touring this farm and when we ask them what we use barley for, they simply don't know. One of them even suggested that we turned it into glue!'.

For a barley farmer that was nothing short of an insult. For a beer lover, which Teddy also confesses to being, it amounted to a serious challenge. The fact that the origins of our national drink had become lost in the mists of time troubled him so much that, in 2004, he set about re-establishing beer's field-to-glass roots by opening his own bottle-conditioned beer shop right in the middle of his farm. 'We need to educate people about the connection between these beautiful fields of barley and the wonderful real ale produced locally from it,' he says.

The Real Ale Shop on Branthill Farm, near Wells-next-the-Sea, has been a hit from day one. Its focus is on beers from Norfolk, many of which are brewed from Teddy's own barley. He's now extended the concept by opening a second shop in Suffolk, where the focus is on beers from that county, and the seed that Teddy planted has seen further green shoots in that Nick Dolan, who worked closely on setting-up the original

348

Equipment from the 1950s in Hunt's Brewery

shop, is today the innovative proprietor of Real Ale, a specialist beer retailer in Twickenham, London. It's a success story on several levels, from educational to commercial, helping the farm diversify in times of agricultural downturn, providing valuable outlets for local brewers and giving beer lovers new oases of choice.

Teddy is not the only farmer to see his role as going beyond that of producer of agricultural goods. Martin Bazeley, who farms on the hills above Portsmouth harbour, has also recognized the value of bringing the finished product back to its origins by creating Suthwyk Ales, which contracts brewers to brew beer from barley grown on Martin's land. In 2005, Martin went a step further by opening a bottled beer shop in an historic brewhouse in the village of Southwick, close to his farm. The listed building had lain dormant since 1957, when Dick Olding, the last brewer of Hunt's brewery, took off his apron, laid down his tools and shut down the operation for the last time. The equipment remains intact and offers a rare, authentic insight into brewing in the 1950s. The bottled beer shop presents a few hundred choices, so a visit is a double treat: you can enjoy a little brewery archaeology at the same time as picking up some great beer.

Martin Bazeley's brewhouse bottle shop in Southwick, Hampshire

History and bottled beer retailing also go hand in hand at Tucker's Maltings in Newton Abbot, Devon. This century-old business enjoyed a major overhaul in the early 1990s, when the working maltings opened its doors as a tourist attraction, with appeal for all the family. The icing on the cake was the introduction of a specialist bottled beer shop in the reception area, offering dozens of beers from small British breweries alongside some interesting imports. It's a great

349

example of lateral thinking: how to generate additional income from an already successful business.

The same open-mindedness has brought success to other unlikely businesses, as the concept of the specialist bottled beer shop has spread across the country. In the pretty Thames-side village of Goring, on the border of Berkshire and Oxfordshire, there's a well-established grocery called Westholme Store. From the outside, it looks just like any other Londis outlet and, indeed, when you enter, the first things that catch the eye are the usual newspapers, breads, detergents and cans of beans. Step a little further inside, however, and perceptions change dramatically as a sea of bottled beers runs away to the back of the shop, pushing aside breakfast cereals, toilet rolls and jars of jam. Jack Patel is the owner and he spotted the potential in becoming a specialist beer retailer. After running the shop for 18 years, he was worn down by having to compete on unequal terms with major supermarkets and was looking for something different, an area in which he could outperform the big guys and hopefully bring in new punters. He found what he was looking for on the internet, in an article that raised the question of why little corner shops didn't think more about stocking a good range of interesting bottled beers. Now, with hundreds on his shelves, his little shop has become a focus for beer lovers from miles around.

Bottled beer brings vital diversity to today's retail market. People are becoming more discerning about what they drink. They are experimenting more, and are more open minded about beer. They also like the idea of small producers. For retailers bottled beer brings in business that otherwise might not have come, and the new customers are likely to shop for other items while they are there. Garden centres and delicatessens see the value in offering a selection of small-brewery beers from their region, and even breweries themselves have recognized the importance of variety, selling not just their own output but beers from other breweries as well. The lead set by Hogs Back Brewery in Surrey, with its excellent shop, has now been followed by Triple fff Brewery in Hampshire.

Beer stores, it seems, are popping up everywhere. At The Lade Inn in Scotland's loch land, The Scottish Real Ale Shop has become a tourist attraction in its own right. At London's Borough Market, the Utobeer stand is a magnet for beer lovers from across the capital, and beyond. In Yorkshire, it seems as if every market town now has a dedicated beer shop.

If, as Teddy Maufe has shown with his Real Ale Shop, you can sell bottled beer right next to a field of barley in the middle of the Norfolk countryside, you can probably sell it anywhere.

Beer Shops

Shopping for good bottled beer has never been easier. Even the major supermarkets now offer a wide variety of beers, with bottle-conditioned beers from both the UK and overseas prominent in their displays. Some have supply deals with local brewers, which add more colour to the otherwise national and regional range on offer. The pick of the major retailers is Booths (www.booths-supermarkets.co.uk), a small chain in North-West England that offers an exceptional range and is always worth a visit. However, for a wider selection than presented by most supermarkets and chain off-licences, it often pays to seek out a specialist independent off-licence, such as those listed below. These generally stock dozens – in some cases hundreds – of interesting beers, and are well worth a detour. Some of these also offer mail order services, as indicated by the symbol ✉ after the address. Additionally, there are a number of internet companies that offer mail order beer sales and a selection of these can be found after the list of shops.

Bedfordshire
Parkland Wine Co
142 High Street, Cranfield MK43 0EL
☎ (01234) 751528

Berkshire
Vitality Farm Shop
Pangbourne Road, Theale RG7 5EA
☎ (0118) 930 5159
🌐 www.vitalityfarm.co.uk

Bristol
The Bristol Wine Company
Transom House, Victoria Street,
Bristol BS1 6AH ✉
☎ (0117) 373 0288
🌐 www.thebristolwinecompany.
   co.uk

Corks of Cotham
54 Cotham Hill, Cotham BS6 6JX
☎ (0117) 973 1620
🌐 www.corksof.com

Humpers Off-Licence
26 Soundwell Road, Staple Hill
BS16 4QW
☎ (0117) 956 5525

Buckinghamshire
The Grape & Grain
84 Broad Street, Chesham
HP5 3ED
☎ (01494) 791319

Cambridgeshire
Bacchanalia
79 Victoria Road, Cambridge
CB4 3BS ✉
☎ (01223) 576292

Bacchanalia
90 Mill Road, Cambridge
CB1 2BD ✉
☎ (01223) 315034

**La Hogue Farm Shop &
Delicatessen**
La Hogue Farm, Chippenham,
Ely CB7 5PZ
☎ (01638) 751128
🌐 www.lahogue.co.uk

Wadsworth's
34 The Broadway, St Ives PE27 5BN
☎ (01480) 463522
🌐 www.wadsworthwines.co.uk

Cheshire

DeFine Food & Wine
Chester Road, Sandiway, Northwich
CW8 2NH ✉
☎ (01606) 882101
🌐 www.definefoodandwine.com

Holly Tree Farm Shop
Chester Road, Over Tabley,
Knutsford WA16 0EU
☎ (01565) 651835
🌐 www.hollytreefarmshop.co.uk

Scatchards
19 Charles Street, Hoole, Chester
CH2 3AY
☎ (01244) 317094
🌐 www.scatchardswinemerchants.
   com

Cumbria

Open All Hours
5 St Johns Street, Keswick
CA12 5AP ✉
☎ (0176 87) 75414

Derbyshire

Goyt Wines
1a Canal Street, Whaley Bridge
SK23 7LS
☎ (01663) 734214
🌐 www.goytwines.co.uk

Original Farmer's Market Shop
3 Market Street, Bakewell
DE4 1HG ✉
☎ (01629) 815814
🌐 www.thefarmersmarketshop.
   co.uk

Red Zebra Drinks Company
2–3 Queen Street, Cathedral
Quarter, Derby DE1 3DL
☎ (01332) 607607
🌐 www.redzebradrinks.com

Devon

Fermoy's Garden Centre
Totnes Road, Newton Abbot
TQ12 5TN
☎ (01803) 813022

Green Valley Cyder at Darts Farm
Clyst St George, Exeter EX3 0QH
☎ (01392) 876658

Moor & More Beer
11 Frankfort Gate, Plymouth
PL1 1QA ✉
☎ (01752) 222220
🌐 www.moorandmorebeer.co.uk

Trumps of Sidmouth
8 Fore Street, Sidmouth
EX10 8AQ ✉
☎ (01395) 512446

Tucker's Maltings
Teign Road, Newton Abbot
TQ12 4AA ✉
☎ (01626) 334734
🌐 www.tuckersmaltings.com

Wines of Gaia
Unit 1, Indoor Food Market,
Newton Abbot TQ12 7RJ ✉
☎ (07875) 124921

Hampshire

Bitter Virtue
70 Cambridge Road, Portswood,
Southampton SO14 6US ✉
☎ (023 80) 554881
🌐 www.bittervirtue.co.uk

General Wine Company
25 Station Road, Liphook GU30 7DW
☎ (01428) 727744

Southwick Brewhouse
Southwick PO17 6EB
☎ (023 92) 201133
🌐 www.southwickbrewhouse.co.uk

Triple fff Brewery Shop
Unit 3, Old Magpie Works, Station
Approach, Four Marks GU34 5HN
☎ (01420) 561422
🌐 www.triplefff.com

Hertfordshire

Wine World Off Licence
2 Canberra House, 17–19 London
Road, St Albans AL1 1LE
☎ (01727) 830322

Kent

The Bitter End
107 Camden Road, Tunbridge Wells
TN1 2QY ✉
☎ (01892) 522918

The Cask & Glass
64 Priory Street, Tonbridge
TN9 2AW ✉
☎ (01732) 359784

Lancashire

Hop & Vine Experience
2 Queen Victoria Road, Burnley
BB10 3DH
☎ (01282) 454970

Rainhall Drinks
18–22 Rainhall Road, Barnoldswick
BB18 5AF
☎ (01282) 813374
🌐 www.rainhalldrinks.co.uk

Real Ale Shop
47 Lovat Road, Preston
PR1 6DQ ✉
☎ (01772) 201591
🌐 www.realaleshop.net

Leicestershire

Melton Wines
Unit 5, Bell Centre, Nottingham
Street, Melton Mowbray LE13 1PJ
☎ (01664) 410114
🌐 www.mailorderwine.co.uk

Metro Wines
1286 Melton Road, Syston, Leicester
LE7 2HD
☎ (0116) 260 0868

The Offie
142 Clarendon Park Road, Leicester
LE2 3AE ✉
☎ (0116) 270 1553
🌐 www.the-offie.co.uk

Lincolnshire

The Beer Cellar
2 Gordon Road, Bailgate, Lincoln
LN1 3AJ ✉
☎ (01522) 524948

Greater London

The Bitter End
139 Masons Hill, Bromley
BR2 9HW ✉
☎ (020) 8466 6083
🌐 www.thebitterend.biz

Kris Wines
394 York Way, N7 9LW
☎ (020) 7607 4871

Nelson Wines
168 Merton High Street, Merton
SW19 1AZ
☎ (020) 8542 1558

Real Ale
371 Richmond Road, Twickenham
TW1 2EF ✉
☎ (020) 8892 3710
🌐 www.realale.com

Utobeer: The Drinks Cage
Unit 24, Borough Market, London
Bridge SE1 1TL (Thurs and Fri pm
and Sat only) ✉
☎ (020) 7378 9461
🌐 www.utobeer.co.uk

Greater Manchester

The Bottle Stop
136 Acre Lane, Bramhall SK8 7PD
☎ (0161) 439 4904

Carringtons
322 Barlow Moor Road, Chorlton-
cum-Hardy M21 8AY
☎ (0161) 881 0099

Carringtons
688 Wilmslow Road, Didsbury
M20 2DN
☎ (0161) 446 2546

Unicorn Grocery
89 Albany Road, Chorlton-cum-
Hardy M21 0BN (organic beers)
☎ (0161) 861 0010
🌐 www.unicorn-grocery.co.uk

Norfolk

Beers of Europe
Garage Lane, Setchey, King's Lynn
PE33 0BE ✉

(01553) 812000
www.beersofeurope.co.uk

Elveden Ales
Elveden Estate, Thetford IP24 3TQ
(01842) 878922
www.icenibrewery.co.uk

Humpty Dumpty Brewery
Church Road, Reedham NR13 3TZ
(01493) 701818

Iceni Brewery
3 Foulden Road, Ickburgh IP26 5BJ
(01842) 878922
www.icenibrewery.co.uk

The Real Ale Shop
Branthill Farm, Wells-next-the-Sea
NR23 1SB ✉
(01328) 710810
www.therealaleshop.co.uk

Samphire
The Estate Barn, Blickling Hall,
Aylsham NR11 6NF
(01263) 734464
www.samphireshop.co.uk

Uncle Stuart's Brewery and Shop
Wroxham Barns, Tunstead Road,
Hoveton, Norwich NR12 8QU
(01603) 783888

Northamptonshire
Country House Fine Foods
The Old Farmyard, Castle Ashby,
Northampton NN7 1LF
(01604) 696742

The Food Hall
60 St Giles Street, Northampton
NN1 1JW
(01604) 233313

Glebe Farm Shop
Rothwell Road, Kettering NN16 8XF
(01536) 513849
www.glebefarmshop.co.uk

Wakefield Farm Shop
Wakefield Country Courtyard,
Potterspury NN12 7QX
(01327) 811493
www.wakefieldfarmshop.co.uk

Oxfordshire
Bellingers Service Station
Station Road, Grove, Wantage
OX12 0DH
(01235) 770548

Classic Wines and Beers
254 Cowley Road, Oxford
OX4 1UH ✉
(01865) 792157

Westholme Store
26 Wallingford Road, Goring-on-
Thames RG8 0BG
(01491) 872619
www.beersnale.co.uk

Shropshire
Ludlow Food Centre
Bromfield, Ludlow SY8 2JR
(01584) 856000
www.ludlowfoodcentre.co.uk

The Marches Little Beer Shoppe
2 Old Street, Ludlow SY8 1NP
(01584) 878999

Riverside Wines
47 Underhill Street, Bridgnorth
WV16 4BB
(01746) 768631

Somerset
Dunster Village Shop and Deli
11 High Street, Dunster TA24 6SF
(01643) 822078

Open Bottles
131 Taunton Road, Bridgwater
TA6 6BD
(01278) 459666

Staffordshire
Amerton Farm Shop
Stowe by Chartley, Stafford
ST18 0LA
(01889) 270294
www.amertonfarm.co.uk

The Beer Emporium
38 Market Place, Burslem,
Stoke-on-Trent ST6 4AR

(01782) 815556
www.thebeeremporium.com

The Country Larder
Unit 2, Trentham Retail Village,
Trentham, Stoke-on-Trent ST4 8AX
(01782) 659080
www.country-larder.com

Suffolk
Alder Carr Farm
Creeting St Mary, Ipswich
IP6 8LX
(01449) 720820
www.aldercarrfarm.co.uk

Barwells Food
39 Abbeygate Street,
Bury St Edmunds IP33 1LW
(01284) 754084
www.barwellsfood.com

Memorable Cheeses
1 The Walk, Ipswich IP1 1DL
(01473) 257315

The Real Ale Shop
Priory Farm, Wrentham
NR34 7LR ✉
(01502) 676031
www.suffolk.therealaleshop.
co.uk

Suffolk Food Hall
Wherstead, Ipswich IP9 2AB
www.suffolkfoodhall.co.uk

Surrey
Hogs Back Brewery Shop
Manor Farm, The Street, Tongham
GU10 1DE ✉
(01252) 783000
www.hogsback.co.uk

Osney Lodge Farm
Byers Lane, South Godstone
RH9 8JH
(01342) 892216
www.osneylodgefarm.co.uk

Wrights Lion Brewery
57 West Street, Farnham
GU9 7AB
(01252) 715749

Sussex (East and West)
The Beer Essentials
30a East Street, Horsham
RH12 1HL ✉
(01403) 218890
www.thebeeressentials.co.uk

Southover Wines
80–81 Southover Street, Brighton
BN2 9UE
(01273) 600402

Trafalgar Wines
23 Trafalgar Street, Brighton
BN1 4EQ
(01273) 683325

The Wine Store Ltd
50A America Lane, Haywards Heath
RH16 3QB
(01444) 456600

West Midlands
Alexander Wines
112 Berkeley Road South, Earlsdon,
Coventry CV5 6EE ✉
(024 76) 673474

Bernie's Real Ale Off-Licence
266 Cranmore Boulevard, Shirley
B90 4PX
(0121) 744 2827

Global Wines
2 Abbey Road, Smethwick,
Birmingham B67 5RD
(0121) 420 3694

Rai Wine Shop
337 Harborne Lane, Harborne,
Birmingham B17 0NT ✉
(0121) 472 7235

Stirchley Wines and Spirits
1535–37 Pershore Road, Stirchley,
Birmingham B30 2JH
(0121) 459 9936
www.stirchleywines.co.uk

Wiltshire
Abbey Stores
30 Salt Lane, Salisbury SP1 1EG
(01722) 336984
www.abbeystores.co.uk

Magnum Wines
22 Wood Street, Old Town, Swindon
SN1 4AB
☏ (01793) 642569
🌐 www.magnumwineshop.co.uk

Worcestershire
Hop Pocket Wine Company
The Hop Pocket Craft Centre,
New House, Bishops Frome
WR6 5BT
☏ (01531) 640592
🌐 www.hoppocketwine.co.uk

Tipplers
70 Load Street, Bewdley DY12 2AW
☏ (01299) 402254

Weatheroak Ales
25 Withybed Lane, Alvechurch
B48 7NX
☏ (0121) 445 4411
🌐 www.weatheroakales.co.uk

Yorkshire
Ale Shop
79 Raglan Road, Leeds LS2 9DZ
☏ (0113) 242 7177

Archer Road Beer Stop
57 Archer Road, Sheffield S8 0JT
☏ (0114) 255 1356

Beer-Ritz
Victoria Buildings, Weetwood Lane,
Far Headingley, Leeds LS16 5LX ✉
☏ (0113) 275 3464
🌐 www.thebeerboy.co.uk

The Bottle
48 Stonegate, York YO1 8AS
☏ (01904) 640001

Drinks Well
34 Market Place, Ripon
HG4 1BZ ✉
☏ (01765) 607766
🌐 www.drinkswell.co.uk

Dukes of Ingleton
Albion House, 6 High Street,
Ingleton LA6 3EB ✉
☏ (0152 42) 41738
🌐 www.dukes-of-ingleton.com

Hi-Spirits
17 Market Place, Knaresborough
HG5 8AL ✉
☏ (01423) 862850
🌐 www.hi-spirits.co.uk

The Jug and Bottle
Main Street, Bubwith YO8 6LX
☏ (01757) 289707
🌐 www.jugandbottle.co.uk

Wells Wine Cellar
94–100 St Thomas Street,
Scarborough YO11 1DU
☏ (01723) 362220
🌐 www.wellswinecellar.co.uk

Wharfed Ale
8–10 Bondgate, Otley
LS21 3AB
☏ (01943) 465309

York Beer and Wine Shop
28 Sandringham Street, York
YO10 4BA
☏ (01904) 647136
🌐 www.yorkbeerandwineshop.
    co.uk

Scotland
Cornelius Beer & Wine
18–20 Easter Road, Edinburgh
EH7 5RG
☏ (0131) 652 2405

Earthy Food Market
33–41 Ratcliffe Terrace, Edinburgh
EH9 1SX
☏ (0131) 667 2967

Edinburgh Wine Merchants
30b Raeburn Place, Edinburgh
EH4 1NH
☏ (0131) 343 2347
🌐 www.edinburghwine.com

Great Grog
2 Dalkeith Road, Edinburgh
EH16 5BP
☏ (0131) 667 2855

JA Mackay
4 Traill Street, Thurso, Highland
KW14 8EJ ✉
☏ (01847) 892811

Peckham's
(licensed delicatessen with
several branches in Glasgow
and Edinburgh: ✉)
☎ (0141) 445 4555
🌐 www.peckhams.co.uk

Perthshire Visitor Centre
Bankfoot, Perth PH1 4EB
☎ (01738) 787696

Real Foods
8 Brougham Street, Edinburgh
EH3 9JH
☎ (0131) 228 1201
🌐 www.realfoods.co.uk

Real Foods
37 Broughton Street, Edinburgh
EH1 3JU
☎ (0131) 557 1911
🌐 www.realfoods.co.uk

Scottish Real Ale Shop
The Lade Inn, Kilmahog, Callander,
Perth & Kinross FK17 8HD ✉
☎ (01877) 330152
🌐 www.theladeinn.com

Wales
Bacchus
1a Beaufort Street, Crickhowell,
Powys NP8 1AD ✉
☎ (01873) 812229

Conwy Fine Wines
19 High Street, Conwy LL32 8DB
☎ (01492) 573050

Discount Supermarket
97 Whitchurch Road, Heath,
Cardiff CF14 3JP
☎ (029 20) 619049

Gwin Llyn Wines
Unit 2, Y Maes, Pwllheli, Gwynedd
LL53 5HA
☎ (01758) 701004

The Jolly Brewer
Stall 21, Butcher's Market,
Henblas Street, Wrexham
LL13 8AD
☎ (01978) 263338
🌐 www.jollybrewer.co.uk

Meadow Farm Shop
Tintern, Monmouthshire
NP16 7NX
☎ (01291) 680101
🌐 www.meadowfarm.org.uk

Stenson's
Cross Street, Holt, Wrexham
LL13 9JD
☎ (01829) 271192

Northern Ireland
The Vineyard
375–377 Ormeau Road, Belfast
BT7 3GP
☎ (028) 9064 5774
🌐 www.vineyardbelfast.co.uk

The Vintage
33 Church Street, Antrim
BT41 4BE
☎ (028) 9446 2526

Internet Sites
The following companies sell a
selection of beers via the Internet.
Some of these are connected to
shops listed above.

🌐 www.artisanbeers.co.uk
🌐 www.beermerchants.com
🌐 www.beersofeurope.co.uk
🌐 www.drinkswell.co.uk
🌐 www.hi-spirits.co.uk
🌐 www.hogsback.co.uk
🌐 www.hoppocketwine.co.uk
🌐 www.livingbeer.com
🌐 www.onlyfinebeer.co.uk
🌐 www.orchard-hive-and-vine.
   co.uk
🌐 www.realale.com
🌐 www.realbeerbox.com
🌐 www.thebeeressentials.co.uk
🌐 www.theladeinn.com
🌐 www.the-offie.co.uk
🌐 www.therealaleshop.co.uk
🌐 www.tuckersmaltings.com

Bottled Beer Dictionary

A quick reference source for the technical terms used in this book and on bottle labels.

80/-: see Shilling system.

ABV: Alcohol by Volume – the percentage of alcohol in a beer ('the strength').

Abbey beer: a beer brewed in the style of monastic beers by commercial companies. Only authentic Trappist monasteries have the right to call their beers 'Trappist'; others producing beers in similar style under licence from a clerical order have adopted the term 'Abbey'.

Adjuncts: other cereals and sugars which are added to malted barley during brewing, often to create a cheaper beer but sometimes for special flavours or effects.

Aftertaste/afterpalate: see Finish.

Ale: a top-fermenting beer (the yeast mostly sits on top during fermentation).

Aroma: the perfumes given off by a beer.

Barley: the cereal from which malt is made, occasionally used in its unmalted form in brewing, primarily to add colour.

Barley wine: a very strong, sweetish ale.

Bitter: a well-hopped ale.

Body: the fullness of the beer, generally related to malt content.

Bottle-conditioned: beer which undergoes a secondary fermentation in the bottle ('real ale in a bottle').

Brewery-conditioned: beer with a fermentation completed at the brewery and usually pasteurised.

Bright: racked or filtered (often pasteurised) beer.

Burtonize: to adjust the salts in brewing water to emulate the natural, hard waters of Burton-upon-Trent.

Carbon dioxide: a gas naturally created by yeast during fermentation and vital to the drinkability of a beer; see also Condition.

Cask: container for unpasteurised beer.

Cask-conditioned: beer given a secondary fermentation in a cask ('real ale').

Condition: the amount of dissolved carbon dioxide in a beer. Too much and the beer is gassy; too little and it is flat.

Decoction: a continental mashing system in which parts of the wort are moved into a second vessel and subjected to a higher temperature, before being returned to the original vessel. The aim is better starch conversion into sugar.

Dry hopping: the process of adding hops to a beer after it has been brewed, usually in the cask or in a conditioning tank prior to bottling, in order to enhance the hop character and aroma.

Dubbel: a Trappist or Abbey 'double' ale of about 7% ABV, generally dark brown and malty, with low hop character. Tripel ('triple') beers are stronger (around 8–9%), fruity and often pale in colour.

Esters: organic compounds comprised of an alcohol and an acid, produced during fermentation. These have unusual

– often fruity – aromas and flavours.

Filtered: a beer with its yeast and other sediment extracted; sterile-filtered beer has passed through a very fine filter.

Finings: a glutinous liquid that attracts yeast particles and draws them to the bottom of a cask (or a conditioning tank in the case of many bottled beers), leaving the beer clear. Finings are usually made from the swim-bladder of a tropical fish. Also known as isinglass.

Finish: the lingering taste in the mouth after swallowing beer.

Framboise/frambozen: see Kriek.

Green beer: beer that is not fully matured.

Green hops: hops picked fresh from the bine and used without undergoing the traditional drying process that allows them to be stored for months. Green hops provide a pungent, sappy character.

Grist: crushed malt ready for mashing. The term also refers to a mix of cereals, or hops, used in the brew.

Gueuze: see Lambic.

Hop: fast-growing plant, a relative of the nettle and cannabis. Its flowers are used to provide bitterness and other flavours in beer. Hops also help preserve beer.

Isinglass: see Finings.

Keg: a pressurized container for storing usually pasteurised beer. Brewery-conditioned beers, or 'keg' beers, need gas pressure to give them artificial fizz.

Kräusen: to add a small quantity of partially fermented wort to a beer in order to provide fresh sugars for the yeast to continue fermentation. It helps generate extra condition.

Kriek: a Belgian lambic beer undergoing a secondary fermentation with the addition of cherries or cherry juice. Similar beers Incorporate raspberries ('framboise'/'frambozen') and other fruits. See also Lambic.

Lager: a bottom-fermented beer (the yeast sinks to the bottom of the wort during fermentation) that is matured for several weeks (months in the best instances) at low temperatures.

Lambic: a Belgian wheat beer fermented by wild yeasts and aged in casks. Blended lambic is known as gueuze. See also Lambic.

Late hopping: the process of adding hops late to the copper boil, to compensate for any aroma that may have been lost from hops used earlier in the boil.

Malt: barley which has been partially germinated to release vital starches and enzymes for brewing, then kilned to arrest germination and to provide various 'baked' flavours.

Malt extract: commercially-produced concentrated wort, used by some brewers to save mashing, or to supplement their own wort.

Mash: the infusion of malt and water in the mash tun, which extracts fermentable materials from the grain.

Mild: a lightly-hopped, usually lowish-strength ale, often dark in colour.

Mouthfeel: the texture and body.

Nose: see Aroma.

OG: Original Gravity – a reading taken before fermentation to gauge the amount of fermentable material in a beer. The higher the OG, the more fermentables and the greater the likely strength of the finished brew.

Old ale: a strong, dark beer; traditionally, a beer set aside to mature.

Original gravity: see OG.

Oxidation: the deterioration in beer caused by oxygen, usually manifested in a wet paper or cardboard taste.

Palate: the sense of taste.

Parti-gyle: method of brewing more than one beer at the same time, using one standard brew that is then adapted – often by adding water to change the strength, or by using the first runnings from the mash tun to make a heavy beer and later runnings for a lighter beer.

Pasteurised: beer which has been heat treated to kill off remaining yeast cells and prevent further fermentation.

Porter: a lighter-bodied predecessor of stout, usually dry, with some sweetness.

Priming: the process of adding extra fermentable sugars to a beer to enable a secondary fermentation in the bottle.

Rack: to run beer from a tank or a cask.

Real ale: an unpasteurised, unfiltered beer which continues to ferment in the vessel from which it is dispensed ('cask conditioned' or 'bottle conditioned').

Sediment: solids in beer, primarily yeast but also possibly some proteins.

Shilling system: a Scottish system of branding beers according to style and strength, derived from Victorian times when the number of shillings stated referred to the gross price payable by the publican on each barrel. 60/-, or light, is the Scottish equivalent of a mild; 70/-, or heavy, is a Scottish bitter; and 80/-, or export, is a stronger beer again.

SIBA: The Society of Independent Brewers, a trade body representing the interests of the small brewing sector.

Single-varietal: a beer using just one strain of hops or one type of malt.

Sterile-filtered: see filtered.

Stock ale: a very strong beer intended to be kept and matured for several months.

Stout: traditionally, a strongish beer, usually dark in colour and tasting dry and bitter, often with roasted barley flavour.

Sunstruck: beer which has been over-exposed to bright light. This can cause a chemical reaction, leading to unsavoury aromas and flavours.

Trappist ale: see Abbey beer.

Tripel: see Dubbel.

Weissbier: a Bavarian style of wheat beer, known for its fruit-and-spices character. Hefeweissbiers are naturally cloudy; kristalweissbiers are filtered to be clear. Also called weizenbiers.

Wheat beer: a style of beer originating in Germany and Belgium, brewed with a high percentage of wheat and often served cloudy with yeast in suspension.

Witbier: a Belgian-style, spiced wheat beer; also known as bière blanche.

Wort: the unfermented sweet liquid produced by mashing malt and water.

Yeast: a single-celled micro-organism that turns sugar in wort into alcohol and carbon dioxide.

Index

Marks & Spencer Norfolk Bitter Woodforde's 76, 335
Marks & Spencer Sussex Bitter Hepworth 92, 292
Marks & Spencer Welsh Honey Bitter Conwy 237, 278
Marks & Spencer Yorkshire Bitter Cropton 280
Marld Bartrams 266
Marmalade Cat Fat Cat 285
Marsh Mild Fulstow 288
Martha's Mild Teignworthy 27, 325
Massive Ale Sharp's 170, 319
The Mayor's Bitter Nailsworth 304
Maypole Mild Oakleaf 25, 307
Meadow Brown Old Chimneys 25, 308
Meadowland Tunnel 328
Megalithic Ale Bartrams 267
Melbourne Bitter Tollgate 327
Melton Mowbray Oatmeal Stout Belvoir 268
Men of Norfolk Iceni 295
Men of Suffolk Elveden 284
Mercian Shine Beowulf 117, 268
Merlins Brew Ffos y Ffin 286
Merry Ale King 213, 298
Merry Andrew Adur 148, 264
Midnight Nutbrook 307
Midnight Stout Woodlands 336
Midsummer Ale Concrete Cow 84, 277
Mild Blackfriars 270
Mild Tindall 326
Woodlands 336
Mill Lane Mild Hoggleys 24, 293
Minion of the Moon Cambridge Moonshine 274
Mitre Gold Blackfriars 270
Moat Mild Castle 275
Molly's Chocolate Stout Hilden 292
Molly's Secret Brandon 272
Monarch IPA North Cotswold 140, 306
Mongrel Nutbrook 307
Monkey Hanger Poachers 312
Monkman's Slaughter Cropton 280
Moon Rocket Tipple's 327
Moor Ale Little Valley 300
More Nutbrook 307

Morrisons The Best Freeminer 119, 287
Mother in Law's Tongue Tied Bartrams 161, 267
Mother McCleary's Milk Stout Bartrams 267
Mud City Stout Windsor Castle 261, 334
Mulberry Dark Conwy 22, 278
Munich Style Lager Tunnel 328
Mustang Mild Green Tye 290
Mutley's Revenge Spinning Dog 68, 321
Muzzle Loader Cannon Royall 51, 275
Mynzamild Stationhouse 322

N

N1 Wheat Beer Pitfield 230, 312
Napper Tandy Brandon 272
Narrowboat Shardlow 318
Natterjack Frog Island 287
Naughty Nell's Mayfields 302
Navigator Bees 267
Nector Rooster's 316
Nelson's Blood Fox 240, 287
Nelson's Column Tunnel 156, 328
Nelson's Revenge Woodforde's 77, 335
Nerabus Ale Islay 213, 296
New Year Daze Bartrams 267
Night Beacon Breconshire 180, 273
Night Mail Stationhouse 322
Night Rider Kelham Island 298
Nightlight Mild Elmtree 24, 284
Nina's Mild Fox 287
No.1 Buckle Street 273
No.1 Kingstone 191, 299
No.3 Ramsgate 313
No.17 Bitter McGivern 302
No.17 Pale McGivern 302
Noble Eden Ale Heart of Wales 291
Norfolk Black Beeston 268
Norfolk Gold Iceni 295
Norfolk Honey Ale Why Not 260, 333
Norfolk Lager Iceni 295
Norfolk Nectar Humpty Dumpty 244, 295
Norfolk 'n' Good Tindall 326
Norfolk Nip Woodforde's 171, 335
Norfolk Nog Woodforde's 29, 335

371

Books for Beer Lovers

CAMRA Books, the publishing arm
of the Campaign for Real Ale, is the
leading publisher of books on beer
and pubs. Key titles include:

Good Beer Guide 2010
Editor: **Roger Protz**

The *Good Beer Guide* is the only guide you
will ever need to find the right pint, in the right
place, every time. Now in its 37th year, the
Good Beer Guide is fully revised and updated,
with information on more than 4,500
recommended pubs, and a unique section
listing all the breweries – micro, regional and
national – that produce cask beer in the UK.

£15.99
ISBN 978-1-85249-266-3

A Beer a Day
Jeff Evans

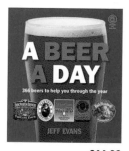

Written by leading beer writer Jeff Evans,
A Beer a Day is a beer lover's almanac,
crammed with beers from around the world
to enjoy on every day and in every season,
and celebrating beer's connections with
history, sport, music film and television.
Whether it's Christmas Eve, Midsummer's
Day, Bonfire Night, or just a wet Wednesday
in the middle of October, *A Beer a Day* has
just the beer for you to savour and enjoy.

£16.99
ISBN 978-1-85249-235-9

100 Belgian Beers to Try Before You Die!
Tim Webb & **Joris Pattyn**

100 Belgian Beers to Try Before You Die!
showcases 100 of the best Begian beers
as chosen by internationally-known beer
writers Tim Webb and Joris Pattyn. Lavishly
illustrated throughout with images of the
beers, breweries, Belgian beer bars and some
of the characters involved in Belgian brewing,
the book encourages both connoisseurs and
newcomers to Belgian beer to sample them for
themselves, both in Belgium and at home.

£12.99
ISBN 987-1-85249-248-9

300 Beers to Try Before You Die!
Roger Protz

300 beers from around the world, handpicked
by award-winning journalist, author and
broadcaster Roger Protz to try before you die!
A comprehensive portfolio of top beers
from the smallest microbreweries in the
United States to family-run British breweries
and the world's largest brands. This book
is indispensible for both beer novices and
aficionados.

£12.99
ISBN 978-1-85249-213-7

Good Beer Guide Belgium
Tim Webb

The completely revised and updated 6th edition of the guide so impressive that it is acknowledged as the standard work for Belgian beer lovers, even in Belgium itself. The *Good Beer Guide Belguim* includes comprehensive advice on getting there, being there, what to eat, where to stay and how to bring beers back home. Its outline of breweries, beers and bars makes this book indispensible for both leisure and business travellers a well as for armchair drinkers looking to enjoy a selection of Belgian brews from their local beer store.

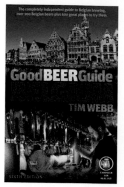

£14.99

ISBN 978-1-85249-261-8

Brew Your Own British Real Ale at Home
Graham Wheeler

The perennial favourite of home-brewers, *Brew Your Own British Real Ale* is a CAMRA classic. This new edition is re-written, enhanced and updated with new recipes for contemporary and award-winning beers, as well as recipes for old favourites no longer brewed commercially. Written by home-brewing authority Graham Wheeler, *Brew Your Own British Real Ale* includes detailed brewing instructions for both novice and more advanced home-brewers, as well as comprehensive recipes for recreating some of Britain's best-loved beers at home.

£14.99

ISBN 978-1-85249-258-8

Cider

Photography by **Mark Bolton**

Proper cider and perry – made with apples and pears and nothing but, is a wonderful drink – but there's so much more to it than that. *Cider* is a lavishly illustrated celebration of real cider, and its close cousin perry, for anyone who wants to learn more about Britain's oldest drink. With features on the UK's most interesting and characterful cider and perry makers, how to make your own cider, foreign ciders, and the best places to drink cider – including unique dedicated cider houses, award-winning pubs and year-round CAMRA festivals all over the country – *Cider* is the essential book for any cider or perry lover.

£14.99
ISBN 978-1-85249-259-5

Peak District Pub Walks
Bob Steel

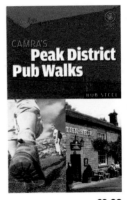

A practical, pocket-sized traveller's guide to some of the best pubs and best walking in the Peak District. This book features 25 walks, as well as cycle routes and local attractions, helping you see the best of Britain's oldest national park while never straying too far from a decent pint. Each route has been selected for its inspiring landscape, historical interest and welcoming pubs.

£9.99
ISBN 978-1-85249-246-5

Order these and other CAMRA books online at www.camra.org.uk/books, ask your local bookstore, or contact: CAMRA, 230 Hatfield Road, St Albans, AL1 4LW. Telephone 01727 867201

It takes all sorts to Campaign for Real Ale

CAMRA, the Campaign for Real Ale, is an independent not-for-profit, volunteer-led consumer group. We promote good-quality real ale and pubs as well as lobbying government to champion drinkers' rights and protect local pubs as centres of community life.

CAMRA has 100,000 members from all ages and backgrounds, brought together by a common belief in the issues that CAMRA deals with and their love of good quality British beer and cider. From just £20 a year – that's less than a pint a month – you can join CAMRA and enjoy the following benefits:

A monthly colour newspaper informing you about beer and pub news and detailing events and beer festivals around the country.

Free or reduced entry to over 140 national, regional and local beer festivals.

Money off many of our publications including the *Good Beer Guide* and the *Good Bottled Beer Guide*.

Access to a members-only section of our national website, www.camra.org.uk, which gives up-to-the-minute news stories and includes a special offer section with regular features saving money on beer and trips away.

The opportunity to campaign to save pubs under threat of closure, for pubs to be open when people want to drink and a reduction in beer duty that will help Britain's brewing industry survive.

Log onto **www.camra.org.uk** for CAMRA membership information.

**CAMPAIGN
FOR
REAL ALE**